Medieval Academy Reprints for Teaching

18

Medieval Academy Reprints for Teaching

ROMILLY JENKINS

Byzantium
The Imperial
Centuries
AD 610–1071

Published by University of Toronto Press
Toronto   Buffalo   London
in association with the Medieval Academy of America

©Medieval Academy of America 1987
Printed in Canada
ISBN 0-8020-6667-4

First published by Weidenfeld and Nicholson in 1966
Reprinted by permission of the publisher

CELINAE VXORI

CONTENTS

MAPS

PREFACE

This book has been written, not for the scholar and specialist in Byzantinism, but for the student and general reader. It is designed to give the latter, by way of an introduction to the subject, a connected account of what actually went on in the East Roman, or 'Byzantine', Empire during the four and a half centuries between the accession of Heraclius and the Battle of Manzikert. Several good books exist in English which deal with this Empire on an 'analytical' plan: that is to say, by sections devoted to separate aspects of its culture (political theory, administration, art, literature and so on), regardless of, or not primarily regarding, chronological sequence. I have here no wish to challenge comparison with these, or to add to their number.

The title chosen calls for a word of explanation. In the eyes of the Byzantines themselves the seventh to the eleventh centuries were no more or less 'imperial' than any other of the fourteen that elapsed between Augustus Caesar and Constantine XI. But, as we shall see, the modern historian divides the eleven centuries from the foundation of Constantinople in AD 324 to its fall in AD 1453 into three distinct epochs: the fourth to the seventh, the seventh to the eleventh, and the eleventh to the fifteenth centuries. The first period was indeed 'imperial', but is better denominated 'Late Roman' than 'Byzantine'. The third period as a whole can scarcely be called 'imperial', except by courtesy. To the second period alone can both terms be properly applied: and indeed an alternative title might well be 'The Rise and Fall of the Middle-Byzantine Empire'.

In a work of this nature, documentation poses some problems. The beginner does not wish to be choked by a mass of primary and secondary sources. On the other hand, if he wishes to pursue the subject, he must be given the opportunity of doing so. On the whole, it has seemed best to limit the primary sources to half a a dozen chief historical texts that cover the period; and the secondary to half a dozen of the best modern histories. These secondary sources have been chosen, not merely because they are good in themselves, but also because they are themselves fully documented.

Texts and editions are given in the accompanying Bibliographical Note; but a word on the modern works there cited will not be amiss. First and foremost stands the classic *Geschichte des byzantinischen Staates* of Georg Ostrogorsky, now in its third German edition. There are two English-language editions of it, but these are less up to date. This work, one of the greatest achievements of all time in this field, is distinguished by sound judgement, minute accuracy, masterly arrangement and compression, and a wealth of reference to every important source, both primary and secondary. The *Vie et mort de Byzance* of Louis Bréhier gives a detailed and well-written narrative of very great value, and, here too, the judgement is admirable; but it is not quite so well articulated, and more difficult to use owing to a complicated and perverse system of references. A. A. Vasiliev's *History of the Byzantine Empire* has been deservedly popular, and cites in translation many opinions of Russian historians whose works the general reader has no occasion to study. The two works of J.B. Bury, though both of them more than fifty years old, are still indispensable sources for the period AD 610–867, and are a monument to the industry and skill of the greatest of English Byzantinists. Finally, the forthcoming re-edition of *Cambridge Medieval History*, volume IV, is certain to be of immense value, and cannot be omitted from even so short a list as this.

Admirable as these works, and very many others, are, they are not books for beginners: and that is my excuse for trying to supply one.

I wish to acknowledge my gratitude to the Cambridge University Press for allowing me to reproduce Chapter 23 substantially as it appears in *Cambridge Medieval History* volume

xii

IV (new edition, 1966); and also to Mrs Fanny Bonajuto for most valuable help in preparing this book for the press.

The dust-jacket illustrates a tenth-century Byzantine ivory now in the Dumbarton Oaks Collection, Washington, D C. It shows an emperor, in full imperial dress, who is probably Constantine VII Porphyrogenitus. It is reproduced by kind permission of the Dumbarton Oaks Research Library and Collection, Harvard University.

ROMILLY JENKINS
Washington, D C

CHAPTER ONE

THE HISTORICAL BACKGROUND

Let me begin with a quotation:

Of the Byzantine Empire the universal verdict of history is that it constitutes, with scarcely an exception, the most thoroughly base and despicable form that civilisation has yet assumed. . . . There has been no other enduring civilisation so absolutely destitute of all the forms and elements of greatness, and none to which the epithet *mean* may so emphatically be applied. The Byzantine Empire was pre-eminently the age of treachery. Its vices were the vices of men who had ceased to be brave without learning to be virtuous. Without patriotism, without the fruition or desire of liberty, after the first paroxysms of religious agitation, without genius or intellectual activity; slaves, and willing slaves, in both their actions and their thoughts, immersed in sensuality and in the most frivolous pleasures, the people only emerged from their listlessness when some theological subtilty, or some rivalry in the chariot races, stimulated them into frantic riots. They exhibited all the externals of advanced civilisation. They possessed knowledge; they had continually before them the noble literature of ancient Greece, instinct with the loftiest heroism; but that literature, which afterwards did so much to revivify Europe, could fire the degenerate Greeks with no spark or semblance of nobility. The history of the Empire is a monotonous story of the intrigues of priests, eunuchs and women, of poisoning, of conspiracies, of uniform ingratitude, of perpetual fratricides. . . . At last the Mohammedan invasion terminated the long decrepitude of the Eastern Empire. Constantinople sank beneath the Crescent, its inhabitants wrangling about theological differences to the very moment of their fall.

This passage from Lecky's *History of European Morals*, written in

1869, is interesting from several points of view, but principally from two. It is dictated, first by ignorance, and second by prejudice. As for the matter, it is, 'with scarcely an exception', a tissue of mis-statements, half-truths and downright absurdities which an historian – let alone a great and learned historian – should have been ashamed to write. This is the fruit of *ignorance*, and it may serve as a warning to even the most gifted of us not to write about what we do not understand. But the *prejudice* is equally illuminating and important. The language is such as a western Crusader of the twelfth century might have held, and often in fact did hold, about Byzantium. It is the outcome of that deplorable strife between Eastern and Western Christendom which begat in the West a long-enduring hatred of Byzantium, still plainly discernible in the pages of the historians Gibbon and Voltaire, and of the novelists Walter Scott and George Eliot. There was, assuredly, much in the East which the West could look upon with justifiable abhorrence. But Byzantium, monopolist as she was, had no monopoly in vice; and the vices of the medieval West, though different, seem on an impartial survey no less odious and contemptible.

One misapprehension common in the West during the eighteenth and nineteenth centuries (we find it in Lecky's diatribe) was the notion that, because the official language of the Byzantine Empire was a form of Greek, this implied that those who spoke it were in some way lineally connected with Classical Hellas, and must therefore be regarded as degenerate offspring from a noble ancestry. This notion the true Byzantine would have rejected with scorn, and very rightly. The Roman Empire, which he claimed to perpetuate, was multiracial, as all empires must necessarily be. The only elements which it had in common with Classical Hellas (whose people were long defunct) were a bastard and artificial version of the classical Attic dialect as the tongue of administration and literature, and the writings of Greek antiquity, on parts of which its secular education was based. It was not until the collapse of the 'universal' empire of East Rome was seen to be imminent, in and after the time of the Emperor Michael VIII (died 1282), that the Byzantines, or rather a few of their antiquaries, put out the utterly erroneous theory that they were descended from the Hellenes, and exchanged the imperial heritage of Rome for the cultural heritage of Ancient Greece.

Let us try to get rid of this notion of 'decline' and review some centuries of Byzantine history, during which the state, far from being in decline, was in a process of rapid improvement and a career of striking magnificence and glory. Let us review the aims and the achievements of the Christian Romans of the Bosphorus, without any but theoretical reference to Augustus or Trajan, and without any reference at all to Pericles or Leonidas. Let us try to put these into the focus of historical perspective; and draw our own conclusions.

Our theme is the internal and external history of what is nowadays called the 'Middle' Byzantine Empire during four centuries and a half: from the accession of the Emperor Heraclius in 610 to the defeat of the Emperor Romanus IV at Manzikert in 1071. In justifying our choice of this temporal period, we might well be content to rest on the now classic definition of Georg Ostrogorsky. He writes:

The years of anarchy under Phocas [Heraclius' predecessor, 602–10] mark the last phase in the history of the late Roman Empire. The late Roman, or early Byzantine, period came to an end. Byzantium was to emerge from the crisis in an essentially different form, freed from the heritage of decadent political life, and fortified by new and vigorous sources of strength. Here [in AD 610] Byzantine history properly speaking begins, the history of the medieval Greek empire.[1]

We might leave it at that. Yet, as we know, history is continuous rather than fragmentary; and what appear at first sight to be its most decisive breaks will on more mature consideration be found to exemplify the dictum of 'plus ça change'. As in the development of species, so in the development of ideas or moulds of thought, sudden and radical change is unknown. We are not without a specimen of this truth in our own day. At first sight, nothing could, and did, appear more revolutionary than the triumph of a form of Marxism over Tsarism, and the transmogrification of Holy Russia into the Union of Soviet Socialist Republics. The bad old world, it was passionately asserted, had been swept away; mankind was setting out on a wholly new track. However, forty years' experience of the USSR suggest that, both in theory and practice, the changes are far less striking than the continuity, and that the sudden and violent imposition of a new creed is powerless to modify, in any material respect, national instincts and policies

3

whose growth has been the work of centuries. The modern Russian state, in its rejection of personal freedom, in its spiritual pride, in its monopoly of orthodoxy (that is, 'right belief'), in the restless and encroaching spirit of its imperialism and expansion, in its unalterable conviction of a pre-ordained world-domination, merely carries on the tradition of Tsarist days, and is utterly unlike any polity dreamt of in the gloomy philosophy of Marx or Engels. Orthodox Christianity has become 'Socialism': and the Will of Almighty God is now denominated 'Historical Necessity'. But behind this re-titled façade the age-old structure is essentially the same, save for some restorations which make it stronger and more durable than ever. Its new, universal religion has abolished the strife between orthodox and catholic. It will not surprise the thoughtful observer that this structure is, very recognizably, the Byzantine Palace of the Third Rome.

With respect to the new or renovated structure of the Emperor Heraclius, we have to be even more careful to subject each of its phenomena to a comparative scrutiny, and to estimate the freshness of its leaven: in as much as, in the eyes of the medieval Byzantine, the continuity of the empire was far more important than its innovations, which he regarded as superficial and incidental. The strongest and most universally held tenet in the Byzantine thought-world was a conviction of Rome's divinely sanctioned claim to universal empire, and the divinely ordained decree that in God's good time this empire must be achieved. The change of creed from paganism to Christianity, initiated by Constantine I (died 337) and consummated by Theodosius I (died 395), had served merely to corroborate the fundamental postulate. The command to rule and the gift of supremacy came long before, from Jupiter. In the mystical accents of the poet, the *imperium sine fine* – empire without limit in space or time – was accorded to the Eternal City: and the *fiat* was enunciated in lines which none of us can afford to forget or ignore:

> Others may softlier mould the breathing brass,
> Or from the marble coax the living face;
> Others more eloquently plead than thou,
> Or trace the heavenly orbits, name the stars.
> Thine, Roman, be the empire over man!
> Be these thy arts! Impose the law of peace,
> Sparing the meek, and trampling down the proud!

These words of Virgil, in their thunderous expression of the might, the duty and, above all, the divine sanction of Rome to rule over the less fortunate races of mankind, breathe the very spirit of the great conquerors and governors, of Sulla and Pompey, of Pilate and Gallio. Did it greatly matter whether the sanction was that of Jove or Jesus?

However, the reign of Constantine the Great (324–37) was marked by two reforms, each of which was of lasting importance. First, the religion of Christ was grafted, with startling ingenuity but not everywhere with absolute harmony, on to the existing imperial idea. Second, the centre of imperial government was transferred from Rome to the Bosphorus. The modifications entailed by the first of these reforms were, politically speaking, more spectacular than fundamental. The old dogma of the unity of the world beneath the elect of Jupiter, a dogma universally accepted by the Mediterranean world and its peripheries, was, for practical purposes, modified by the simple substitution of Jesus for Jove. The younger, more mystical Divinity replaced the older and more effete, with an increase in imperial authority and prestige. Almighty God, it was now stated, at the very time when Augustus was unifying the temporal empire and giving it the inestimable benefit of universal peace, had sent on earth his Divine Counterpart, Jesus Christ, who was also the Prince of Peace. The *Pax Romana* was reinforced by the *Pax Dei*. The unity of the Roman Empire was the reflection of the celestial unity, over which the One True God governed in perfect law and order, backed by a heavenly hierarchy and a standing army of invincible strength. It was God's Will, as His Son had explicitly stated, that the world should be similarly governed. Anyone who disagreed with this was God's enemy as well as Rome's. Anyone who refused to submit to the Roman sceptre was automatically a rebel, a disturber of God's Peace, in short, a warmonger, to be dealt with righteously as God has dealt with Lucifer-Satan. God's minister for the unification and pacification of this world was the Roman emperor, whom He himself elected and crowned, with the concurrence of the old Roman estates of senate, army and people, and the newer, though not indispensable, sanction of the Christian Church. Hitherto the emperors, following Hellenistic tradition, had themselves been deified, and in this single particular their newer status as Christian rulers was diminished. But, in practice, their position as the elect and representative of the One True God was more authoritative than their automatic membership of a rather disreputable Hellenistic pantheon. Such, then, was the conception of the Roman's destiny and place in the universe which endured until 1453, and, in its essence, long afterwards. The harnessing to imperial destinies, both in Ancient Rome and in Modern Russia, of the two religions of humility, created in each case an entity which the founders of those religions would have contemplated with amazement and consternation.

And here we may note in passing that this dogma of divinely prescribed unity is one which differentiates the mind of Classical Greece in its heyday from the mind of late antiquity and the middle ages. Plurality was acceptable, and indeed fundamental, to the thought-world of the Ancient Greeks. Their divinities and their communities were legion. Much of their intellectual activity was devoted to differentiation and definition. It was the opinion of the philosopher Heracleitus that life itself consisted in the tension of opposite forces. This tendency is certainly reflected in the political configuration of Hellas, with its multifarious states at war, or at all events at rivalry, with one another.

However, as one of the most brilliant of the early Greek philosophers very justly observed, tendencies towards plurality and towards unity run in temporal cycles. And even by the time of Plato and Isocrates (fourth century BC), the opposite motion was setting in. According to the former thinker, who detested democracy and idolised absolute power in a carefully organised and graduated society, the plurality of the world of sense is illusory: it serves merely to elevate a properly adjusted mind to a hierarchy of supersensible forms, themselves subordinate to a single monarchical principle, the 'Good', which dominates the world of being as the sun dominates the sensible firmament. This doctrine, as developed by the Neo-Platonists, reached its logical conclusion in the belief that unity is morally good and plurality intrinsically evil: which is merely another way of saying that orthodoxy is good and heresy bad. It can easily be seen that this dogma, or, better, this way of thinking, became the strongest prop of universal empire in the minds of late Roman and medieval man. The very notion that one single empire of all the world with one single orthodoxy is the best and ultimate constitution because it *imitates* the supersensible constitution of Heaven is more Platonic

6

than Christian; although of course the Lord's Prayer could very easily be made to square with it. And the Empire of Rome was the only possible candidate for the position in the world of sense.

But now, as regards the second reform of Constantine the Great, the transfer of the administrative centre from the Tiber to the Bosphorus: this was an eminently judicious step, alike from political, economic and – as it proved – ecclesiastical aspects. If it had not been taken in time, it seems very doubtful whether the empire could have survived the Dark Ages; and it would certainly not have known the centuries of increasing stability, riches and glory which it experienced in the Middle-Byzantine era. But the transfer had one other important consequence. It brought the centre of imperial administration and society into the area of Greek speech. Greek, in its various forms, as the medium of education, religion, commerce and everyday communication, had won so firm a grasp over the coasts and cities of the Near East during the long rule of the successors of Alexander, that its predominance in those parts, though twice challenged, was never seriously threatened by the Latin; and in the seventh century, the Latin, as the language of administration, was officially abandoned. Asia, Syria, Palestine and Egypt, though never by any means monolingual, remained in the sphere of Greek speech. This meant that the education and cultural tradition of the empire of New Rome were exclusively Hellenistic: and the enormous pride which was felt by the Byzantine in his possession of this splendid, if very imperfectly understood, cultural inheritance increased his sense of his divinely ordained superiority over the rest of the world. The linguistic division was at last fatal to the unity of the old Roman Empire: perhaps more fatal than any differences of belief or character. After the seventh century Catholic West and Orthodox East literally could not understand one another: and ignorance bred, on both sides, arrogance and contempt. The doctrinal differences which divided, and still divide, Catholic from Orthodox Christians appear, to an impartial observer, trivial and even infinitesimal by comparison with the great body of Christian belief which has never been questioned by either. It is certainly arguable that if all Mediterranean countries had been latinised in speech by Rome, as Italy, Gaul and Spain were latinised, a common tongue would have preserved a common faith, and even a unified empire. This could not be.

The decisive factors in the disintegration of the Mediterranean, or 'universal', empire of Rome, which led to the formation of the truly Byzantine state, a compact and solid rump of the old dominion, in the seventh century, were the invasions of Germans, Slavs, Huns and Arabs or Saracens, the scope and direction of which we must consider in some detail. Not only the losses of territory, but also the fundamental administrative reforms of the century, are directly attributable to this cause. It is certainly true that, by the time of Justinian I (527–65), the process of barbarisation had during some centuries been continuous. Spain and North Africa were already occupied by Visigoths and Vandals. The Salian Franks were masters of North Gaul. Much of Italy was governed by the Ostrogoths. The eastern part of the empire itself had absorbed a large Gothic element, which had intruded into the fabric of society and the machinery of government. But this earlier, Germanic, inundation differed in principle from the later inundations of Lombards, Slavs, Bulgars and Saracens. The Gothic rulers of Italy, and the Frankish rulers of Gaul, were content, at least in name, to form parts of the old empire, and to derive their titles, if not their policies, from Constantinople. The empire itself in the sixth century was still strong enough to envisage the reconquest of Spain and north-west Africa. But the Lombards, Slavs and Saracens never integrated themselves into the old imperial scheme. The Saracens had their own religion and formed their own empire. The Lombards were conquered, not by the Roman, but by the Frankish empire. The Balkan Slavs, except those of Hellas, remained generally speaking outside imperial control. Nothing of this, of course, disturbed the *faith* in Roman unity and universalism; but faith and fact now began markedly to diverge, and were to remain divergent.

The last forcible attempt of the empire at a reassertion of its control over the dominions of Augustus was made by Justinian I who has consequently been called, by Francis Bacon among others, 'the last of the Romans'. This title does violence to the Byzantine concept of the continuity of the Roman imperial tradition throughout the middle ages, though it is true that Justinian, in contrast with his successors, spoke Latin and shaved his chin. During a very brief period of his long reign he was master of Rome and Italy, of all North Africa, and a corner of Spain; but this brief restoration of Roman authority, which survived him by three years only, was a meagre return for the fearful ruin and loss brought about by his profuse expenditure of money and men. It was in 533 that he undertook to recover the western half of his empire from a century-old German occupation. In each theatre of operation – Africa, Italy, Dalmatia – initial success was followed by years, or decades, of tough warfare, which even the genius of his generals Belisarius and Narses could not curtail. After twenty years the end seemed to be in sight. Gelimer, Vitiges and Totila were taken or slain. Africa and the Danubian frontier were held down by costly and (as it proved) useless fortifications. But by this time both men and money were exhausted. The large treasure amassed by the Emperor Anastasius (died 518) had long been dissipated; and plans for fresh taxation of trade and agriculture were stultified by malversation or sheer inability to pay. Some at least of the discontent sown in the once prosperous provinces of the east, which showed itself in the increasing intransigence of the so-called 'monophysite' heresy, is attributable to economic rather than to doctrinal causes; though we should certainly err in regarding the latter as mere symptoms of dissatisfaction. More serious still was the catastrophic decline in manpower. The numbers of men sacrificed in Justinian's wars must be told in millions. To make matters worse, in 542 the bubonic plague broke out with unexampled severity. The historian tells us that at its height the mortality in Constantinople alone reached ten thousand a day. The bearing of such wars, and of such a pestilence, as these on the fate of the empire during the next century must be appreciated. Repopulation was the condition of survival.

The last years of Justinian's reign were indeed not troubled by military wars. But internal religious dissensions were never at rest. Justinian's designs in the west had at first compelled him to champion the orthodoxy of Chalcedon against that large section of his eastern subjects who claimed that the Saviour had had but one Single Nature, that is, the 'monophysites'. Later, circumstances forced him to shift his ground; and he at length found himself committed to a position which scarcely differed from that of the outermost and most mystical fringe of monophysitism itself. Nothing would serve. He had piped unto them and they would not dance. Justinian had restored the empire of the Mediterranean. He had brought order to the civil code. He had built St

Sophia's cathedral, the 'eye of the universe'. But he was powerless to impose on men the views which they should adopt as touching the nature of the Divine Incarnation. This absolutely irreconcilable conflict, in an empire of which religious unity was a fundamental postulate, was ominous of political disruption. Three whole centuries were to pass before the problem, in one form or another, could be settled, and the religious unity essential for stability be achieved.

Justinian achieved much. Yet the structure at his death resembled a vacuum. He had recreated a system which there were no longer the men or the money or the general and popular will to sustain. It was subjected to multifarious external pressures, any one of which was powerful enough to pierce the shell, and shatter the globe into fragments. This dangerous situation was abundantly clear to his contemporaries, and their gloomy pessimism over the future was a sad return for so much effort and so much that had seemingly been achieved. The historian John of Ephesus thought that the end of the world was nigh : and so, in one sense, it was.[2]

Italy was the first, though not the most important, part of Justinian's empire to disappear. It was, when the emperor died in 565, already both disaffected and indefensible. The tyranny and extortion of the Byzantine Governor-General Narses were already arousing the loud-voiced protests of those who felt the Byzantine finger thicker than the loins of the alien and heretical Ostrogoths. The Germanic occupation soon returned. In 567 the Lombards, a gifted but primitive tribe then settled in Pannonia, reached an agreement with the Hunnic people of the Avars, who had pushed westwards across Thrace and into the lands of the upper Danube, in search of habitation. The Lombard Alboin and the Avar Khan Baian agreed jointly to extirpate the tribe of the Germanic Gepids who lived in Dacia, on the left bank of the Danube. The Avars were to settle on the Danube. The Lombards, taking one half of the spoils, were to invade Italy. Both plans were carried out, with lasting effects. The Avar kingdom was for a century the source of widespread devastation south of the Danube. And the Lombard invasion of Italy, which began in 568, changed the face and to a considerable extent the population of that peninsula.

It is significant of the exhaustion and unpopularity of the restored Roman régime in Italy that the Lombard advance met with little or no opposition. The invasion was gradual rather than sudden; and was in fact not properly consummated until the eighth century. But it was inexorable. The Roman power was contracted into the peripheral regions of Venice, Ravenna and Calabria-*cum*-Sicily. The Lombards took Milan and Pavia, and, further south, set up the duchies of Spoleto and Benevento. The invasion was in the long run decisive for the fate of Old Rome also, where the papacy, no longer under the direct and continuous political control of Constantinople, developed its independence and at last its distinctively western orientation. The Spanish Visigoths soon recovered the small but important territories seized by Justinian, and remained masters of the country until the Saracen conquest of the eighth century.3

It was during the same sixth century and in the beginning of the next that an even more momentous immigration of foreign races engulfed the ancient homeland of the Hellenes. The factual truth of this very simple event was long obscured, partly by the paucity of direct evidence (which, however, scanty as it may be, is unanimous), but even more owing to a very absurd and frustrating controversy aroused during the nineteenth century by the publication of the facts. During the War of Greek Independence (1821-7) the cause of the insurgents had prevailed owing to the support given them by the Great Powers of Europe; and this support had been accorded in decisive measure because of the delusion then prevalent in the West, that the contemporary inhabitants of old Hellas were the racial descendants of Homer and Sophocles and Plato. When, shortly after the war ended, it was pointed out that this could not be so, the popular revulsion, both in Greece and Europe, against this unpleasant truth completely befogged the issue; and even scholarship itself, which should be exempt from passion and prejudice, was drawn into the maelstrom of recrimination and error. Gradually the mud began to settle, though resentment at any suggestion that new Hellenes were not old Hellenes writ large was still fierce in Greece at the end of the nineteenth century, when the learned Gelzer could write: 'For this reason, all attempts to convert the honest Neo-Hellenes to a recognition of historical truth is literally labour in vain. However, this need not stop us from expounding it'. We live in an age when, as at Byzantium, religious and political controversies have once more taken the place of racial: and this at least has the advantage that racial origins need no longer be discussed amid a babel of abuse and objurgation.

The invaders of Italy were Lombards. The invaders of the Balkan Peninsula were Hunnic Avars, whose strength lay in the uncountable hordes of Slavs which now make their impact on Mediterranean history. The Slavs were an eminently hardy, but peace-loving, unambitious and industrious people. Their tribes were reluctant to combine, and they seldom acted in unison except under foreign leadership such as that of the Avar and the Bulgarian. They were not town-dwellers; yet it would be very erroneous to class them as nomads, like the Turkic tribes of the Steppe. They had developed agriculture to a high degree of efficiency. They were bee-keepers on a large scale. They were skilful huntsmen and fishermen. They were, as the Byzantine emperors soon found, well qualified to be immigrants into waste or underdeveloped territories; and it is to their industry and agricultural skill that much of the recovery in the Byzantine rural economy in and after the seventh century must in fairness be attributed. The contention of a recent historian has much to be said for it: namely, that if the Slavs had been permitted to infiltrate peaceably into the waste lands of the Balkans, they would have been welcomed there by the Byzantine government as they were welcomed into Asia Minor. But the savagery of the Avars under whose leadership the Slav tribes pressed southwards made this impossible; and it is to the Avar element in the Avaro-Slav invasion that we must probably attribute that merciless extermination of the remnants of rural life recorded by contemporary historians.

During the 570s to 90s the Roman forces of the Emperors Tiberius and Maurice, with the slenderest resources but with indomitable perseverance and courage, were fighting desperately to contain the Avars beyond the frontier and to defend the key fortresses of Sirmium on the Save and Singidunum on the Danube. But this could not last. Both fortresses succumbed, and the way was open for the barbarian invasion of Dalmatia, which Byzantine records state to have been either Avaric or Slavonic: in fact it was both. The eastern half of the peninsula was scarcely defended except from behind the walls of a few impregnable fortresses.

A particularly vicious raid on Mainland Greece in about 587 destroyed most of what was left of Athens and Corinth outside their acropoleis. The invaders poured into Peloponnesus and by 623 were raiding from it as far south as Crete. The natives, such as they were, sought refuge under the walls of Monemvasia, but up to those walls the inundation rolled. During a period variously estimated at between 50 and 200 years Byzantine control of Greece was non-existent. In Peloponnesus there was not even a framework of Roman administration. In Mainland Greece only the garrison forts held out. The rest was 'sclavinica terra'.4

Italy, Dalmatia and Old Hellas were divided from the empire by the year 615, which Isidore of Seville marks as the final step in the Slavonic conquest of Greece. This in itself was a revolutionary break with the past, and the inauguration of a new epoch. But it was a mere beginning to the changes which the Eastern Empire was shortly to undergo. I do not here wish to describe the Arab conquests at length, since they began only in the latter years of Heraclius' reign and were consummated during the next half century. Suffice it to say that in a few decades, Syria, Palestine, Cyprus, Egypt and North Africa fell to the Saracens. Armenia was overrun; and shortly afterwards first Crete and then Sicily were occupied. The Aegean islands were devastated afresh, and the very coasts of Asia Minor fearfully harassed. The youthful and growing might of the Bulgars was fixed permanently to north and south of the Balkan mountains. And the nightmare of John of Ephesus, that the end of the world was nigh, was realised in an age most justly denominated 'dark'. It seemed that the great heritage and tradition of the Graeco-Roman world, and even the Christian culture of the later Empire, might be extinguished. The miracle lay not in the collapse of the Roman Empire but in its survival and ultimate recovery as the dominant power of the Near East. With the loss of Syria and Egypt, trade and economy were disrupted, for the one had been the great manufactory, the other for centuries the granary, of the Eastern Empire.

What was left? The kernel of the empire, Asia Minor, with its capital across the Bosphorus, was what remained as the raw material of recovery. So long as these survived, there was a hope, if only a slender one. But at least two emperors of the seventh century thought of abandoning the city of Constantine and establishing an imperial capital in Carthage or Sicily. Nor should

13

we blame their faintheartedness, but rather applaud their apparent good sense.

What measures, military, economic, demographic and administrative ultimately stemmed and turned back the tides we must try to summarise below. But, to answer the question posed at the beginning, the empire of the House of Heraclius, though unchanged in theory, was radically different from that of Justinian in the practical respects of territory, population and administration. And the survival, though in a very different form, of the culture of the successors of Alexander and of the Rome of Augustus must be attributed primarily to the new settlers in the Eastern Empire: to the genius and valour of Hellenised Armenians and to the industry and adaptability of Hellenised Slavs.

NOTES

[1] Ostrogorsky, 72.
[2] Ostrogorsky, 57–66.
[3] Bury, LRE, 145 ff.
[4] Bury, LRE, 117–20; Ostrogorsky, 68–70; Vasiliev, 176, 179.

CHAPTER TWO

HERACLIUS

When Justinian died in 565, at the age of eighty-three, his death was not, as seemed probable, followed by the immediate collapse of his empire. The *status quo*, except in Spain, Italy and Greece, was preserved during about forty years, and at some points — on the Danube and in the East – the position of its defence appeared even to show some signs of improvement. This was no mean achievement, with discord rife at home, the religious feuds as ardent as ever in Syria and Egypt, an empty treasury and armed forces chronically undermanned and underpaid. It is plain that talents of no mean order were at the helm; and a superficial view of Byzantine history between the two pre-eminent figures of Justinian and Heraclius often loses sight, very unjustly, of the abilities of the Emperors Tiberius II (578–82) and Maurice (582–602). Tiberius, it is true, after a distinguished career in the army, reigned no more than four years. But his successor and son-in-law Maurice, the last emperor whose line reached back to the days of Old Rome, governed for twenty years and showed a devotion, industry and competence which have only been appreciated in our own day. That his successes in the field could only delay, rather than prevent a major catastrophe was not his fault. He did what he could, and it is truly astonishing that he did so much. Nor were all of his activities ephemeral. In two very important departments, those of administrative and military organisation, his reforms were lasting; and Heraclius often receives credit for some ideas which were in truth those of Maurice. The senseless profusion of Justinian had so totally ruined the finances of the empire that

Maurice was compelled to economise at home, and this was his undoing. Moreover, though in early life a brave and skilful soldier, he was unable, when emperor, to keep in touch with his forces in the field. Had he led his men on the Danube or in Armenia, he would certainly have been as successful as his generals Priscus and Philippicus, and would have won the love of the very men who at length turned upon and overthrew him. His mistake was not repeated by Heraclius, who totally disappeared with his troops into the fastnesses of Persia for years at a time, judging rightly that where the emperor and his army were, there was the Roman empire.[1]

To Maurice, it would seem, more than to any one man, must be given the credit for the conception of the Middle-Byzantine system of provincial government – the so-called *thematic* system – which in our own time has been, and still is, the subject of widespread controversy. That Heraclius developed this system in the vital areas of Asia Minor, I believe, with the greatest of living Byzantinists, to be true. But the organisation of the so-called *exarchates* of Ravenna and Carthage, which in all essential points prefigures the system of the *themes*, was the work of Maurice. This system of provincial organisation was the only answer to the ever worsening military situation. It was the conception of an empire based on martial law. The military and civil functions had hitherto, since the time when fighting had been confined to the frontiers and the great body of the Mediterranean Empire was in a state of profound peace, been kept carefully distinct. The structure of the empire as devised or modified by Diocletian and Constantine was a civilian structure. The armed forces had their own organisation, and their areas of deployment did not necessarily correspond with those of the civil government. This system, in a state of affairs in which war, and war in any of half a dozen areas at the very heart of the empire, became chronic, was increasingly unworkable. Even Justinian, deceived in his hope of restoring universal peace to a united empire, had begun to see that some frontier districts must be put under martial law, and that the governor must be in one person controller of justice, army and finance. The initial reform of Maurice was precipitated by the Lombard invasion of Italy (568) and by the constant menace of the Berbers in North Africa, at a time when communication between those areas and the capital, though not severed, had become precarious by sea and by land. Hence arose the so-called *exarchates*, or vice-royalties, of Ravenna and Carthage in the 580s and 90s. The *exarch* was a military governor who corresponded in all essentials to the later *strategos* of an imperial *theme*, and indeed his lieutenant, at least in Africa, went by the title of *hypostrategos*, or vice-governor. His power, so long as he retained his office, was absolute over every department of both the civil and the military administration, and he was the sole representative of the emperor, to whom he was directly responsible. His *exarchate* was organised in a manner which is highly instructive for an understanding of the later *thematic* system, about whose origins our information is very meagre. The Italian *exarchate* of Ravenna was divided into several territorial circumscriptions which corresponded to the political exigencies of the moment. These subdivisions were called 'duchies', and the military administrator of each was appointed by the *exarch*, and called a 'duke' or *magister militum*. Each duchy in turn was subdivided into forts and garrisons commanded by a tribune or lieutenant, and the troops or 'bands' who manned it were no longer regular soldiers drafted thither by a central command, but local populations conscripted for service. They were *milites*, or 'soldiers'. The close correspondence of this organisation with the later *thematic* system of the empire as a whole, as we find it in full working order in the eighth and ninth centuries, needs no emphasis. Its introduction was a positive *renovatio* of empire – in its military, territorial and economic aspects. It is intimately connected with Byzantine survival and recovery, just as its dissolution in the twelfth century is intimately connected with the Byzantine collapse.[2]

The soldierly and statesmanlike talents of Maurice were principally occupied with the running sore of the eastern frontier. During the whole of its existence the properly Byzantine state, although in theory still Mediterranean or even ecumenical, was, willy-nilly, turned eastward, and its main preoccupation was to hold the eastern frontier from Chaldia to Tarsus. It is easy to see the reason for this. Territorial losses and disruptions in Spain or Italy or even in the Balkans, much nearer home than either, were no doubt blows to the prestige of the Roman Empire, but in practice they were very little more. It was not so with Asia Minor. Any protracted occupation or diminution of that fertile and prosperous homeland must in the end be fatal. Manpower,

agriculture, minerals, all depended on control of Anatolia, or
'Romany' as it came to be called. Moreover, Anatolia is the key
to an area almost equally important to Byzantium, that is, to
Armenia. It is a highly significant circumstance that one of the
first and largest of the provinces into which Asia Minor was
parcelled by the reforms of Heraclius was given the name
Armeniakoi, which is, being interpreted, the Province of the
Troops of Armenia. Armenia was for centuries not only the
source of the finest fighting men of Byzantium, but also, there is
good reason to believe, the chief source of her precious metals,
especially gold. The Byzantine economy was, as we know, a
money economy. The empire stood or fell with the solidity of her
gold bezant, which was not only the symbol of stability and
purity in commerce, but also the symbol of imperial might. The
trader who carried this symbol was – as it were – under the protection and jurisdiction of the throne. The barbarian customer
who received it became, in one sense, the subject of the Caesar
whose image and superscription it bore; and the gold *solidus* (or
nomisma, in the Greek language) ranked with the imperial
images and the imperial bulls as tokens of universal imperial supremacy. Byzantium was thus always acutely sensitive to her
north-eastern frontier. More than one war with the Persians is explicitly stated to have arisen in quarrels over the control or lease of
Armenian goldmines. And when we contemplate the vast and
continuous efforts of the Heraclian, Isaurian and Macedonian
dynasties which were devoted almost uninterruptedly to the
maintenance of, and expansion beyond, the eastern frontier, we
must always remember the compelling reasons for this preoccupation.

One of the chief and certainly the most destructive of the agents
which brought the empire of Justinian to the verge of extinction
was the Sasanid Empire of Persia. This dynasty had always been a
menace to Roman Asia since its establishment in the early third
century. For nearly a century, between 531 and 628, this realm
was governed by Chosroes I and his grandson Chosroes II. They
were ambitious and encroaching despots. Justinian, whose designs in the west made a peaceful eastern frontier an absolute
necessity, made treaty after treaty with the first Chosroes, each
one entailing territorial concessions and vast sums of gold. Each
time the faithless Persian broke the pact and renewed the war.

Nothing decisive was achieved, and in 561 the final treaty was made and kept, though at the price of 200,000 pieces of Roman gold.

Maurice inherited this problem, but his resources for coping with it were drastically curtailed. Subsidies could not be paid, for there was no money left. Soldiers were few, and very often mutinous. It was with great difficulty that an army of 4,000 could be mustered to meet the invaders. Yet, for ten years, the frontier was maintained by the courage and genius of the imperial generals Philippicus and Heraclius, father of the future emperor, whose services were rewarded with the *exarchate* of Carthage. At last, in 591, diplomacy achieved what force could not. A revolt broke out against the Great King, Chosroes II, as he fled for refuge to the Romans. Maurice, by a brilliant stroke of policy, restored him to his throne, where he reigned at peace during the next ten years, surrounded by a Roman bodyguard.[3] Maurice was thus able to turn his attention to the next point of danger, the Avar menace on the Danube. This menace was not so easily contained, and fearful losses of territory were suffered in the Balkan Peninsula. At length, lack of money and supplies precipitated the cataclysm. In the year 602 Maurice was compelled to order his Danubian army to winter across the river in Avar territory and to live off the country. They mutinied and chose one of their own officers, Phocas, to be their *exarch*. Phocas at once marched on the capital. Maurice, owing to his self-will and parsimony, was the object of universal dislike, a dislike which he had by no means deserved. Deserted by the city militia and abandoned by the army, he slunk away with his family to Chalcedon; and there he and four of his sons were butchered on 26 November 602. The army crowned Phocas, who entered the capital in triumph.

The days of the 'tyrant' Phocas (602–10) were few and evil. His reign of eight years is generally regarded, and with good reason, as the nadir of the empire, the point at which the only alternatives left were extinction or reform. His administration is remarkable for nothing but disaster abroad and bloodshed at home: and people said commonly that it was doubtful whether the more destructive enemy were the Persians without or the emperor within. His energies were wholly absorbed in keeping his throne against repeated treasons and conspiracies, which he repressed with continual and bloody reprisals. King Chosroes of

19

Persia flew to arms to avenge his benefactor Maurice, whereupon the only capable Roman general threw in his hand. The Persian advance was nearly unopposed, and it was ominous for the fate of the eastern provinces thirty years later. Mesopotamia and Syria were overrun, and Cappadocia and Paphlagonia, in the very heart of Asia Minor. At last the Persian host pushed to the very walls of the capital, and laid siege to Chalcedon. In the face of this Phocas could think of no expedient but a singularly ill-timed attempt at a forcible conversion of the Jews of Antioch, which caused a violent and destructive revolt in that city. Egypt was in disorder and the corn supplies to Constantinople were suspended. Famine and pestilence ravaged the capital. Phocas himself, said Bury, broods like some hideous nightmare over an exhausted and weary realm. It was hard to see whence salvation was to come.4

In the end it came from Africa. The single part of the empire which at that time enjoyed peace, prosperity and good government was the *exarchate* of Carthage. The *exarch* was the elder Heraclius, who had done brilliant service in the Persian campaigns of Maurice. Heraclius saw that if anything was to be done, he must do it. He accordingly equipped a fleet, which he put under the command of his son Heraclius, and at the same time dispatched his nephew Nicetas with a strong force by land. One or the other would get to Constantinople and whoever got there first would take command. In September 610 the young Heraclius sailed into the straits of Helle. The miserable Phocas had scarcely a friend, and Heraclius was welcomed with open arms as a deliverer. On 4 October the tyrant was seized and dragged aboard Heraclius' galley. 'And it is thus,' said the conqueror, 'that you have governed your empire?' 'Are you sure,' said his victim, 'that you will be able to do any better?' He was instantly cut to pieces, and his remains were burnt in the Forum of the Ox.

The personage who now essayed the task of restoration was one of the most remarkable men ever to mount the Roman throne. Heraclius was in all probability of Armenian stock, and this, if true, is highly significant, since from now on nearly all the great rulers of Byzantium came of this race. A devout and orthodox Christian, he imparted a mystical tinge to his duties, and was capable of inspiring himself and his subjects with a sense of his divinely appointed mission. Like most rulers who govern through inspiration rather than steady force of character, he tended to act

by fits and starts, in bursts of irresistible energy alternating with
fits of depression and inertia. To his sense of devotion was added,
we must infer, a capacity for civil and military organisation of a
very high order. On every department he left his mark : he found
his realm in ruins and he bequeathed it to his posterity in a state
which, if not renovated, at least ensured survival and promised
restoration. During thirty years he laboured, and the tragedy of
his life is that at the end of it he seemed to have achieved nothing.
It is indeed painful to contemplate his latter days, as, a discredited
general and an incestuous uncle, with his structure seemingly in
ruins, he sat idly day after day, shrinking in vertiginous terror
from the gently heaving waves of the Bosphorus.[5] But the tragedy,
though personally severe, was more apparent than real. Heraclius
was one of those who build upon the rock, and his fame both as a
ruler and as a soldier was deeply, and very justly, venerated for
centuries in Byzantine memory.[6]

The arrival of Heraclius at Byzantium in 610 and his assumption
of supreme power caused no immediate improvement. On the
contrary, during nine uncomfortable years, things got very much
worse. The emperor's first attempt to stem the Persian advance
was abortive. And then disasters came thick and fast. Cilicia was
occupied in 613. In May 614 Jerusalem was stormed and sacked
by the Persians, the patriarch Zachary taken prisoner, and the
Holy Cross, the most sacred relic of Christendom, carried off to
the Persian capital. In 615 the Persian army was again at Chalcedon
and in the same year the Greek Peninsula was regarded as finally
lost to the Slavs. In 617 began the Persian invasion of Egypt.
Alexandria fell ; and the Egyptian granaries which had for so long
fed the capital with cheap corn were at length closed to her for
ever.[7]

It was in all probability this final catastrophe which convinced Heraclius that the game was up. In 618 he announced his
decision to leave Constantinople and withdraw to Carthage where
alone men and means might be found for a counter-attack on
Egypt. The announcement was momentous. The citizens were in
uproar. They refused to be deserted. Sergius the patriarch persuaded the emperor to swear that he would never abandon the
Queen of Cities.[8] Heraclius was quick to seize the occasion. That
moment saw the renewal of the covenant between the emperor
and his people. Whatever he chose to demand, they would

unhesitatingly supply. The Church turned her fabulous treasures into gold pieces. Rigorous financial economies were imposed without a murmur of discontent. A new army was raised, and a programme of military training was put in hand. Heraclius himself would lead the soldiers of God.

It is at this conjuncture that we are compelled to return to the problem of the date and origin of the organisation of the empire into military provinces, or *themes*. The problem is this : was this organisation the work of Heraclius ? Or was it virtually in operation before him ? Or did it not properly exist until the days of his great-grandson ? In short, was Heraclius the author of a far-sighted economic and social reform ? Or had Heraclius nothing whatever to do with the matter ? Astonishing as it may seem, the paucity of our evidence makes it possible to adopt either of these extreme positions, as well as all sorts of compromises intermediate between them.

According to one view, Heraclius founded the Armeniac and Anatolic provinces, or *themes* (which then occupied most of eastern and central Asia Minor), before his Persian campaigns began in 622. He designed them to function more or less as we know them to have functioned two or three centuries later: namely, on a basis of martial law, decentralised authority and soldiers' estates among a free peasantry, where the head of the family gave military service and the rest of the family tilled the soil. This was the reform by which Heraclius strengthened the armed forces, revitalised agriculture, and brought prosperity to the countryside and relief to the central treasury.

The directly contrary position is also stiffly maintained. There was no reform but merely a gradual process brought about piecemeal by changes in the population. No soldiers' estates are in fact mentioned in our sources until the tenth century; therefore they did not exist. *Pas de documents, pas d'histoire*. As for Heraclius, since there was no conscious and deliberate reform, he was no reformer. And indeed his reputation as a statesman and a soldier is ludicrously exaggerated.

My own view, for what it is worth, is that the first position is almost certainly the right one, and that the *thematic* system was in fact introduced into Anatolia by Heraclius. Theophanes, writing of the year 622, explicitly states that Heraclius went out into the region of the *themes*; and though the word *thema*, in this martial organisation, means an army corps as well as the area where it is quartered, it is easier to suppose the latter to be the meaning here. Moreover, writing of the year 627, Theophanes mentions a *turmarch* of the Armeniakoi, which seems to prove that by this time at least the military organisation characteristic of the *themes* was in operation: for *turma* was the new title for the subdivisions of a *theme*, just as in the west the 'duchy' was the subdivision of the *exarchate*. The evidence of Constantine Porphyrogenitus, who wrote three centuries later, is indeed vague and dubious; but he does say, 'I believe the name [*Armeniakon*] dates from the time of Heraclius the emperor and from the years after him'. This shows that old tradition did connect Heraclius with the origin of the older *themes*. Who are we to contradict it?[9]

As for the basis of the whole reform, which rested from the first on peasant-soldier freeholders, it is true that, if we confine ourselves to purely Byzantine documents, we cannot prove the matter one way or the other. But we have more light from the development of the *exarchate* of Ravenna, where, as we saw, the people who lived in the circumscription of a fort and supplied its garrison, were in fact local residents and were denominated 'milites'. Heraclius, who himself came from Carthage, knew all about the organisation of an *exarchate*, and had seen with his own eyes its success and prosperity. Indeed, it was to Carthage that he proposed to transfer his capital in 618. The great probability – as I see it – is that during the years 619–22 he did in fact consciously and successfully transfer this system to Asia Minor, merely altering some of the Latin terminology existing in Africa and Italy. It was he who reorganised the whole state on a military footing and in doing so saved the empire.

The next six years were devoted by Heraclius, with inflexible purpose, to the destruction of the Persian monarchy. Nothing else mattered. The Balkan provinces were abandoned. The West was nearly forgotten. Efforts to create diversions in his rear went unheeded, and even the fearful danger of the combined Perso-Avar attack on the capital in 626 could not draw him home. But, present or absent, he seemed to inspire his countrymen to ever new achievements. And their destruction of the Slavonic fleet in the Golden Horn on the night of Thursday, 7 August 626, one of the most glorious and memorable exploits in Byzantine history, and attributed to the direct intervention of the Mother of God, was at least indirectly attributable to the influence of Heraclius. We cannot follow his eastern campaigns in detail; but he won a series of astonishing victories with a new army that never failed him, often against odds in difficult terrain. In the latter part of 627 the decisive battle was fought near Nineveh. The emperor, mounted on his dun charger Dorkon, hewed down three captains with his own hand. The Persian general Razatas was killed, and his force was annihilated. The emperor's unbroken success at last discouraged the Persians. A revolt broke out and Chosroes II was murdered by his own son. Peace was made in 628. The True Cross was retaken at Ctesiphon and at length restored to Jerusalem. The emperor announced his triumph in a dispatch which commenced 'O be joyful in the Lord', and this was read from the pulpit of St Sophia. In the autumn the Lord's champion appeared in person in his City, and a solemn service of thanksgiving was made more solemn still by the presence of the True Cross.[10]

The Roman Empire as restored by Heraclius may be considered, in a historical point of view, the truly Byzantine Empire; and it may be well to consider briefly at this point two important features of its culture. The unifying factors of its heterogeneous folk were Orthodox Christianity and Hellenistic letters. The latter every educated person was proud to acquire: and to thousands of clerks and bureaucrats, knowledge of Greek was the source of their livelihood. With Heraclius, Greek becomes the official language of the state. The emperor becomes the *basileus* (emperor), a title henceforth reserved for the master of the world, and never shared, except under the most stringent pressure, with foreign princes. The Greek education was chiefly in grammar and rhetoric, as codified in the Hellenistic age. It was a barren discipline, and Byzantine writing as a whole is nearly devoid of literary merit. But it was a thorough discipline. It gave to a population which came from a hundred non-Hellenic stocks a common cultural inheritance. And as a factor making for cohesion in the reformed state its importance is considerable. Centuries, however, were to pass before the Byzantine felt or wished to feel any relationship with the ancient inhabitants of Hellas. He was simply a Greek-speaking Roman. And when Heraclius returned from his Persian wars, he was hailed, not as the new Alexander, but as the new Scipio.

The sense of belonging to the Chosen and Orthodox People of

the Roman Christ was also a factor which ultimately made for imperial unity in the high middle ages, and it was of course not confined to the educated class. Yet, for many centuries, the Christian religion appeared to be a pretext, if not a fundamental cause, for disruption. To understand or divine the meaning and importance of theological speculation to the East Mediterranean during these centuries demands a great effort of historical imagination. The points at issue are of unbelievable complexity, all of them arising from efforts to explain the Incarnation of God in a human body. Even where the arguments are intelligible – and this is by no means always the case – they appear very frequently too grotesque for the acceptance of a rational being, and too trivial for his serious consideration. That such questions should have been the lifelong study and passion of the subtlest minds, and should have been so fervently espoused by the masses as to provoke savagery, slaughter and political change, appears to a modern mind so incredible that many have been tempted to regard them as mere colouring which masked social needs or racial antipathies such as we are familiar with in our own day. But this simple solution cannot be received without qualification. That monophysitism tended to be strong in provinces seized by the Saracens, and that disaffection caused by imperial persecution contributed to this seizure, are undoubted facts. But the theological issues involved in this and other disputes must be taken at their face value. They really were what mattered. 'If,' said St Gregory of Nyssa in the fourth century, 'you ask change for your money, you get a lecture on the difference between the Father and the Son. If you ask the price of a loaf of bread, the baker will tell you that the Father is more than the Son. If you ask if the bath is ready, the reply is that the Son is born of nothing!'

The most powerful and menacing of the christological heresies, the one which more than any had during two centuries divided the minds of men, was that of Eutyches. His contention was that the Saviour had possessed one single, divine nature : and hence his heresy was known as 'monophysite'. The orthodox view, as formulated at Chalcedon in 451, was, on the contrary, that the Saviour was complete in humanity as well as divinity, one and the same Christ in two natures, without confusion or change, division or separation, each nature concurring into one Person and one Substance.

25

This was the controversy that all the despotism of Zeno (474–91) and Justinian had been unable to allay. No formula could be devised, no edict promulgated, which could heal the divided body of the Spouse of Christ. The final attempt was made by Heraclius at the very hour of the Saracen cataclysm. After long cogitation, Heraclius in 639 suggested to the Syrian sectaries that the Saviour, whatever the number or condition of His natures, had been animated by a single *energy* and a single *will*. For a moment it seemed that this solution might be the panacea for which emperors and churchmen had sought so long. The monophysites accepted it, and even Pope Honorius did not condemn it. Yet it was no more than a makeshift, and the political purpose of its promulgators was to mask the dispute rather than to settle it on any strictly theological grounds. The orthodox patriarch of Jerusalem Sophronius condemned it and the pope finally disavowed it, as he was bound to do. Persecution followed, both in Syria and Egypt. The new solution was ratified by Heraclius in a document known as the *Ekthesis*, or 'Exposition', but this too was rejected by orthodoxy. In any case, solution came too late. By 639 the Saracens were undisputed masters of Syria and on the road to Egypt.[11]

For, at the exact moment, in 622, when Heraclius was embarking on his first campaign against Chosroes, an event far less spectacular, but of incalculably greater significance, was taking place one thousand miles to the south. Here in the city of Mecca had dwelt for rather more than fifty years Mahomet, the Prophet of God. His origin and early life are obscure, and so much incrusted with legendary and apocryphal matter that, when we have said that he came of a minor clan of the ruling tribe of the Koraish, that he was born in humble circumstances about the year 570, that he established his fortunes by marriage with a widow much older than himself, and that he suffered intermittently from mental disturbances afterwards diagnosed as epilepsy, we have said very nearly all about them that can be regarded as historical.

The culture of Arabia was at that time on a very low level. The comparatively high and civilised religions of Judaism, Zoroastrianism and Christianity had passed it by, except in the Yemen, at its south-western extremity. Here Judaism had been established; and here the Roman empire had striven, with the help of the Axumite rulers of Ethiopia, to implant Christianity. The Emperor

Anastasius I sent these Himyarites a bishop. The Emperor Justinian sent them a missionary, and with him, it would seem, a code of laws. However, in a year close to that of Mahomet's birth, the Persians invaded Yemen, and these endeavours ceased for ever.

Elsewhere in the peninsula the Arabs practised idolatry of a very primitive and far from uniform character, although the Kaaba, or 'Cubic House', of Mecca had some claim to being regarded as the centre of a national religion : where, among other idols, a holy stone or fetish was kissed, stroked and adored by the worshippers.

How much of the great spiritual revolution which was consummated by Mahomet during the ten years of his Hegira (622–32) can be attributed to his original inspiration, and how much of it was derived from foreign religious beliefs, is again disputed. But it seems certain that he was influenced by Jewish ideas, and perhaps also by Christian ; and these he might have found among the embers of those creeds yet glowing in the Yemen. At all events he early became convinced of two important principles : the first, that there was but one God, and the second that he, Mahomet, was God's prophet. That he regarded himself as the founder of a sect which was destined for world conquest is not probable, since, like Jesus, he was himself preoccupied with the imminence of the Judgement Day, on which the evil would go to a very Christian sort of Hell and the good to a carnal Paradise which obviously derives from his own fervid imagination. Convinced of these propositions, he began, under the direct inspiration of God, to devise a whole series of moral precepts and injunctions which were a very decided improvement on those prevailing among his contemporaries, and are the most valuable part of his doctrine. This doctrine he began to teach to a few relations and intimates, but, for about ten years, he had little success. His fellow citizens eyed him with indifference or misgiving, and the widespread acceptance of his teaching began only with the event already alluded to, his 'emigration', or *hegira*, to the city of Medina, in the summer of 622. Here for ten years 'his heresy', as the Christian writers put it, 'prevailed', and he began to assume the significance of a temporal as well as of a spiritual leader. Gifted and influential men, who afterwards became those generals and caliphs who spread his creed over the Near East, joined his standard. In 628 he was able to occupy Mecca and formally to expel the idols, with the exception of the stone fetish of the Kaaba. Four years later he died,

27

but his work was done. In a few decades the tide of Islam (the 'Surrender to God') had poured irresistibly over Persia and most of the eastern and southern areas of the Graeco-Roman world.[12]

The great revolution which thus changed the face of the East, and incidentally determined the shape and fate of the Byzantine state, must be followed in more detail when we come to speak of the Heraclian and Isaurian sovereigns who bore the brunt of it. But we may make one or two observations of a general character which may help us to understand its sudden and overwhelming success. Internally the Arabian peninsula was in Mahomet's time both divided and impoverished. The great majority of the population consisted of nomadic tribes at feud with one another and scarcely conscious of ethnic or religious relationship. Islam realised the economic need for expansion by providing religious and thus national unity. A few early successes in the field were sufficient to rally the nomadic Beduin by thousands to the standard. The exhaustion of both Byzantine and Persian empires did the rest. In 636 and 637 each empire succumbed on the critical and terrible fields of the Yarmuk and Cadesia.

The Roman provinces of Syria, Palestine and Egypt were ripe for the sickle. The Semitic and Coptic races of those parts had been compelled, for a thousand years, to live under a Hellenistic yoke and a Hellenistic culture, imposed in turn by the successors of Alexander and the successors of Augustus. Their state had never been happy and their fusion was always incomplete. Much of the religious controversy which, ever since its adoption of Christianity, had rent the Roman world may be attributed to peculiarities of racial character, and to the conscious or unconscious repugnance of the East against conformity to one more Graeco-Roman orthodoxy imposed from without. The monophysite heresy ardently espoused by Syrian Jacobites and Egyptian Copts surely shows a racial, that is an oriental, tendency towards monotheism and mysticism, which regarded with genuine aversion the subtle distinctions of Chalcedon and the emphasis laid on the human component of the incarnate Deity. The maladroit policy of the successors of Justinian exasperated these sentiments to a dangerous degree. Opinions may differ as to the expediency of persecution, but at least it is clear that a persecutor must be strong to be effective. Maurice and Heraclius, able as in many ways they were, remained blind to the hopelessness of imposing by the sword a religious unity which even the powerful arm of Justinian had failed to enforce. The obstinacy of Sophronius of Jerusalem in rejecting all compromise, and the cruelties of Cyrus, the orthodox patriarch of Alexandria, showed themselves on the very eve of the Saracen eruption. It is probably an anachronism to suggest that the eastern provinces voluntarily or consciously seceded out of any racial, still less national, feelings of antipathy to the Roman government. But it is very certain that they had no interest whatever in struggling to maintain the existing order. And when a headlong wave of Semites, propelled by a doctrine of strict monotheism which they could at least understand even if they did not share it, promising moreover and practising religious toleration for all shades of Christian belief, rolled upon them, they went under without resistance. Nor is it true to say that the eastern provinces were inundated by a horde of savage strangers with whom they had been previously unacquainted, as happened with the coming of the Slavs into Greece. On the contrary : Saracens had been settled for decades on both sides of the Byzantine–Persian frontier, where, having as yet no settled loyalty or faith of their own, they served either power and professed either religion. Thus, the Saracen assumption of empire was speedy and relatively bloodless in the east, and the rectified balance of power now swung, no longer between Byzantium and Ctesiphon, but between Byzantium and Damascus, and, thereafter, between Byzantium and Bagdad.

Syria, Egypt and North Africa became Arab lands, still are so, and will in all likelihood so remain.

NOTES

[1] Bury, LRE, 79–94.
[2] Ostrogorsky, 80–4.
[3] Bury, LRE, 95–113.
[4] Bury, LRE, 197 ff.
[5] Nicephorus, 25–7.
[6] Bury, LRE, 208–10.
[7] Ostrogorsky, 79.
[8] Nicephorus, 12.
[9] Theophanes, 303, 325; Ostrogorsky, 80-4.
[10] Bury, LRE, 227 ff.
[11] Ostrogorsky, 90–1.
[12] Vasiliev, 202–10.

CHAPTER THREE

THE SARACEN CONQUESTS

The dominating facts of Byzantine history for the hundred and fifty or two hundred years following the death of Heraclius (641) are: externally, the rise and consolidation of the Arab empire, first under the Omayyad caliphs of Damascus and later under the Abbasids of Bagdad; and internally, the struggle with icono-clasm. To both of these phenomena we must give some thought. At first sight the caliphate, the empire of the 'representatives' of the Prophet, might seem to have stepped into the shoes of the Sasanid empire of Persia: and indeed it is possible to see in the rise of the Abbasid caliphs, after the middle of the eighth century, a revival of specifically Persian influence. Hence, if we look to the east only, we might believe that the old balance of power between two empires of rival ambitions and faith was merely perpetuated. Yet it is obvious that a militant power such as the Saracen, which, in a very few years, became undisputed master of Persia, Iraq, Syria, Egypt, North Africa and Spain; which then created strong navies and thus established an empire in the very heart of the Mediterranean, based on the great islands of Sicily and Crete; which occupied for many years a substantial part of Southern Italy; which from its Cretan base, ravaged southern Greece, the west coast of Asia and the Aegean Islands; which for centuries pushed its marauding bands annually or biennially into the heart of the Byzantine homeland; which sacked Thessalonica; and which on two occasions besieged Constantinople herself by sea and land with uncountable multitudes – it is, I say, obvious that such a power presented problems more searching and had effects more profound than any which the Sasanid menace had ever produced. The very extent of the Saracen power did indeed necessitate its fragmentation into the autonomous caliphates of Bagdad or Kairouan or Cordova; but this fragmentation was never, in the period of which we speak, decisively advantageous to Christendom. The Saracen might and did ally himself with a Christian power against other Christians; but he was reluctant to ally himself with a Christian power against other Saracens. So overwhelming was the Saracen superiority in the Mediterranean during the seventh to the ninth centuries that the Belgian historian Pirenne, as is well known, maintained the thesis that this supremacy was a principal cause of the ultimate division between eastern and western Christendom: the two halves, he thought, simply could not get at one another.[1] This thesis has, to be sure, been shown to be greatly exaggerated. Maritime communications between Anatolia and the west were never wholly interrupted, either for war, or for negotiation, or for commerce. But they were certainly endangered and hampered. And it is certainly a fact that eastern and western Christendom never succeeded in combining effectually against Islam, though plans of this kind were in the minds of more than one emperor of the east.

The eruption of Arab military might which followed the death of the Prophet was by no means the planned and organised manoeuvre that its startling speed and success might suggest. When Mahomet died in 632 his movement was in its infancy still, and had not won anything like universal acceptance even in the Arabian Peninsula itself. The conquest of that peninsula, which was completed by the first of the caliphs, Abu Bekr, was a war against religious rather than political dissent. The earliest attacks on the Roman province of Syria were carried out in a piecemeal and sporadic fashion which suggests no coherent strategic plan. It was not until the total victory of the Saracens at the Yarmuk river in 636, and their second and permanent occupation of Damascus, that the Caliph Omar was persuaded of the inevitability of imperial grandeur and imperial responsibilities.

If we seek for the proximate causes of Saracen success, these are to be found in the unbounded ardour of the desert tribesmen, and in their sagacity in choosing as battle-sites their familiar desert surroundings, in which opportunity for manoeuvre militated against the close order of the Roman war machine. And assuredly

31

the Roman generals might have found much matter for reflexion in the records of the destruction of 40,000 of the best troops in the world by the Parthians at Carrhae in 53 BC. Above all, the great conqueror Heraclius himself, though, as has recently been shown, by no means as idiotic in his Saracen campaign as the results of his strategy would lead one to suppose, seems to have suffered a long period of inertia and exhaustion after his sustained efforts, both mental and physical, against Persia. Meanwhile, the Arab forces were led by men of enormous vigour, enterprise and genius. Khalid, Abu Obaida, Amr and Moawiya, the generals of the Caliphs Abu Bekr and Omar, were all men of splendid abilities in the field.

The Saracen campaign of 634 in Syria seems to have been in the nature of a tentative rather than of an invasion in due form. Three separate Saracen forces participated. Amr entered the coastal strip of Palestine: Abu Obaida pushed northwards to the Sea of Galilee, where at the line of the Yarmuk river he was held by the Roman fortification. Meanwhile Khalid, who had been operating in Iraq, boldy crossed the desert and in March appeared under the walls of Damascus. At this conjuncture it was learnt that a serious Roman attempt would be made to cut the enemy off piecemeal, and that a strong Roman army was advancing from the north along the coast to destroy the isolated force of Amr. Khalid acted with an energy contrasting with the languid operations of the Romans. He fell back on the Yarmuk river and, with the Arab force already in position there, made all haste south-westwards to join Amr. In this he succeeded. In July the Roman army confronted the joint forces of the Arab commanders at Ajnadain, which lies in the plain midway between Gaza and Jerusalem. The enthusiasm of the tribesmen was victorious; and the Roman army was destroyed.

If Heraclius had until now not realised the full extent of the threat, the ensuing months made it painfully clear. The victorious Saracens returned northwards to the Yarmuk and after some months succeeded in forcing open the gate of Syria. Homs and Damascus capitulated, and at Damascus the prudent and judicious administration of the conquerors bore out their professions and assured their ultimate success. The monophysite Christians welcomed the tolerance shown to their religion and the respect shown to the centres of its worship. In truth the notion that the

Saracen conquerors offered the three alternatives of Islam, tribute or the sword must be received in the sense that of the three, they infinitely preferred the second. Religious fanaticism was certainly a part of their creed, but wholesale and forcible conversion to it was not. The Semites, whether Jew or Arab, are not a proselytizing race. Whereas the Byzantine believed in 'compelling them to come in', since conquest necessarily implied conversion to orthodox Christianity in order to fit the conquered into the imperial scheme of one empire and one faith, the Arab was content to remain one of the dominant caste of the Faithful, to tax the infidel at a higher rate than himself, but to leave him otherwise free to worship as he chose. It is not difficult to see the effect of such policies when these became generally known in areas where the policy of the Roman government had been for centuries, and still was, religious coercion frequently enforced by active persecution.

Meantime Amr, left behind in the south, laid siege to Jerusalem. The situation was serious, but not as yet desperate : no worse indeed than it had been fifteen years before, when the Persians had been masters of Palestine and Egypt ; and in some ways decidedly more hopeful. In the year 636 Heraclius, still at Antioch, made a final and convulsive attempt to crush the invader. He collected an army which has been estimated at 80,000 men, though this is probably an exaggeration. At least it outnumbered any force which the Arab chieftains could muster to oppose it. The Roman army included several thousand Armenian troops, belonging, it may be, to the regular *thematic* force of the Armeniakoi ; and also a strong contingent of Christian Arab cavalry. Theodore the Treasurer commanded in chief.

In face of this formidable threat the Arabs evacuated Homs and Damascus, united their forces and fell back seventy miles southward to the river Yarmuk, an affluent of the Jordan, which runs westward across the Deraa Gap, between the Sea of Galilee and the lava slope of the Jebel Hauran. Theodore's troops followed closely and occupied the gap. Then, from May until August, they remained inactive. This was fatal. The Arab commanders acted with their usual energy. They sent for reinforcements and began by forays and skirmishes to turn the Byzantine position to east and west. The Armenian contingent of the Roman army grew sullen and mutinous at this inaction and demanded that their countryman Baanes should take the chief command. At length the westerly infiltration of the Arabs reached and occupied the bridge over the Wadi-al-Rakkad, which lay right in the rear of the Byzantine army and across one of its lines of communication with the north. The decisive moment arrived on August 20, when a sandstorm began to blow from the south and into the faces of the Roman troops. The impetuous Saracens seized the moment and charged the Roman line, which gave way and was cornered in a position from which no escape was possible. They fell nearly to a man, and Theodore was among the dead.[2]

The result of the celebrated battle of the Yarmuk river, on 20 August 636, decided once for all the fate of Syria, and of much more than Syria : of Persia also, and Egypt. The emperor, old and ailing, perhaps already the prey of that horrible disease which ultimately put an end to his life, abandoned the east, and made his way back to the capital, which, seven years before, he had entered in triumph.

No further resistance was possible in the field. Homs and Damascus were re-occupied by the Arabs. The fortress of Jerusalem, never an easy place to capture, was defended by the Patriarch Sophronius, whose obstinate bigotry had destroyed any hopes of putting an end to religious division by means of the solution of one Will and one Energy. By the autumn of 637 he saw that the Holy City must capitulate. The Arabs were prepared to treat on their usual generous terms : for respect to be shown to Christian worship and churches. Sophronius, however, would not make any agreement except with the caliph personally and, strange as it may seem, this august personage undertook the journey from Medina. The story of his appearance in his ragged and patched cloak (for the caliphs of Medina, in contrast to their successors of Damascus or Bagdad, preserved the strictness and austerity of the Prophet's rule) is familiar from the Greek sources, and need not be doubted. The Caliph Omar entered the city, and was conducted on a tour of its monuments by the courteous patriarch, who held his bridle but was secretly disgusted at the ragged garb of this new Master of the Orient. And, on seeing his guest in the Church of the Holy Sepulchre, he is said to have exclaimed, 'Lo the Abomination of Desolation, spoken of by the mouth of the Prophet Daniel, that standeth in the Holy Place'.[3]

The capitulation of Jerusalem had been preceded by an engagement at Cadesia, on the Euphrates, between Khalid the Conqueror and Rustam, the Persian general of the youthful King Yastagerd. This engagement far surpassed Ajnadain and the Yarmuk in length and endurance. But at last the Saracens were, as usual, totally victorious, and Persia was inevitably as much theirs as Syria.

The invasion of Egypt, where substantial Byzantine military and naval forces were still able to operate, seems to have been agreed upon between the Caliph Omar and his general Amr at Jerusalem in 638. But it was not until the end of 639 that Amr entered that country, with a force which appears wholly inadequate for the operation. However, the prestige of the Beduin warrior and the feebleness of the Byzantine leadership supplied the place of myriads. Pelusium fell in a month. The strong fortress of Babylon at the nodal point of the Nile Delta seemed likely to hold out. But Cyrus, the patriarch of Alexandria, who was in that fortress, lost heart, and the news of the death of Heraclius, in February 641, completed the demoralisation. The place was handed over in April. The strong and rich city of Alexandria which, so long as the Byzantines had control of the sea, could and should have held out for years, first negotiated a truce and was finally occupied in September of 642.4

NOTES

1 Vasiliev, 390.
2 Theophanes, 337–8.
3 Theophanes, 317.
4 Bury, L R E, 263–71.

CHAPTER FOUR

THE SUCCESSORS OF HERACLIUS

Heraclius married twice. His first wife Eudocia died early, leaving a son, Constantine, who became co-emperor with his father as Constantine III. The second wife of Heraclius was his own niece Martina. His union with this lady lasted nearly thirty years, until his death in 641. It was regarded by the church and people as incestuous and Martina was, throughout her husband's life and after it, the object of violent animosity in the capital. The ultimate defeats and cruel death by disease of Heraclius were thought to be Heaven's punishments for his sin in marrying her. Heraclius wished his son by Eudocia, Constantine, and his son by Martina, Heraclius or Heraclonas, to succeed him as joint rulers. But this plan was instantly seen to be unworkable. The popular clamour was for the succession to be secured to the elder branch of the family, to the exclusion of the younger. Constantine II indeed died within three months of his father: but his son Constans was at once put forward as co-emperor with his step-uncle Heraclonas, and by the end of the year 641 an uprising had banished Martina and Heraclonas, one with a slit tongue, the other with a slit nose, for ever.[1]

The youthful Constans II (641–68), who now emerged as sole ruler, reigned for twenty-seven years. He was a responsible and energetic sovereign, and his designs, though frequently ill-chosen and nearly always, so far as our records show, unsuccessful, at least arose from a clear view of the needs of his empire. To read the chronicles is to get the impression that the first seventeen years of his reign were nothing but a catalogue of ignominious and total defeats by land and sea at the hands of invincible Saracens. Yet in 659 the all-powerful Moawiya, the emir of Syria, bought him off with a truce for the high sum of 1,000 gold pieces a day. It appears certain that Constans rebuilt the fleet, though all we hear of this is its defeat in 655. He is certainly responsible for settling Slav captives and immigrants in large numbers in Asia Minor. If he devised the revolutionary plan of transferring his capital back to the west, this was surely due not to fear of a hostile population in Byzantium, but to profound, if mistaken, policy: for it might well seem that the Old Rome would serve better than the New as a centre of defence against the westward-spreading tide of Islam. Of all his policies that which appears to us the most wrongheaded is his insistence on persecuting the orthodox up-holders of the two Energies of Christ, since the question had ceased to have any practical importance and was in fact composed in the orthodox sense by his own son at the Sixth General Council of 681.

The Islamic thirst for conquest was by no means slaked by the capture of Egypt and Alexandria. An abortive attempt by the Byzantines to reoccupy Alexandria in 646 was instantly overcome by Amr; and, with scarcely a pause, the Saracens swept on to the west of Africa. In the following year the *exarch* of Carthage, the treacherous Gregory, ventured with a large Roman force to bar their passage. But this force was totally defeated, and the *ex-archate* put under tribute to the conquerors. Yet the main threat to the very life of the empire lay in the ambitious designs and enormous abilities of the Omayyad Moawiya, the military governor and viceroy of Syria, who had his seat at Damascus. He was the first of the Saracen war-lords who had his eye firmly fixed on the conquest of Constantinople; and during his forty years of rule, first as emir, then as caliph, he never lost sight of this objective. With Moawiya begins the systematic invasion and ravaging of Asia Minor itself, which rapidly became an annual in-stitution, and called for that close system of frontier defence and reprisal characteristic of the frontier *themes*. But the sagacious emir saw that no land attack by itself could bring down the empire. Fleets must be built in the dockyards of Tripolis and Alexandria. Hitherto the Caliph Omar had forbidden this necessary adjunct, on religious grounds. But his successor Othman sanctioned it, and a new and terrible weapon was forged against Byzantium. The reform was put into effect with the energy characteristic of the Saracen power in all its departments at this explosive epoch. In less than five years the land power had taken to the sea. In 649 Cyprus, and in 650 the important commercial island of Aradus were attacked. In 654 a worse disaster befell. The large island of Rhodes was taken and sacked, and the colossal bronze statue of the sun-god, which had been reared eight centuries before over that proud commercial harbour, but which had, for nearly as long, sprawled in ruin like Satan in *Paradise Lost*, was hacked up and sold to a Jewish contractor. Meantime Constans, faced by this maritime threat, was paralysed by the simultaneous revolt of Byzantine Armenia, and an army sent by him to recover this all important area was cornered and destroyed.

Next year, however, the year 655, something had to be done, for the threat was now within measurable distance of the capital. A large Saracen fleet was collected at Tripolis, and though delayed by a gallant exploit on the part of some Roman prisoners in the place, was able to set sail for the west, while Moawiya himself, inaugurating the tactic followed by his successors, of a joint thrust by land and sea, drove into Cappadocia. The Roman fleet met the enemy off Phoenix, on the Lycian coast. The importance attached by the Romans to this encounter can be judged by the fact that the emperor went on board and took command in person. A battle took place in which the Roman fleet was decisively worsted, and Constans himself escaped only by subterfuge.[2]

There is no doubt that, but for a very lucky accident, the emir's fleet would in the next year or so have been able to anticipate by twenty vital years the sustained attack on Constantinople in 674, at a time when the capital was far worse prepared to meet the assault. But in 656 the Caliph Othman was murdered and Moawiya was during five years embroiled in a struggle for power with Ali, the son-in-law of the Prophet. This contest preoccupied him with home affairs until his own appointment as caliph in 661, and the establishment of the hereditary line of the Omayyads. It was during this struggle that Moawiya concluded with Constans the truce already referred to, which sufficiently indicates his belief that Roman intervention would be ruinous to his power.[3]

Constans did not intervene. Instead, he used his respite to make an expedition in the opposite direction, and this can have only one meaning. 'In this year [657]', says the chronicler, 'the emperor invaded the Slav regions, and took many prisoners, and reduced them'.4 The note is meagre, but it can only mean that Constans II was in urgent need of the 'many Slav prisoners' he took, in order to settle them in Asia. That, with the Saracen threat poised over him, he should have wasted time in forays into Macedonia to gain some cheap glory is quite incredible. It is rather a rare glimpse of that imperial policy of repopulation of the newly organised *themes* by transfer of a healthy and industrious stock of free peasants, to whom the empire owed its revival and prosperity. Constans of course, as a heretic, gets no credit for this among his contemporaries, who are much more interested in the circumstance that the same year was marked by his persecution and mutilation of Maximus the Confessor.

The ecclesiastical policy of Constans II was certainly mistaken and needlessly despotic. It will be remembered that, after long cogitation, his grandfather Heraclius had hit on a final expedient, a final face-saving formula, to heal the breach between orthodoxy and monophysitism. This was the doctrine known as the 'single will', or 'single energy', exercised by the Saviour. At first sight this seemed a harmless proposition. The monophysites did not know, and the pope seems not to have cared, what it meant: so that for a moment it passed current, and, as the modern phrase has it, 'papered over the cracks'. But already the catholics, on closer inspection, had discovered that 'monotheletism' or 'monoenergism' was in fact unorthodox: and indeed, given the natural interpretation of the definition of Chalcedon, it is hard to see how they could have reached any other conclusion. The Saracen conquests which had supervened had rendered the reconciliation of orthodox and monophysite, politically speaking, a matter of secondary importance ; and it would undoubtedly have been wise in the Constantinopolitan church to let the matter rest, and to consign the *Ekthesis* to a decent oblivion. Wisdom, however, is never a characteristic of religious controversy. The audacious polemic Maximus the Confessor moved the African church in 646 to ask the pope to take cognisance of the monotheletism professed, of necessity, by the Patriarch Paul of Constantinople. Paul, sounded by the pope, answered that it was indeed his conviction that the Saviour had been animated by one single will. The pope replied that this was a manifest heresy, and declared the patriarch excommunicated.

The youthful emperor resented this insult to his patriarch and to the memory of his grandfather in the highest manner. To provoke disturbance in his own capital by a forthright corroboration that the doctrine of monotheletism was correct would have been madness. Instead he promulgated in 648 an imperial edict, the celebrated *Type* – that is, the 'Rule' – which in the most peremptory fashion abolished the whole controversy. No one henceforward was to discuss the question of one will or two, one energy or two, on pain of deposition, excommunication, expropriation, flogging or banishment, as the case might suggest. No such instance of imperial absolutism over the church had been seen since the death of Justinian ; and even the *Henoticon* (or 'Act of Union') of Zeno, published 165 years before, was not couched in such absolute terms.

This instrument was not likely to be tamely received by the catholics. Pope Martin, who had been elected to the throne of St Peter without imperial sanction, instantly summoned a synod at the Lateran in 649, which condemned the *Type* and asserted the single truth of the 'Two Wills'. While the Fathers were deliberating, down came the imperial *exarch* of Ravenna upon them, with instructions that the *Type* should be put to instant and rigorous application. It is said that the pope himself narrowly escaped assassination, which, in view of what he subsequently had to endure, might have been a more merciful fate.

To provoke and carry on a factious dispute of this sort at the very moment when Abdulla was pushing towards Tripolis and the fleets of Moawiya were heading for the Dodecanese, may seem to us singularly ill-timed. It might, we may think, have occurred to both emperor and pope that a question even more pressing than Christian definition was that of Christian survival. But this was not the medieval view of the matter. For, as Pope Martin wrote to Constans, 'the safety of the state is contingent on right belief, and only if you rightly believe in Him will the Lord grant success to your arms.'

Constans was not to be trifled with. Four years after the Lateran council had reaffirmed its orthodoxy, the *exarch* of Ravenna once more came to Rome, seized the person of Pope Martin and shipped him to Constantinople. After long months of imprisonment and privation, the pontiff was brought before the imperial tribunal and accused on a trumped up charge of high treason. He was convicted, sentenced to death and shamefully humiliated. The sentence was commuted to banishment in the Crimea, and there the old man died in September 655.

Nor was Maximus the Confessor, who had been the prime mover in flouting the imperial will, allowed to remain unmolested. He too was brought from Italy and subjected to many trials and places of banishment; though, with the toughness which martyrdom seems to produce, he survived to die a natural death at the age of 80. The real significance of this unedifying episode does not lie on its surface: for the issue of monotheletism *per se* was of small importance, and in fact was abolished in 681. But, by his promulgation of the *Type*, the emperor was by implication vindicating a right to define dogma, which, though claimed by other emperors as part of their prerogative, has never been conceded by the Church. It is true that by refusing to publish any definition that displeased him the sovereign could in practice control dogma. But this was held to differ from a substantive promulgation of doctrine on the part of a secular ruler. And claims to do so, as made by Justinian I or Leo III, in virtue of the imperial office, were always fiercely resisted by the spiritual arm.[5]

Far more important from the point of view of political history was the decision of Constans II to leave the capital and establish himself in the west. This decision was made in 662. The reasons for it are not stated in our records, or, if they are, they appear manifestly absurd – such as that he had murdered his brother and was troubled by nightmares. The true reason was almost certainly political, or rather strategic. That Constans felt himself to be unpopular in Constantinople is no doubt true enough, but he had little reason to suppose himself any more popular in Italy. His plan was, no doubt, to set up a stable, central system of defence against an imminent Saracen invasion of Europe from Africa. If Italy and Hellas were to go the way of Syria and Egypt, while the Saracen fleets at the same time dominated the Aegean, what was likely to be the fate, at no long interval, of Constantinople herself?

That he had this in mind seems to be clear from the fact that on his way to Italy he spent nearly a year in Greece, visiting Thessalonica and Athens and probably Corinth, with the obvious intention of putting the Roman fortresses in a proper state of defence. His plans for this country, whatever they may have been, were abortive, and after his departure with his troops the whole province, but for a few fortresses, seems to have relapsed into Slav occupation, in which no traces of Byzantine administration are to be discerned for about a century and a half.

The arrival of Constans in Italy in 663 was followed by operations against the Lombards, carried out energetically but with only partial success. He visited Rome, but evinced no desire or intention of living there: and indeed the object of his whole expedition could only be achieved by a strategic occupation of Sicily, the base of all operations in Africa. He succeeded in relieving Carthage; but, as was to happen so often in future Byzantine history, his reoccupation was accompanied by such stringent taxation that he became odious to the very Christian population whom he set out to redeem. His final years seem to have been ineffective, and we cannot say what precise schemes he had in mind. In 668 he was murdered in his bath at Syracuse, and with his death the centre of interest moves back again to the eastern Mediterranean.[6]

The death of Constans II was followed by the peaceable accession of his son Constantine IV (668–85), who had during several years administered the eastern empire while his father resided in the west. He was the third member of this great dynasty to reign effectively, and, like his father and great-grandfather, he was a man of energy and ability. It is true that his triumphs are largely attributable to the sane policies of his predecessors in reforming the military and economic organisation of Asia Minor, which, in the life and death struggle which distinguished his reign, showed amazing powers of resistance and recuperation. And these, aided by one decisive stroke of luck, which may be regarded as the latest triumph of Hellenistic inventiveness, combined to make the next ten years (668–78) a turning point in the history of mankind.

For, by the year 668, it was clear that the settled strategy of the Saracen caliphate was the destruction of the Roman Empire itself. Moawiya, triumphant over his rival Ali, had in 661 established himself as caliph at Damascus, which now supersedes the far off and parochial Medina as the centre of the Saracen power. His design of completing the conquest of the Roman Empire was conceived with fair hopes of success; and, with the examples of Damascus and Alexandria before him, he had little reason to suppose that Constantinople would not be as easily captured. Not merely was he baulked of his design : his gigantic efforts, shrewdly prepared and skilfully executed, met with total disaster and ruin. This is surely a phenomenon which must engage the particular notice of the historian.

Moawiya made his advances during many years, by land and by sea. The naval approach up the coast of Ionia was relentlessly pursued. The island of Cos was occupied, and then Smyrna. Finally, in 672, the Saracens took Cyzicus, on the Bithynian coast of the Marmara, and turned it into a strong base-camp. All was now ready. In the spring of 674 the siege was begun by land and sea.

Absolutely nothing was achieved. The walls of Constantinople, that enduring monument of Roman engineering, could laugh at any assault mounted by the most enthusiastic of the Faithful. At the same time by sea a revolutionary innovation in tactics struck dismay into the hearts of the besiegers. Shortly before this time Callinicus, an architect and chemist of Heliopolis, in Syria, escaped to Constantinople with plans of an invention which during centuries gave maritime supremacy to the Byzantines, and was of no small service to them in siege operations by land. The secret of the so-called 'Greek Fire' was so jealously and success-fully guarded that its precise ingredients and the means of its ignition and discharge cannot be certainly known. The chief ingredient, however, was certainly petroleum, which could be obtained in large quantities from surface deposits in the Caucasus and Armenia, without the necessity of boring. This substance was projected by means of a pump or siphon against and around an enemy vessel. The results of ignition were terrific. Flames shot up to envelope the doomed vessel. And what made the operation more terrible was the fact that the substance burned with equal ardour on the surface of the sea ; nor could it be extinguished save by the application of sand or urine or vinegar.

Never was a secret weapon more timely discovered. The tubes and ammunition were speedily manufactured. The weapon was brought to play on the Saracen vessels, with catastrophic results. But, even so, a lengthy siege was inevitable. In September 674 the besiegers withdrew across the Marmara to Cyzicus for the winter, and their commanders even further afield. In 675 the assault was renewed, with equal spirit but with equal lack of success. The persistence and determination of the Saracens show to what an extent the caliph had set his heart on the scheme. Massive reinforcements were sent, and for three more whole years the assaults continued. Finally, the besiegers, decimated by losses in battle, by hunger and by disease, were compelled to desist. The fleet sailed away. The army set off homeward across Anatolia. But the Byzantine resistance showed no sign of exhaustion. The Saracen ships, further reduced in numbers by shipwreck, were encountered by the Roman provincial navy near the south-west coast of Asia Minor and finally destroyed. On land the provincial armies, under Florus and Petronas, engaged the retreating Arab forces and put thirty thousand of them to the sword.7

The effect of this splendid victory, coming after so many decades of uninterrupted retreat and disaster, was enormous, both within and without the empire. Moawiya was stricken to the heart. All his fine schemes of conquest had merely demonstrated that his empire was not invincible, and that it had still to deal with a power as formidable as its own. He evacuated Rhodes, Cos and Cyprus. He made an ignominious treaty, by which he undertook to pay to the emperor an annual tribute of three thousand gold pieces, forty slaves and fifty fine horses : a tribute trifling in itself, but of very great moral significance. A year later he died. Equally significant was the psychological effect in the west. East Rome was once more established in western eyes as the champion of Christendom. The Khan of the Avars, the Lombard dukes, perhaps even Frankish and Anglo-Saxon princes, sent embassies of congratulation to Constantine iv. And the Roman imperial idea was given a lease of life in the west which endured for another century. So, 'profound peace prevailed, in East and West'.

This remark of the chronicler Theophanes is in fact more true in spirit than in practice. It is true that the Saracen expansion to the west and their depredations into Asia Minor were checked for about fifteen or twenty years, and were not renewed until the banishment of the second Justinian in 695. This respite was of great value in allowing the Byzantine government to develop their provincial organisation, and it is in this period that several revealing references to new *themes* are made. But, by contrast, the northern frontier was threatened ; and in an endeavour to counter this menace Constantine assured, if he did not create, the establishment of the Bulgarian kingdom which for centuries was to tax

44

Byzantine strategy on the north, as the Saracen empire was to do in the east. We have seen that by the time of Heraclius, and by the year 615, the Balkan peninsula as a whole was regarded as a *Sklavinia*, or *Sklaviniae*, an area or areas inhabited and controlled by Slavonic tribes. These Slavs had been turned into conquerors owing to their exploitation by the Avars : and, not content with occupying, settling and cultivating Roman territories, they developed a taste for aggression, piracy and plunder. Thessalonica, which after the Saracen conquest of Alexandria had become the second city in the empire, was repeatedly besieged by them, and it is not at all surprising that one of the most sustained and determined of the Slavonic efforts to capture the place coincided with Moawiya's siege of Constantinople. Two formidable assaults were made by the Slavs of Thessaly in 675, and again in 677, when they were supported, or more probably led, by Avars and Bulgarians ; but, owing to the miraculous interventions of St Demetrius, they were repelled. Twice more before the end of this critical decade the same Divine assistance was required, when, as is stated, the emperor could do little or nothing to assist. We can therefore count no fewer than four separate assaults, one of them lasting two years, between 675 and 681, and must thus conclude that Thessalonica was as closely and as continually invested as Constantinople herself.

The significant feature in these accounts, legendary in detail but true in substance, of the Slav assaults at this time is that the Slavs were supported by Bulgarians. The Bulgarians seem to have been in origin Huns, who may well have formed part, and survived as a rump, of the hordes of Attila in the fifth century. Both in the sixth and seventh centuries we find them, in small detachments, allied with Avars and Slavs across the Danube. In the time of Heraclius the so-called Onogur Bulgarians are found in large numbers somewhere between the Kuban and the Volga rivers, and here they formed a considerable power independent of Avar control, with which Heraclius, always on the look out for support against the Avars, was not slow to ally himself. In the middle of the seventh century, however, this concentration of Onogur Bulgars joined the unending conveyor-belt of tribes forced westwards across the steppe by more powerful neighbours in the rear. The motive power in this instance was the expansion of the empire of the Turkic Chazars, which spread from the Volga to the

Crimea, and which during the eighth and ninth centuries was the lynch-pin of Byzantine foreign policy to the north of the Black Sea. The Bulgarians, at this time without Slavonic accretions, wandered westward into Bessarabia and were in the 670s established on the north bank of the lower Danube. Their restless and enterprising spirit led them across the river and into contact with the solid Sklavinia that lay between the Danube and the Balkan Range. The details, as usual, are lacking; but we shall not be wrong in supposing that their mischief-making among the pastoral Slavs must have constituted a serious danger to the Byzantine government. Constantine IV, flushed with his triumph over Moawiya and incensed by the repeated attacks on Thessalonica, supposed it to be his duty to scotch this threat from the north before it became uncontrollable. In the year 680 he embarked his victorious troops and sailed in force for the Danube delta. 'The emperor [says Theophanes] learning of the sudden settlement across the Danube of this dirty, filthy tribe, ordered all his provincial troops into Thrace and proceeded to the Danube'. The Bulgars, as was natural, took fright at this imposing demonstration. They retreated into their fortifications, which were protected by the marshes of the delta and thus could not be assaulted.

The emperor, whose staff-work does not seem to have been very good, dawdled away four days, and was then seized by an acute attack of the gout. He thought he could leave his officers in charge of so simple an operation, with instructions to lure the enemy on to the solid ground and defeat them, or else to starve them out. He then set sail, to take the waters at Mesembria. And now occurred one of those incidents which, repeated over and over again in later operations against the Bulgarians, were nearly fatal to the Byzantine arms. The emperor's withdrawal was misunderstood. A panic ensued. The Byzantine cavalry turned round and galloped for the river. The astonished Bulgars seized the moment. With their chief Isperich, they pursued and cut down the fleeing Romans and passed with the remnant across the Danube. Once across the river, they were not slow to appreciate the advantages of a territory protected on three sides by mountain, river and sea; and, moreover, thickly inhabited by no fewer than seven tribes of peaceable and industrious Slavs. These they quickly mastered, and set to work for them. Constantine IV made the best of a bad job.

46

He acquiesced in the settlement and gave the Bulgarians an annual subsidy. Such is the simple account[8] which the chronicler gives of the origins of that great and ferocious power which the Byzantines were to know so well through the terrific names of Krum and Symeon and Samuel. And there is no doubt that the account is substantially true. But the ill-fated expedition of Constantine merely precipitated an event which could in any case not have been long delayed. All the same, Theophanes is witness to the astonishment generally felt that the conqueror of the strongest power on earth – the Saracen – should submit to defeat and ransom at the hands of these 'vile, upstart' savages. He can only explain it by supposing that his orthodox hero rejected further hostilities in his eagerness to get down to the really important task of abolishing the doctrine of the single energy and the single will of the Saviour.

For [he continues] Constantine kept the peace until his death, since it was his most particular care to unite the holy Churches of God which had been everywhere divided since the years of his great-grandfather, the Emperor Heraclius, and those villains Sergius and Pyrrhus, who most unworthily had sate in the stool of Constantinople, and had declared one Energy and one Will in our Lord and God and Saviour Jesus Christ: whose follies desiring to overthrow, that Most Christian Emperor gathered together an Ecumenical Synod of 289 bishops in Constantinople, which confirmed what had been taught in the preceding five Ecumenical Synods; and the pious doctrine of the two Wills and Energies was approved by that same holy and most correct Sixth Ecumenical Synod, over which the same most pious Emperor Constantine, with his hierarchs, presided.[9]

The convocation of the Sixth Council, the Council *in Trullo*, as it was called, was a statesmanlike measure. Constantine's letter to the pope, proposing the synod, was written in August 678, when the victory over, and withdrawal of, the Saracens can only just have been completed. Constantine's good sense is manifest in his realisation that the makeshift doctrine of 'One Will', whether as discussed in the *Ekthesis* or as forbidden all discussion in the *Type*, was in a political point of view more hindrance than help. A monophysite who accepted it would remain a monophysite; and no catholic, after the unlucky blunder of Pope Honorius forty-five years before, could be found to accept it at all. Pope Vitalian in 668 revived the orthodox objections to it, but did not proceed with the arrogance of Martin, which had moved the wrath of Constans II. Constantine IV reacted to this with equal tact. He invited Pope Agathon to send delegates to a general Council in Constantinople, at which the other patriarchs, or their representatives, should also be present. The Council met on 7 November 680 and sat until 16 September 681. The emperor presided when he could find the time, as it was his undoubted right and duty to do. But he took no sides. The whole proceedings were orderly and dignified. Almost the only dissentient was the patriarch of Antioch, who used the phrase 'a theandric [God-Man] energy', without specifying whether this were single or double. This was an ambiguity of which certain monophysites, or their defenders, had availed themselves in the past: for, if Christ was 'a single Nature of the Divine Logos made Flesh,' as they contended, did not the very addition of 'made flesh' denote a second, human nature? The decision was nearly unanimous that the doctrine of One Will was a doctrine which tended to the prejudice of the Saviour's humanity; and that the truth is that 'there are two natural Wills and two natural Energies, without division, alteration, separation or confusion'. With this decision both the emperor – now once more the *orthodox* emperor – and his patriarch concurred. In the list of those anathematised in the final session occur, together with the Byzantine Patriarchs Sergius, Cyrus and Pyrrhus, also the name of Pope Honorius: *Honorio heretico anathema*! This would appear to present some problems for the nineteenth-century doctrine of papal infallibility.[10]

Constantine IV died in the year 685. His achievements were more spectacular than those of his father, and he seems in any case to have been a better statesman. The repulse of Moawiya makes his name immortal; and we may give him some personal credit for this. To preserve the morale of a great city during five years of constant siege by a power until then thought to be irresistible was undoubtedly the work and the glory of the emperor; and many must have been reminded of the siege of 626, over which his great-grandfather, though not present, shed his benign and inspiring influence. It is one of the losses incurred by our dearth of sources for this period that they give us little or no inkling of the personalities of these gifted Heraclian rulers. If we knew more about them as men, we should understand their policies better.

To at least one very unpleasant feature of imperial family life, fast becoming imperial tradition, Constantine IV was no conscientious objector. He slit the noses of his brothers, Heraclius and Tiberius, for having dared to demand a share of the rule with him. The mutilation was regarded as a brand or stigma, to denote that the victims were incompetent to rule. But if this disfigurement was generally held to be a bar to governing, a ruler was coming who would demonstrate that the general opinion was mistaken. The story of the attempt of Heraclius and Tiberius to associate themselves with their brother's power is told in characteristic fashion by Gibbon :

At their secret instigation the troops of the Anatolian theme approached the city, demanded for the royal brothers the partition or exercise of sovereignty, and supported their seditious claim by a theological argument. They were Christians (they cried) and orthodox Catholics; the sincere votaries of the holy and undivided Trinity. Since there are three equal persons in heaven, it is reasonable that there should be three equal persons upon earth. The emperor invited these learned divines to a friendly conference and they obeyed the summons. But the prospect of their bodies hanging on the gibbet in the suburb of Galata reconciled their companions to the unity of the reign of Constantine.[11]

I recount this anecdote rather for its historical implication than for its historical importance, and will add another for the same reason. At the fifteenth session of the Council in Trullo one of the very few convinced monothelites was a certain Polychronius, 'religiosissimus monachus'. He penned his definition of faith in a memorial to the Emperor Constantine, and claimed that proof of its truth could be tested by placing the document on a corpse, which would then return to life. He was taken at his word. A dead body was laid on a silver bier and placed in the atrium of the Bath of Zeuxippus. The reverend Fathers, and a large crowd of other spectators, assembled to watch the proceedings. Polychronius placed his scroll on the body, but it remained inanimate. In vain did the practitioner, during several hours, mutter incantations into its ears. The result continued to be negative. Why, now, asked the exasperated delegates, surely you will admit that your doctrine is false ? But not at all. Polychronius maintained it was true still, and he would adhere to it. He was anathematised as a heretic.[12]

These contemporary stories are worth remembering : the first as an illustration of the literal-mindedness with which simple folk could apply the imperial dogma that the terrestrial was a copy of the celestial empire; the second as an indication of the degree of credulousness prevalent even among educated men at that time. That two hundred and eighty of the best and wisest men in the empire should seriously attend and follow the antics of a mountebank is a fact of some significance for an assessment of the intellectual climate of the seventh century. And both anecdotes may, in their several ways, help us to understand the iconoclastic controversy, which broke out half a century later.

Constantine IV was only thirty-three when he died in 685. The state of his empire was not unfavourable or menacing. The Saracens had been humiliated, at least for the time. And the restoration of amicable relations with the papacy undoubtedly strengthened the position of the Italian *exarchate*. Constantine's son, Justinian II, who now inherited the empire, was the fourth and last effective ruler in the succession from Heraclius, and seemed by no means ill-qualified to continue the recuperative work of his ancestors. Like them, he was energetic and conscientious; and like them he appears to have duly appreciated the internal needs of the empire. But he was unwisely despotic and tactless in his relations both with his own subjects and with foreign powers. It was probably a mistake to have christened him Justinian, since this seems to have attracted him to the policies of his great predecessor of that name, policies which, as his own father could have told him, were no longer practicable. To have embroiled himself at once with the caliphate, with the Bulgars and with the papacy, in the short space of ten years, suggests that whatever may have been his talents as an organiser – and these were not contemptible – he was signally lacking in those of a statesman. A morbid streak in his mentality, which may have afflicted, in a lesser degree, all his line, declared itself unmistakably in the years of his second administration, when, if he is not misrepresented, he indulged in sentiments and freaks which suggest positive derangement.

His first acts, however, were auspicious. The fifth caliph of the Omayyad house, Abdalmalik, contending with internal troubles, was for a time an easy prey to Byzantine reprisals. Justinian pressed home his advantage. He sent expeditions both to Armenia and Georgia (vital spheres of Byzantine influence), and also to

Syria, where for a time he reoccupied Antioch. His sturdy allies in this area were the Mardaïtes, a tribe of Christian monophysite highlanders, warriors and freebooters, who for some years had been the scourge of the Saracen administration right up to the walls of Damascus. The embarrassed caliph asked for a renewal of the treaty of 680: and this was granted by Justinian in 688, on favourable terms for the Romans. The revised treaty contained some remarkable provisions. One was, that the island of Cyprus and the Armeno-Caucasian area should be taxable in equal proportions both by the emperor and by the caliph. This implies that the empire had now become aware that the balance of power on its eastern border had, in the course of fifty years, become stabilised; and collaboration or *condominium* in buffer states, was a policy not merely feasible but advisable. How, and for how long, the provisions were applied to the north-eastern area, we are not informed. But of the results in Cyprus during the next two hundred and eighty years we know a good deal. The island was demilitarised, and allowed much local autonomy. Neither empire claimed it as a possession, and maintained in it only such a skeleton administration as was necessary to keep the peace and collect the revenue. Its harbours were at the disposal of the navies of both powers; but, for the rest, it formed a no-man's land, to its own great benefit and relief. The Greek-speaking inhabitants were not subject to compulsory military service, and they were moreover exempt from the iconoclast persecutions of the eighth and ninth centuries. The Byzantine government used the island as a place of banishment for undesirables, just as it used Cherson and Athens, both of which at this time were in remote areas outside its own direct administrative control. The islanders seem to have been aware of their fortunate position, and evinced no desire whatever for reunification with their co-religionists on the mainland. The whole transaction reflects a good sense and far-sightedness not often seen in Arabo-Byzantine political relations.[13]

Another provision of the treaty was viewed at that time with greater misgiving. It was that the emperor should remove the Mardaïte marauders from the Lebanon and receive them within his own borders. This provision was carried out in 689 by the emperor personally, who disposed twelve thousand of these excellent soldiers and sailors mainly at Attalia, on the south coast of Anatolia, where they formed a *corps d'élite* of imperial marines independent of the military or naval governor of the province. Justinian was much castigated for weakening his Syrian frontier in this way. But he knew what he was doing. He strengthened his sea-defences in a vital area; and his transfer of the Mardaïtes was only one feature in his widespread activities in repopulating the homeland.

For his settlement of the Mardaïtes must be regarded in conjunction with his expedition at nearly the same time westwards into Sklavinia. It is clear that this expedition was principally a slave-raid, designed to capture or allure fresh settlers for Asia Minor. Justinian pushed his way to Thessalonica, which he entered in triumph, and, says the chronicler, 'many masses' of the Slavs were either taken prisoner or else came over to his side. These he ferried across the straits at Abydos, and settled in the *theme* of Opsikion (Obsequium) which corresponded roughly to old Bithynia, an area which had been fearfully devastated during the five years' siege of Constantinople by the Saracens. The twofold object of importing Slavs as warriors and farmers in the *thematic* organisation is here very manifest, since we are told that four years afterwards, in 692, no fewer than thirty thousand of these Slavs had been drilled into soldiers, and were ready to take the field. This figure implies at least a hundred thousand for the immigration of 688, and gives a very vivid impression of the enormous scale on which the population of Anatolia was renewed.

Justinian's plans did not stop short here. In 691 he is said to have transplated the (Greek-speaking) population of Cyprus and settled them on the Marmara at Cyzicus, which had been the Saracen base of operations fifteen years before; and also on the southern and western coasts of Anatolia. But here we do not know the numbers involved, and this migration was in fact abortive. Seven years later, the usurping emperor Tiberius repatriated the Cypriots, probably because their removal from Cyprus very seriously reduced both the Roman and the Saracen receipts from the taxes of that island. Lastly, we hear, during the same years, of an influx of famine-stricken refugees from Syria. These facts are of the utmost importance for the history of Byzantine recovery in the following centuries. It seems likely that Justinian alone, in the short space of five or six years, imported and established a minimum of two hundred and fifty thousand new settlers into the empire. If, as we are entitled to do, we assume this progress to have gone on, with greater or less impetus, for at least a century, since the time when Maurice imported thirty thousand Armenian cavalry, we get an idea of the disastrous depopulation that went on during the wasteful reign of Justinian I, and also of the thorough-going change, from a racial point of view, of the raw material of the Middle Byzantine Empire. The new structure was architecturally similar to the old; but the building materials were quite different.[14]

It is in the reign of Justinian II that we get the first clear picture of the *thematic* organisation as it was beginning, after seventy years, to crystallise: for to his reign is now almost universally attributed a document of the first importance, the so-called 'Farming Law'. This document contains a code of instructions reflecting the state of agricultural and rural society then prevailing; and certain very clear and very significant deductions can be drawn from this. To begin with, the basis of territorial occupation is no longer, as in pre-Heraclian days, the large agricultural estate worked by serfs tied to the property, but is now the rural commune of freehold lots, moderate at first in extent and bounded by communal pastures and woods. The human element consists no longer of the serf but of the 'free' peasant, who is no longer tied but mobile. He was indeed still a 'slave', but in servitude to the emperor's treasury, not to a private master. This system brought solid advantages, agricultural, economic and military. In the first place, the *theme* grew its own food, to support both its inhabitants and its army: and the relative freedom of the peasantry led, as it always does, to a healthy increase in the population and to a consequent expansion of the area which could be put under cultivation. In the second place, the rural commune, in addition to its social advantages, formed a taxable unit, so that – in theory at least – the revenue was ensured of its income, whoever owned this plot or that, and tax-collection was vastly simplified. In the third place, the head or eldest son of each 'military' family was a regular soldier, responsible for providing his own cavalry charger and equipment, for getting adequate training at the local garrison headquarters and for giving active service when this was required, as it often was. By this means the government had in every *theme* a local, independent force of troops which could, if necessary, muster quickly and operate independently under its military governor and his lieutenants; and this again meant an economic as well as a strategic gain, since the large forces of highly paid mercenaries, which had hitherto drained the treasury, could be and were drastically reduced. Finally, the *thematic* troops fought as local units with all the sentiments of local patriotism : often literally for hearth and home, if not, as was maintained by the imperial propaganda, for faith and emperor. Such is the new organisation as we see it at work in the Farmer's Law of Justinian II.[15] It is known that, by the end of the seventh century, Anatolia was divided into the Armeniac, Anatolic and Obsequian (or Bithynian) *themes*; the *theme* of Thrace was founded by Constantine IV contemporaneously with the establishment of Bulgaria south of the Danube. The *theme* of Hellas was founded by Justinian II, no doubt in connexion with his policy of Slavonic recruitment. The maritime province of the Aegean was organised into the Seamans *theme*, the 'Karavisianoi'. These too large jurisdictions were subdivided by later emperors, but this was merely a matter of policy. The system was there and it was the Heraclian house that made it.

Controversy (not always edifying or unprejudiced) has long raged over the question of what part the new settlers, especially the Slavs, played in this great revolution. Some Slavonic scholars have maintained that the rural commune itself originated with the Slavs, and that they lived in the empire as they had heretofore lived outside it. There seem to be few if any grounds for this belief. The system of inalienable freeholds was not a Slavonic conception, and almost certainly originated within the empire itself. It is true that much of the territory comprised by the commune was land held in common, but there is no trace of any periodic distribution of holdings such as we find in seventeenth-century Russia. What, however, can be said with absolute certainty is that the coming of enormous numbers of Slavonic settlers, already with a high standard of agricultural skill and technique, hardy, laborious, patient and comparatively free, revolutionised the rural economy, and brought about that agricultural prosperity on three sides of the Aegean Sea which is characteristic of the Byzantine Empire during the eighth to the eleventh centuries.

Justinian II, like his father, was a keen theologian, but, unlike his father, he had not the sense to let well alone. It was represented to him that certain administrative matters in the church had not been covered by previous rulings; and he determined, without papal support, to call a synod.

The Quinisext Synod – for so it was denominated from its intention to regulate details of ecclesiastical administration left undetermined by the Fifth (quintum) and Sixth (sextum) ecumenical Councils – was convened in 691. The 102 Canons approved by the Fathers are to us among the most trivial, and among the most interesting and informative, ever discussed by a synod. The canons regulating the lives of the clergy do not reveal any startling degree of laxity among that body. Chastity among the higher orders was rigidly enforced, from which we may infer that it was frequently violated. And clergy are forbidden to attend horse-races and theatrical performances. But these excesses scarcely betoken more than the laxity of the fox-hunting, card-playing parsons of Victorian England. Of enormously greater interest are the interdicts on practices of a superstitious and pagan colour among the rural populace, among whom festivals or celebrations indicating survival from antiquity seem to have been prevalent. The folklorist who examines these with a professional eye will be on his guard against postulating direct and specific continuity from Rome, still more from classical Hellas. The festivals of the vintage, the telling of fortunes, the interpretation of omens, and a score of other superstitions, have an origin which is nearly as ancient and as wide-spread as the human race. In every age and clime the simple have been at the mercy of charlatans who peddle their tufts of bear's fur or their amulets, or predict the course of the future from natural phenomena. The Quinisext ordinances illustrate in the seventh century the prevalence of pagan superstitions which may equally be traced in the seventeenth. The church fought a noble rearguard action against such charlatanry and imposture, but to no effect whatever; and merely confirmed that superstitions and practices – travesty, masking, dancing, mumming – which preceded by whole millennia the foundation of anything that can properly be termed a religion, were not, and could not be, eradicated. [16]

Unhappily, not all the decisions of the council were equally harmless. Marriage was stated to be permissible among the secular clergy; and fasting on Saturdays in Lent, approved by the catholics, was condemned. When the proceedings of the synod were published, the pope, who was not represented at the

Council, very naturally refused to approve them, and his refusal exasperated Justinian, who, like his grandfather, regarded the bishop of Rome as his subject and vassal. He instructed the *exarch* of Ravenna to arrest the pontiff, and convey him for judgement to Constantinople, as Constans II had conveyed and judged Pope Martin. The result was unexpected. The Roman populace rose in defence of their shepherd, and it was only by the papal intervention that the imperial official avoided being lynched.

Justinian had enemies to contend with at home, no less than abroad. It has been suggested that his wholesale settlement of communes of free Slavonic peasantry in Anatolia outraged the larger land-holders, but this, though probable, is not supported by concrete evidence. But the odium excited by his extortionate fiscal policy is a proved fact. Unlike his more prudent predecessors, he was a spendthrift; and like his celebrated homonym, the first Justinian, he pillaged rich and poor alike. His finance ministers were as ruthless as John of Cappadocia : and the odious system of torture to exact revenue, notable among his successors, was especially invoked under his administration. It says much for his ruthlessness and profusion that he, the descendant of a much loved and beneficent dynasty, which had governed for eighty-five years, had by the year 695 rendered himself so universally hated that a revolt against his authority could have been successfully promoted, with scarcely any opposition. An undistinguished general named Leontius, who had been haled from prison, and was on the point of being exiled to the west with the empty title of military governor of Hellas, could with only a handful of supporters drawn from the praetorium gaol proclaim himself emperor and be accepted with relief. Justinian was seized. His nose and tongue were slit, but it would appear that these operations were, at least in his case, perfunctory. And he was banished to Cherson, a remote and at that time self-governing city in the Crimea.[17]

His removal inaugurated an era of anarchy during which, in twenty-two years, no fewer than seven emperors, including himself, followed one another in quick succession. With the end of Justinian's first reign, we say farewell to the continuous rule of the house of Heraclius. In the eighty years of its direction the empire had undergone fundamental changes, and these changes though they were consummated below the surface, as it were, were essential in the preservation of what was unchanging – the majesty, the might and the prescription of the Empire of Caesar Augustus.

NOTES

1 Ostrogorsky, 93–5.
2 Theophanes, 345–6.
3 Ostrogorsky, 97.
4 Theophanes, 347.
5 Ostrogorsky, 100–1; Bréhier, 59–61.
6 Bury, LRE, 299–307.
7 Theophanes, 353–4; Ostrogorsky, 103–5.
8 Theophanes, 356–9; Nicephorus, 33–5.
9 Theophanes, 359–60.
10 Ostrogorsky, 106–7.
11 Bury, LRE, 308–9 and note 3.
12 ibid., 318.
13 Theophanes, 363; Ostrogorsky, 108.
14 Theophanes, 364–6; Nicephorus, 36; Ostrogorsky, 108–11.
15 Ostrogorsky, 111–6.
16 Ostrogorsky, 116; Bréhier, 67.
17 Theophanes, 368–9.

CHAPTER FIVE

THE EARLY 'ISAURIANS'

Justinian II was driven from his throne in 695. During the next twenty-two years (695–717), confusion at Byzantium led to a revival of the Saracen power, and started it on the second great surge of expansion. During this period it was clear to everyone that the repulse of the Arabs from Constantinople in 678 had been no more than a check, and that a second, equally powerful, wave would shortly launch itself on the citadel of the empire. Happily for Christendom, a hand as powerful as, and a brain more subtle and cunning than, those of Constantine IV would be present to repel it. But, meanwhile, things had gone very wrong indeed for the Romans.

The three-year reign of the upstart Leontius (695–8) is remarkable only for the final occupation of Carthage by the Saracens, and the final extinction of the African *exarchate*. His successor Tiberius III (698–705), a seaman, showed some signs of administrative ability. He strengthened the naval defences of southern Asia Minor, repatriated the Cypriots, and repelled the Saracen invader both in Armenia and in Cilicia. Had he been suffered to remain on the throne, he might have anticipated some of the triumphs of Leo III without plunging the empire into religious disarray. It was not to be. The banished Justinian had, for ten years, led a life of wandering and adventure which would not come amiss as the plot of a picaresque novel. Pursued by the suspicions of the usurper Tiberius, he was driven out of Cherson, and threw himself on the protection of the Chazar prince, whose empire had already spread to the eastern shore of the Sea of Azov.

The khan welcomed the fugitive, and gave him his sister in marriage; and from this time date the very close relations that subsisted between the empire and Chazaria during about two hundred years. Even in this sanctuary, Justinian was not beyond the reach of the usurper's arm, and he was once more compelled to shift his ground. This time he turned westward, and, sailing to the mouth of the Danube, took refuge with Tervel, the prince of the Bulgarians. He proposed to Tervel that the Bulgarians should help him back to his throne, and Tervel, who had everything to gain by such a scheme, readily fell in with it. In 705, after ten years of exile among the barbarians, the last of the Heraclians reached the walls of his capital. The people evinced no very great eagerness to welcome him home, and their apprehensions were just: for he had left them an arrogant and wilful, but still a responsible, despot; he returned to them little better than a homicidal lunatic. He effected an entrance by means of a ruse, surprised Tiberius, seized the palace, and began a holocaust of revengeful slaughter not seen in the capital since Phocas had been hewn in pieces before Heraclius.[1]

The two pretenders, Leontius and Tiberius, together with their followers, were apprehended and executed. But for the city of Cherson, which had expelled him six years before, was reserved his chief hatred and vengeance. Nothing less than total extermination of the ruling families of this city, men, women and children, would satisfy his lust. His first expedition spared the youth of the place: but a second was at once sent to rectify the omission. When this large armament foundered, with the loss, it is said, of more than seventy thousand men, the emperor received the news with a roar of delight, and set about organising a third. Ravenna, for reasons yet more frivolous, was punished scarcely less cruelly than Cherson. It is melancholy to record such lunacy in the last, and not the least able, of the great house of Heraclius.

The inevitable revolt broke out in 711. Justinian was beheaded, and an Armenian general named Bardanes was proclaimed emperor. But it was doubtful, in an imperial point of view, whether the remedy were not worse than the disease. The new sovereign was not merely idle and incompetent, but a monothelete heretic to boot, and this seemed to threaten all the good work of the Sixth Council. Some have thought Bardanes to have been feeling towards iconoclasm. If it were so, it was lucky that this revolution was not entrusted to such feeble hands as his. He was deposed and blinded in 713 and Artemius, renamed Anastasius II, held power during the next two years.[2]

It would have been strange indeed if the great foes of Byzantium had not taken advantage of such instability and demoralisation. The Bulgarians, who were beginning to feel their strength, twice appeared at the gates and had to be bought off by Justinian and Bardanes. But the Saracen threat was far more persistent. The annual invasions recommenced in 706, and continued during the next ten years. Tyana was sacked and Dorylaeum and Antioch in Pisidia, together with many towns of Isauria. The most serious feature of these depredations, on a long term, was the wholesale deportations which accompanied them. The Saracens seemed fully to realise the value of the Heraclian policy of repopulating the *themes*, and resolved to undo it by removing this invaluable asset to their own dominions. But by 714 more ominous rumours were abroad : that the Caliph Walid was about to renew the assault of Moawiya, on the capital city itself.

It is in connection with this second, and, as it proved, final, Saracen assault that we must pause to do justice to the work of Anastasius II. During the years of the locust (695–717) only he and Tiberius III can claim to have been conscientious and capable emperors. Naturally, such an assault as that which was meditated could not be set on foot without lengthy preparation, and rumours of this began to filter into the empire as early as 713. In 714 Anastasius sent an embassy, led by the Lord Mayor of Constantinople, Daniel of Sinope, to Damascus, ostensibly to conclude a treaty or truce, but in fact – says the chronicler[3] – to discover the nature and extent of Saracen preparations. Daniel brought back a report which confirmed the worst. Preparations were afoot on the argest scale, both by land and sea. Anastasius instantly set about putting the capital into a state of defence. He reinforced the land-walls with artillery of every description. He issued orders that all citizens should collect and store supplies of food which would last three years : and, with the siege of 674–8 in mind, his order was prudent. All who could not afford to do this were required to billet themselves on the countryside. The imperial granaries were filled to capacity and carefully sealed. And a programme of ship-building was put into immediate operation. It was well that these orders were made and carried out. For when Leo III took over the empire in March 717, only four months' grace were given him before the siege was set, and this short interim would have allowed only very inadequate preparations to repel it.4

The state of the provinces, however, was less satisfactory. In 715 Anastasius very rightly determined to try and destroy the Saracen fleet in its home waters, and thus nip the whole operation in the bud. His navy was adequate and loyal; but the provincial army of the Opsikian *theme* revolted against him. The revolt spread – we cannot say why – and Anastasius, whose civilian training gave him no moral authority over his troops, was toppled from the throne. The soldiers set up a feeble creature called Theodosius, who had nothing but his name to qualify him for rule. And during two crucial years the Saracen preparations went on unhindered. Had it been left to Theodosius III to meet the blow, it might well have been mortal, despite the prudent measures taken by Anastasius. This mercifully did not happen. The period of indecision and anarchy was nearly over, and a dynasty scarcely less remarkable than that of Heraclius was to seat itself on the throne and deliver the empire.

The family of Leo III, who now dominates the scene, were early said to hail from Isauria, a mountainous district lying between the old provinces of Pisidia and Cilicia, in southern Asia Minor. Hence he, his son and his grandson, are termed the 'Isaurian' emperors. This is certainly a misnomer. A more trustworthy account says that Leo was born much further east, at Germanicia in Commagene, beyond the Taurus. We have express testimony in Arab sources that Leo was bilingual, in Greek and Arabic, which would be natural enough in a native of Upper Syria but improbable in an Isaurian. His close familiarity with Arabic policies and personalities is of the utmost significance both for his political and (as we shall see) for his religious schemes. In 694, when he was a youth, his family either migrated or was, in accordance with the resettlement schemes of Justinian II, forcibly transplanted to Thrace, and established itself near the Bulgarian border, at Mesembria. Here it prospered. In 705 it was fortunate enough to be on the right side when Justinian re-entered his empire from Bulgaria. The young Leo attracted the emperor's notice, and was taken into the imperial service. His eminent talents, his knowledge of the east and his command of Arabic suggested his employment in diplomacy in that area; and soon afterwards, perhaps about 710, he was dispatched to the Caucasian Alans, to try his hand in that perennial game of inciting one buffer-state against another, which was the ruling principle of Byzantine diplomacy between the Caucasus and the Adriatic. In these parts he spent the next three years and, with very little support, showed a combination of courage, coolheadedness and duplicity among Alans, Abasgians, Armenians and Arabs, which insured sub-stantial gains for the empire and his own safe return to Con-stantinople. Justinian and Bardanes were already deposed, and Anastasius was on the throne. The governorship of the all-important Anatolic province was vacant, and Anastasius, quick to appreciate Leo's qualifications, appointed him to the post, pro-bably in 715. Shortly afterwards, as we saw, Anastasius himself was dethroned in favour of the incapable Theodosius. In the following year, the Saracen preparations were complete, and two great armies, commanded by the caliph's brother Maslama, and the caliph's namesake Suleiman, poured over the border, and laid siege to Amorion, the capital of the Anatolic province.

What followed between the Byzantine governor-general Leo and the Saracen war-lords is known mainly from a confused account which may well go back to a report of Leo himself.[5] The only certain conclusion to be drawn from it is that Leo over-reached the Saracens at every point, and contrived to save Amorion from Saracen occupation. But a further conjecture can be made with great probability : that it was the plan of Suleiman and Maslama to make Leo into a puppet emperor, to induce him to revolt against Theodosius, and finally themselves to take over the empire through his instrumentality. It was not the first time such a plan had been adopted, and it was by no means the last. A whole string of malcontents, beginning in 668, and continuing through Thomas the Slav in 821 and Bardas Sclerus in the late tenth century, accepted Saracen support and undertook to subdue the empire to Saracen domination. We have at least two Arab docu-ments which explicitly state that Leo undertook the same. His ready wit, his great authority, his known aversion to the usurper Theodosius, and his fluent command of Arabic, marked him out as a man to tamper with : and the Arab commanders could only learn by bitter experience the depth of his dissimulation. Suleiman caused him to be proclaimed emperor by the garrison of Amorion : and Maslama obtained promises from the troops of Cappadocia, also in the Anatolic province, that they would support his usurpation. The result of these manoeuvres was that, during the winter of 716–7, the two great Saracen hosts withdrew eastwards. This step seems explicable only on the hypothesis that their generals had obtained an express promise from Leo that, once he had secured the capital, which he could do with less opposition if not seen to be backed by a Saracen army, he would play in with the enemy.[6]

Temporarily freed from danger in the rear, Leo hastened to the Bosphorus. He defeated an imperial force sent against him, but did not choose to waste his meagre resources in assailing the impregnable city. Instead, he lay all the winter at Nicomedia, and opened a negotiation with the patriarch and the senate. He doubtless represented to them the imminence of the Arab invasion, and that he alone was able to meet it. By March 717 they had made up their minds. Theodosius, ineffectual to the last, made no resistance and was allowed to withdraw into a monastery at Ephesus. Leo entered the city and was crowned. His dynasty remained in power for eighty-five years.

In August Maslama headed the long heralded invasion. With eighty thousand men he crossed Asia Minor and passed over into Thrace. Here he collected the harvest, piling the corn in such heaps in his camp that they could be seen from the walls of the city. In September Suleiman with 1,800 ships of war sailed into the Marmara. The fleet endeavoured to establish a blockade of the city both east and west; but they were cruelly harried by the Byzantine Greek-fire ships, which spread destruction and demoralisation. The land-force could make no impression on the walls. Winter came on, and with great severity. The Arab stores failed. The soldiers were reduced to eating the most nauseous and obscene compounds, and died by thousands of cold, famine and disease. Reinforcements scarcely less imposing than the first armada arrived in the spring from Egypt. But a large part of this fleet was manned by Christian slaves who deserted to the emperor, and the blockade was smashed. The decisive blow was struck by the Bulgarians, who opportunely arrived to assist Leo and massacred about twenty thousand of the besiegers. In August, just a year after the siege had commenced, the Caliph Omar ordered retreat. The land forces retired in tolerable order; but once again the fleet met with shipwreck and destruction, and it is said that of that great armada no more than five vessels reached the home ports.[7]

Such in sum is the Byzantine account of this memorable repulse. But Arab accounts differ from it in some important particulars. According to these, Maslama was tricked and outwitted at every point by the cunning emperor, whom he had set up. Leo, it is said, was in constant communication with the Saracens, always promising and advising, but never performing: until, at last unassailable, he threw off the mask and declared he had used them merely as tools in his elevation to power. It was he – says the Arab account – who persuaded Maslama to destroy his grain supplies before the winter, in order to convince the Byzantines that an overwhelming assault, rather than a long siege, was to come, and thus induce them to lay down their arms. However this may be, it seems certain that diplomacy played a large part in this victory; and we may trace the results of these devious manoeuvres both in the desertion of the Egyptian fleet and in the timely arrival of the Bulgars. The brilliant exploits of the Byzantine navy did the rest. However menacing the Saracen power might continue to be, the safety and survival of the Queen of Cities were assured. And for this achievement the so-called 'Isaurian' house shares the glory with the Heraclian.[8]

As we saw, the Arab land-force was able to withdraw with comparatively little loss to Syria. It resulted from this that during the rest of Leo III's reign, Anatolia was subject to more or less continual raids, as it had been for more than fifty years. Cappadocia was ravaged and Caesarea actually taken. And this is perhaps the moment to ask ourselves how it came about that a country so continuously invaded, century after century, by plundering and exterminating hordes, was able so long to preserve, and even to increase, its economic stability. The reason surely is that invaders, however persistent, are like tourists, in that they keep to a beaten track. To spread far and wide over the countryside would have been dangerous, and would have taken too long. Hence we may conclude that the devastation, severe though it was, touched comparatively small areas on either side of the trunk-roads, where of course defence was concentrated. The largest part of the agricultural inhabitants of Anatolia seldom saw an invader, except when they were mobilised to repel him elsewhere. The cities and townships undoubtedly suffered, and were rapidly diminished into fortresses. But the fact remains that at the end of the Isaurian rule the countryside as a whole was much more prosperous than at its beginning. And the enemy which was ultimately to destroy the *thematic* system was not foreign invasion, but economic imbalance arising from social revolution.

It is further of interest to notice that about this time, after the second repulse from the city, the Saracen and Byzantine empires were settling down into that equilibrium or balance of power which had formerly existed between Byzantines and Persians. The eastern frontier of Asia Minor begins to develop an independent existence of its own, where Byzantine local governors and Saracen emirs meet in an atmosphere of heroism, chivalry and even sometimes friendship, with only sporadic interference from their central governments. This strange world of the 'frontiers' witnessed its own exploits, which gradually gave rise to a whole cycle of popular epic and ballad, centring about certain chieftains of historical origin, but whom later legend transferred easily from century to century, and made into figures closely resembling King Arthur or Roland. In the year 739, Leo III and his son Constantine won a great victory over the Saracens at Acroïnium, in central Asia Minor. The chronicler Theophanes mentions that among the slain was a Saracen commander named Battal. It is universally conceded that in this person we must see the historical origin of the mythical hero Sayyid al-Battal, whose exploits are celebrated in both Turkish and Spanish legend. Just fifty years later, in 789, during the reign of Constantine VI, the same chronicler records the death in a border skirmish of one Diogenes, *turmarch* or brigadier of the Anatolikoi. Applying the parallel of Battal, Grégoire has suggested, as I think with great probability, that the brigadier Diogenes is the historical figure lying behind the celebrated hero of Byzantine legend, Digenes Acritas, 'Twice-Born the Frontiersman', whose fame spread all over the Greek-speaking world. 'Twice-Born' was his name, for he was in the legend of part-Byzantine, part-Saracen stock. And this is by no means an improbability : it is in point to remember the very strong affinities of Leo III himself with the Saracens of Upper Syria.[9]

In the brief space between the repulse of the Saracens and the renewal of their incursions into Anatolia, Leo III took the most fateful step of his career. In 726 he made his first overt attack on Christian pictures and images. The theoretical origins and bases of the so-called 'iconoclastic' movement need a separate discussion. Here I wish merely to point to some of the political consequences, both disastrous and advantageous, which his policy entailed. The campaign began, then, in 726, with the destruction of a venerable picture of Christ in the porch of the Great Palace known as Chalke. Its destruction provoked a riot in which some soldiers were killed by fanatics, and was received with horror in the image-worshipping west. The first reaction to its destruction was a revolt, in 727, of the great naval command of the Karavisianoi (Seamen), a command which extended from the southern shores of Asia Minor over the whole of the Aegean Sea. The rebels were joined by the Helladics, or garrison troops of the *theme* of Hellas. The armament which the rebels were able to put on the sea was brushed aside with contemptuous ease by Leo III. But the reaction of these parts to iconoclasm showed clearly that the struggle would be between the remains of the old Graeco-Roman culture of the Aegean and the religious instincts of the Syro-Semitic orient.

Three years later (730) Leo put out his edict against images, which was his first and only legal pronouncement against them. That a large part of his Asian militia, especially in the Anatolic province, was behind him goes without saying; and that the whole institution of monasticism was against him to a man, is equally obvious. The last word here rested with the military arm. But in the Balkans and Italy the revolution brought about changes of which the significance, both short term and long, can scarcely be exaggerated. Whether or not it be true that at least one of the motives for the emperor's policy was to confirm his spiritual as well as his temporal absolutism, he was determined to vindicate this throughout his dominions. Even before the edict of 730, the *exarchate* of Ravenna and Pope Gregory II were informed of the imperial decision, backed by the tremendous claim of the Emperor Leo to priestly as well as administrative authority. His mandate caused an explosion of unmeasured ferocity. The *exarch* Paul and the Neapolitan duke were murdered. Paul's successor fled to Venice; and Ravenna was for a time in the hands of the Lombards.

Pope Gregory naturally refused to recognise the imperial authority in matters spiritual, or to countenance the heresy imposed by it. His resistance precipitated what the chronicler, prematurely but still justifiably, calls the 'apostasy' of Rome and Italy from the empire. The emperor at first thought he could deal with the matter as Constans II had dealt with Pope Martin; and he sent a strong fleet to Italy, which, however, foundered in the Adriatic. His next measures were of far wider import. In 731 he confiscated to the imperial treasury the so-called 'patrimonies of St Peter', a papal tax levied on the churches of Calabria and Sicily which brought in annually three and a half hundred-weights of gold. And, probably in the following year (the date is not quite certain), he transferred from the Roman to the Constantinopolitan see the bishoprics, not merely of Calabria and Sicily, but also of the whole area comprehended by the old prefecture of Illyricum. This area comprised nearly all the Balkan Peninsula, between Dalmatia and Thrace, from the Danube as far south as Crete, and included such historic centres of Graeco-Roman civilisation as Thessalonica and Athens and Corinth and Patras. This was a long step towards the severance of eastern from western Christendom. The annexation, so far as it concerned Illyricum at this time, was more of a form than a fact: since, owing to the occupation of this area by autonomous and pagan Slavs, their ecclesiastical organisation was for the moment theoretical rather than practical. Nevertheless, the sees annexed to Constantinople were such as would one day fall into the Byzantine sphere of political influence: and the ultimate adhesion of the Balkan Slavs to the Orthodox faith was in great part a result of this enactment. On the other hand, the South Italian areas of old Magna Graecia formed linguistically a more suitable adjunct to the see of Constantinople than to that of Rome. The patriarchate of Constantinople now formed a single administrative unit from the Saracen border to Naples (since, at the same time, the bishoprics of Isauria were detached from the jurisdiction of Antioch), and therefore nearly coincided with the territorial limits of the empire. The Roman Church, on the other hand, saw much of its power and resources curtailed. In the Photian-Ignatian quarrels of the ninth century, the papacy throughout kept half an eye on which party in the dispute was more or less likely to restore Illyricum, with Bulgaria, to the See of St Peter. In fact neither party did, or could have done. But if, in the long and growing estrangement between East and West leading inevitably to the schism of Cerularius, to the Fourth Crusade, and ultimately to the fall of Constantinople in 1453, we wish to pick on any specific incident as more influential than another in rendering the breach irreparable, Leo III's edicts of 731 and 732 must claim pride of place.[10]

Leo III has been the subject of many judgments in modern days, which differ as his judges are orthodox or catholic, freethinkers, nationalists or socialists. The fact that so many, and so widely divergent, views of him are possible is due to the scanty historical witnesses of his reign. He has by some been regarded as the great renovator of his realm, who tried to reform, and in great part succeeded in reforming, the state from top to bottom. His aims – it is said – were the repulse of superstition, the subjection of aristocracy and church to the absolute sovereignty of the emperor, the promotion of secular education, the curbing if not the extermination of monasticism (both for economic and spiritual reasons), the restoration of discipline to the armed forces, the revival of agriculture, and the promulgation of a code of laws, civil, criminal, commercial and rustic, which could be understood and applied in the provinces. Some of this is inference from results which may well have been secondary or fortuitous. What is quite certain is that Leo was a most gifted ruler and also a singularly uncompromising one. Whereas, at a comparable crisis, his great predecessor Heraclius had done all he could to heal religious dissension, Leo III appears to have gone out of his way to provoke it: and that at a time when Anatolia itself had no overwhelming majority in his favour. That divers advantages, with many more disasters, attended his policy was what he could not have foreseen. A lesser statesman would have made shipwreck: a greater would have run clear of the rocks.

Leo's son Constantine V (741-75), known to his ecclesiastical opponents as Copronymus, or 'called from dung', was a ruler yet more daring and capable. Even his traducers cannot conceal his greatness. His military talents were of the first order; and to these he added an intellectual energy and a firmness of purpose which, if he had reigned two centuries later, would have brought him to the pinnacle of glory. Moreover, though his age was sterile in all but ecclesiastical literature, there is reason to think that Constantine was fond both of music and of non-representational art. It is certainly an error to regard the early iconoclasts as a kind of proto-Calvinists or proto-Puritans – I mean, as gloomy enthusiasts who renounced art and letters as sinful. Constantine himself had a tendency towards what Puritans themselves would have called 'worldliness'. Finally, he was more highly strung than Leo; and even such traces of compromise as can be discerned in the father are altogether lacking in the son.[11]

The reign began unhappily. Constantine V, a youth of twenty-one, was at once opposed by his much older brother-in-law, the veteran general Artavasdus, who succeeded in getting control of the capital. Constantine fell back on Amorion where, owing to their proud memories of Leo III, the Anatolic troops were devoted to him. In less than a year Constantine had three times routed the forces sent against him by Artavasdus, had reduced Constantinople, and was back on his throne. The most important feature of Artavasdus' revolt is that he promised to restore the images, and had already set about doing so. And though he was defeated, it is surprising to find that the soldiers of the Armeniac province fought bravely in his defence. Iconoclasm, as we shall see, is by no means an easy question. The revolt probably had the result of inflaming to something like madness the emperor's hatred of image-worship, and he indulged in systematic persecution, which his father never did.

The reign continued inauspiciously during some years. Hardly was Constantine securely in command, when his empire was ravaged by a most cruel visitation of the bubonic plague, which lasted from 745 to 747. It was lucky that the two most formidable foes of Byzantium, the Saracens and the Bulgars, were at that time preoccupied with internal upheavals: otherwise the consequences might well have been disastrous. In Constantinople itself the living were too few to bury the dead. One of the most terrible features of the pestilence was its incidence among the populations of the maritime cities and garrisons, for the disease was sea-borne, and followed the routes of commerce and shipping. It was at this time that all Byzantine authority was extinguished in Peloponnesus, where, until that time a Byzantine garrison had held out in the south-east, at Monemvasia; but, as early as 722, the whole hinterland seems to have been controlled by Slavs. Constantine V, faced with this appalling scourge, applied the same remedy which had been invoked by the house of Heraclius: the wholesale reception of Slav settlers. Many, we are told, came to Constantinople from Hellas; while, a year or two later, Bithynia was repeopled with – if our source is reliable – no fewer than two hundred and eight thousand Slavs who emigrated from Bulgaria. We cannot doubt that these were wise moves, and the ultimate prosperity of agriculture under the Isaurians, as well as the Heraclians, is striking proof of this.[12]

Meanwhile events of world importance were taking place, both east and west. The Omayyad caliphate of Damascus had for thirty years been subject to internal pressures, religious, financial and nationalistic. The movement which ended in 750 with the extinction of the Omayyad house and the succession of the Abbasids might no doubt bring with it a restoration of rule to the family of the Prophet: but, more important, it brought the victory of the Persian over the Arab of Syria. The vast empire which the successors of Mahomet had built up could no longer be governed by a nationalist clique of Arabs, whose rulers depended for their authority more on tradition than on ability, able as many of them were. The empire of the Abbasids was in spirit much more akin to the Byzantine: with an administration open to the talents, more indiscriminate mixture of all racial elements, and a wider distribution of the special privileges which the Arab had hitherto enjoyed. The removal of the capital in 762 from Syria to Iraq was a logical outcome of this revolution.

Instead of intervening in the struggle between Mervan II and as-Saffah, Constantine V contented himself with rectifying the eastern frontier, and consolidating his position at home, which had been shaken by revolt and pestilence. He was also busily engaged in preparations for his iconoclastic Council which was to set the seal on thirty years of reform. But these years of comparative inaction witnessed in Italy a series of events no less momentous than the transfer of power from the Omayyads to the Abbasids. The Byzantine *exarchate* of Ravenna had been under the Lombard menace ever since its foundation two hundred years before. By 750 it was gravely, if not fatally, threatened. Constantine lifted not a finger to save it. The Lombard King Aistulf next turned his eye upon Rome. Pope Stephen II sent repeated appeals for aid to his lawful, if heretical, master at Constantinople, but these were answered only by the dispatch of an imperial envoy. By 753 the pope saw that, if Rome was to be saved at all, it must be by an arm more powerful and prompt that that of the Byzantine Caesar. In the depth of winter he stole away across the Alps, and on 6 January 754 held his historic meeting with Pippin, king of the Franks, and Pippin's young son Charles, afterwards 'the

Great'. From this step followed directly the emergence of the papacy as a temporal power, the Frankish conquest of Italy, and the establishment of the Holy Roman Empire. Yet even at this pass there is reason to think that the pope had still no thought of dividing the divinely sanctioned unity of the empire of Rome. It seems to be clear that the notorious forgery known as the Donation of Constantine, whereby temporal sovereignty or overlordship of the western empire was said to have been conveyed by Constantine I to Pope Silvester and his successors in perpetuity, did not formally emerge for half a century after 754; and also that, by conferring on Pippin the title of *patricius Romanorum*, the pope was consciously enrolling him in the Roman imperial hierarchy. The revolutionary innovators were not Pope Stephen and Pippin, but Pope Leo III and Charles the Great. Yet it is hard to overestimate the importance of Pope Stephen's initiative. Pippin carried back Pope Stephen to Rome at the head of his army. King Aistulf was overawed and rendered tributary, and the pope stepped as temporal sovereign into the shoes of the *exarch* of Ravenna.[13]

Hitherto Constantine V has not appeared to much advantage as a military man. He abstained from interference in two transactions to east and west of him, in either of which his interference might have been fruitful, though it probably would not have been lasting. But Constantine had other preoccupations. A threat more grave than the Moslem or Frank lay closer at hand, and in 756 Constantine had to begin an exhausting struggle with Bulgaria which occupied the remaining twenty years of his life.

It should seem that in the century which had elapsed between the Bulgarian occupation of the trans-Danubian Sklavinias and the era of Constantine V, the process of fusion between the Hunnic aristocracy and the Slavonic tribes had gone on apace; and the Hunnic overlords had played among the Slavs the part played by the Avars in the sixth century: that is, they had turned them from docile agriculturalists into ferocious aggressors. Bulgaria was now a compact and populous neighbour, destined henceforward to play a dominant role in Byzantine affairs. The history of the first Bulgarian empire is a history of bloodshed and destruction on such a scale that it seems nearly incredible that a state of this dimension could have wrought it. No reverses could check, no exhaustion could discourage, no concessions could satiate their restless savagery. And when we come to assess the causes of the breakdown of the Middle Byzantine Empire, we must attribute a substantial part of this breakdown to generations of Bulgarian slaughter and rapine.

Constantine v at least was under no illusion as to the seriousness of the position. He was compelled to confront it in no fewer than nine campaigns, in most of which he was triumphant. It is fair to say that, between the seventh and tenth centuries, no Roman general took the measure of this enemy as he did. He was constantly in the field. His dispositions were prudent. His orderly mind and his growing experience, backed by a stern discipline, were everywhere victorious. And it was small wonder that after he was dead his people, sickened and terrified by the havoc wrought by Khan Krum against Roman folly and incompetence, surrounded his tomb and implored him to come out and lead them once more to victory.[14]

Such were the external achievements of the great 'Isaurians', who carried on the work of the Heraclians. The imperial territories, shorn of the *exarchate* of Ravenna, were a little smaller than before, but what was left was in good case, both militarily and economically. In the economic field both Leo and Constantine were good managers who spent nothing profusely. Their agricultural policy was prosperous. The cost of living went down substantially. The enemies of Constantine attributed this to a drastic policy of deflation, which, by restricting the supplies of minted money, ensured an increase in the purchasing power of the gold *solidus*. Economists must tell us whether this expedient is probable, or even possible. But simpler minds, who can forget about religious heresy, will probably conclude that the reason why food under the Isaurians was cheaper than heretofore was because there was more of it, and this in turn was due to the extension of cultivated lands. The revealing testimony of an Arab source shows that between 718 and about 800 the corn-growing of Thrace doubled and trebled. For, says this source, 'nowadays if a besieging army at Constantinople wanted corn, the dealers could bring all and more than all it wanted from quite close at hand'.

The most striking tribute to the energy, ability and devotion of Leo iii and his son is found in the very last place in which we should look for it: in the Acts of the Seventh Council of 787, which anathematised and undid all their work in the religious sphere. The synod's *porte-parole*, the deacon Epiphanius, while reflecting very bitterly on the blasphemous and adulatory language applied by iconoclast churchmen to those sovereigns, yet added:

Though these clerics might rather have extolled their courage, their victories, their overthrow of the barbarian, exploits which many have commemorated in pictures and on walls, and have thus drawn the beholders to loyalty and affection: aye, and their care for their subjects, their counsels, their trophies, their secular reforms and their civil administration, and the cities which they rebuilt.

When we call to mind the malice and rancour of the iconodule party in general, and the rooted belief of those days that unorthodoxy automatically entailed disaster, we shall not fail to accord due weight to this eloquent testimony, which provides an excuse, if not a full justification, for the comprehensive eulogies bestowed by many modern scholars on the first two 'Isaurians'.

NOTES

1 Theophanes, 368–74; Nicephorus, 40–3.
2 Theophanes, 380–1; Ostrogorsky, 119–21.
3 Nicephorus, 49.
4 Theophanes, 384.
5 Theophanes, 386–91.
6 Bury, LRE, 374–86.
7 Theophanes, 395–8.
8 Vasiliev, 236.
9 Ostrogorsky, 124; Vasiliev, 369–70.
10 Ostrogorsky, 142.
11 Bury, LRE, 461–2.
12 Theophanes, 422–4, 429; Nicephorus, 69; Ostrogorsky, 140.
13 Bréhier, 84.
14 Ostrogorsky, 140–1; Bury, LRE, 470–5.

CHAPTER SIX

ICONOCLASM

I have thought it necessary to discuss in a separate chapter the first of those great religious struggles whose origins are traceable to the period which we are reviewing. The monophysite heresy goes back in origin at least to the middle of the fifth century, if not to the third, and we have thus, while allowing it due weight, at least politically, not been under the necessity of tracing it to its source. The iconoclast movement was indeed closely connected with the monophysite, and may have originated directly – as some believe – from that creed: at bottom, both were a protest against the material element in the divine Incarnation. The most determined and intellectual champion of image-breaking, the Emperor Constantine v, was almost certainly a monophysite, if not an out and out manichee. But it is convenient to deal with iconoclasm as a separate entity, whatever its affinities or inspirations may have been. The political consequences of its establishment were of prime importance. While it was the creed of a dynasty which saved Byzantium from the recrudescent Saracen and the emerging Bulgarian powers, it was productive of violent, enduring and deleterious cleavages in Byzantine society for more than a century. We are therefore bound to make a special effort to explore its origins and importance.

It should be said at once that, on the wider bearings of iconoclasm, there is no agreement among scholars, even today. Some say that behind the official policy of the iconoclast sovereigns there lay a desire to strengthen the absolute control of the crown, by depressing the orthodox clergy and vindicating for the emperor sacerdotal as well as imperial functions: the definition, that is, as well as the defence, of faith. Such were indeed the results of iconoclasm, but were they its causes? Others will have it that the whole programme was anti-clerical and anti-monastic: in other words, that the sharp-sighted 'Isaurians' were alive to the strains on the economy caused by excessive and expanding church properties and by the ever larger numbers of youthful and vigorous males, needed as fathers, soldiers and cultivators, who embraced the infertile life of monasticism. Here again, it is true that Constantine v at least was a fanatical hater of monasticism, who later in his reign forcibly secularised and forced marriage upon many of that profession; but can we regard these as the prime objects of his policy? Or were they simply the logical outcome of it? Others, again, regard the movement as scarcely religious at all, but entirely economic: as a blow against the landed and orthodox aristocracy, and as a single item in the programme of *thematic* development – an intensification, that is, of the system of the rural communes and of soldier-peasants, directly dependent on the central imperial control. Once more, it is certainly true that, despite costly wars, the Isaurian sovereigns were successful in bringing prosperity to the countryside, improving agricultural production and thus bring down the cost of living. But was that simply what they were after, all along?[1]

It is a modern tendency, in an age when religious dogma and precision are no longer burning questions (and I mean, literally, 'burning' questions, a phrase which survives from an epoch when anyone who took the wrong side in such questions might find himself at the stake), it is, I say, a modern tendency to regard such questions as a mere mask or outward expression for other interests – social, political, economic, nationalistic – which the present age finds more absorbing and therefore considers more important. Marxism, which pervades modern historical thinking to a far greater degree than most of us would care to admit, has been largely instrumental in giving this tendency a modern interpretation, and has thus corrupted the right attitude to the religious movements of history. According to this way of thinking, when a man said that Christ had but one divine Nature, or that His Nature was indescribable, what he really meant was that he had not enough bread in his belly or clothes on his back. One Marxist interpretation of iconoclasm regards it as a kind of proto-revolutionary and popular movement, in the Marxist sense, against economic exploitation and religious obscurantism: so that Leo III and his son appear almost as medieval forerunners of Lenin: men who defended the interests of the small man in the rural areas as well as the industrial (and heretical) proletariate of the capital. This theory, however, leads to some difficulties. In the second period of iconoclasm (815–43), the Slav Thomas led a formidable revolt against the iconoclast régime of Michael II. This movement must be described as eminently 'popular', if ever any movement was. And yet Thomas pronounced himself decidedly in favour of images, and indeed claimed to be the image-worshipping Emperor Constantine VI. And whatever we may say of Leo III and Constantine V, they were certainly not religious *pococuranti*, to whom one belief was as good as another. Their policies sprang from settled, preconceived religious convictions: and not their religious convictions from their practical policies.

Perhaps on the whole it is best to go back to things as they were and as our sources depict them; and to trace what the men of those times thought significant, rather than what we, in our enlightened days, imagine they must have meant by their expressions of belief. A far safer line of thought – it seems to me – is to regard the whole struggle as one more clash between the settled beliefs and philosophical moulds of thought of the old Graeco-Roman world, and the oriental mysticism and monotheism of the eastern provinces: at bottom, polytheism against monotheism, philosophic relativism against literal communion, Athens against Jerusalem. We might go further: and see it as a struggle between two distinct eras of human development, the era of magic and the era of religion. Such a view helps us to explain why the two positions, at first sight far from irreconcilable by judicious compromise, were in fact definite and final. They were the outcome of two separate traditions, neither of which even understood the other. One or other must be victorious, where no basis for composition existed. To take the most striking example of this divergence, to which we shall return: the iconoclasts believed, as the Jews of the Old Testament believed, that in painting or carving an image, one was *creating* either a false god or else something of the same substance with the divine personage depicted: and this was of course the very crime forbidden in the most positive fashion by the Second Commandment. The icon-worshippers, on the other hand, believed that an icon was an indispensable step in the progress of spiritual contemplation upwards from the things seen to the things unseen, a conception first formulated by Plato in his *Symposium*, and established unshakably in the thought of the Hellenistic world by the Neo-Platonists and the pseudo-Dionysius. No bridge could span this gap; and there were other chasms equally unbridgeable.

In origin, the conflict between support of graven images and their rejection was as old as the beginnings of Christianity. The Judaic origins of the faith would naturally not permit any representation of a divine personage. When the faith spread to the gentiles, this aversion to images was one of the features which marked out the early Christian from his fellow-citizens, whom, in their worship of a pantheon depicted in thousands by the brush or the chisel of the finest artists of antiquity, he denounced as idolaters. And one of the chief causes of early martyrdom was, as is notorious, the Christian's refusal to offer decent respect to the *image* of the reigning sovereign, a duty incumbent on all subjects, neglect of which was construed as treason.[2]

Nevertheless, it is in the imperial cult that we must trace the origins of the Christian worship of images. According to the Roman imperial theory, the emperor was regarded as Universal Providence, which implied his omnipresence. As he could not, in actual fact, be in a thousand places at once, his presence was supplied by his images, which were regarded as a literal substitute for it: just as his image on a coin denoted his power and authority wherever that coin was passed. All the ceremonial which would have been performed before him had he been manifest in the flesh was, of course, transferred wholesale to his likeness, which was adored, prayed to, carried in procession, illuminated and incensed.

The acceptance of the Christian religion by Constantine the Great and his successors made no difference at all to this procedure; nor could it have done so, without convulsing the framework of secular society. There is ample evidence that fourth and fifth-century Christians had long withdrawn all opposition to a practice which their predecessors rejected with obstinacy and abhorrence. 'The emperor', says St Gregory of Nazianzus himself, 'must have adoration, whereby his dignity is increased: and not only that "adoratio" which he receives in person, but also the "adoratio" that he receives in his statues and pictures, so that the veneration paid to him may be without boundary or limit.'

It is not difficult to see the effect of such a procedure on more specifically religious practice, once the Christian empire had been established by Constantine and its *mystique* had been formulated by Eusebius. If the emperor, who is Christ's deputy, receives adoration through his images, does it not follow – or did it not follow at least in a pre-christological age – that pictures and statues of the great God-Man should be similarly venerated? Fourth-century Christian apologists, representative of the old traditions of the faith, were manifestly uneasy about the new tendency brought about by the imperial-religious fusion of human and divine. An early and celebrated statue of the Saviour (or, more probably, of the Emperor Vespasian) at Paneas in Palestine had been given sanctuary in a church: but, explains Philostorgius, this was a mere mark of respect: no 'adoratio' was paid to it by the faithful, who regarded it merely with expressions of joyfulness. Austin was not deceived. He viewed with deep misgiving the *picturarum adoratores*. Epiphanius of Cyprus, his contemporary, was more outspoken still. A convinced opponent of Christian images, he explains in a revealing phrase what was going on. 'They put up their images', he says, 'and then perform the practices of the pagans before them.'

It is obvious that, in a spiritual point of view, the danger of such practices rests not so much in the practices themselves but in the mental attitude of the practitioner. It may be true, as later icon-worshippers were to urge, that an image, by instructing, stimulating and elevating the mind, may lead it on to contemplation of eternal verities. It may also be true that the worshipper may approach it in a spirit of grovelling and superstitious idolatry, as a savage approaches his fetish. The moment that the worshipper begins to attribute a separate life and power to the material object before his eyes, the safety point is passed, and idolatry, animism and mere magic have usurped the place of religion.

It is safe to say that, whatever the theoretical defenders of images may have affirmed, the vast majority of their worshippers regarded them with superstitious veneration. The doctrine of spiritual elevation to higher things demands an intellectual effort and training of which the ordinary worshipper was – and perhaps is – totally incapable. The cult of relics, as opposed to that of images, had been widespread from earliest time among Christians, for these were not images; and they had from the first been invested with magical powers. It was an easy transfer of these powers to the much more attractive and intelligible *likeness* of Deity or saint or martyr, and the ordinary man did not trouble his head as to how such transference could be justified by philosophical or theological arguments. The sixth century, especially the latter part of it, is remarkable for the proliferation of its wonder-working images, images that were independent sources of action or subjects of passion, images which wept or bled, punished or healed. Nor were these by any means such as administered help of comfort in individual cases only. Many became civic palladia or talismans, as had, in pagan days, been the Wolf of Romulus or the Fortune of Antioch. To such talismans were committed the weal or woe of the whole city. The miraculous Christ of Edessa was a notable example, and, of course, the Hodegetria of Constantinople itself, which, in 718, on the very eve of iconoclasm, was to deliver the capital from the Saracen hordes of Suleiman.3 Suitably paraded and escorted by the adorants, the object itself would emit blinding light or consuming flame to repel the invader or confound the infidel. No churchman would have declared that the power of the Virgin Mother of God, the guardian, general and guide of the Queen of Cities, resided in the tangible icon of the Hodegoi or of the Blachernae: nonetheless, to the credulous populace, these tangible representations, like the tangible robe of the Virgin, were no mere reminders of a celestial power but the actual, visible repositories of it. And Christian people kissed and adored the man-made images with a fervour equal to, and sentiments scarcely differing from, those with which the Beduin stroked the sacred stone of Mecca.

The growth of superstitious belief during the sixth century has been noted, and proved, by scholars in the fields both of Byzantine art history and Byzantine culture. It is a phenomenon which we do well to mark, as one more symptom of the death of the old, rational standards of life, and the birth of the new age of faith.

There are abundant signs that in the seventh century the rulers of the Heraclian house not merely approved, but actively encouraged, the propagation of images of the Saviour, as the manifest source and protector of their throne and empire. Emperors down to Justinian I were more Romans than Christians. No doubt they were believers, and devout believers; but, as the source of their power, they believed rather in the temporal dominance and fortune of Rome than in its sanction by the God of the Christians. The political circumstances of the seventh century altered the emphasis here. In the short space of eighty years, New Rome had lost about three-quarters of her territorial empire. On at least two occasions (626 and 674) her own survival as a Christian city was in doubt. As we have seen, the theory of universal Romano-Christian autocracy was not altered by these diminutions. But, in the article of emperor as viceroy of Christ, it is not strange that in these doubtful times greater emphasis should be laid on the divine than on the human element in the dyarchy; or that imperial policy should have been at pains, by the spread of images, to familiarize their subjects with the divine Appearance as it had once been seen on earth, and thus to inspirit them by reminders of an awful Power that was pledged to their support. By the 82nd canon of the Quinisext Council, convened by Justinian II in 691, it was enacted that, in future, representations of Christ in the form of a lamb were to be forbidden, and only anthropomorphic depiction of the Saviour permitted, 'So that', proceeded the Fathers, in a very orthodox fashion, 'we may perceive through this the depth of the humiliation of God, and be led on to the remembrance of His life on earth, of His Passion and of His Death unto Salvation, and of the Redemption which these brought among us.' Was this, one wonders, the only reason for the enactment? Was it not also that the people might gain strength from beholding the awe-inspiring and terrific features of Him who was All-Powerful to save? The same sentiment is doubtless behind a significant change in the coin-types of this same Emperor Justinian II. On his money appears for the first time the image of God along with the image of Caesar; and they are denominated respectively 'Rex regnantium' and 'Servus Dei'.

This encouragement of images, if not of actual image-worship (though it is hard to distinguish in practice between the two), may very probably have strengthened the imperial arm by giving renewed faith and confidence in it to the people. But it was not without its perils in another direction: since, by accentuating the divine control and favour, it gave additional authority to the department of state which claimed to define and interpret the conditions under which that control and favour could be claimed and enjoyed: I mean, the Church. There had always been a body in the Christian empire to which the claim of the emperors to absolutism over church as well as state had been difficult of digestion, a body which remembered that earlier emperors had for centuries cruelly ravaged the flock of Christ. The emperors down to Justinian I, and even to Constans II, had regarded the pontiffs as their vassals and had bullied them as they bullied recalcitrant civil servants. This absolute authority now appeared to be weakened; and it is hard to deny that at least one of the most important consequences, if not one of the motives, in the coming iconoclast policy was a return to imperial authority over matters spiritual as well as temporal, and the reduction of the church establishment to a simple department of the imperial bureaucracy.

The very great increase in the number, sanctity and worship of images during the seventh century, whether this was due to superstition or policy or both, was viewed with apprehension by more than one element in the population, and especially by those of oriental extraction. The Saracen conquests had indeed relieved the empire of many monophysites; yet their number within its borders was still not inconsiderable. And the monophysites could never accept the making of images. As the Saviour had had, they thought, but a single divine nature, it was impossible to circumscribe it within the limits of a picture, and it was impious to try to do so. They were also strongly opposed to Mariolatry, since they reduced to a minimum, often indistinguishable from naked dualism, the human element in Our Lord; and the respect due to His earthly Mother naturally waned in consequence. As for pictures of saints, these 'lumps of matter' were an insult to the bright choirs of Heaven and bred nothing but idolatry. The Armenian Christians naturally took the same line, and the Armenian Paulicians (Dualists) went far beyond it. There is, however, good reason to think that a non-Christian impulse was at least as much responsible as any Christian for the explosion of hatred and violence which took place in 726. The Jews, powerful in the Saracen empire, were always on the look-out for a handle against the caliph's Christian subjects. The Saracens themselves, smarting from their inglorious repulse in 718, found their tolerance of large Christian minorities under some strain. It is likely that these elements fused to produce what most people then, and many people now, regard as the opening shot in the iconoclastic campaign: the edict promulgated by the Caliph Yazid II, in July 723.[4]

The actual terms of this Saracen edict are no longer extant; and the various accounts of its promulgation – Byzantine, Latin, Syriac, Armenian and Arab – that have come down to us are, in parts at least, legendary. These accounts boil down, in sum, to the following common elements: shortly after his accession in 720 the Caliph Yazid fell ill. Whereupon a Jew of Tiberias, a magician, and a savage hater of the Christians, whose name is variously given as Visir or Tessarakontapechys (the Greek for forty cubits), approached his bedside and promised him a further thirty or forty years of life and rule if he would issue an order that all representational pictures of whatever sort or kind, whether in churches or in markets, should be destroyed throughout his dominions. The edict was issued at once, and the destruction of all representational art in every Christian church in Saracen territory followed. However much of this account may be legend, the destruction at this time is certain: for a delegate at the Seventh Council at Nicaea in 787 stated, 'I was a boy in Syria when the Saracen caliph was destroying the pictures'.

For the rest of the story, we may accept that the caliph was directly or indirectly inspired to act thus by Jewish influence, since the accounts are unanimous that this was so, and there is not the smallest reason to doubt it. Jewish influence had induced the Caliph Omar I to remove Christian symbols in 644. It is even possible that a Jewish doctor (here called a magician) of the caliph advised the step. The nomenclature used is, however, odd. Tessarakontapechys is a Greek word, and can hardly have been the name of a Jew at Tiberias. And as for Visir, it is close to the Arabic title vizier, though the office does not seem to have existed before 749.

The edict of the Caliph Yazid was put out in 723. The first action of Emperor Leo III against icons in the Byzantine empire followed in 726. It is asking too much of human credulity to suppose that the two steps were wholly independent of one another. Leo III was universally condemned by the icon-worshippers as *Sarakinofron*, that is, 'Saracen-minded', in his religious policy: so that they at least drew the obvious deduction. Moreover, until that time, Leo III had been, if not a warm, at least an orthodox, supporter of icons, as is clear from his letter, now regarded as genuine, to the Caliph Omar II, which was written before 720; and there is evidence that during the Arab siege of 718 he had made use of the miraculous icon of the Virgin Hodegetria to repel the invaders. Thirdly, there is some evidence that this iconoclast revolution at Byzantium was precipitated by the intervention of one Tessarakontapechys, one of his strenuous agents in the affair, and it is impossible to dissociate this person from the one who bore the same peculiar name and had been active in persuading the Caliph Yazid in the same direction three years previously. As we saw, he is said to have been a Jew. And the fact that Leo III's hostility to icons was not, like his son's, based on christological arguments but on the simple Mosaic interdict against graven images, points to Jewish influence here too.

The whole question, it is true, bristles with difficulties. The action of Yazid II against the Christians of Syria constituted a severe blow to their rights, and one would have supposed that Leo III, the victor over Omar II, would have protested in the strongest manner against it, instead of adopting what amounted to the same policy in his own dominions. In adopting the iconoclast creed, Leo knew well that he was flying in the face of orthodox Christianity, and imperilling his relations with Italy and the papacy. That he made head against, and ultimately profited from, this opposition, was what could not possibly have been foreseen. The only rational explanation of his revolutionary conduct is that which lies on the surface: namely that, owing to predisposition, to the remonstrances of some of his Phrygian bishops, and possibly to advice from the shadowy Tessarakontapechys, he was sincerely *converted* to a belief in the wickedness and impiety of sacred pictures. All other consequences were of secondary importance. A severe volcanic eruption, which to his mind seemed to be God's condemnation of idolatry, is said to have hastened his decision. And in 726, by the public destruction of Christ's image in the Brazen Porch of his own palace, he opened the conflict.5

He proceeded at first with much caution. After the initial outburst of image-breaking in 726, he waited four years before calling a *silentium* and issuing his one and only edict against the pictures. During these four years his Patriarch Germanus, an orthodox icon-worshipper, remained at his post and administered his see apparently without interference. In 730, of course, he had to go. Yet the extreme fury of the monkish opposition, to whom posterity is indebted for almost the only information it has about Leo III's internal administration, cannot attribute to him the savagery of per-

83

secution of which it accuses – we fear, with too much reason – his more brilliant but less stable son Constantine v. Of one charge, as Bury saw,[6] Leo must be acquitted at once: that of strangling higher education. The story is that he destroyed the ecclesiastical academy of the Ecumenical Didaskalos (a kind of Professor of Theology, or Moderator) for refusing to obey him: and this, by lighting a fire and burning building, books and professors all together. Whatever germ of truth there may be in this report (and it is probably a very small one), certain it is that during the middle of the eighth century education, at least in Constantinople, was at a far higher level than in the middle of the seventh. And polished, refined scholars like Nicephorus or Tarasius or Theodore of Studius, or a hundred others who heralded the dawn of culture's rebirth in the ninth century, are sadly to seek in the days of Justinian II and Leo III himself.

The doctrinal disputes which the iconoclast controversy aroused during the first period of iconoclasm – we may date it from 726 to 787 – are of two very different kinds, the first simple, the second highly complex; the first roughly corresponding to the reign of Leo III, the second to that of Constantine v.[7] The ground on which Leo III and his advisers took their stand was primarily that of the Mosaic law, with its prohibition of the making of idols. Even in this primitive form we note the oriental belief that the painting of an icon was the actual creation of a false god, which lay at the root of the Jewish interdict. The orthodox image-worshippers got over this initial hurdle very easily. The Mosaic law had been put out in days long before the divine Incarnation, before the Deity had revealed Himself to mankind in a recognisable, tangible, and hence representable shape. By making idols in those days, the people no doubt were making unto themselves false gods, monsters and demons. This was what was prohibited. But, since the appearance of God on earth, and that of His Holy Mother, and those of His apostles, witnesses and saints, their true forms had been revealed to mankind, which was thereafter allowed, and indeed encouraged, to make representations of them: for these, by recalling their true appearances to succeeding generations, led up the hearts of their worshippers to the suprasensible truth on high.

The second phase of the controversy, which elevated it to the sphere of abstruse christological definition, was precipitated by the intervention of the greatest theologian of that century, an Arab

Christian named Mansur, who is better known as John of Damascus. After holding high office at the caliph's court, he retired to a monastery in Palestine, and there set himself to confute in detail, from a far higher standpoint, the iconoclast heresy. It seems at first sight remarkable that he should have remained free to indulge in a polemic which was directly counter to the policy of the Caliph Yazid; but it must be remembered that the edict of Yazid had been revoked by this time, and that the Saracens themselves were ready to condone any efforts which might tend to weaken the interior condition of the Byzantine empire.

It was John who, in the years immediately before and after 730, initiated the arguments on which the whole defence of icon-worship was subsequently to rest. It was he who developed the neo-platonist conception that the function of pictures was mediatory between man and the supersensible world, a conception which derives ultimately from the doctrine of the wise Diotima of Plato's *Symposium*: where it is explained that visible beauties are essential, but merely transitory, stepping-stones towards the knowing and contemplation of that absolute beauty which is apprehended only by the soul. Upon this doctrine John of Damascus grafted the Christian doctrine of the Incarnation. Christ's manifestation in bodily form was the indispensable, but initiatory, step in raising men's souls to a knowledge of God. To deny the value and significance of a material picture was to deny the value of Christ's own Incarnation. The one implied the other.

This brilliant and profound reasoning naturally involved the further question of the nature of the Incarnation itself· and thus the iconoclasts of the second, or Constantinian, dispensation were thrown back into the christological tempests which had convulsed the church of the fifth and sixth centuries. Contantine v himself was an ardent theologian, if a not very subtle one. He was, by conviction, a monophysite, if not worse. Many anecdotes of his remarks and behaviour make this quite certain. He had all the monophysite disgust for Mariolatry, hagiolatry, efficacy of relics and intercessory prayer. He refused to speak of the Blessed Mother of God, but only of 'Mary': if his own iconoclast Patriarch Anastasius is to be believed, he once said with an oath, 'Mary gave birth to Christ just as my mother Mary gave birth to me'. As an older man, in 764, when his council of 754 had fortified his position, he is said to have remarked to the Patriarch Constantine,

'Why, my lord, what harm does it do to call Mary the Mother of Jesus rather than the Mother of God?' The patriarch was flabbergasted. 'For Heaven's sake, your Majesty', he said, 'don't talk so! Don't you see how Nestorius is universally condemned and anathematised for saying just this'? 'Well, well', said the emperor, 'I only asked, to hear what you would say. The decision naturally rests with you.' Nonetheless, the title *Theotokos* (Mother of God) was odious to him, and if an old courtier tripped up and let fall the expletive 'Help, Mother of God!', he did not pass without reprimand. Constantine even baulked at the words 'Saint', or 'Holy', applied to churches; and it became usual to say, 'I'm going to the Apostles', or 'The Forty', or to 'Theodora's', or 'George's'.[8]

This convinced opponent of images and image worship saw that, if his opponents were effectually to be met, it must now be on their own ground, that of Christian apologetics, and no longer by simple reference to the Mosaic law. He summoned a council in 754, which called itself the Seventh Ecumenical Synod, but of course was deprived of this title as soon as images re-established themselves. Before the council met, the emperor thought it wise to brief the delegates upon his own views of the question. He therefore drew up a schedule of articles which he circulated to the bishops in the form of an imperial rescript. His exposition is lost, but, luckily, some of its most fundamental contentions have been preserved to us, apparently verbatim, by the apologist St Nicephorus.

The first proposition of the imperial theologian was as follows: Christ, as we know, was of two natures, a human and a divine, and these natures coalesced in a single, if unconfounded, union and a single person. How can this be depicted? If we say we make a picture of Him, one of two consequences must follow: either we are depicting the divine nature, but this by definition is indescribable, or, more properly, uncircumscribable; or else, if we are depicting His human nature only, then a separate person is created out of His flesh, the Godhead is increased by one to a monstrous committee of four, and Christ, deprived of His divine nature, becomes a simple creature like other men. To be short, an icon of Christ must either purport to circumscribe the uncircumscribable, or else to divide His indivisible natures and so to upset the doctrine of their unconfounded union.

This view of the case was – as, considering its source, is not surprising – substantially accepted by the council. Their main preoccupation, while decisively rejecting the images, was to avoid running foul of the Charybdis of unorthodoxy. Constantine had indeed, in his rescript, paid lip-service to the two natures of Christ; but certain expressions of his draft, with their emphasis on the single person, seemed to smack of monophysitism. These expressions were toned down in the definition. It was now stated that no one could make an image without contracting the taint either of monophysitism or of nestorianism. If he described the divine, he confounded the natures: if he described the human only, he severed them: and each was heretical according to Chalcedon.

But the most interesting of Constantine's propositions is one already alluded to: 'If [he said] this is right, then the image is *of the same substance* with the imaged'. The image one makes is, as it were, transubstantiated. This curious and typically oriental doctrine explains why, according to iconoclast belief, the Sacrament alone was the true material icon of the Godhead, as Christ had ordained it to be. Christ himself had stated the Sacrament to be of His substance, His own flesh and blood. He had not stated that lumps of wood or other humble materials did or could partake of His divine Essence.9

As to the images made of the Virgin and the saints, these were indeed not obnoxious to the christological arguments against images of the Saviour. But they served only to degrade their originals by subjecting them to dead matter and besides promoted idolatry. These too were abolished.

Against all this, the opposition had a ready answer, the neoplatonic answer already outlined by John of Damascus. An image was not *consubstantial* with its original, but merely a Platonic *mimesis* (imitation) of it, having in itself no independent significance, except in so far as it *partook* of the divine form and led the soul up to the latter. But, in this, its function was all-important and indispensable. As for the Christ-image, Christ had appeared in two natures on earth, in a shape which obviously had been describable – witness the holy tile of Hierapolis or the holy towel of Edessa. His likeness was in fact extant in more than one object not made with human hands, but by His own divine emanation. The doctrine of the degradation of matter, in which the icon-worshippers, not without reason, had detected manichaeanism, was false, or at all events obsolete since the Incarnation. By taking on flesh the Godhead had not degraded Himself, but sanctified the material element. The material icon, once stamped with His likeness, was similarly made holy.

So, on the higher planes of philosophical reasoning, the battle was fought out. The rival arguments seem less important than the practical realities behind them: the clash of two worlds, of two irreconcilable instincts or points of view. That image-worship, with all its cultural and aesthetic advantages, finally prevailed over iconoclasm, was doubtless a gain for European civilisation. But we must never forget that the iconoclasts had a case, and a strong one, in the field of polemic: and that their temporary victory, though a setback for the arts and also for the enlightenment of the un-educated portion of society, was accompanied by solid advantages in the economic and military fields, without which there might well have been no chance for unity or for final recovery.

Constantine v was no man for half-measures. He has, naturally, suffered severely at the hands of orthodox historians: and no histories presenting the iconoclast point of view survive, if any were in fact written. His morals were laid under the cruellest of stigmas. He was a homosexual (though thrice married), and a pervert. He enjoyed secular music. He trafficked with demons. No one can say how much of this stuff has any foundation in fact, though, since none of it is alleged of Leo III, we are tempted to believe him at least a more complex and more violent character than his father. That he was a determined persecutor can scarcely be denied. After the council had pronounced its decisions by the mouth of 338 bishops in 754, Constantine set to work with a will to put them into execution. At least six confessors, of whom the best known is St Stephen of Mount Auxentius, were executed. It is noteworthy that at least one victim was lynched by the Con-stantinopolitan mob, and this may indicate that the industrial pro-letariat, some at least of whom were dualists, took the icono-clastic side. But in the 760s the venom of Constantine's persecution was directed, not so much against individuals, as against the whole monastic order, which he seems to have dreamt of extirpating root and branch.[10] He succeeded in making considerable inroads on mon-astic properties. He paraded monks and nuns, and expelled them from their seats. His vigorous governor Lachanodracon is said to have exterminated monasticism in the Thracesian province, and this, if true, was no small achievement in that fertile and populous area of the Ionian coast. It cannot be doubted that these secularisations and expulsions benefited both the army and agriculture. Many monks opted for exile, especially in neutral Cyprus, as well as in Sicily and South Italy, where they reinforced the Greek-speaking element of those areas. But many did not so choose, and opted instead for marriage and a return to the world.[11]

Constantine was one of the few sovereigns strong and determined enough to fight against the entrenched power of the monks. But even he had no permanent success. His son reversed his policy, and his daughter-in-law annulled the decisions of his council. Yet he could not have done what he did without a devoted army, which he seldom led to defeat, and very widespread popular support. The one was conciliated by his victorious operations against the Bulgarians. And the other, we can scarcely doubt, was due in large measure to a strong element of personal magnetism.

NOTES

1 Vasiliev, 251–3.
2 Ostrogorsky, 134, notes 1 and 2.
3 DAI, 92.
4 Ostrogorsky, 135.
5 Bréhier, 79.
6 Bury, LRE, 433–4.
7 Ostrogorsky, 142–6.
8 Theophanes, 415, 435, 442.
9 Ostrogorsky, 143 and notes 2–4.
10 Bury, LRE, 460–8; Vasiliev, 251–63.
11 Theophanes, 445–6.

CHAPTER SEVEN

CONSTANTINE VI AND IRENE

Constantine v died in 775, leaving a strong homeland, a victorious army, a semblance of religious unity, a sound economy, and six sons. The eldest son, Leo, born of a Chazar princess and hence commonly called Leo the Chazar, now succeeded as Leo iv. Leo had none of his father's ability: and it is probable that even at his accession he was suffering from the disease which killed him five years later. He had been married in December 769 to Irene, daughter of a noble family of Athens. The union appears at first sight an odd one, and it is to be asked what Constantine v had in mind in choosing such a daughter-in-law. What remained to Byzantium within the pale of the Athenian fortress was known to be solidly image-worshipping, that is, hostile to the official policy of iconoclasm. And the young empress herself never made any secret of her fondness for the pictures. It can only be, that the choice was dictated by a desire to conciliate image-worshipping opinion, and the name which she was given at her marriage – *Irene*, or Peace – suggests that this was so. Whatever hopes the Emperor Constantine may have entertained in this direction were sadly belied. The lady brought not peace, but the sword. She was destined to rule, on and off, for twenty-two years after her husband's death, and they were years of almost unrelieved disaster. She was, by any standards, medieval or modern, a bad woman; and, what was worse, an incapable and irresponsible prince. It was unfortunate for Byzantium that her reign (780–802) coincided with those of the greatest of the Franks, Charlemagne (771–814), and the greatest of the Abbasid caliphs, Harun al-Rashid (786–809).

Leo IV was by upbringing an iconoclast. But he was at once faced with the fact that his realm was fatally divided. Only the strong arm of his father had been able to hold the opposition in check. Leo began the policy of concession which was continued on one side or the other up till 843, in the hopeless attempt at securing unity by consent. The long centuries of failure to solve the monophysite controversy might have made it plain to everybody that religious unity in the Byzantine church could never be won by agreement so long as there were two churchmen left to take opposing sides. Even the final abandonment of iconoclasm in the mid-ninth century brought no peace, for a feud was continued for centuries between two wings of orthodoxy. At all events, Leo IV was disposed to see what moderation could do, and he began by concessions to the monks.

As we saw, Constantine V had execrated the monks with a sustained fury scarcely distinguishable from mania. To him they were the 'unmentionables'. They were the slaves of sexual lust. Their order of life was the doctrine of hell. They either fled or were deported wholesale. Their properties were confiscated, their precious pictures destroyed. There can be no doubt that this radical policy excited great resentment, at least in the countryside, where all that there was of culture and education resided in monasteries. Leo IV, though far from sympathetic to monkish views and practices, reversed this policy. The monks were permitted to return to their monasteries, and might once more discreetly venerate a picture of the Virgin without having it broken over their heads.[1] The ribald and blasphemous disrespect of the Blessed Virgin herself was discontinued, and Leo was hailed among the orthodox by the rather surprising title of 'Friend to the Mother of God'. In this policy he was doubtless influenced by the convictions of his wife, and possibly by the attitude of his Patriarch Nicetas, a Slav, who may, because of his race, have escaped that taint of fanaticism evinced by the two main parties to the controversy. However it may be, the emperor had no mind to go farther in his concessions, and his last year was signalised by new persecution of prominent lay image-worshippers: nor is there reason to doubt that, had Leo lived, this persecution would have been intensified. As it was, after five years of undistinguished rule, and after exacting a promise from the army, the senate and the populace, that they would remain loyal to his infant son Constantine, Leo IV died (780).

The Empress Irene now succeeded to the real mastery of the empire. Her son, who came to the throne as the Emperor Constantine VI, was only ten years old, and was for eleven years completely under the thumb of his mother. The image-worshipping proclivities of the empress were notorious: and, even if they had not been, her initial acts would have made them so. The splendid military organisation bequeathed to Leo IV by Constantine V was still intact, but its commanders were of course all of the iconoclast persuasion. The empress might have waited to see what would be the reaction of the military towards the reformation she was working to produce. But there is evidence[2] that she dismissed the experienced military governors almost at once, and replaced them by inexperienced orthodox. Instantly a revolt broke out which was said to be in favour of one or other of her five brothers-in-law, *fainéant* princes who passed dreary lives moving from one confinement and mutilation to the next, whenever a conspirator took their names in vain. The movement was repressed and the princes, who probably knew nothing about it, were tonsured as monks. But this was made an excuse for further dismissals of officers. The effects of this tampering with the military machine were soon apparent. Elpidius, the governor of Sicily, threw off his allegiance, and, when attacked, went over to the African Saracens. In Asia Harun, son of the Caliph al-Madi, invaded the empire at the head of a hundred thousand men. Once again demoralisation and treachery were apparent in the defection of the Armenian general Tatzates to the Arabs with all his men. The Romans were compelled to make an ignominious and very expensive peace. The writing was on the wall. The single item of military glory which attached to the new régime dates from the year 783. Irene, who hailed from Hellas, was more concerned than her father-in-law had been about the reclamation of this territory. She sent a large force – the first large-scale operation in that area since Justinian II's expedition of 688 – to Hellas under the command of her chief minister and adviser, the eunuch Stauracius. He is said to have marched on Thessalonica, reduced the Slavs of Hellas, and even pushed into Peloponnesus, whence he took 'many prisoners and much spoil'. It seems likely that the *theme* of Hellas, as a working administrative unit, dates from this time; whereas the terms 'prisoners' and 'spoil' used of the Peloponnesian venture show that this peninsula was still foreign territory: and in fact there is reason to think that its history as a *theme* dates only from the following reign of Nicephorus I (802–11).3

Meanwhile the empress was moving, slowly but surely, to the main task of her life, the restoration of image-worship in her dominions. However eager she might be to act, common sense compelled caution, and it was not until six years after the death of Leo IV that a council could be convened (786), and seven years before a decision could be published (787). It is hard to gauge the strength of the opposed parties at this time. That revived monasticism was behind the empress to the last man goes without saying. It seems equally clear that the armed forces, trained to conquer in the faith of the great 'Isaurians', were chiefly of the opposite persuasion. On the other hand, many of the provincial levies, especially in Bithynia, were of Slav extraction, who probably did not feel nearly as strongly about the matter as the officers and men of the Anatolic province; while the western garrisons of Hellas, and the bulk of the Italian province of Calabria (its population swelled by orthodox fugitives from Asia), were certainly in favour of reaction. The revolt of the troops in Constantinople at the opening of the council in 786 was the work of a hard core of loyal iconoclasts recruited by Constantine V to garrison the capital. By disbanding and cashiering this splendid body Irene undoubtedly weakened the empire's defences: but the very fact that it could be disbanded shows that substitutes of one sort or another could be found to take their place. The objection to Irene's armies is that they were bad armies, not that there were no armies at all.

In 784 died the Patriarch Paul IV, an iconoclast churchman who had been appointed in 780 by Leo IV. The caution of Irene is well illustrated by the fact that he held his throne during the first four years of her reign. The choice of a successor, who should carry through a most difficult and thorny reformation, demanded more than usual discrimination. And the appointment of Tarasius, who governed the church for twenty-two years (784-806), showed ability and shrewdness in the empress's counsellors, if not in herself. Tarasius had not been bred a churchman. He was one of that line of patriarchs, which included his successor Nicephorus and his grand-nephew Photius, whose early training was in civil administration and diplomacy. These appointments were fiercely resented by the monastic wing of the church, which regarded them merely as worldly and time-serving prelates who looked on the things of Caesar as of at least equal importance with those of God. But in the eyes of a sovereign this was their greatest virtue.

Tarasius was in 784 head of the imperial chancellery (or 'secretary of state'). He was a man of high birth and exceptional diplomatic ability. Diplomacy was now needed: and Tarasius was the man for the post. Had Irene been foolish enough to appoint a fanatical monk to the patriarchate, the cause of compromise would have been foredoomed, and the result chaos, if not civil war.

Tarasius began by inviting Pope Hadrian to send delegates to an ecumenical council at Constantinople, which should undo the work of the heretical council of 754. The pope received this invitation in August 785 and replied to it in October. The council was convened in August 786, and its sittings were to be held in the Church of the (once more 'Holy') Apostles. The number of the delegates was about 350, including several who represented, or said that they represented, the patriarchal sees of Antioch, Alexandria and Jerusalem. But the most elaborate precautions were vain. Stimulated – as was said – by iconoclast delegates, the city garrison burst into the first session, and with drawn swords dispersed the pious conclave. The papal delegates at once took leave and departed by ship for Sicily. It was clear that the local forces of iconoclasm had been underestimated.

The imperial government acted with cunning. The mutinous garrison of Constantinople, on pretence of an expedition against the Saracens, was carried across into Asia as far as the base camp at Malagina. They were then ordered to lay down their arms: and, deprived of their officers, they did so. Their place in the capital was supplied by troops from Bithynia, who could be trusted. And negotiations were resumed for gathering together once more the assemblage which had been so rudely scattered. At length in September 787 it met at Nicaea, under conditions of strict security; and the historic Seventh Ecumenical Council could begin. The acts are preserved, and include some invaluable material from the lost acts of the Council of 754. The fourth, fifth, sixth and seventh sessions were devoted specifically to settling the question of the pictures: and at the sixth a bulky tome, compiled by Tarasius himself, was read on the subject. At the seventh session the *Horos*, or Definition, was read and approved: it concluded thus:

Wherefore we define with all strictness and care that the venerable and holy icons be set up, just as is the image of the venerable and life-giving Cross, in as much as matter consisting of paints and pebbles and other materials is suitable to the holy Church of God, on sacred vessels and vestments, on walls and panels, in houses and streets: both the images of our Lord and God and Saviour Jesus Christ, and of our undefiled Lady the Holy Mother of God, and of the honourable angels, and of all the Saints. *For the more continuously these are seen by means of pictorial representation, the more their beholders are led to remember and to love the originals,* and to give them respect and honorable obeisance: not that we should worship them with the true worship which is appropriate only to the Divine; yet still with offering of candles and of incense, in the same way as we do to the form of the live-giving and venerable Cross and to the holy Gospel-Book, and to other sacred objects, even as was the pious custom in ancient days also.[1]

Now at last the feud which had raged during sixty years in the bosom of the church, with its accompaniments of deprivation, cruelty, exile and alienation, might be felt to be healed. But the appearance, as always, was delusory. At the very opening of the Seventh Council a new rift appeared, which in its consequence was hardly less deadly and enduring than the former. As we have hinted, this was the rift between the moderate and the die-hard wings in the orthodox camp itself. It is probably an error to regard this rift as a mere continuation of the iconoclast-iconodule controversy, under a new name. But at least the new quarrel derived certain features from the old. The die-hard or monastic wing of the church had its kernel in the steady resistance of the monks to imperial or secular dictation of any kind, whether in spiritual or political matters. These men were the direct successors of those who had suffered for righteousness' sake under two generations of heretical sovereigns, and they were therefore absolutely opposed to any undue exercise of imperial power, even if those who exercised it were indisputably orthodox. They were themselves the repositories of divine truth, taught to them in long years of meditation and austerity. Upon this truth they were stiff and intransigent. Any compromise on what they believed to be right was anathema. 'What hath Christ to do with Belial?', was a question commonly in their mouths. Among this body the monks of the monastery of Studius held during many years an unquestioned pre-eminence.

It is plain that, in a state whose chief postulate was unity under the emperor as elect of Christ, this line of thought was at best disquieting, and at worst disruptive and treasonable. Secular and ecclesiastical government at Byzantium were constitutionally two departments of state; and, in this very imperfect world, government cannot be carried on at all without a certain amount of give and take, or, as the Byzantines called it, *economy*, or dispensation. That an important church party should arrogate to itself the right to scrutinise, reject and disobey any imperial order which did not conform to a private and arbitrary standard altogether independent of the secular authority, was the negation of unity and an open incitement to faction. And when this church party espoused the cause of Rome – as it often did – against its own emperor and patriarch, its policy might not unfairly be construed as rebellion. In the course of the next two centuries, the emperors for obvious reasons tried to avoid appointing a patriarch from this party. They much preferred a secular politician as patriarch, who would collaborate with them. The one or two exceptions to this rule were disastrous. Ignatius by his stiffnecked obstinacy opened or reopened the breach, and had to be deposed. And Polyeuctus was only saved from deposition by the death of his exasperated master.

The party of what we may call 'broad' churchmen, on the other hand, who from this point onwards gave the church her ablest statesmen, was closely connected with, and often sprang directly from, the educated lay bureaucracy. The Patriarchs Tarasius, Nicephorus, Photius, Stephen, Nicholas I and Theophylact, had all had either a lay career in civil administration, or else were brought up in the palace. They thus knew the principles and needs of imperial government. It would be grossly unfair to say that such men were the lineal descendants of the time-serving and often simoniac churchmen whom Leo III and his son had recruited to carry out their iconoclastic policies. Their orthodoxy was above reproach, and they would all have resisted, as some actually did resist, any attempt on the part of the sovereign to compromise that orthodoxy. But in this at least they did represent and carry on the traditions of their iconoclast predecessors: they thoroughly understood the necessity of cooperating, in all possible ways, with the imperial government. They saw that if the church was to offer systematic opposition to the emperor on points which did not affect the spiritual salvation of his people, all government must come to a standstill. Hence they were not severe, for example, on cases of sexual irregularity in the imperial house, especially where this irregularity was indulged for the higher purposes of confirming the dynasty, and hence giving stability to the realm. The quarrels which rent the church during the ninth and tenth centuries over the second marriage of Constantine VI, the adultery of Caesar Bardas and the fourth marriage of Leo VI, all sprang from a conflict between the more liberal and 'dispensing' attitude of the one party, and the strict austerity and 'accuracy' of the other.

This new division in the church, which followed the first restoration of images in 787, is a most important feature in the Middle Byzantine Empire, and we shall have occasion to refer to it over and over again in the future. For the present, it is enough to note that even at the Seventh Council itself, where the desperate need for unity against the common enemy, iconoclasm, might seem to override all secondary considerations, there were yet ominous signs of conflict to come. The first shots were fired over the question of those iconoclast bishops who were ready to recant and to rejoin the fold. The president, the statesmanlike Tarasius, was clear that they should be allowed to do so: but the Studite monk Savas was equally clear that they should not. With the threat of an iconoclast reaction looming close, the council compromised on this point, and Tarasius got his way. But opposition again burst out over those iconoclast prelates to whom the charge of buying or selling church preferments (simony) had been brought home. And here at last Tarasius, who had stood firm for pardon after a period of repentance, was compelled to give ground.5 Within eight years a more lasting ground of ecclesiastical dissension was to appear, in the second marriage of the young Constantine VI; and here we must go back a little to the history of that emperor's relations with his despotic mother, in order to see how this dispute arose.

Constantine VI at the age of twelve – that is, in 782 – had been betrothed to Rotrud, daughter of Charles the Great, king of the Franks. The relations between east and west at this period will form the subject of future discussion. It is sufficient here to note that both Irene and Charles favoured the match, and that a tutor was despatched from Constantinople to Aachen in order to instruct the princess in the rudiments of the Greek language. The match was renounced by Charles in 786, possibly owing to his resentment at not having been consulted over the Seventh Ecumenical Council, and owing to his knowledge that the images were to be restored at that Council: whereas he himself, as he later showed unequivocally at the Council of Frankfort in 794, inclined far more to the iconoclast than to the orthodox position.

In 788 the empress forced her son, now eighteen years of age, into a distasteful marriage with Mary of Amnia, who came of a wealthy provincial family of Paphlagonia. This imperial marriage is the earliest of those between 788 and 900 at which the bride was supposedly chosen by the bridegroom at a concourse of the most beautiful girls in the world. Needless to say, the election was nearly always rigged, the result being arranged beforehand. But the custom itself, never repeated after 900, is interesting. There is a probability that it was introduced into the Byzantine court, along with other customs, from the court of Chazaria.

The total exclusion of Constantine VI from all affairs of government lasted until his twenty-first year, in 790. Then, signs of dissatisfaction began to show themselves. The empress now demanded that her own name should appear before that of her son. This was too much. A plot was laid in Constantine's interest to banish the empress to Sicily. It was disclosed and suppressed. Constantine himself was confined; and an oath of allegiance to the empress mother personally was exacted from the military. This caused an explosion. The Armeniac troops rose in revolt. They forced the government to liberate the lawful emperor, who forthwith deposed his mother and exiled her eunuchs from the Palace.

The game was now in Constantine's hands, had he had the skill to play it. But he was no Constantine v. He was at once called on to show his mettle in the field, but his campaigns in April and October of 791 against the Bulgars and Saracens made it clear that he had no talent for command, and doubtful if he possessed the common courage of a soldier. He was the prey of unscrupulous counsellors and charlatans – of anyone, in short, who could get his ear. In January 792 he was so deplorably misguided as to restore to his mother her share in the imperial government. This piece of folly appears too gross even for Constantine, and it seems likely that weightier reasons were behind it than were allowed at that time to appear. The welcome given to Constantine by the troops shows pretty clearly that these troops were still in the main iconoclasts, and that they hoped the young emperor would revert to the policies of his grandfather and revoke the ordinances of the Seventh Council of 787. It was probably represented to Constantine, with some show of reason, that if he adopted this policy, a civil war would be inevitable. And that only a recall of the empress who had put back the images could put his own orthodoxy beyond doubt. It is certain that he long toyed with the idea of throwing himself into the iconoclast scale. But in this case, wiser counsels, or what appeared to be such, prevailed.

Constantine's marriage with Mary of Amnia, forced on him in 788, had been neither happy nor fruitful. One single daughter had been born of the union, who survived to be the empress of Michael II thirty years later. There was no son. In January 795, church and laity alike were shocked to learn that the emperor had divorced his wife and that she had withdrawn into a nunnery. In August of the same year, at the palace of St Mamas outside the city, Constantine went through a form of marriage with a lady in waiting called Theodote, who, on 7 October 796, presented him with a male child. Hence arose the celebrated *moechian*, or 'adulterous', scandal which bedevilled the church during the next twenty years. It was, in fact, never forgotten, and had a deep influence on the yet more celebrated scandal of Leo VI's fourth marriage a century later.

There is no reason to believe that either Constantine VI or, later, Leo VI, married again for any but dynastic reasons. The principle of hereditary rule vested in the eldest son of the reigning sovereign was as strong in the 'Isaurian' as it was to be in the Macedonian house. And the reason is obvious. It was a matter of practical policy. It can be taken as certain that Constantine prepared the ground as carefully with the Patriarch Tarasius as did Leo VI with his Patriarch Nicholas Mysticus. Tarasius, true to his principles of cooperation and conciliation, was prepared to go as far as he reasonably could in condoning the affair. It is highly significant that his compliance was assisted by the open threat of the Emperor Constantine to return to the iconoclast heresy if it were withheld. To perform the marriage himself Tarasius could not consent. But the marriage was celebrated by one Joseph, abbot of the monastery of Cathara. And after it had been performed

Tarasius admitted both the adulterous pair, and also the celebrant, to the communion. In other words, he exercised *economy*, or dispensation, by regarding the matter as exceptional, in view of the compelling circumstances of the case. But the opposition from the die-hard churchmen, who had never forgiven the moderate policy of Tarasius at the Seventh Council, was immediate and fierce. At its head were Plato, abbot of Saccoudion in Bithynia, and his nephew Theodore, recently appointed abbot of the Studius. They loudly proclaimed that the second marriage of Constantine VI fell under the ban of Holy Gospel (Mark 10, 11) against adultery. They altogether denied that the emperor, *qua* emperor, constituted any special case whatever – far less that he stood above the law – and that therefore dispensation was sinful. A charge of heresy was prepared against Tarasius; and the monks withdrew themselves from communion with him.

In view of the fact that these zealots represented an influential part of the church, and in view also of the fact that the new Empress Theodote was own cousin to Theodore Studita himself, the government were bound to take a serious view of the matter. The emperor himself seems to have been disposed to argue the matter out with his cousins-in-law, who, however, declined to meet him. Sterner measures were then employed from which a wiser sovereign might have recoiled. The commander-in-chief was sent to arrest the obstinate monks. They were brought to Constantinople. Plato was shut up in a palace chapel. Theodore and the rest were banished to Thessalonica.[6]

And what part did the most pious Empress Irene, who owed her return to power and influence entirely to her son's generosity or feebleness, play in all this ? It is to the subtle, intriguing character of this woman, to her selfish ambition, implacable resentment and unnatural cruelty, that much of the unenviable reputation acquired by Byzantine methods of government in later ages can be set down. There is evidence that she had deliberately encouraged her son to persist in his unlawful second marriage, knowing full well the odium this would excite in the breasts of her own favourites, the monks. Her intrigues against him came to a head in the following year, 796. By representing her son in the worst possible light, as well as by lavish bribery, she formed a civil and military party against him which, if he had been a man of foresight and resolution, would scarcely have been formidable, but which was sufficient to sow treason against him in all his under-takings. In the spring of 797 he seemed to be about to make himself unassailable through military successes. He won a victory against the Bulgars. Then with twenty thousand picked troops from the Armeniac and Anatolic *themes*, devoted to his person and his house, he moved against the Saracens. The cunning empress was too much for him. Her agents persuaded him that the Saracens had dispersed before him, and he returned without fighting. Shortly before, he had received news of the death of his infant son. In June, all was in train for the final move against him. He gave his enemies the slip and set out for the east: but once again treachery was his undoing. He was seized and shut up in the Palace of Porphyry; and on Tuesday, 15 August 797, at 3 o'clock in the afternoon, by orders of his own mother, his eyes were put out. He died shortly afterwards. 'And [says Theophanes] the sun was dark-ened during seventeen days, and gave not his light, so that ships ran off course and drifted, and all men said and confessed that because the emperor was blinded, the sun had put away his rays. And in this way power came into the hands of Irene, his mother.'7

It is not necessary to make any moral reflexions upon this, one of the most atrocious murders in recorded history. Yet at first sight it seems no less politically inexplicable than ethically indefensible. To put the matter on no higher ground, Irene must have known that her action would cause widespread horror and consternation at home and abroad: and so it did. Alcuin, the English adviser of Charlemagne, is witness to the shudder felt at it as far off as France. Why then was it necessary? The blinding in itself was to make the emperor incapable of further office; but Theophanes tells us it was deliberately done in such a way as to kill him. Why? To my mind there can be but one explanation, and that is the one to which we must hold as a guide or clue throughout all these difficult times: the religious explanation. There either was, or seemed to be, a serious danger that Constantine VI would annul the acts of the Seventh Council and revert to those of 754. He had, in a wordly point of view, everything to gain by doing so, and nothing to lose. The monks, who cursed him as an impious adulterer, could not have said worse of him if he had been an avowed iconoclast: he had nothing to hope from their aid and little to fear from their alienation. His grandfather Constantine V had married three times, and if his iconoclast bishops raised any protest, we do not hear of it. Moreover, as we have seen, the strength of the eastern army lay still in its iconoclast troops, with whom, because of his name, he was immensely popular. If he had escaped and put himself at their head, what could the monks of Saccoudion have done to stop him ? In his own capital those who hated him worst were most convincedly orthodox. Lastly, there is some evidence in western documents to show that at the very time of his blinding, in 797, he was in direct diplomatic contact with Charles the Great, who received his envoy Theoctistus with great favour and respect. What was this embassy about ? Charles' own virtually iconoclastic standpoint, and his vigorous condemnation of the Seventh Council in 794, were by this time notorious in east and west. Is it not possible that Constantine was treating for alliance between east and west on the basis of a religious *concordat*, which would imply on the part of Byzantium a turn-over to something like the anti-icon position of 754 ? With all this in mind, does it not seem likely that Irene had very good reason to regard her son, not merely as a troublesome obstacle to her own supremacy, but also as a dangerous heretic, likely, unless instantly and decisively checked, to undo her life's work and plunge his empire once more into darkness and sin ? This line of thought would enable us to regard that empress, not indeed as other than cruel and unnatural, but as something short of an odious and capricious monster.

Constantine's murder brought about consequences at that time unforeseen, but of much importance thereafter. To start with, by his death or incapacity, and by his want of a male heir, the throne of the world was now, in the eyes of the Franks and of the papacy, vacant. This circumstance had a direct bearing on the form, if not on the fact, of the imperial coronation of Charles the Great in Rome on Christmas Day 800, three years later. The probability is that Pope Leo III supposed that he was crowning, not just an emperor of the Franks or of the West, but the Roman Emperor, the successor of Augustus, which, had Constantine VI been still reigning, or even alive, could not have been so. In western eyes a woman was incapable of rule. The deficiency was corrected by the expulsion of Irene and the coronation of Nicephorus I in 802. After this, and only after this, is it correct to speak of an Eastern and a Western empire.[8]

In the next place, it was more than a question whether the east itself recognised such a phenomenon as a sole empress. At least it had never done so before, and scarcely ever did so there-after.[9] The original fusion of imperial with military power might be held, and was by the army held, to exclude a female from the throne. The flatterers and favourites of Irene said that she had the mind of a man, and perhaps she had; but it was undeniable that her body was female. She was compelled to sign her documents by the anomalous title Irene *Emperor* of the Romans: and it is certain that the die-hards of the church would not have countenanced this had she not been their defender and protectress.

The five years of Irene's autocracy (797–802) were years of disaster without and misguided favouritism within. The murder of their emperor had demoralised the armies of the east, and the Saracens seized the moment for an extensive and destructive raid (798). Their forces overran the rich provinces of Cappadocia, Galatia and Lydia, and reached Ephesus on the Aegean coast. The Armeniac and Anatolic levies seem to have been stunned; but the Count of the Opsikian *theme* opposed the invaders with all his troops, and was resoundingly defeated. The empress was glad to buy a shameful truce from Harun which was to last four years.

At home her government was a continual dog-fight between the two chief eunuchs, Stauracius and Aetius, the latter of whom emerged victorious; yet his only success seems to have been in stultifying the negotiations in progress between Irene and Charles the Great. To allay the general discontent, Irene initiated a quite irresponsible programme of tax relief. She remitted the city-tax levied on the inhabitants of Constantinople. She halved the customs dues receivable on imports at Abydus and in the Narrows. And she abolished the tax on receipts, an impost hateful more for the capricious and extortionate nature of its collection than for the severity of its incidence. For these reliefs, which were in the highest degree impolitic if not downright ruinous, she is of course extolled to the skies by her monkish adulators.[10]

But such mismanagement could not last. The armies were disaffected. The high officials were scandalised by the regiment of a woman, and even more alarmed at the possibility of a pact of union with western barbarians. The treasury saw nothing but ruin ahead, with taxes no longer collected, or only half levied. It is altogether significant that the usurper who overthrew the empress, in October 802, was her Minister of Finance. Irene succumbed with a good grace, and in a short speech attributed her downfall to her own sins.[11] Many will probably agree with her. She was exiled to Lesbos and died in 803.

NOTES

[1] Nicephorus, 71.
[2] Bury, LRE, 485–6.
[3] Theophanes, 456–7, 486.
[4] Theophanes, 458–63; Ostrogorsky, 149; Bury, LRE, 494–8.
[5] Bréhier, 90; Ostrogorsky, 149; Vasiliev, 264.
[6] Theophanes, 464–71; Bury, LRE, 483 ff.
[7] Theophanes, 472.
[8] Ostrogorsky, 155; Bury, LRE, 506-7.
[9] Psellus, 2, 72–3.
[10] Theophanes, 474–5.
[11] Theophanes, 478.

CHAPTER EIGHT

'HAEC DUO IMPERIA'

In her relations with the west and with the papacy during the last quarter of the eighth century, Byzantium was naturally faced by an overwhelming fact – the Frankish empire (though not yet so called) of Charles the Great. The rise of the Salian Franks, their conquest of Gaul and their foundation of the modern French nation were the work of Clovis and his sons in the first half of the sixth century. The second great period of Frankish expansion, which far surpassed the first, began with the accession of the Great Charles, in the year 771, to the kingdom over all the Franks.

The origin of the Frankish intervention in Italy lay, as we saw, in the pope's need for protection against the Lombards, and in his desire for a temporal sovereignty, if not over all Italy, at least over the territories of the fallen *exarchate* of Ravenna. It was these desires which promoted the journey of Pope Stephen II across the Alps in 753, and his coronation of Pippin the Short as king of the Franks in July 754. Twenty years were to elapse before the Frankish intervention became decisive, though Pippin twice answered the call of the pope to beat back the aggressive Lombards. But, in 773, Charles broke into the peninsula, seized the Lombard capital at Pavia, made himself king of the Lombards, and established the pope as a temporal ruler over most of the lands then claimed by him. It might now appear that Charles was well on the road to a planned restoration of the western empire of Rome, and that the event of Christmas Day 800 was merely the last, logical step in a process of long development. But this is not so. The key to his whole policy was and remained the aggrandizement and corroboration of the Kingdom *of the Franks*; and his resolve was to be independent of dictation from either emperor or pope. To be king of the Franks, as Alcuin assured him in a celebrated letter of 799, was superior to being either; and all his life, his seals bore the simple inscription, 'Christe protege Carolum *regem* Francorum et Langobardorum'.

Thus, from the purely political point of view there was no reason why a *modus vivendi* should not have been arranged between Byzantium and the new western empire – or dominion – of Charles; and such an arrangement was sincerely desired by at least one of the parties, Charles himself. The territorial interests of the two states scarcely conflicted. At the beginning of the ninth century there were some inconsiderable clashes in Dalmatia, Venetia and Southern Italy; yet, when a political compromise was effected in 812, it was Charles who, for all his preponderating power and the temporary weakness of his eastern rivals Nicephorus I and Michael I, drew back, in return for the ostensible recognition of his *imperium* over the Franks and of its parity with East Rome. The real issue was thus not so much political as ideological; it was the question of the theoretical status of the temporal and spiritual sovereigns, and of the authority by which they purported to govern: whether, in short, they were doing the work of their Divine Master in preserving the unity of the Roman State and thus ensuring that His will should be done on Earth as it is in Heaven. This unitary doctrine was at first accepted by all parties: but it was susceptible of various interpretations which amounted to three in number. There was the traditional interpretation of the successors of Constantine the Great, who sat on the throne of the world at Constantinople; there was the interpretation of Charlemagne himself, both before 800 and after 802; and lastly there was the interpretation of the papacy, which, sundered from the East by the heresy and aggression of the iconoclast emperors of the eighth century, and once more by the heresy and weakness of Byzantium in the early part of the ninth, took refuge in the extraordinary claims of the *Constitutum Constantini*, the Donation of Constantine, that celebrated forgery which can now be attributed – at least in its final and definitive form – to the fertile genius of Pope Leo III and to the year AD 804. Any attempt therefore to understand the literally epoch-making clash of convictions during the ninth century must be preceded by a summary of each of these three distinct positions.

The Byzantine imperial theory was based on the union of the historical fact of the Roman world-state with the Christian belief in the redemption of the world through Jesus Christ. This union of Roman power and Christian belief had been consummated, once for all, by Constantine the Great, the successor of Augustus and the elect of Christ, the thirteenth apostle who combined in his own person supreme earthly power with unique celestial sanction. From that point onwards the Roman emperors were the successive appointments and earthly embodiments of Christ, with the overriding duties of preserving Roman unity and Christian orthodoxy throughout the world. This grandiose conception naturally carried with it several corollary axioms of great import: first, that there can be but *one* single emperor on earth, as there is but one divine Ruler in heaven; second, that there can be no legitimate earthly power independent of the emperor, either temporal or spiritual; third, that the emperor's sanction was literally divine, and hence that any challenge to his sole and imprescriptible authority was not merely rebellion but also blasphemy; and fourth, that his people, the people of the Byzantine state, was the 'peculiar people', the Chosen Race of the New Covenant, entrusted by God with the election of His own mortal vice-regent, and with the spreading of his authority: to the end that civilisation (that is to say, Roman law and Hellenistic culture), and peace and subordination should be imposed on the gentiles, and should, ere Christ Himself should come again, be extended to the uttermost parts of the earth. It cannot be too strongly insisted upon that these vast claims were no mere abstract and theoretical concepts, but the living faith and conviction of every Byzantine from emperor to peasant during at least eight centuries; and that they were the fixed and activating principle, not only of imperial pretensions, but also, where possible, of practical, day-to-day imperial policies.[1]

This *Weltanschauung*, which made Christianity interdependent and coterminous with imperial sovereignty, was, until the ninth century, the undisputed conviction of the western no less than of the eastern Mediterranean. If we were to study the course of west European history between the fifth and ninth centuries without reference to the east, we might reach the superficial conclusion that after the establishment of the Gothic and Frankish powers, and even more after the final collapse of Justinian's ephemeral empire in Italy, the west pursued what was to all intents a separate course of its own; that the Byzantine emperors, engrossed by their own desperate struggles for survival against the Slav and the Avar, the Bulgarian and the Saracen, and sundered from Italy by increasing difficulties of land and sea communication, lost interest in developments in the west; and that only the papacy preserved a tenuous filament of spiritual and political contact with the east. No conclusion could be more erroneous. Such a hold over the minds of men had the tradition of a single, universal Roman sovereignty, promoting and protecting a single, universal orthodox church, that for many centuries, marked as they were by the most radical political changes, any deviation from it was unthinkable. The rise of the Frankish kings was due in no small measure to the fact that they had, from the first, kept a prudent eye on Constantinople, and, in theory, at least, acted as the emperor's nominees and vice-gerents. The emperors, for their part, true to the traditions of an age-old imperial diplomacy, were not slow in lending the weight of their influence to an orthodox power against its rebellious and heretical rivals. Our knowledge is hampered by the paucity of documentary evidence; but we know enough to be certain that, between the fifth and seventh centuries at least, communication between Byzantium and the Franks was frequent and cordial. The Emperor Anastasius I (491–518) was in direct touch with Clovis, who won his victories against the Goths in the guise of the emperor's representative and, after his conversion, with the full support of his orthodox clergy; it is well known that in 508 he accepted the title of consul and the rank of *patricius Romanorum* conferred on him by imperial codicil. It was by an act of imperial cession that the Franks made good their possession of Provence. It was in virtue of his alliance with Justinian I that Theodebert invaded Italy; and it was in conscious imitation of the imperial ritual and procedure of Constantinople that the same prince, now a rebel, presided in state over the games at Arles, and committed the treason and blasphemy of striking gold coins with his own image and superscription. It is beyond question that in 584 the Emperor Maurice, harassed as he was by Persian assault and Avaro-Slavonic inundation, yet found time to intrigue with the picturesque adventurer Gondowald for the recovery of Francia; and between 584 and 590 he repeatedly admonished his spiritual son Childebert to intervene in Italy on behalf of the empire against the Lombard invaders. It is true that for the century and a half which elapsed between the last known contact of Heraclius with King Dagobert and the conferment of the Roman patriciate on Pippin the Short, evidence of east-west contact is lacking; but this does not prove that such contact ceased, nor is there any reason to believe that it did.[2]

The period in question, from the death of Heraclius to the end of the eighth century, is, as we have seen, a period of enormous disruption, both political and religious, which would certainly lead us to expect that the political schism between east and west was now an established fact. It is with astonishment that we learn that when in 753 Pope Stephen escaped to France and invested his protector Pippin with the title of *patricius Romanorum*, he did so with the authority of the iconoclast Emperor Constantine v, and, having done so, called down the blessings of St Benedict upon 'the apostolic see, the empire of the Romans [i.e. Constantinople], and the glorious patrician'. In fact, Pippin stood to Constantine v precisely in the relationship in which, two and a half centuries before, Clovis had stood to Anastasius. So deep and lasting was the impression made by the theocratic world-order of Constantine the Great, overriding all considerations of practical politics and even of religious orthodoxy.

In truth this respect of the primordial claims of the single Roman world-empire persisted during another half century, and at the end of that time, by an odd twist of fortune, they came within an ace of being realised in fact: not by Constantinople, but by Charles the Great. The familiar story of the papal initiative in crowning Charles emperor on Christmas Day 800, and the familiar problem of the precise degree of participation or acquiescence on the part of Charles himself, need not here be rehearsed. The significant features of the incident for our purposes are, first that, after the coronation and unction, Charles was saluted as emperor *of the Romans*; and second, that the pope prostrated himself, for the last time in history, before a temporal sovereign. This meant that the papal design was to crown a single emperor of the world in the old Roman tradition, and to reclaim for the old capital the function of election by senate, army and populace of Rome, exercised during nearly five centuries by Byzantium. Only a highly unusual circumstance could render this possible. The Empress Irene occupied the Byzantine throne as emperor or *basileus*, and thus the throne was, in the eyes of both the pope and of Charles, vacant. Charles himself, who possessed a powerful and original intelligence and was able to emancipate himself almost wholly from the dead weight of the Roman tradition, had in principle no desire to govern his empire as the elect of the pope, or to interfere with the rights and prerogatives of the eastern sovereigns: indeed, he said as much. But on the matter of female incompetence to rule, he had very decided opinions, and for a few brief months he acquiesced in the pope's designs, for the sake of a prize of such tremendous importance that it would barely have been possible to turn his back on it. The prize was no less than the actual, practical restoration in his own person of the empire of Augustus. The aged emperor of the west made an offer of marriage to the aged empress of the east; and there is reason to believe that she was as much entranced by the proposal as he. If this alliance had been concluded, and it very nearly was concluded, the consequences for the future of Europe could not have been other than momentous. Irene's only son was dead, or at any rate incapacitated to rule after her; her marriage would have involved the automatic union of the vast empire of Charles with that of the east, and Charles and after him Lewis the Pious would have occupied the seat of Constantine the Great. At all events, it was not to be. In 802, even while Charles' envoys were present in the capital, Irene was surprised and deposed; and Nicephorus I seized the throne of the east. From that moment some would date the death of the ancient world: from, that is to say, the *de facto* repudiation of a dogma eight centuries old, and the birth of a state of affairs in which two empires maintained an uneasy co-existence.3

For now Charles, after his brief vision of universal domination as the elect of Christ, at once reverted to his original concept of a western empire *of the Franks*, on a basis of parity of esteem and privilege with the eastern. He withdrew himself from the papal influence and authority, and fashioned his state closely on the Byzantine model. He had already arrogated to himself the right to promulgate religious doctrine. He now ceased to claim the empire *of the Romans*, which he agreed was the heritage of Constantinople. But he demanded spiritual 'brotherhood' with the Byzantine emperor, instead of the spiritual sonship hitherto accorded to him as king. In true Byzantine style, he exalted the authority of the imperial family, resisting the papal claim to unfettered rights of election: he created his sons kings, and in 806 parcelled out his dominions among them without reference to the pope; and in 813, again without reference to the pope but again according to Byzantine practice, he crowned his eldest son Lewis co-emperor of the Franks.

Before considering how these apparently reasonable but in fact inadmissible and even blasphemous proceedings were received by the Constantinopolitan emperors, we have to summarise the view of the third great party to this dispute, those of the papacy itself. The papacy, unlike the upstart empire of the Franks, was coeval with the settlement of Constantine the Great, and was supported or cumbered by the same age-old tradition. During the three centuries between the breakdown of Roman rule in Italy and the elevation of the Emperor Nicephorus I in the east, successive pontiffs had continued to be, and to feel themselves to be, integral factors in the one undivided empire of Christ on earth, whose lieutenant was the Byzantine sovereign. On the postulate of temporal unity depended the preservation of the spiritual unity of the Spouse of Christ. Yet this position, loyally as it had been maintained by the papacy, had been subject to fearful shocks, both temporal and spiritual. The manifest inability of Byzantium, since the sixth century, to defend the papacy against barbarian aggression had at length been compensated by the recognition successively of Pippin and Charles the Great as protectors of Rome. The spiritual shock resulting from the first period of eastern iconoclasm (730–87), and the transfer of the sees of Sicily, Calabria and Illyricum to the see of Byzantium, were sterner tests. The restoration of orthodoxy by the Empress Irene in 787 could not, except superficially, mend the position: since the Byzantine power was still too weak to act as a decisive counterweight to the Frank, even in South Italy; and the attitude of Charles in the iconoclast controversy was nearer to that of Leo III and Constantine V than to that of Irene.

In these unhappy circumstances, when the brilliant plan of Pope Leo III to unite east and west beneath the rule of his elect finally failed in 802, the same pope – there seems to be little doubt – devised or perfected a pronouncement which should, on apparently unassailable authority, put beyond question, not only the primacy of the see of St Peter, but also the supra-imperial power of the pope (as heir to the privilege of binding and loosing accorded by the Saviour to St Peter himself) to elect and invest the emperor *of the Romans*, the temporal ruler of this world. The Emperor Constantine the Great – such was the tenor of the 'Donation of Constantine' – , recognising that the heir of St Peter was true emperor, thought it unsuitable that the temporal sovereign should rule in the domain of his spiritual superior. He accordingly retired to wear his temporal crown in the 'province' (the word is full of meaning) of Byzantium, leaving to Pope Silvester his own imperial crown, which Silvester was not to wear (though he and his followers were to be, in fact, also temporal sovereigns to the west), but keep in his gift for whomsoever he should elect to be secular or administrative emperor of the Romans. This 'stupendous falsehood', which, surprisingly enough, seems to have been accepted as genuine in the east as well as the west until exposed by Laurentius Valla in 1440, by implication killed half a dozen birds with one stone. First, it accorded to the pope an authority above all emperors. Second, it left the imperial crown in his gift. Third, it vindicated by implication the superiority of any western emperor so crowned over the eastern emperor, who, though in virtue of succession from Constantine the Great he could not be absolutely denied an imperial status, was degraded to the position of a provincial or Greek emperor. Fourth, it claimed for the western emperor the empire *of the Romans*. Fifth, it set the pope in the position not only of spiritual but also of temporal overlordship above the said emperor of the Romans. And sixth, it bound the western emperor to the territorial area of Rome itself, and in so doing restored the Eternal City from a local western bishopric to the centre and head-spring of the universe.

At the beginning of the ninth century, therefore, we find these three great powers, each with a different view of the origins and extent of their authority: Byzantium, jealously guarding her exclusive tradition of continuity from Augustus and the thirteenth apostle Constantine the Great; Charles the Frank, renovator of the *Frankish* kingdom, claiming for his empire on the one hand parity of imperial status with the east, and on the other its independence of papal authority; and lastly the pope, claiming for himself a power above that of all temporal sovereigns, and the superiority above all others of that sovereign who had been invested and anointed by himself. Of these mutually irreconcilable claims the third (resting on a blatant forgery) was manifestly the weakest: and it is salutary for the moralist to reflect upon the causes why, of these three great institutions, the third alone should have survived in a recognisable form to the present day.

The claims of Charles the Great to imperial status, to brotherhood and to parity of esteem with Byzantium, were very naturally received by the latter with incredulous horror, and were summarily rejected by the ambassadors of the Emperor Nicephorus I in 803. As well might one postulate two Christs in heaven as two emperors on earth. But unhappily this rejection automatically provoked a war with Charles, which Byzantium had almost no resources to meet. As so often before and after, she was already heavily engaged on two fronts, in the east against the Caliph Harun al-Rashid and in the north against the Bulgarians. Charles seriously menaced her position on the north-east of the Adriatic, and in 809 his son Pippin, king of Italy, tore Venice from her empire and laid it under tribute to the Franks. This could not be allowed to go on. Peace must somehow or other be made; and, after long negotiations, made at last it was in 812. The utmost skill and finesse of the Byzantine Foreign Ministry were employed in devising a formula which, while seeming to concede everything, in fact conceded very little, and that little only temporarily. Charles was perforce allowed the status of emperor, and was so saluted at Aachen by the Byzantine envoys; and he was further granted a fraternal instead of a filial relationship with the Roman emperor, the only concession which survived into the tenth century. But everything was done to soften the blow, and to leave the door open for shuffling out of this hateful and unparalleled usurpation. Charles was to be emperor, but only of the Franks; the true emperor *of the Romans*, that is, of the Roman world, remained at Byzantium, and from the year 813 the adjunct *ton Rhomaion* (of the Romans) was officially appended to the Byzantine imperial style. Moreover, Charles was emperor only in virtue of his personal rule over all the nations of the west: as the Emperor Constantine Porphyrogenitus wrote in his *De administrando imperio* one hundred and fifty years later: 'This Charles, the Elder, was sole ruler over all the western kingdoms, and reigned as an emperor in Great Francia':4 that is to say, his imperial status was recognised only so long as the territorial integrity of his empire was preserved: and, as the Byzantines maintained, it was vested solely in his person. After the partition of Verdun in 844, and still more after the re-partition of 855, the imperial status, in the Byzantine view, automatically lapsed, though it was not formally abrogated by Byzantium until 871. Even Lewis the Pious (Charles' eldest son) was addressed by the Emperor Michael II as 'King of the Franks', 'whom' – he grudgingly added – 'they call their *imperator*'. But despite all these safeguards, hesitancies and mental reservations, every Byzantine realised that the concession wrung from them marked a turning point of enormous significance: it might be treated with ridicule, or it might be treated with grief, but ignored it could not be. The contemporary Byzantine historian Theophanes describes the coronation of Charles in a tone which is manifestly ironical: 'In this year the pope crowned Charles the king of the Franks, as emperor of the Romans, in the temple of the Holy Apostle Peter, smearing him with oil from head to foot, and putting imperial robes and a crown on him, month of December 25, Indiction 9'[5]. But others saw that this act, and its consequences twelve years later, could not be so laughed away: and even in the twelfth century tears filled the eyes of the Byzantine historian Cinnamus whenever he thought of that hideous profanation.[6]

In one particular, however, the rise of the Frankish empire and its claim to parity seem to have obtained a lasting concession from Byzantium, which in the lapse of time became almost respectable. The same imperial author from whom I have quoted says in another part of his work; 'No emperor of the Romans shall ally himself in marriage with a nation of customs differing from and alien to those of the Roman order, especially if it be with one that is infidel or unbaptised, unless it be with the Franks alone; and why is it ordained that with Franks alone of foreigners the Romans may intermarry? Because of the traditional fame of those lands and the nobility of those tribes'.[7] Now, it is perfectly true that projects for such marriage alliances between the imperial families of the east and the Carolingian and Ottonian houses were quite frequently approved, though they were hardly ever consummated; and it is equally true that they were approved with far less trouble than were marriages with other, orthodox, Christian states, such as Bulgaria or Russia. These unions were, of course, always devised with a contemporary political object in view, sometimes with the very obvious, if chimerical, hope of re-uniting east and west beneath a single imperial house. But these political objects were not good enough excuses for a step which appeared in the eyes of every Byzantine as a derogation of the holy imperial dignity: and this expressed exception in favour of the Franks, who, be it noted, were since 866 regarded as heretical, does in fact seem to have been based, albeit tacitly, on the claim of Charles, and later of Otto I, to rule, not as kings, but as emperors, in Great Francia. It is a startling tribute to the prestige of Charles himself that a union between him and the pious Irene was not merely considered at Byzantium but was also in a fair way to being brought about, a union which, as an ingenious German historian has put it, must have appeared as bizarre to a Byzantine of the eighth century as a union between the Empress Maria Teresa and the Negus of Abyssinia would have appeared to a Viennese of the eighteenth.

Yet, after all, Charles' empire was the seed sown upon the stony ground where there was not much earth. His conception, much as it owed to Byzantium, was rootless and self-destructive. His renunciation of the single word *Romanorum* from his style divorced him from an almost millennial tradition which was still immensely powerful both in the east and the west. The division of his empire, by himself in 806 and by his grandsons in 844 and 855, were not less potent elements of dissolution. All this had been plain from the first both to Byzantium and to the papal Curia. A bare half-century after Charles' death, the whole position was reversed. The basis of Charles' empire and imperial status was, as we saw, his real and effectual power over all the western kingdoms. All this had vanished. Lewis II, a simple king of Italy, and not a very secure one at that, threatened as he was by the Byzantine, the Saracen and the Lombard, could make good his imperial status only by a complete surrender to the authority of Rome, and by declaring himself, at papal insistence, emperor of the Romans. By then it was too late. The balance of political power between east and west had by then swung decisively in favour of the east; and the growing might of the Macedonian house could look with amused contempt on the feeble pretensions of Charles the Bald and Charles the Fat, Arnulf and Berengar.

NOTES

1 Ostrogorsky, 154–5.
2 Bury, LRE, 159–66.
3 Vasiliev, 265–9; Bury, LRE, 490.
4 *DAI*, 108.
5 Theophanes, 472–3.
6 Ostrogorsky, 166–7.
7 *DAI*, 70–2.

CHAPTER NINE

NICEPHORUS I AND MICHAEL I

The Emperor Nicephorus I, who rose to power by the downfall of the Empress Irene in 802, found his empire in a weaker and more precarious state than it had been for nearly a century. This was almost wholly due to the incompetence of his predecessor. The main cause of this weakness was financial. The manipulation, for religious reasons, of the splendid military organisation of Constantine V had brought disaster both from the Saracen and the Bulgarian; and both of these had had to be bought off with a ruinous annual tribute by the most pious empress. The incursions into Asia of the armies of Caliph Harun, on a far wider scale than had been undertaken before, had begun to disrupt the rural economy, with the result that the fiscal economy also was breaking down. The countryside, and the capital itself, were swarming with penniless defaulters, who had abandoned their smallholdings, and with these their military and financial obligations to the state. This condition of affairs played directly into the hands of the acquisitive landowners, and especially into those of pious foundations, which the irresponsible Irene seems to have exempted from payment both of capitation and of property taxes. The urban economy was crippled by the remission of the residence tax, and by the drastic reduction of customs dues on imports from east to west. It was moreover at just this moment that the empire was put under strong pressure to deny the whole basis of its existence by granting the imperial title to Charles the Frank. Refusal meant war, and war meant defeat. Both ensued.

Nicephorus himself was not ill-equipped to confront these

perils. In many ways he was an excellent choice. His career had been in the Treasury, and he had during some years been finance minister, or 'logothete of the general'. He was thus qualified to see where the finances ailed and how best to put them right. But he was no mere administrative reformer. He was also familiar, or else made it his urgent business to become so, with the military needs of the empire. In the tradition of the Isaurian monarchs, he led his troops in person, and though not a successful, was, by at least one account, a capable and even outstanding commander in the field. His religious orthodoxy could not be impugned, and the worst crime that could be laid to his charge was that, for political reasons, he showed some toleration of heresy. The accusations that he was himself a heretic, an iconoclast, or a mere atheist, may be dismissed. Like all emperors who properly understood the Byzantine constitution, he regarded the church as a department of state; he therefore welcomed Tarasius as his patriarch, and, on the death of Tarasius in 806, appointed one as much like Tarasius as possible – the civil servant Nicephorus, the historian and confessor. This policy naturally aroused the resentment of the fanatical monks of the Studius and indeed of the whole order, who coveted the patriarchate for one of themselves, and were still further incensed by the financial measures of the emperor which put the monastic properties once more under contribution to the treasury.

The Emperor Nicephorus has been described by the chronicler Theophanes, a contemporary and one of our very few sources for his reign, with a venom usually reserved by that chronicler for iconoclasts. Some modern historians have been puzzled by this, and have suggested that there must have been a personal motive for this dislike. But his financial policy amply accounts for it. If there was one thing which the church resented more than another, it was the smallest interference with her revenues and her real estate. Only the strongest emperors – Heraclius, Romanus I, Nicephorus II, Basil II, Alexius I, – cared to disturb them, and then only in the direst and most urgent crises. Nicephorus I dared to touch them, and the church cursed him to his face.

His first year was disturbed by a revolt, which happily proved abortive. One of the pressing needs of the empire was financial economy; and one of the most costly and humiliating drains on the treasury was the tribute paid to the Saracens and Bulgars by agreement with Irene. Nicephorus thought himself strong enough to discontinue these payments. He therefore wrote to the Caliph Harun saying that no more tribute was forthcoming, and even demanded repayment of what had been disbursed by his feeble predecessor. Nicephorus, however, mistook his man. Harun wrote a curt and insulting message to 'the Greek dog', and instantly set his troops in motion. The emperor appointed as *generalissimo* over his eastern forces a competent and distinguished Armenian officer named Bardanes Turcus, who was supported by a staff of equally capable subordinates. Unfortunately, the plan miscarried. In July of 803, with the Saracen armies already on the frontier, Bardanes revolted and had himself proclaimed emperor. Almost at once he seems to have regretted his action. He took three of his officers, Michael of Amorion, Leo the Armenian and Thomas the Slav, all of whom were later to distinguish themselves, and went off to consult a hermit of Philomelion, supposedly endowed with the gift of prophecy. The hermit shook his head. The scheme of Bardanes was doomed. Then, his eye lighting on the three henchmen, he foretold how two of these would in fact ascend the imperial throne, while the third would attempt, but fail, to do so. Such was in fact the destiny of Leo v, Michael II and Thomas. The whole story reminds one of the encounter of Macbeth and Banquo with the weird sisters. The revolt of Bardanes naturally collapsed.[1]

The emperor next set about putting the finances, and with them the rural economy, in order. In one of his most valuable passages, the chronicler Theophanes enumerates ten separate financial 'vexations' imposed by Nicephorus on his empire. The provisions are highly informative, and seem to have been dictated by sensible and sound principles of finance. Two are concerned with the reoccupation of Hellas and the coast of Asia Minor, through compulsory purchase of smallholdings and forcible transfer of peasantry. A third covers the enrolment of destitute ex-cultivators into the regular army at the cost of their more prosperous neighbours, who had to make up a sum of $18\frac{1}{2}$ gold pieces for the equipment of each of these recruits. It seems at first sight a hard provision, but we have to remember that in these village communities no one became poor without someone else's becoming richer, by acquisition of the alienated property: and we must see in this regulation the first of many efforts to preserve an equilibrium in the communes. Two more 'vexations' concern tax-reassessment and removal of tax-reliefs. Then comes the edict on which most stress is laid: the families of serfs attached to monastic and charitable foundations are to be subject to the poll-tax; and the imperial land-commission is authorised to confiscate certain properties belonging to such foundations without affording corresponding tax-relief, so that their taxes often went up by as much as 100%. We cannot doubt the substantial truth of this report; on the other hand we have no reason to doubt either its equity or its necessity. Three more articles concern tax-avoidance, death-duties and the customs duty on slaves. The last forbids private loans to traders, and confines shipowners to borrowing from the state at an interest of $16\frac{2}{3}\%$. 'These few examples out of many I publish in summary form', says Theophanes, 'so as to illustrate the fertility of his invention for extortion.' No one – it is true – likes a cheeseparing ruler, and no one likes paying taxes: but on occasion both are unpleasant necessities, and this was one such occasion. Though his contemporaries gave him no credit for his good sense, posterity can afford to be more generous.[2]

At all events, money was desperately needed for defence. The dreary battle on two fronts, Saracen and Bulgar, was carried on throughout the reign, although the Saracen front was more active in the former, the Bulgar in the final and fatal part of it. A fearful infestation of a hundred and thirty-five thousand Arabs led by the Caliph Harun in person took place in 806; and resulted in the loss of Tyana, and in the payment of fifty thousand gold pieces of ransom money. The great caliph, who added insult to injury by negotiating with Charlemagne on equal terms, died in 809, and thereafter a civil war between his sons relieved the pressure on Byzantium's eastern front. But the fact is that by now the annual plundering raids were promoted from Tarsus or Melitene, irrespective of what might be the internal political state of the caliphate. Meanwhile the Bulgarian menace was becoming very grave indeed. In 805 the khanate was occupied by one of the great Bulgarian conquerors, Krum. In 808 he led his hordes across the Balkan, which formed his southern frontier, and drove into Strymon and Macedonia. In 809, Krum got possession of the key-point of Byzantine defence in the area, Serdica, which is the modern Sofia, and slaughtered the Byzantine garrison. This was not to be borne. Nicephorus collected an army, hurried northward to Pliska, the Bulgarian capital, and sacked it. But his success had no lasting result. And his plan to recover Serdica was frustrated by a mutiny of his troops, who seem never to have loved him. Meanwhile, on yet a third front the war with the Franks, a naval war provoked by Nicephorus' flat rejection of Charles' offers of diplomatic compromise, resulted in the capture, or at least the reduction, of Byzantine Venice by Charles' son Pippin in 809. Here, at least, nothing was to be gained by prolonging hostilities, and everything, except prestige, to be gained by making peace. Byzantium had no chance whatever of checking the Franks on land: while, if she acceded to Charles' very moderate terms, she would recover Venice and Istria, and also reestablish Francia as a western barrier to Bulgarian ambitions. It was a bitter pill. But Byzantine diplomacy chewed it up very small indeed, so that it was less painful to swallow it at last. In 811 serious peace negotiations between *haec duo imperia* were opened between Nicephorus and Charles.

The Bulgarian threat must be considered the operative factor, here as elsewhere, at this date. Let us review the position of the Balkan Peninsula. At this time the province of Hellas, though nominally incorporated by Justinian II in 690, was scarcely more than a paper province. Athens and Demetrias – and of course Thessalonica – were still, and remained, in Byzantine hands; but whether Thebes, the later administrative centre of the *theme*, was effectively controlled by Byzantium, remains very doubtful indeed. The countryside was virtually independent. Of Peloponnesus there had, since the great pestilence of 745-7, been no Byzantine occupation at all. The very fact that no trace, even theoretical, of Byzantine provincial organisation is discernible before about 810, shews very plainly that this southern part of the peninsula was regarded, like Cyprus or Cherson, as altogether outside the effective control of the central government. The Slavonic settlers of the peninsula were, if left to themselves, of a pacific and industrious nature. And since the seventh century they seem to have preferred a settled and quiet agriculturalism to military adventures. But now, with the influx of the savage and hostile Bulgarians of Krum into the Slavonic regions of Macedonia, this pacific settlement was likely to become gravely disturbed. Was it not probable that, unless vigorous Byzantine efforts were made to control them, the Bulgaro-Slavs would very speedily form a warlike and menacing block extending from the Danube to Cape Taenarum? The reality of the threat may be very plainly seen in the subsequent exploits of Tsar Symeon between the years 921 and 924, when the Bulgarians did actually become masters of the Hellenic peninsula, and demanded its permanent cession to the Bulgarian 'emperor'.

Spurred on by this danger, the Emperor Nicephorus made the first systematic attempt to recover and christianise Hellas and Peloponnesus. The first step was to organise the latter area into a *theme*, and it was done about this time. The exact date of its incorporation is not known. But a military governor, one Sclerus, is found in the reign of Michael I, that is, in 812, and the organisation itself is attributable with virtual certainty to Nicephorus.

The recovery of the historic Hellenic homeland from its Slavonic occupation gave rise to some legends which doubtless contain a germ of truth. A document known as the *Chronicle of Monemvasia*, dating from the ninth century, tells us that, after the Peloponnesus had been totally occupied by Slavs during 218 years, so that no Roman had been able to put his foot in it, Patras (at the mouth of the Gulf of Lepanto) was at length refounded, in the year 805, by the descendants of those Peloponnesians who had, in 587, been expelled thence and had taken refuge in Southern Italy. This story, improbable as it may be in detail, is substantially true. Peloponnesus was in fact resettled by Nicephorus, who transplanted thither Greek-speaking Byzantines from all over the empire. The resurgence of Patras is moreover commemorated in a legend preserved for us by Constantine Porphyrogenitus in his *De administrando imperio*.3 According to this, Patras was besieged by Slavs in the time of Nicephorus, and applied to the military governor of the *theme*, who resided at Corinth, for relief. These two anecdotes preserve memories both of the establishment of the *theme* of Peloponnesus and of the resettlement of its western district. The factual truth of this resettlement is told by Theophanes, under the year 810–11:

In this year Nicephorus ordered Christian colonists from every province to move into Sklavinia, and to sell their holdings: this was worse than captivity: many despaired and blasphemed, or prayed for an enemy invasion, others wept over the tombs of their fathers and blessed the happy lot of the dead. Some hanged themselves to escape so dreadful a fate. Poor and rich alike were helpless. This forcible migration was begun in September 810, and was completed by the following Easter.[4]

It would seem that a sojourn in Hellas was in those days not so popular as it has since become. When Theophanes says that the Byzantine settlers came 'from every province', he no doubt includes Calabria and Sicily, where Saracen incursions were causing a retromigration of Greek speakers to Hellas. Confirmation of this is found in the legend of the miraculous deliverance of Patras from the Slavonic besiegers: for in this legend the Greek speakers are called, not Peloponnesians, or Helladics or Rhomaioi, but *Graikoi* or Greci, that is, Greek speakers from Italy.

It is therefore to the Emperor Nicephorus that we must give credit for initiating the byzantinisation and conversion to Christianity of the Slavs of Hellas, a process which was virtually complete a century later. In the later ninth century the picture of Peloponnesus is one of enormous agricultural and commercial prosperity, so much so that barren Hellas was even for a time an exporter of grain. The imperial purple-fisheries were reactivated. Parchment was manufactured for the imperial chanceries. Superb carpets and tapestries were woven on the looms of Patras. Nowhere is the genius and adaptability of the new Slavo-Byzantine, when put to good use, better exemplified than here.[5]

The religious events of the reign do not present so happy or promising a picture. The quarrel between the two church parties – the moderate pragmatists and the die-hard theorists – of which we have already noted the origins as early as 787, burst out with great violence in the year 806, and continued during the rest of the reign. The proximate cause appears unbelievably trivial. It will be remembered that Constantine VI had been married to his second wife, Theodote, by an abbot called Joseph. The patriarch Tarasius had at first refused to condemn Joseph; but, after the blinding of Constantine himself, he had, under pressure from the Studite monks, consented to Joseph's excommunication. Joseph, however, remained in the government service, and in 803 performed a most signal service for the Emperor Nicephorus. He it was who had been sent out to negotiate with the rebel Bardanes; and had succeeded in inducing him to lay down his arms. In return for this the emperor resolved that Joseph's excommunication should be annulled. While Tarasius lived, nothing could be done, since that patriarch could scarcely be required to change his mind yet again in the matter. But in February 806 Tarasius died, and Nicephorus appointed his own namesake, Nicephorus the secretary, to the patriarchal chair.

This patriarch is celebrated for more than one reason. He became so for his courageous opposition to resurgent iconoclasm in 815, and for his subsequent deposition and exile over this dispute. He became so as the author of one of our few reliable sources for seventh and eighth-century history, the so-called *Breviarium*, which treats of Byzantine history from Heraclius to Constantine V, and is an invaluable supplement to the *Chronicle* of Theophanes. Like Tarasius, Nicephorus had been bred a layman and a civil servant. On April 5 he received the tonsure: on the 9th he became deacon; on the 10th presbyter, and on the 12th he was ordained bishop and ecumenical patriarch.

This sudden procedure, though not illegal, was wormwood to the monastic party, who abominated this secularisation of the holy office. It was plain that they would need only an excuse to withstand him; and the excuse was soon forthcoming. The ban on the abbot Joseph was removed at the emperor's instance, and he was admitted to the sacrament. The monastic party instantly took alarm, and the whole *moechian* scandal, apparently dead since 797, flared up once more. The die-hards were led, as before, by the now aged Plato, and his two nephews, Theodore of Studius and Joseph, archbishop of Thessalonica. They once more condemned in the most absolute style the infringement of canon law which Constantine VI's second marriage had involved: they denied the right of Nicephorus to dispense the sin: they sneered at the new patriarch as a mere steward of Caesar: and they flatly refused to communicate with the rehabilitated Joseph. The emperor resented their contumaciousness in the fiercest manner. The archbishop of Thessalonica was summoned before the imperial secretary of state. 'My quarrel,' said his Grace, 'is not with the emperor but with the abbot Joseph who wedded the adulterer.' 'Ah', said the minister, 'then let me tell you that their imperial Majesties have no further use for you, either in Thessalonica or anywhere else.' He was dismissed from his see. Theodore and Plato were brought before a mixed tribunal of laymen and secular clergy. 'You are talking utter nonsense:' the committee told Theodore, 'this is a simple case of dispensation, as practised by the Saints, and the blessed Tarasius.' Theodore gave them a lick with the rough side of his tongue. He stiffly maintained that Joseph was a 'coupler of adulterers'. At the dreadful word, the tribunal gnashed with their teeth upon him as though they would swallow him down. He was anathematised and sent into exile once more, where he remained until the reign of Michael I.

It cannot be emphasised too strongly that the quarrel, though trivial in itself, is important for what lay behind it: which was nothing less than the fundamental and perennial question of the Byzantine polity – who was to be master in the church, the emperor and his party, or the zealots. It will appear strange that the Emperor Nicephorus in years when the Bulgarian menace was hardly more acute than the menaces of Saracen and Frank, should have deliberately provoked and kept up this internal dispute, with the consequent disunion and weakness in the empire. The probability is that – as Bury long ago suggested – Nicephorus regarded it as a test case. He made it perfectly plain that he was not asking the Studites to approve the marriage of Constantine VI and Theodote: he disapproved of it himself. But what he must vindicate beyond any doubt at all was the right of the church to give 'dispensation' in special cases where the emperor so demanded. This was the heart of the matter. The Studites maintained that infringements of canon law were not to be so dispensed. And this was exactly the situation which recurred over the fourth marriage of Leo VI in 906.[6]

The last appearance of the emperor Nicephorus on the stage of history was dramatic to a degree. The devastation caused south of the Balkan by the Bulgar Krum was such that an exceptional effort must be made to put a stop to it. The emperor, his son and co-emperor Stauracius, and his son-in-law, Michael Rangabe were to go on a joint expedition into the heart of the enemy's country; and in May 811, they crossed the Bulgarian border. The army marched north and appeared in overwhelming strength before Krum's capital at Pliska. Several thousand Bulgars remained to defend the place, but were cut down to the last man. The rest fled. Then, it is said, something like mania overtook the emperor. He was apparently master of all he surveyed. He sacked and burnt Pliska to the ground, announcing that he should build a city of his own name on the ruins. He then turned his steps westwards towards Serdica. However, his mania progressed, until he remained shut up by himself, completely isolated from his generals. In vain did they send Stauracius to remonstrate with his father. Nicephorus repelled his son and threatened to flog him. As was natural, the Roman army got out of hand, and wandered widely in indiscriminate slaughter and pillage. The Bulgarians were the very last enemy to be treated in this contemptuous fashion. They blockaded the mountain pass with a high barrier of wood. Below the pass ran a marshy river, and beyond the river straggled the invading army, encamped by regiments at a too great distance from one another. At dawn on Saturday, 26 July 811, the Bulgars attacked the emperor and his guards from the rear. There was no resistance in that demoralised host. The cavalry fled into the river and there were drowned by scores, while their comrades galloped over them. The emperor was slain in his tent. His son got away but received a mortal wound in the neck. He was carried back in awful agony to Constantinople, where he lingered six months and died in the odour of sanctity. The skull of Nicephorus was retrieved, and Krum lined it with silver to serve as a drinking-cup for the honouring of royal toasts at his banquets. It was one more out of a hundred examples of the dependence of the whole Byzantine military machine on the wariness and sobriety of its commander-in-chief. There are no 'soldiers' battles' in Byzantine history.7

The dying Stauracius was now sole emperor. He was childless. His sister Procopia was married to Michael Rangabe, who was probably a Slav and certainly an incompetent. Stauracius endeavoured, during the few weeks left to him, to govern from his bed. His brother-in-law Michael, who had also campaigned at Pliska, had returned with him unhurt. The overriding question was to determine the succession. The obvious choice, in a legitimist point of view, was Michael; but to him Stauracius had, for reasons not altogether clear, a strong antipathy. He seems to have thought of devising the crown on his wife, or widow, Theophano. It would be hard to think of a sillier plan. To put a woman on the throne, with Krum at the gates, would have been fatal: and to restore an 'Irene basileus', just when the negotiations with Charlemagne were in a critical stage, would be to invite some much more peremptory and far-reaching demands from the Franks. At this conjuncture an active part was played by the Patriarch Nicephorus. On his own initiative he represented to Michael the absolute necessity of Michael's declaring himself emperor. This was undoubtedly true, and Michael saw that it was so. On 2 October 811, a show of election by senate and garrison was gone through and Michael I was crowned. Only after the ceremony was the unhappy Stauracius informed of what had been done. He must now be tonsured and removed to a monastery, there to await his end. As the patriarch approached him, Stauracius looked bitterly on one whom he thought to have betrayed him. 'You will find no better friend than me', he said. He lingered on in fearful torment, and died on 11 January 812.[8]

His successor was wholly unfit for his position, both as a general and an administrator. But these considerations, in the eyes of the patriarch, were outweighed by the fact that Michael was his nominee and could in ecclesiastical matters be forced or persuaded into acting at the patriarch's dictation. The Patriarch Nicephorus was able to make it a condition of the emperor's coronation that the emperor should give a written undertaking to uphold orthodoxy, and to keep his hands off priests or monks: and these safeguards were clearly dictated by the very real risk of a return to iconoclasm. To meet the danger it was obviously essential to heal the rift between the two wings of orthodoxy, and Nicephorus at once secured the release and recall of the Studite monks.

Michael I reigned from October 811 to July 813. His short reign is memorable for a single event: the conclusion of peace, after twelve years of negotiation, with Charles the Great. In anticipation of this event, Charles had already, in 811, restored Venice to the empire. Early in 812 the imperial envoys set out for Francia: a bishop and two diplomats, Theognostus and Arsaphius. At Aachen they were conducted to the cathedral, and there, says the German chronicler, 'scriptum pacti ab eo (sc. Charles) in ecclesia suscipientes, more suo, id est graeca lingua, laudes ei dixerunt, *imperatorem eum et basileum appellantes*'. Two empires were thus established: how long would it be before the spiritual body, in its turn, would be split in two corresponding halves, for ever?

The rest of Michael's reign was marked by disastrous follies, both in diplomacy and in the field. Krum the Bulgar, following up his victory, pushed into Thrace and seized Develtus. Michael, at the head of his army, marched out to confront him, but the troops were rotten with disaffection, owing in all probability to their dislike of Michael's orthodoxy. They mutinied, and Michael had to fall back, leaving Thrace and Macedonia at the enemy's mercy. Krum, however, was not disposed to get by fighting what he could get without it, and he offered peace. The terms were not oppressive, and should have been accepted at once. But unfortunately they included a demand that Bulgarian refugees, of whom there were many in Bithynia, should be repatriated. On this the Studite monks, who had no concern whatsoever with foreign affairs, but could never resist an occasion for meddling, objected that to return fugitives to Bulgaria would be to contravene the words of Our Lord: 'He that cometh unto me, I will in no wise cast out'. Incredible as it may appear, this appeal to Scripture carried the day with the pious emperor. The terms were rejected, and the war recommenced. Mesembria followed Develtus. A fresh attempt was made to face the invader. The troops of Asia, Armeniacs and Anatolics and others, were brought over into Europe, and in May the two armies established contact at Versinicia in Thrace. Meanwhile, a significant event took place in the capital. The patriarch led the people in prayer for victory, in the church of the Holy Apostles. During his ministrations, an unseemly fracas arose. A large number of disbanded veterans invaded the imperial chapel, surrounded the lordly sepulchre of Constantine v and with tears besought him to arise and rescue the ruined state. They called on him – 'as they were inspired to do by the Father of Lies' – as on a prophet and conqueror. There is not the slightest doubt that by this time the fumbling and feeble policies of the orthodox Irene, Nicephorus and Michael had enormously enhanced the prestige of iconoclasm, which was now connected in the public mind with victory, and hence with piety. It could easily be foretold what the result of any further defeat would be.

But defeat was unavoidable. For weeks the imperial driveller manoeuvred, with a much superior force, in front of the Bulgars at Versinicia. At last, on 22 June 813, Michael was forced by his officers to give battle. And the troops of Asia ran away. Krum could not believe his eyes. But at length he dashed forward and a fearful slaughter ensued. There can be no doubt that treachery was at the bottom of it, and this treachery must be brought home to the governor of the Anatolics, Leo the Armenian. He, it will be remembered, had accompanied Bardanes to the seer ten years before, and had been promised the imperial crown. This was his way to secure it. He was wholly successful. A fortnight later he was proclaimed emperor by the army, and on July 11 he entered the city. Michael gave in at once. He and family were exiled, and his male offspring – one of whom was the future Patriarch Ignatius – were emasculated. On July 12, Leo, after giving an unofficial assurance of orthodoxy, was crowned by Nicephorus the patriarch: but even as the patriarch placed the diadem on Leo's head, he felt, as it were, the pricks and stings of innumerable thorns. However, as so often before, the desperate crisis had brought the responsible ruler, for Leo was a man of real energy and ability. His talents were of a high order. But alas, he was an iconoclast.[9]

NOTES

[1] Theoph. Cont., 7–8; Bury, ERE, 11–2.
[2] Theophanes, 486–7; Ostrogorsky, 157–60; Bury, ERE, 213–7.
[3] DAI, 228–33.
[4] Theophanes, 486.
[5] Ostrogorsky, 160–3.
[6] Bury, ERE, 34–9.
[7] Ostrogorsky, 124, notes 1–3.
[8] Theophanes, 492–5.
[9] Theophanes, 493–503; Ostrogorsky, 165–8; Bréhier, 99–102; Bury, ERE, 350–2.

CHAPTER TEN

LEO V AND THE ICONOCLAST REVIVAL

Leo the Armenian (813–20), who now ascended the throne as Leo v, was certainly of Armenian stock on one side. He is said to have been 'Assyrian', that is, Syrian, on the other: but this is perhaps attached to him owing to his heretical and iconoclastic beliefs, and to the fact that he modelled himself on the great iconoclast conqueror Leo III, to whom Syrian descent was more certainly attributed. His heresy excited widespread loathing among the orthodox, both in his lifetime and after his death. Hagiography is full of his crimes and cruelties. Yet, though he is nowhere given justice, new methods and standards of historiography cannot conceal all his merits. That he was unscrupulous in obtaining power and ruthless in exercising it, cannot be doubted. But it is equally indubitable that he was shrewd, conscientious and energetic. The most pressing tasks, those of strengthening defence and restoring discipline to the demoralised armies, he undertook in person, and with a large measure of success. And the later testimony of the Patriarch Nicephorus, whom he deposed, was to the effect that, by Leo's death, heretic as he might be, the empire had lost an able and courageous defender. It has to be remembered that his restoration of iconoclasm can only have been undertaken by him to meet an urgent requirement of state. He was no convinced fanatic like his 'Isaurian' predecessors. He saw that the strength of the armed forces still lay in the fundamentally iconoclast levies of the Armeniac and Anatolic provinces, who would not fight, or would fight only with half a heart, for an orthodox emperor such as Nicephorus or Michael. Once his choice was taken, he pressed it with vigour and cruelty. But we firmly believe that this choice was taken not so much out of personal religious conviction as in the best interests of the state, as he saw them.

Leo's first task was to deal with the victorious Krum, who, after the shameful rout at Versinicia, swept down on the capital, and, less than a week after Leo's proclamation, was encamped outside the Golden Gate. The trembling inhabitants gazed with awe from the walls at the strange rituals and abominable sacrifices carried out by the heathen barbarian. However, Krum could make no impression on that gigantic fortress, and for the second time he proposed peace: he would take some gold and women, and would go home. The emperor proposed a personal meeting outside the wall near Blachernae, on the Golden Horn. Krum, accompanied by three retainers, came to the rendezvous and was joined by Leo, who came up the Horn in his barge. The party sat down and the negotiations began. Krum's brother-in-law, a renegade Byzantine, acted as interpreter. Suddenly, one of the Byzantine delegates hid his face in his hands. It was a signal to some assassins planted in a nearby house to rush out and murder the Bulgarian. Krum, however, was too quick for them. He leapt into the saddle and galloped off to his lines, pursued by a hail of darts from the walls. The crestfallen emperor returned to his palace.[1]

He must bitterly have execrated his wickedness and folly. Krum, in his fury, began a systematic destruction of everything outside the walls – palaces, churches, houses, men and beasts. From Hebdomon to Pera, and from Pera far up the smiling coast of the Bosphorus, ranged his exterminating barbarians. The booty was enormous. Only when they could take no more did the host fall back and lay siege to Adrianople. This, one of the most important cities in Thrace, was perforce abandoned to its fate. Ten thousand prisoners were taken: and these were driven off to the far north, to till Bulgarian soil on the Danube river. Among the captives was one who had a remarkable progeny. He was an Armenian boy who became the father of the Emperor Basil the Macedonian.

These horrible disasters stirred Leo into activity. Some counterstroke was vital for his own prestige. Late in the year 813, he followed the retreat of Krum's victorious army to the Bulgarian frontier at Mesembria. Here, by another clever stratagem, which this time succeeded, he was able to enter the Bulgarian camp by night and kill many of the enemy. Krum retaliated by the unusual step of a winter campaign, which resulted in the deportation of a further fifty thousand prisoners. It is worth noting that this wholesale importation of foreigners and Christians into Bulgaria had no small effect in building up the resources of the Bulgarian economy, and also in preparing the way for the Bulgarian conversion to Christianity, which took place just fifty years later. Still the terrible khan was not satisfied. In the spring of 814, an enormous army of Slavs, eager to share in the rich plunder of Thrace, was massed under his standard, and this time his army was supplied by his engineers with all manner of siege equipment. Leo hastily repaired walls and dug trenches to repel the assault. But, by a *coup de théâtre*, on April 14, Krum sustained a cerebral haemorrhage, and died. His successor, the Khan Omurtag, whose own position was not too secure, offered peace, and peace at last was made in 815. The new boundaries of the two states were defined and the Slav refugees were returned to Bulgaria, another indication of the Bulgarian need for repopulation. The peace was made binding for thirty years. And the whole empire breathed a heartfelt sigh of relief: it had, despite considerable losses of territory, got off more cheaply than it deserved.[2]

The remaining years of Leo's reign (814–20) passed in one of those very rare ages when the eastern empire enjoyed profound peace. The internal disturbances of the Bagdad caliphate which arose on the death of Harun kept his successor Mamun from any considerable enterprise abroad between 814 and 829. Charles made an application to Leo for confirmation of his title to the empire over the Franks, and this was conceded. The respite was sorely needed. Thrace was devastated: and Thrace had since the eighth century increasingly become the granary of Constantinople. The streets of the capital were full of destitute soldiers.

This last was a feature which, we are bound to suppose, was of some significance in impelling Leo v on the course which he now adopted, the revival of iconoclasm. The orthodox Patriarch Nicephorus gives us some interesting information as to the sort of persons who supported this revival in the city. They included (he says) common clowns of the kind called *mimes*, loungers, brothelkeepers, beggars and the vulgar generally. Then, he goes on, there were the broken soldiers. Who were they? There is some evidence, and a strong degree of probability, that these troublemakers were destitute ex-freeholders of the eastern provinces to whom the Emperor Nicephorus, in one of his celebrated financial 'vexations', had given relief, by enrolling them as regular soldiers at the expense of their more prosperous neighbours. A large body of these troops was quartered in the capital and employed as a city militia. Here however, in 814, we find them disbanded. It was probably they who had created the iconoclastic disturbances in 813, while the orthodox Emperor Michael was fumbling with the Bulgarian problem in Thrace. No doubt Michael disbanded them and threw them on their own resources. These men, says Nicephorus, were more attached to iconoclasm than anything else: and, as they were probably recruited from the eastern provinces, where Saracen depredations had made them destitute, this is understandable enough. They had until a year or so before lived on the imperial rations; but now, disbanded and impoverished, 'they have reached the limit of penury, and are publicly begging from the passers-by'. Large, starving mobs are uncommonly effective in forcing governments to act; and it is small wonder if they gathered in public places and called 'Down with the icons': not because they had any very strong theological prejudices on the subject, but simply because a reversal of religious policy would throw open to them again the ranks of military service from which the orthodox government of Michael I had excluded them. When we add to this state of affairs what we have emphasised before, that success and victory were now firmly associated in the public mind with iconoclasm, and failure, defeat and starvation with image-worship, we begin to see the extent of the pressure building up on the government to annul the definitions of the Seventh Council. And we can afford to smile at the anecdotes that the emperor consulted a soothsayer, who prophesied that God would root out Leo v if Leo v did not root out the detested pictures: or that another wizard promised him he would reign till the age of seventy if he consented to the reform.

Leo v, like Leo III, began cautiously.3 He was no theologian and never pretended to be one. His first move was the appointment in June 814 of an iconoclastic research committee, which was to sit in secret in the Palace, and to examine every document of scriptural and patristic writing which might seem to bear on the subject. They were to have the run of the palatine and patriarchal libraries. Every passage which could be cited in support of the iconoclastic position was marked by a slip inserted into the codex. Six months were allowed for the committee to conclude its work. By far the most remarkable member of it was the abbot of the monastery of Sts Sergius and Bacchus, John Morocharzamius, or John the Grammarian, at that time about thirty years old. He was probably the best scholar of his age; and an iconoclast from conviction, not opportunism. He was almost certainly an Armenian. He served three iconoclastic sovereigns, Leo, Michael II and Theophilus, both as a scholar and a diplomat; and ended up as the last iconoclast patriarch of Constantinople (837), before his deposition in 843. Joined with him was Anthony, bishop of Syllaeum, whom his orthodox traducers characterised as a debauched old rip who kept the monks in fits of laughter by his naughty stories and buffooneries. Two monks and two laymen completed the quorum.

At the end of six months, that is, in December 814, the commission submitted its conclusions. It does not appear that they had done much more than the commission of Constantine V, but at any rate they had confirmed the earlier findings. The emperor thought it time to act. He summoned the Patriarch Nicephorus and said to him, 'People are worried about these images. They say we ought not to worship them, and that that's why the barbarians defeat us. Come now, make a small concession to the people! Let us remove the ones that are set low down! If not, then explain to us why you worship them, when there is no scriptural injunction to do so.' This was moderate enough; but Nicephorus could not see his way. As for worship of images, he said, he worshipped them as he worshipped the Cross and the Gospel-Book, neither of which acts of reverence was enjoined by scripture. It was, he added, idle to ask if the practice were written or not: the church accepted many beliefs without any scriptural authority for them: indeed her so-called *dogmas* were of this kind, which she had received by direct inspiration of the Holy Spirit.

Having failed with Nicephorus, Leo determined to act on his own account, but he did so in a typically tortuous and underhand fashion. The scene chosen was the Chalke Gate of the palace where, eighty-eight years before, Leo III had pulled down the picture of the Saviour. This picture had been restored by Irene, but was now to be desecrated once more. On the secret orders of the emperor, some guardsmen gathered at the porch and began to throw stones and mud at the image, uttering the most fearful imprecations. Out came the emperor: 'We had better take that down', he said, 'lest the soldiery dishonour it'. And down it came.

The book of citations compiled by the commission was next put into the patriarch's hands, and he was told to answer them if he could. On Christmas Eve 814 he assembled a synod of divines at the patriarchate and read them the document. They pronounced by a majority that the doctrine contained in it was false: and they swore an oath to abide by their orthodoxy unto death. Next day the emperor summoned the patriarch and his synod to the palace. He began mildly: he did not disagree with the orthodox, but there were many who did. Why not argue it out with them, and he would be arbiter? The bishop of Cyzicus asked what the emperor had to do with it? 'Why, I am a son of the church', said Leo, 'and shall listen to both parties and decide between them.' The bishop then accused the emperor of favouring the iconoclasts by giving them shelter in the palace. 'Not at all', said Leo; 'as I tell you, I don't disagree with your side. But of course if you won't argue the matter, the opposition will say, with good reason, that you have no arguments to put against theirs.' Whereupon up spake Theodore, the fiery abbot of Studius: 'To your Majesty are entrusted politics and the armed forces. You look after those, and leave the church to us. For even if an angel from Heaven told us to change our faith, we should not listen to him, and we shall certainly not listen to you.' He added that it was useless, and very likely harmful, to argue with a heretic.

The emperor's patience was exhausted. He acted as Leo III would have acted. He deposed Nicephorus. The patriarch, sick in mind and body, took leave of his flock. Through rioting crowds, bellowing for the destruction of images and for his own blood, he was escorted to the shore, and banished across the Bosphorus. He never came back again. Leo appointed Theodotus Cassiteras, a connexion of the Isaurian house, and a good, mild man, to succeed him.

At Easter in 815 a council was convened in St Sophia. It was packed with iconoclast bishops. It began by accepting the ruling of the iconoclast council of 754, and thus rejecting those of 787. Then some orthodox bishops were introduced for examination. Shameful and unedifying scenes were enacted. The orthodox were thrown down, kicked, pummelled and spat upon. The council ended with its *Horos*, or Definition, which though definite enough in its prohibition of image-worship, cannot be compared in doctrinal subtlety with that of 754. Indeed, it seems clear that the revival of iconoclasm brought with it no fresh intellectual stimulus, such as had been added to the controversy by the thought and originality of Constantine v and his council of bishops. This may perhaps fortify the conclusion that the chief motives of the Emperors Leo v, Michael ii and Theophilus were political and social rather than religious. Indeed, the chief emphasis of the Council of St Sophia in 815 was not on christology at all, but on the degradation and blasphemy incurred by representing the holy and divine figures of the Christian hagiology in – or on – pieces of dead and corruptible matter: which was something like a return to the original and very simple position taken up by Leo iii, that the icons were nothing but graven images. It is true that the council did not stigmatise the painting and worship of images as 'idolatry': there were, it was said, greater and lesser degrees of evil. But it did very plainly evince its conviction that to make an icon was to incorporate into perishable material what should be worshipped by the heart alone.

So was iconoclasm restored for the second and last time. It endured only twenty-eight years, and indeed its fate was already sealed, as soon as the great movement forward in secular education was under way. This movement, by reviving and developing men's knowledge of a part of the classical heritage, won the victory for western over eastern modes of thought in the minds of the Byzantine educated class. Once this victory had been won, pictures returned as a matter of course, with comparatively little opposition. In this, as in so much else, the ninth century was a turning-point for Byzantium. The persecution which followed the Council of St Sophia is described by the hagiographers in terms which suggest that it was the cruellest onslaught upon the faithful since the time of Diocletian. But their accounts must be received with much caution. Those who deliberately set out to make martyrs of themselves found the government ready to oblige them. But those who kept quiet were not molested. Theodore the Studite was naturally the object of much imperial resentment. He was flogged – it seems, more than once – and imprisoned. But his insulting carriage and uncompromising attitude marked him out for punishment. There was also something else in his conduct of which the imperial government was doubtless aware. Theodore was in touch with Pope Paschal at Rome. It was characteristic of the monastic and die-hard wing of the church that they looked up to the bishop of Rome, rather than to their own emperor, as the supreme arbiter in ecclesiastical affairs. This tended to get them into trouble, especially as the division between east and west grew ever wider, and the Roman Catholic church became more sharply opposed to Eastern Christianity. Theodore was not content with explaining the plight of the faithful to the pope. In one of his letters he seems to suggest that through the papal mediation 'help' might be got from the Emperor Lewis the Pious. The nature of the help is unspecified: but it is plain that words of this kind could easily be regarded as treasonable.4

The Emperor Leo V could now look about him with satisfaction. His empire was at peace. His city was in a strong state of defence. The threat of civil strife had at least temporarily been removed by solution of the religious question. If he was personally odious to some fanatics, he had very little to fear from their malice. And yet this promising reign was to close after only seven years, as the result of a purely personal quarrel.

It will be remembered that in the year 803 the rebel Bardanes visited a hermit with his three staff-officers, Leo, Michael of Amorion and Thomas the Slav. To the first two were promised an imperial crown, to the last an unsuccessful attempt to obtain it. By the Emperor Nicephorus, Leo was raised to be military governor of the Anatolic province and Michael to be his Count of the Tent, or aide-de-camp; while Thomas, who had stood by the rebel Bardanes, took refuge in the dominions of the caliph. Leo and Michael had been fast friends. But it was soon noticed that things were going amiss. Michael, who seems to have become jealous of his friend's promotion, had not the prudence to keep his mouth shut, and became notorious for his criticisms of the emperor. Leo ignored this for some time, but then issued a warning that this criticism must cease. Michael took no notice, and was thereafter closely watched. At last solid evidence was procured that he was hatching a treasonable plot. On Christmas Eve 820, he was seized and examined. His guilt was undeniable, and he was sentenced to be burnt there and then in the palace furnace. It would have been well for the emperor if this sentence had been carried out. But the Empress Theodosia, on hearing of it, came down in her nightgown and persuaded her husband to grant a respite, since the morrow was Christmas Day, and he could not easily take the sacrament with so cruel an execution on his conscience. The prisoner was therefore put in irons, and handed over for safe-keeping to the palace steward.

Night fell, but the emperor could not sleep. His mind was disturbed by omen and vision. At last he rose, and, through long corridors and barred entrances, he made his way alone to the room where his prisoner was confined. Both Michael and the gaoler were asleep. The emperor repeatedly shook his fist at them and stole silently away. But he had been observed by a youth hiding under Michael's bed, who had noted the purple boots which none but the emperor wore. No sooner was the emperor gone than this lad woke Michael and told what he had seen. There was, clearly, no time to be lost. Under pretence of fetching a priest, the gaoler went out of the palace, and warned the other conspirators that now was the time to strike. If they held back, Michael would reveal their names to the emperor.

The dawn service on Christmas Day began at 4 a.m. in the palace chapel of St Stephen. The officiating clergy spent their night of vigil in their own houses, and entered the palace shortly before the hour. The conspirators, dressed as priests, entered along with them. It was bitterly cold. The emperor, muffled to the eyes, his head covered with a peaked cap of fur, entered the chapel. He had a fine, melodious voice, on which he prided himself. He began to sing his favourite hymn, 'In their love of the Almighty they despised the things of this world'. The conspirators suddenly surrounded him. But Leo was not one to give in without a struggle. He seized the ceremonial cross, or else, as some had it, an incense-burner, and strenuously defended himself. At length a sturdy ruffian dealt him a fearful cut which severed his arm. Leo fell, and was dispatched, at about 4.15 a.m. on Tuesday, 25 December 820. The conspirators hastened to liberate their friend. He was still ironed and, as a blacksmith could not at that hour be found, he was seated at once on the imperial throne with these very unusual insignia still fastened to his legs. So the third prophecy of the seer of Philomelion was fulfilled. The body of Leo was dragged naked to the Hippodrome and exposed to the insults of the holiday-making crowd. Then it was conveyed, with the widowed empress and her sons, to the island of Prote in the Marmara. At midday on the same day of Christ's birth, Michael, washed and free of his fetters, was taken to the cathedral, and crowned master of the world by the Patriarch Theodotus.[5]

I have told this story at some detail because it well illustrates the more literary character of our tenth-century source, and its preoccupation with striking and dramatic incident. On the murder itself it is scarcely necessary to comment. No removal of an emperor, not even of Maurice, was more unjustifiable than this. No religious principle could be pleaded, for Michael was as much an iconoclast as his victim. Personal jealousy, and naked treason, were the sole motive and means.

Between the murder of Constantine VI and the murder of Leo V, twenty-three years had elapsed. During this short period five emperors had ruled, of whom two only, Nicephorus and Stauracius, had come from the same house. Two had been deposed, two killed in battle, and the other one murdered. Never was a more obvious lesson to be learnt than the value, the absolute necessity, of a settled dynasty on the throne.

NOTES

[1] Theoph. Cont., 764-5; Theophanes, 503; Bury, ERE, 354 and note 2.
[2] Theoph. Cont., 24-5; Ostrogorsky, 168-9.
[3] Bury, ERE, 56-76.
[4] Ostrogorsky, 168-70; Vasilicv, 283-9; Bréhier, 103-4.
[5] Theoph. Cont., 33-40; Bury, ERE, 48-55.

CHAPTER ELEVEN

MICHAEL II AND THEOPHILUS

The Emperor Michael II, the first emperor for fifty years who did succeed in dying in his imperial bed, and, what was more, in leaving behind a healthy son to succeed him, came of humble farming stock from Amorion, the North Phrygian capital of the great Anatolic province. As an iconoclast, if not a particularly enthusiastic one, he is disliked by Byzantine historians; but he was demonstrably a man of courage and considerable military experience. His appearance at the head of affairs throws an interesting light on the progress of the *thematic* system as organised by the house of Heraclius: for Michael obviously started as one of those sturdy peasant-soldiers who from the seventh century onward had formed the backbone of imperial defence. The Continuator of Theophanes, with his eye to the importance of personal characteristics, has this to say of him:

However, Michael was well versed in his own pursuits: that is to say, he could tell of a litter of pigs which would grow healthy and strong, and *vice versa*. He knew how to stand up close to a kicking horse, and to get out of the way of the heels of a kicking donkey. He was an excellent judge of a mule, and could tell you which was better for a baggage-animal and which for a rider. He could distinguish between speed and stamina in a war-horse, and say which of your cows and sheep would be best for breeding or supplying milk. . . . Such were the tastes of his youth and age, and on these he prided himself in no small degree.[1]

Of course it is said with a sneer; but, from the passage, we can see of what sterling stuff the peasant-soldier of the provinces was made. It is further said that he was of Jewish blood, and this is perfectly possible, if not likely. He spoke Greek with a strong lisp, and was therefore nicknamed Michael the Lisper. The splendid aesthetic and intellectual endowments of his son Theophilus, and the erratic waywardness of his grandson Michael III, may be pointers in the same direction. There are certainly elements in the psychological configuration both of son and grandson which suggest a more cultivated streak than would be expected from the peasant stock of Phrygia. He had early married Thecla, daughter of a military governor who had been moved to select this rustic son-in-law on the strength of the prophecy that he would one day be emperor. And by her he had his son Theophilus, who, at the time of his father's accession in 820, was about sixteen years old. He very wisely crowned the boy co-emperor in 821, and married him to a Paphlagonian lady of distinguished birth in the same year. Shortly afterwards, on Thecla's death, he fortified his own position still further by marrying as his second wife Euphrosyne, the daughter of Constantine VI by his first wife, Mary of Amnia.[2]

Michael's resolution was soon to be put to a severe test. The third member of that triumvirate of officers who had visited the hermit of Philomelion in 803, Thomas, was now to make his bid for the supreme power. There is much in this fateful two-year revolt, as in the rebel himself, which is still doubtful. The main facts are clear enough: but the motives which lay behind them are more than usually hard to determine.

Thomas was, as nearly all are agreed, a Slav: though even here the sources are not quite unanimous. If it was so – and we believe that it was – his origins were against him, for Slavs, though since the seventh century they had regenerated the empire at its base, were never popular among the ruling classes of the empire, and seem to have been especially odious to the new Armenian aristocracy. Thomas, who had stuck by his patron Bardanes in 803, had spent the next ten years in exile in the Saracen dominions. He returned in 813 and was given a military command by Leo V; but he certainly meditated, and probably began, his revolt before Leo V was murdered. Of his person, we know only that he was lame of one leg, and that his manners ('though he was a Slav') were polite and winning.

The genesis of his revolt is shrouded in mystery. He seems to have made a bid for securing the eastern provinces by putting it about that he was the Emperor Constantine VI, who had been dead at least twenty years, and who would, if alive, have been blind. How many people were convinced of this identity it would be hard to say. Constantine VI had been an image-worshipper, at least in profession. Thomas adopted the same profession, and gave out that he came to restore the pictures torn down once more by Leo V. This was no doubt a good war-cry for the west. And yet we hear that no small part of his support came from 'Paulician' heretics from the east, who hated the pictures with a hatred surpassing that of Constantine V. Obscurities do not end here. Thomas felt the need to secure his rear, and with this in mind marched his army into Arab territory and negotiated with the Caliph Mamun. The caliph must have been mistrustful of a rebel who might well repeat the deceptions of Leo III. However, Thomas seems to have promised to hold the empire as a tributary of Bagdad, and the caliph promised his help. Thomas' next step is less easy to understand. At the caliph's instance, he had himself crowned emperor of the Romans at Antioch (then of course a Saracen possession) by the Greek patriarch of that place. Why ? If he had been, as he pretended to be, Constantine VI, no further coronation would have been called for or advisable.

At all events, the invasion of the Anatolian provinces began in the spring of 821. Thomas entered the empire at the head of a motley horde of eighty thousand troops, among whom the Emperor Michael himself mentions Saracens, Persians, Georgians, Armenians, Alans, Zichians and Colchians, as well as some Huns and Goths and Slavs. It is to be noted that nearly all these came from beyond the eastern border of the empire. Among few, if any of them, could the restoration of images be a rallying-cry, and the probability is that most of them served for plunder. On the other hand, their progress nearly unopposed through the once sturdy *themes* of Asia is remarkable, and can only be explained by the disgust felt in those areas at the cold-blooded murder of Leo V and the dislike felt for his murderer. The invading army spread destruction far and wide. The naval *theme* of south-west Asia Minor furnished a fleet, which sailed into the Marmara. Thomas transferred his army into Thrace. And in December 821 the siege of Constantinople was begun by land and sea.

The siege lasted about fifteen months. It was, in essentials, a repetition of the Arab siege of 717, and with the same result.

Once more, as in 626, 674 and 717, the gigantic defences of the city held firm when all elsewhere seemed to be lost. The siege-instruments of Thomas made no impression from the land-side: and the splendid imperial navy wrought havoc among the light-armed ships of the provincials. In the summer of 822 Thomas received timely reinforcement from the ships of Hellas and Pelo-ponnesus, in which provinces he, as a Slav and an image-wor-shipper, enjoyed wholehearted support. But Michael's jets of liquid fire burnt these feeble auxiliaries down to the water-line. He captured the rest. The end came, as in 718, with a Bulgarian intervention. The Khan Omurtag, who had concluded a ten-year truce with the empire in 814, offered his services to Michael. Michael did not positively accept, since he did not wish to incur the odium of setting pagan barbarians on to butcher the Christian levies of Thomas. But he left the matter open, and the khan took the hint. In March of 823 his hordes came down into Thrace. At the Aqueduct, near Heraclea, Omurtag routed the rebels, and re-turned to Bulgaria laden with the spoils of Asia and Thrace. Thomas at once broke off the siege of Constantinople and withdrew his forces – or what was left of them – to the Plain of the Diabasis. At last Michael could take the offensive. The disci-plined regiments of his guards made a bold front against the demoralised rebels, who surrendered without resistance. Thomas was handed over to the victor. He died horribly. The two-year rebellion was over.3

The consequences, both social and political, of the uprising were widespread and lasting. Many rural areas were devastated. The system of small-holdings, whether military or purely agricultural, while in favourable circumstances it could and did succeed, was highly vulnerable in adversity. The essential weakness of the small-holder is his want of capital. His food supply and animals, and his modest sales of produce, will suffice for the nourishment and taxes of the current year. But a long drought, an animal pestilence, or a thorough military devastation may put him wholly out of business. Moreoever, military revolt needs more money to resist it, and more money means more taxes, with less and less ability to pay them. It is a vicious circle. The result is that the small-holder surrenders his land to anyone who will buy it, and decamps to the city, or else works as a serf on the estate that was once his freehold. From the ninth century dates the inevitable, if gradual rise, or rather recovery, of large landed estates, which, in the eleventh century, became the dominant feature of the rural economy, and must be considered a root cause of Byzantine decline. The revolt certainly gave strong impetus to this pernicious tendency in the *themes*.

Abroad, the consequences were hardly less unfortunate. In the year 816, some ten thousand Spanish Arabs, under the leadership of Abu Hafs, either were expelled from Cordova or else left to seek their fortune in more prosperous parts of the inland sea. They sailed eastward to Egypt, seized Alexandria, and, owing to the internal disorders of the Bagdad caliphate, were able to hold it during about ten years. They were then dislodged and took to the sea once more; and, in the words of Constantine Porphyrogenitus, 'they desolated all the islands of the Cyclades, and came to Crete, and found it rich and carelessly guarded, and thus took possession of it, and hold it to this day [949]'.4 The Arabs seem to have had no trouble in occupying this large island, then a Byzantine *theme*, and they held it for one hundred and thirty-five years (826–961). The Christian population merged very easily with the Saracen; and we are told that the invaders took the native women to be their wives. A Christian monk showed them where to build their new city of Chandax, and almost at once the piratical raids of the settlers raised the prosperity of the island to a height it had scarcely known since the days of King Minos. The ease with which it was taken, and the absence of any attempt on the part of the local population to assist repeated Byzantine expeditions to recover it, is one more proof of the unpopularity of the Byzantine government in the west at this time.

The threat of a Crete firmly occupied by daring and ferocious pirates was not to be ignored. Between 827 and 829 no fewer than three separate expeditions were sent by Michael to expel the Saracens. Every one of them ended in failure. Indeed, without the collaboration or neutrality of the local population, Crete is a most difficult island to capture in the face of determined opposition. The Byzantine navies of the Aegean, as the chronicler justly observes, had been weakened by the fighting in the Marmara during the revolt of Thomas, and even the best commanders, Photeinus, Craterus and Ooryphas could make no impression against ten thousand resolute defenders. The importance of its recovery was however never lost sight of. Expeditions continued to be sent, in 843, 866, 911 and 949; but all of them were costly failures.5

Meanwhile the corsairs gradually depopulated the Aegean islands: and spread their raids far along the coasts of Ionia and into the Peloponnesus. For a century the island of Crete was a running sore. The Cretan emirs were practically independent, but the Saracen caliphs so well understood the island's importance as a Saracen base that they would send their navies to its relief, when attacked, both from east and west. It played a capital part in the naval warfare of the early tenth century; and Cameniata, the captive from Thessalonica in 904, has left us a lively account of its slave and booty markets as he saw them on his way in a Saracen galley from Thessalonica to the east.

If such was the state of Byzantine helplessness to redeem Crete, their helplessness to defend the more distant, but no less important, island of Sicily was greater still. The expansion of the Saracens over all the northern coast of Africa necessarily endangered Sicily, and with Sicily all of Italy too. But the revolt of Thomas naturally enhanced the danger, and it is not surprising that Saracen intervention in that island came within a month or two of their occupation of Crete. A daring Byzantine naval commander named Euphemius precipitated their invasion. He turned traitor and decamped to Africa. He invited the emir of Kairouan to come with a Saracen force and take over the island. The invitation was too tempting to be spurned. In 827 the Arabs arrived, and were from that time never ejected. The Byzantine troops were defeated, and compelled to take refuge under the walls of Castrogiovanni. Syracuse was for a time occupied by the Arabs. The total Saracen occupation of the island was not completed for about seventy-five years. But their partial occupation had just the same results in its area as their occupation of Crete had had in the Aegean area. Almost at once the Dalmatian coast, as far north as Cattaro and Ragusa, became the prey of the Saracen corsairs. Far worse, Southern Italy was wide open to their invasion. Taranto fell, and Reggio and Bari. By 840 they were ranging to the borders of the Papal State. The Lombard duchies, chronically at feud with one another and with the nominally Byzantine cities of Naples and Gaeta and Amalfi, were only too ready to call in the invincible Saracens to further their private ends. And this state of affairs lasted until a serious and combined Franco-Byzantine offensive brought it to a halt in 871.[6]

These then are some of the results directly traceable to the revolt of Thomas the Slavonian: and if Constantine VII exaggerates in saying that 'owing to the sloth and inexperience of the Amorians the empire declined to the very verge of extinction',[7] we shall not deny that these results, both at home or abroad, were serious.

Before we pass on to the rule of Michael's far more interesting son Theophilus, it is well to say a word about the emperor's religious policy. He, if any iconoclast emperor, may be classed as a Laodicean. Indeed, had he succeeded to an icon-worshipping empire, it is doubtful if he would have changed its policy. Nothing can better illustrate the strength of iconoclast belief and conviction at this time than the fact that Michael the Lisper confirmed it as the state religion. But he was no persecutor. He released the Studites from their prisons, and allowed them to reside once more in the City. He had some idea that they might, out of principle, side with the rebel Thomas; but he never thought of putting them back in gaol. He hoped – against all hope and experience – that they and their opponents could live peaceably in mutual toleration, but this, of course, was impossible. Only once does Michael seem to have been incensed on a religious matter. The Studites moved the pope to protest against the emperor's iconoclasm, and to impose orthodoxy. Michael strongly resented this intervention from the west; and the pope's emissary, the Greek Methodius, was thrown into prison.[8]

Michael II died in 829, and was succeeded by his son and co-emperor Theophilus. It has more than once been remarked that if Theophilus had not been a convinced iconoclast, he would have gone down to history as one of the most glorious of emperors, comparable in the splendour of his constructions and the urbanity and refinement of his court with Harun al-Rashid or Constantine VII. He is the first emperor since Justinian I of whom we have a satisfactory character sketch in our sources.[9] We know him as a man, as well as an emperor; but his reign still awaits a modern study.

Even at the outset of his twelve years of rule we meet with an enigma which, so far from having being solved, has, so far as I know, scarcely been noticed. The years of Michael II had been years of loss and of ruin for large areas of Anatolia. War against

Thomas, and war against the Saracens of Crete and Sicily, were heavy drains on the exchequer. Yet no sooner does Theophilus ascend the throne than a veritable age of gold begins. The coffers are fairly brimming with gold. Lavish expenditure is the order of the day. And the question is, where did all the gold come from ? Michael II was doubtless tight-fisted, but could not possibly have saved a tenth part of the inheritance of Theophilus. More than this, despite all his extravagance, Theophilus died leaving the treasury even fuller than he found it, and it took all the maniac profusion of his son to squander it. The answer can only be a sudden influx of gold from fresh or reworked mines, probably in Armenia. This is the sort of thing, unfortunately, that Byzantine historians regarded as below the dignity of history, so that we can only follow the influx by means of stray hints; but such are not wanting. As we know, a sudden flood of gold on the market leads to inflation. One anecdote of Theophilus records that a cavalry charger was priced at 144 pieces of gold. We learn from tenth-century sources that in that century the requisition price for cavalry remounts was eighteen pieces of gold. Even if the charger in question was a stallion, the price seems to be enormous. Again, one of Theophilus' preoccupations was the retail price of food in the capital. He regularly visited the markets of Constantinople and enquired the day-to-day prices of bread, wine, vegetables, fish and so on. Now, these prices were normally stable, unless something had gone very wrong indeed. Why should the emperor be so persistently curious in this matter, unless there was in his day a steady inflationary pressure ? At all events, gold there was, and we must see what the emperor did with it.[10]

Theophilus was an aesthete and a romantic. Despite his warfare with the caliph, he had a warm admiration for Arabic culture and art. He may even, in his peregrinations about the city, have been consciously aping Harun the Just, who is credited with wandering about Bagdad at night-time in disguise. It was to Bagdad that Theophilus sent in 830 a diplomatic mission whose magnificence and profusion became legendary. It was headed by the celebrated John the Grammarian, later patriarch. The gifts provided for the caliph were the most magnificent works of art from the hands of Byzantine jewellers and goldsmiths; and, over and above these, John was provided with thirty-six thousand gold pieces to disburse at his discretion. John fulfilled his instructions to the letter.

147

From the moment that he crossed the Saracen frontier, everyone who approached him on the most trivial errand went away with a pocketful of gold. Two large golden bowls, incrusted with gems, were the chief articles of his plate. At a reception he deliberately contrived that one of them should be stolen. Consternation ensued, and was followed by stupefaction when the envoy calmly ordered in the other one. 'In such ways as these', says the chronicler, 'did Theophilus augment his reputation for splendour and magnificence.'[11]

The emperor's buildings were patently inspired by Saracen originals. His splendid palace at Bryas, on the Bithynian coast, was built on the model of the Abbasid palace at Bagdad. His most celebrated building within the Great Palace itself was called the Triconchos, a two storey building with three apses: and this, too, was an oriental type of structure. In the Magnaura Palace, which was the imperial throne-room, Theophilus set those mechanical wonders – the gold lions that roared, the birds that twittered on the brazen tree, the great golden organ – which again imitated similar marvels at Bagdad. The spectacle of a Roman emperor showing such evident admiration for a foreign culture is rare indeed: and we have to wait till the time of Manuel Comnenus, three centuries later, to find another example as striking.[12]

It was indeed remarked of Theophilus that he loved foreigners in general: Armenians, Saracens, Persians, Negroes and others. His detractors said he favoured foreigners more than Romans. He certainly settled them by thousands in Anatolia, thereby intensifying the hybrid character of its population and also repairing some of the ravages of the recent revolt.

Theophilus has also left a reputation for the purity of justice during his reign: and indeed in a late Byzantine lampoon he appears in Hades as a judge along side Minos and Rhadamanthys. His displays of justice were, to be sure, a trifle theatrical, as when he ordered the public and summary chastisement of his own brother-in-law for a very trivial offence; or burnt a merchant ship belonging to his wife on the ground that her participation in a commercial venture degraded him into a huckster. But when we find even his enemies extolling his justice, we may take it as a fact, and a very creditable fact, that he did effect a salutary improvement in its administration.

For the rest, he wrote poetry, composed music, patronised

learning, loved his wife Theodora, though she was an image-worshipper, had a large family of seven children, and insisted on his courtiers having their hair cut. He had a keen sense of humour and, from what we can surmise, seems to have been a brilliant companion and a thoroughly good fellow.

His wars with the Arabs of the east were forced upon him by the aggressive policy of the Caliphs Mamun and Motassim. He would much have preferred a nobler rivalry in arts and sciences. This could not be. The chroniclers record the military exploits of Theophilus as though they were unrelieved failures; but a closer examination suggests that he gave at least as good as he got. Only one terrible disaster, the loss of Amorion in 838, is attributable to his reign. At the very beginning of this reign, the caliph was wrestling with a rebellion in Chorasan, and several thousand of the rebels passed over into Roman territory. They were commanded by an officer with the Greek name of Theophobos, about whom lies an impenetrable cloud of mystery. He seems to have been a relative by marriage of the emperor, but also, in some way, to have been thought to fulfil in his own person an antique Persian prophecy, to which was attributed his influence over his renegade Persians. Theophilus, true to his policy of welcoming foreigners of all descriptions, settled these Persians in the newly created north-eastern *theme* of Chaldia. The interest displayed by the emperor in this area shows that his eyes were on Armenia, and this may be a pointer to the source of his gold.

Two of his victories over the Saracens (in 830 and 837) gave occasion for a triumphal celebration in the capital, of which detailed descriptions survive. As might have been expected of Theophilus, the proceedings were on the most lavish scale and in very good taste. The streets through which the triumphal cavalcade passed were strewn with flowers. Superb carpets, embroidered vestments, and receptacles of gold and silver were hung on the walls. The Saracen prisoners and the Saracen trophies went before the emperor, who rode on a white horse decked with jewels. His dress was gold or gilt. He proceeded for prayers to the Cathedral, and then addressed his people from a rostrum at the Brazen Gate, seated on a golden throne, between a great golden organ and a great golden cross. From the dry description we can reconstruct with striking vividness something of that august pageantry which filled the spectators with reverence and awe, as they gazed on the golden streets of their New Jerusalem, and listened to the words of the golden sovereign whom Christ Himself had crowned emperor of all the world.[13]

However, it was a disaster, the sack of Amorion in 838, that impelled Theophilus to the most far-sighted and grandiose venture of his reign. In this year he opened negotiations with the western Emperor Lewis the Pious, and, after Lewis' death in 840, continued them with his son Lothar. The object of these negotiations was a combined east-west offensive against the Saracens of Asia, Crete, Africa, Sicily and Southern Italy. Details are lacking; but it is likely that Byzantium was to move against Crete (as in fact she did, without success, in 843), and that the Franks were to drive into Southern Italy against the African invaders. Byzantine accounts suggest a yet more startling proposal: nothing less than a massive Frankish descent on Africa itself, and even on Egypt. If this plan was in fact seriously considered by the joint chiefs of staff, it must be regarded as the germ of Crusading strategy three centuries later. It is interesting to note that the initiative, in 838 as in 1094, came from Byzantium. To fortify the east-west alliance, one of Theophilus' daughters was to be given in marriage to Lothar's son Lewis, the future Emperor Lewis II. The death of Theophilus in January 842, together with other causes not altogether clear, brought the scheme to nothing, though negotiations were continued until as late as the summer of 843. It is perhaps to this year (843) that we should date the well known 'Imperial Letter of St Denis', a document still partly extant, which was addressed by the Empress Theodora (in Michael III's name) to the western Emperor Lothar; although good reasons can be adduced for dating it two years earlier, while Theophilus was still living. From this missive it appears that Byzantium was still cherishing hopes of joint action with the young Lewis against the Saracens. Cooperation, however, was more easily proposed than achieved, as the same Lewis was to discover thirty years later. East was east, and west was west.[14]

Theophilus, unlike his father, was an intellectually convinced and pious iconoclast. He was the last of the iconoclast sovereigns, and his attachment to this outworn creed is of a piece with his romantic attachment to Saracen culture. But there can be little doubt that, by the time of his death, the reaction was unavoidable, since, even in his time, the cultural climate had changed towards humanism and the classical spirit. It is a superficial judgement which describes the final victory of orthodoxy as a triumph of the party of monks and women. It was much more than that. And in restoring the images the state was recognising a basic need of cultivated, as well as of obscurantist, society altogether more significant and urgent than any of the scriptural, patristic or sophistical arguments pleaded in its justification. Theophilus, however, remained true to his principles, and even, for the last time over this issue, resorted to persecution. St Methodius was cruelly confined: and two orthodox monks from Palestine were flogged and tattooed on the face with verses of the emperor's own composition. They were bad verses, but quite good enough for them, he said. It is, however, only fair to say that these men were self-confessed trouble-makers who came unbidden from over the eastern frontier; and their punishment, cruel as it might be, was as much political as religious.[15]

Theophilus was happy in his marriage with Theodora, who was as convinced an orthodox as he was an iconoclast. This in itself speaks volumes for the progress of polite manners. One cannot imagine Constantine v with an image-worshipping wife, although, it is true, he chose an image-worshipper for his daughter-in-law. Theodora kept icons in her bedroom and kissed them when she thought no one was looking. On one occasion the court buffoon saw her at it, and asked her what she was doing. She answered that she was playing with her dolls. The jester, all innocence, repeated this to Theophilus, who read his wife a lecture on disloyalty and superstition; but he does not seem to have insisted on the destruction of the 'dolls', far less on a judicial process and enquiry. In return, when Theophilus died, Theodora made it a condition of the restoration of the pictures that her late husband should be exempted by name from the general anathema uttered against the iconoclasts. She encountered opposition from the confessor whom Theophilus had tattooed; but she stuck to her guns. It is pleasant to contemplate this instance of domestic constancy.

Theophilus and Theodora had two sons, Constantine, who died in infancy, and Michael iii who was born in 840, after twenty years of marriage. The baby Michael was at once crowned co-emperor with his father, probably in 840, and reigned with him two years. Theophilus died on 20 January 842, leaving his infant heir to the regency of Theodora and her advisers. Michael's reign was as glorious as his own character and fate were tragic. But in our admiration of the former, we must not lose sight of the very. important preparatory work – cultural, diplomatic, artistic – made by the iconoclast aesthete Theophilus, and of his contriving, not least, to leave a full treasury behind him, wherever the means for this may have come from. We know of him enough to wish to know far more.

NOTES

1 Theoph. Cont., 43–4.
2 Bury, ERE, 78–83.
3 Theoph. Cont., 49–71; Ostrogorsky, 170–2; Bury, ERE, 84–110; Vasiliev, 274–6.
4 DAI, 96.
5 Theoph. Cont., 73–81.
6 Theoph. Cont., 81–4.
7 DAI, 124.
8 Bury, ERE, 111–9.
9 By Theodore Daphnopates: Theoph. Cont., 84–148.
10 Theoph. Cont., 87, 803-4.
11 Theoph. Cont., 95–9.
12 Bury, ERE, 129–35; Vasiliev, 298; Bréhier, 108.
13 Bury, ERE, 127–9.
14 Ostrogorsky, 175 and note 2.
15 Theoph. Cont., 104–6; Bury, ERE, 136–8.

CHAPTER TWELVE

MICHAEL III

With the reign of the ill-starred Michael III we inaugurate that long period of greatness and expansion which is the Middle Byzantine Empire triumphant. We have now passed under review the most significant developments in Byzantine history from the beginning of the seventh up to the fourth decade of the ninth century. These two hundred and thirty years are the story of the struggle for survival against apparently hopeless odds; of wide reaching reforms (military, economic, administrative), consummated without prejudice to the old imperial idea which constituted the mainspring of the whole machine; of gallant defence; of bitter internal feud between two separate and hostile civilisations, two contending traditions, and at last two contending spiritual factions. Four times the very heart of the empire has been threatened by the barbarian and the rebel. Four times the mass of stones piled up by Roman engineering, and the tenacity of the Heraclian, 'Isaurian' and Amorian sovereigns, have beaten off the threat. One by one the most prosperous and, apparently, the most indispensable provinces – Italy, the Balkans, Syria, Palestine, Egypt, Africa, Crete and Sicily – have been amputated from the trunk, and are now controlled by the heretical Franks, or Saracens, or by the pagan Bulgars. Across the Russian Steppe stretches the independent power of the Turkic Chazars. South-east of them are the Georgian and Armenian principalities, which, though Christian, are monophysite and heretical, and subject perforce as much to Saracen as to Byzantine influence. Antioch is gone. Tarsus is gone. The old province of Fourth Armenia is gone. But Anatolia is left, with its fertility and its new population of Slavs, Armenians, Saracens and Persians. Thrace is left, with its ample cornfields and sturdy Armenian and Slav peasantry. The Slavs of the Hellenic homeland are becoming byzantinised and prosperous. Above all, the *thematic* system is left, with its core of fighting soldier-proprietors. Trade from east and west, and now from the north, pours into the market of the great City on the Bosphorus. The spring has been contracted by external pressures until the only alternatives are rupture or recoil. The decay of the Abbasid caliphate and the break-up of the splendid empire of Charles are indications that the latter solution is inevitable. For the first and last time, Byzantium shows a new spirit of expansion, both military and cultural. Just at this moment, too, the final solution of the great spiritual rift which has for four centuries divided the body politic gives the state a unity and determination scarcely known since the days of Ancient Rome. We cease to mark time and prepare to advance.

The widowed Empress Theodora, now regent, governed with the help of a council whose chief members were her relative by marriage Sergius, who was the father of the patriarch Photius, and her able and devoted foreign minister Theoctistus. It was by the advice of these men that the empress, herself orthodox, decided to restore the images. But the extreme caution with which she acted witnesses very clearly the strength of the opposition she expected to encounter.

Theophilus died in January 842. It was not until March 843 that the reform was made. During those fifteen months iconoclasm was the official creed of the empire, and John the Grammarian, the iconoclast patriarch, continued on his throne. Many and anxious were the discussions between the empress and Theoctistus and the monk Methodius, marked out to be the new patriarch, who remembered the fiasco of the Council of 786. The probability is that the deciding factor was the conversion of Theoctistus himself to the orthodox party, since he had till then, during the previous reign, been a loyal iconoclast. He now saw that this policy must be abandoned. At last on Sunday, 11 March 843, a council was summoned. The decisions of the Seventh Ecumenical Synod of 787 were re-affirmed. It was declared that, 'those who adhere maliciously to the word "indescribable", and for that reason are not willing that images should be made of Christ our true God, Who partook of flesh and blood even as ourselves, and are therefore manifest phantasiasts, shall be *anathema*'. John the Grammarian, still titular patriarch, was asked if he would subscribe the tome, and, on his refusal, was deposed. Methodius was elected. Soldiers were sent to eject John from the patriarchate, which they seem to have done with some violence; or so he said. But he was very wisely allowed to go in peace, and to retire to his villa on the Bosphorus where, muttered the superstitious, he vanished underground and indulged in black magic and peered into basins.

It has in our own time been noted how this caution of the empress and her council showed itself in regard to the actual, physical restoration of the pictures. The scarcity of trained painters and mosaicists no doubt had something to do with it. But the fact remains that the first pictures to be restored were set up inside the palace, where they could not be insulted or even seen by the vulgar; and even these do not seem to antedate the 860s. It was not until March 867, twenty-four years after the Council of Orthodoxy, that the apse mosaic (still extant) of the Virgin in St Sophia, the centre of Christendom, could be unveiled.

The appointment of Methodius is altogether in accord with this sane and tentative policy. Though bred a monk, and though at first persecuted by both Michael II and by his son, he had afterwards been reconciled and had lived many years on cordial terms with the emperor, the iconoclast Theophilus, in the palace. Here, without in any way abandoning his principles, he had forgotten to be a fanatic and learnt to be a statesman. Theodora's council saw that a violent revolution, accompanied by a signal vengeance on the iconoclasts, would merely perpetuate the quarrel which they wished to compose. In Methodius they found the very man for the task of conciliation. His orthodoxy was unimpeachable, and he had suffered cruelly for the cause of the images. Yet he was a moderate, out of the same mould as Tarasius and his successor Nicephorus. His very moderation of course aroused the bitterest animosity in the hearts of the men of the Studius, who regarded him, if not as a heretic, at least as a traitor to the cause. His refusal to appoint extremists to the vacant sees drove them to such paroxysms of insult and fury that Methodius took the extraordinary step of excommunicating that fraternity, a step only explicable on the supposition that something must be done to appease the still powerful iconoclasts, and to show that things cannot be all take and no give. Methodius, very unfortunately, died in 847, and the Court, even more unfortunately, was persuaded to choose the monk Ignatius to succeed him. If they thought in so doing to continue the policy of appeasement and conciliation, they were altogether mistaken. Even so, while Theodora's council remained in power (842–56), they were able to keep their nominee in tolerable order.[1]

The three-year-old emperor Michael III, in whose name this salutary reform was carried out, is one of the most controversial figures in Byzantine history. The accounts which we have of his character derive chiefly from the Continuators of Theophanes, among them the Emperor Constantine VII Porphyrogenitus himself. Not merely did these writers compose their books nearly a century after the events which they described; but they also had the best of reasons for misrepresenting the truth, in as much as Michael himself had been brutally murdered by the founder of the very dynasty under which they were writing: and it was thus their task to excuse this murder by representing Michael as a villain so black as to have richly deserved and even courted his fate. The malice and misrepresentation of the tenth-century historians were suspected by Bury,[2] and have in our own time been traced and emphasised by Grégoire, in a series of brilliant, if not always convincing, studies.[3] There is a question of principle here, I suspect. Byzantine history writers seem to me to have distinguished carefully between two faults – those of suppressing the truth and of outright, deliberate falsification: and they thought the first a good deal more venial than the second. Thus, Grégoire clearly convicts the tenth-century writers of ignoring the brilliant naval assault on Damietta in 853, some victories won by Michael on the Euphrates, and some splendid constructions built under his administration, both at Byzantium and in the provinces. But to conclude that, because we can convict these writers of suppressing truth, we are entitled to go on and say that what they do tell us can be dismissed as fiction, is an altogether different and far more questionable matter. The unanimous testimony of our sources is that Michael himself was a dissipated and drunken weakling, a blasphemer and player of obscene jests, successively under the thumb of his mother, his uncle Bardas, and his favourite Basil. On the contrary, we are now told, we are entitled to assume that he was a ruler of charm, ability, and great personal popularity, and a military commander of genius. Again, to cite a more concrete example, Constantine Porphyrogenitus, speaking of his own grandfather Basil I, says that Basil took over Cyprus and made it into a *theme*, which it remained during seven years and then reverted to its old status of a Byzantine-Saracen condominium.4 This is explicit enough, and almost certainly true. Yet some scholars, without a tittle of evidence and on pure inference only, have stated that the incorporation of Cyprus as a *theme* must have been the work of Michael III and Theodora, which Constantine VII is here trying to claim for his ancestor Basil. In my view, we cannoe treat affirmative statements in this cavalier fashion. If we are going to reject plain testimony of this sort, we may as well make up our minds that we can know nothing whatever about the period, and rewrite its history according to our own taste and fancy.

The reign of Michael III falls into three distinct epochs. The first, from 842 to 856, may be called the administration of Theodora and her minister Theoctistus. The second, from 856 to 866, is the administration of Michael's uncle Bardas and Photius. The third, from May 866 to September 867, is the period of the administration of Michael III himself and Basil the Macedonian. The only one of these periods on which Michael may be said to have exerted a personal influence is the last, which was in consequence brief and disastrous.

The principal achievement of Theodora's administration we have already described – the re-establishment of orthodox image-worship. It was the basis, the indispensable prerequisite, of all that was to follow. Without religious unity no settled progress could be made; and for this alone her brilliant successors had good reason to be grateful to Theodora. Her military adventures were various, but not always prosperous. An effort to recover Crete in 843, which we saw reason to think was merely one campaign in a proposed Franco-Byzantine grand offensive, was a failure. Its commander, the minister Theoctistus, got to Crete; but soon took alarm at some news from home, and hastily withdrew his forces from the island, though it does not appear that these suffered much loss. At the same time his namesake Theoctistus Bryennius conducted a punitive raid against the Slavs of Peloponnesus who had risen in revolt. The same Theoctistus Bryennius also overawed the Bulgars, who were threatening to invade the empire. However, the operations of the imperial troops in the east were directed against their most valuable potential allies, rather than against the Saracens.

We have mentioned the sect of heretical Paulicians. These were Armenian dualists, who emerge somewhere about the middle of the seventh century on the eastern borders of Asia Minor, in Commagene. They combined a manichean belief in two opposed principles, of good and evil, with a belief in Pauline Christianity. Their conviction of the baseness of matter was pushed to such an extreme that they maintained that this world had been created, not by God, but by the devil. Thinking thus, they naturally devised a christology very different from the orthodox. As all matter was evil, it was clear that Christ had derived no part of His single and divine nature from the material world. The Mother of God had therefore been no more than a worthless instrument of the divine purpose, through which the divine substance had been poured 'as water pours through a pipe'. They further claimed (and for this they had scriptural warrant) that the Blessed Virgin had gone on to have several more children after serving this function. The Holy Cross was in the same way a mere material instrument, worthy of neither reverence nor adoration. They of course execrated icons and paintings. The Paulician was therefore something compounded of a monophysite and a manichee, and in both characters he was odious to the orthodox. He was also exceedingly cunning and disingenuous in his professions under examination (as he had need to be), for he would own the purest of orthodox doctrines while he reserved a mental proviso which attributed to each article of faith an allegorical signification wholly at variance with those of correct belief.

This body of heretics had been growing in strength since the time of the 'Isaurian' emperors: and indeed it may well be that Leo III's and Constantine V's beliefs derived in part from them. The systematic persecution of Paulicians began under Michael I in 813, and this was continued even under the neo-iconoclasts, Leo V and Theophilus. The restoration of orthodoxy in 843 marked its intensification. An order went out for a wholesale massacre of all who refused to conform. The Paulicians were an eminently brave, sober and hardy folk. They formed a Christian bulwark from Lycaonia to the Armenian borders, and were even established in force as far west as Phrygia, in the centre of Anatolia. Their value as fighting men was very great. They were skilful and industrious settlers. Nor do they seem to have been aggressive proselytizers of their creed, though this was undoubtedly spreading in Asia. The persecution of the Paulicians – almost the only systematic attempt in Byzantine history to extirpate a whole religious sect – was therefore as impolitic as it was cruel. The regiments of Theodora fell on them like wolves. One hundred thousand Paulicians were slaughtered, drowned or hung on crosses. Their lands were confiscated to the treasury. And their remnant, still formidable, escaped eastwards into the territories about Melitene, where the Saracen emirs welcomed them with delight; and where they soon taught their persecutors to curse the day when they had ventured to molest so hardy and resolute a folk. We shall meet the Paulicians again; but it is proper to note the extreme obstinacy of their beliefs, which spread into Bulgaria in the guise of Bogomilism, and into western Europe in the guise of Catharism, and which seemed to Gibbon to carry the germ of modern Protestantism.[5]

An exploit more creditable to the government was a singularly daring and successful naval descent on the Arab dockyard at Damietta, near the mouth of the Nile. Ever since the establishment of Arab naval power by Moawiya, the Arab corsairs, based on Egypt, Laodicea, Tarsus and latterly Crete, had been the terror of all the Aegean Sea. In 853 the Byzantine government, despite its many failures to retake Crete, determined to strike a blow far to the south, in the very heart of the caliph's dominions. On 22 May 853, a strong Byzantine fleet, commanded by one whom the Arabs called 'Ibn Katuna' appeared off Damietta, burned the Arab squadron there, destroyed a store of arms destined for Crete, and sailed off with prisoners. We learn that two other Byzantine squadrons were acting elsewhere at the same time; and in the following year, 854, a second expedition of two hundred ships once more raided Damietta. The minister Theoctistus may have been a poor general, but his care for the armed forces deserves all praise.[6]

But, by 855, the great minister's days were numbered. For fourteen years he and the empress had kept the youthful emperor Michael under close control. He was permitted neither the appearance nor the substance of power. In 855, when he was fifteen years old, he seems to have formed an attachment to a noble lady called Eudocia Ingerina, whose father Inger, or Igor, was almost certainly a Scandinavian. The empress took alarm, for Eudocia was said to be an impudent girl. She broke off the liaison and married her son out of hand to the harmless Eudocia of Decapolis. This piece of high-handedness was an error of judgement. The young emperor, disgruntled and chafing, was ripe for revolt: and there were those who were only too willing to second him. Chief among these was the Empress Theodora's own brilliant brother, Bardas, who felt himself undeservedly slighted by the powerful minister. Uncle and nephew confided their grievances to one another. A conspiracy was hatched. Bardas provoked the minister into insulting him and then had him seized, and carried out of the palace; and he was murdered by the emperor's own command. The empress was thrust into the background, and, after two years of idleness and intrigue, she was tonsured and sent with her daughters to a nunnery. Bardas seized the highest offices in the state: he became chief magistrate and commander-in-chief of all the armed forces. He was emperor in all but name during the next ten years. However, those who rise on the bodies of murdered rivals are vulnerable themselves. As the Duchess of Gloucester in the play very pertinently observed,

> In suffering thus thy brother to be murdered
> Thou showest the naked pathway to thy life,
> Teaching stern murder how to butcher thee.

At the very time of Theoctistus' murder, a young Armenian peasant, just twenty years old, came up from Thrace to seek his fortune in the capital. His name was Basil.[7]

The decade of the administration of Bardas (856–66) was the most brilliant in all Byzantine history. The government everywhere showed a rare combination of energy and foresight. The armed forces were everywhere successful. Secular education was revived with spectacular results. The church was governed, not indeed in peace and quiet, but certainly with wisdom and ability, by the greatest of Byzantine patriarchs, Photius. At the close of this decade there seemed to be no end to the probable progress and expansion. The sense of rebirth and optimism is vividly expressed in a speech of Photius delivered in 864 at the splendid dedication of the rebuilt *capella palatina*, where the genius of Bardas is suitably extolled. If these two great men had been as wise for themselves as they were for others, the horrible tragedies of 866 and 867 might have been avoided, and the throne have descended rightfully to the sons and grandsons of Bardas Caesar. But, in their preoccupation with the state, they neglected one vital factor in it, the Emperor Michael himself.

The accession – for this is what in practice it was – of Bardas galvanised the whole machine into action. I defer for the moment a discussion of ecclesiastical matters, but may here summarise the military. Bardas, and his scarcely less brilliant or disreputable brother Petronas, together with the emperor, opened a series of operations on the eastern frontier, against the Saracens of Melitene and the Paulicians of Tephrike. The government did more than this. They embarked on a grand programme of rebuilding in the cities of Asia; and celebrated inscriptions at Angora and Nicaea attest that the walls of these places were re-erected by the Emperor Michael III.

In 860, Michael III had left Constantinople for his third campaign in the east when a highly dramatic and important incident occurred. As the sun was westering in the afternoon of Tuesday, 18 June, a powerful flotilla glided out of the Bosphorus and swung round the Seraglio Point into the Marmara. It was the first expedition against Byzantium of the terrible Vikings of Kiev. This branch of the great Norman race which had spread far and wide into Europe, Asia and the New World, had earlier in the century established a hegemony over the Slavonic tribes of northern and central Russia, and by this time controlled the great trade-route down the Dnieper river into the Euxine. They were equally renowned for commerce, navigation and fighting. Their trade with the Chazar empire and even with the Caucasus was developed. They called themselves *Rhos*, which appears to be a Scandinavian term for an oarsman, but which the Byzantines equated with the Gog and Magog of Old Testament prophecy. Their ships were the terror of the Euxine coasts as the ships of their cousins were the terror of the coasts of England, Ireland and France. Their vessels were termed by the Byzantines *monoxyla* or single-woods, and some have supposed from this that these ships were canoes hollowed out of single and gigantic tree-trunks. I cannot but think this theory to have been devised by landsmen, who have never envisaged waddling about the Black Sea – not to speak of the Atlantic – in a storm, trying to navigate a hollowed-out tree-trunk. In fact, we know perfectly well what a Viking ship looks like: she is constructed in the fashion known as 'clinker', in which the lateral planks, or strakes, run unbroken from stem to stern: and this no doubt is the meaning of *monoxylon*, at any rate as applied to Viking ships.

This was the first hostile contact of Constantinople with the great race which was to supply her in days to come with her hides, wax, furs and slaves, and with her incomparable Varangian guard. The raid was destructive. The marauders landed in Thrace and Bithynia and did much damage, which is very rhetorically described in a sermon preached by Photius while they still lay in sight. The emperor's army was hastily summoned home. But ere it could arrive, the Virgin Protectress of the City had done her work. Photius paraded the walls with the Sacred Robe of the Mother of God: and the plunderers melted away.[8]

And now, after seven years of planning and organisation, all was in train to strike a decisive blow in the east. The emir of Melitene, Omar ibn Abdulla, had undertaken extensive raids during these years, and his forces were the more formidable in that they were stiffened by the courageous and exasperated Paulician refugees. In 861 they defeated an imperial army; and in the summer of 863 Omar embarked on what was more properly to be called a full-scale invasion than a razzia. He marched, burning and slaughtering, through the Armeniac province; and he took and sacked the important commercial port of Amisus, on the Black Sea coast. This could not be ignored. The command-in-chief was given to Bardas' brother, Petronas. He was supplied with every soldier available, from Europe as well as from Asia. Omar learnt of these preparations, and marched south, some hundred miles, from Amisus to the Halys river. Here Petronas, whose tactics and organisation are highly praiseworthy, manoeuvred to surround him. Three Byzantine armies, numbering together about fifty thousand men, advanced from north, south and west, and by admirable staff-work arrived simultaneously at their positions. Too late the emir saw his danger. His one escape route was dominated by a hill which he endeavoured to occupy in a night-attack. The sharp eye of Petronas had seen the same. A hot engagement was fought to settle the matter, but when dawn came the Byzantine standards flew on the hill-top, and the trap was closed. And now was the moment when some at least of the two-hundred-year debt of rapine and death at the hands of the Saracen marauders was to be paid. Omar selected the division of Petronas as his point of attack, in a desperate effort to fight his way out of the ring. He could scarcely have made a worse choice. Petronas commanded the imperial guards and the tough regiments of Thrace and Macedonia. They stood firm, while the two other Byzantine divisions closed in on the enemy's rear. The long day was scarcely sufficient for the slaughter. The Saracens and Paulicians fell nearly to a man. The emir himself was killed, and the Paulician general Karbeas. Omar's son was taken alive. The battle of Poson – so it was called – took place on 3 September 863, between the Halys river and the Lalakaon, its affluent. It had the same sort of effect which the two repulses of the Saracens from the walls of Constantinople had had in 678 and 718. The relief was profound. The Emperor Michael (who, say the Arabs, was present at the engagement) and Petronas returned in triumph to the capital. The people were mad with joy and pride, and a splendid celebration was made, at which a special hymn of gratitude to the Almighty and His elected vice gerent was sung in the Hippodrome. 'Hail, Lord, by Whom the great Emir was laid low! And Hail, Lord Michael, the destroyer! May God keep thee in the purple, may God hearken unto the prayers of His people!'9

It was instantly obvious that valuable capital could be made of this victory by a wise and politic government. Since the middle of the seventh century the two chief threats to the empire had been the Saracen and the Bulgar. Might not the downfall of the one be used to reduce the other? The moment was propitious. The Bulgar Khan Boris was in negotiation with the western Emperor Lewis II, and it was known that one item of discussion was the possibility of Bulgarian conversion to Roman Christianity. It was vital for Byzantine security that the spiritual centre of the Bulgar nation should be Constantinople and not Rome. The Bulgar army was engaged in the west. At home a famine was raging. On a sudden, the Emperor Michael appeared in Bulgaria at the head of his victorious army. Resistance was useless, and not a blow was struck. Negotiations were at once opened. The Khan Boris agreed to be converted; and, that there might be no doubt which side he was on, he took the name of his sponsor, the Emperor Michael. By the end of 864 all was done, and a new and powerful nation had been added to the fold of eastern Christianity. Seldom have twelve months of war and diplomacy won more spectacular and lasting results.

The triumphs of peace were no less splendid that those of war. While Photius, patriarch since 858, was reforming the patriarchal school for the education of the higher clergy, Bardas had already taken the step with which his name is most honourably associated. He refounded the secular university at Constantinople, which had been neglected, if not absolutely closed, during all the dark age of the seventh and eighth centuries. It would, it is true, be unjust to accuse the iconoclast emperors of totally disinteresting themselves in learning, and, as we saw, the tradition of classical letters was fully maintained by such scholars as the Patriarch Nicephorus and Ignatius the Deacon. But the rise of Photius, a layman until 858, put the whole of learning on a more thorough and systematic basis. It may be that as early as 855 he had compiled his monumental *Bibliotheca*, which brought into focus the knowledge to be gained through the study of literature, theology and above all history. With him were leagued two scholars scarcely less remarkable; Leo the mathematician and astronomer, whose society was coveted by the caliphs of Bagdad, and Constantine the philosopher, linguist and diplomat, whose daring innovation of a Slavonic script brought the sacred books of Christianity to the comprehension of the Moravian and the Bulgar. The very facts that such great scholars as these existed, that Leo the mathematician had until 843 been an iconoclast archbishop of Thessalonica, and that the scarcely less distinguished John the Grammarian had been iconoclast patriarch, is witness that remarkable men could, even in the days of Leo v, get learning if they wanted it. But now they could get it at the state's expense. Bardas opened his university in the Palace of the Magnaura. Leo the mathematician was made rector, and three salaried professors, of geometry, astronomy and grammar or philology, were appointed. The splendid tradition of secular learning which distinguishes the following two centuries springs directly from this beginning.[10]

There were offsets in this brilliant catalogue of achievement and progress. In Sicily, and indeed in South Italy too, the Saracens advanced nearly unchecked. And the spiritual schism between east and west was hastened by the disastrous quarrels of Photius, first with the followers of his predecessor Ignatius, and, arising out of that, with the pope. But the outlook was cheerful. The succession to the throne was apparently secured to the Amorian dynasty: for Michael, though himself childless and by this time incurably alcoholic, had been induced in 864 to create his uncle Bardas 'Caesar'. This gave Bardas the right of succession, and Bardas had two sons. Two of the ablest men in the world, if not the two ablest, were at the head respectively of state and church, and both were in the prime of life. Photius was about forty-five; Bardas not much older. And both worked for the same ends, in perfect harmony. Was it not probable that in twenty years time the same settled administration, hoary, authoritative and beloved, would have come to be the real renovators of the Roman Empire? These prospects were belied. By September 867, Bardas and Michael lay brutally murdered, Photius was in exile, and a peasant desperado was on the throne.

Basil the 'Macedonian' was born at Charioupolis in Thrace, in or about the year 836. His father was certainly an Armenian peasant, and his mother probably a Slav peasant-girl. His first language was Armenian; and to the end of his life he could neither read nor write. On the death of his father, in or about the year 856, he packed his bundle and set out to try his luck in the capital. He had two chief assets, a quick brain and enormous physical strength. His country training had made him familiar with horses, and he took employment as a groom in a noble household related to the court. His master became aware of his strength; and, when a Bulgar wrestler appeared at the court to show his prowess, Basil was called in to cope with him. The contest was brief. Basil picked up the Bulgar champion and flung him bodily the length of the room. The Emperor Michael was delighted, and engaged him on the spot to look after the imperial stables. And from that time, probably 857, his rise was rapid.

The intimate friendship between the Emperor Michael and the Armenian groom is a circumstance which suggests reflexions of a not very pleasing nature. Bad as Michael's character was – weak, drunken, faithless – it seems that we must also credit him with homosexualism: and this is confirmed, both by his making Basil his bedfellow, and by his choice, when he grew tired of Basil, of a pretty boy to succeed him as favourite. Michael's character was of course known to his family, who regarded him with well-deserved contempt. But it is strange that men so wary and sagacious as Bardas and Photius should have been so careless as to forget that their kinsman Michael held one card in his hand which could overtrump the best in theirs. He was emperor. Surely it was unwise to allow this card to be played by a groom, however harmless he might at first sight appear? It was this they forgot when they came to the unwritten bargain that Michael was to amuse himself as he pleased, while they did the governing. The dowager empress saw the danger; but her warning went unheeded.[11]

Basil went to work on Michael, just as Bardas had gone to work on him in 856. By showing him that his uncle regarded him with contempt (which was true), and by insinuating that his uncle meant to put him out of the way (which we cannot disprove), Basil got the unstable emperor into a state of violent resentment against Bardas. In the spring of 866, the military victories of 863–4 were to be rounded off by the capture of Crete. Michael, Bardas and Basil were to join the invading force. They reached the point of embarkation on the Ionian coast. And there, as Bardas came to his nephew's levée, Basil struck him down with his own hand. Michael looked on in apparently stunned amazement.

The armament at once returned to Constantinople. A month later, on 26 May 866, Basil was crowned co-emperor with Michael in St Sophia. Now he had it all, or nearly all. The final murder of Michael, on 23 September 867, was a logical step; but it is probable that Basil had at first no intention of killing his benefactor, if Michael would allow him to govern as Bardas had governed. But Michael did not. Freed from his uncle's tutelage, Michael refused to be restrained by a servant such as Basil, who owed everything to his favour. Though he was but twenty-seven years old, alcohol had brought on mental derangement; and during his final months he was no better than a savage and criminal lunatic. At last his pranks grew so outrageous that no one near his person, least of all Basil, could feel themselves safe for twenty-four hours. Photius openly admitted that he was helpless. Basil remonstrated with his colleague in the strongest terms, but was answered with insult and menace. At last Basil was convinced that Michael was about to treat him as he had treated Bardas. This was the end. One of the emperors had to go; and no one who knew Basil the Macedonian could doubt which one that would be.[12]

NOTES

1 Ostrogorsky, 182–4; Bury, ERE, 143–53.
2 Bury, ERE, 179.
3 Ostrogorsky, 186 and note 2.

4 Ostrogorsky, 198.
5 Theoph. Cont., 165; Ostrogorsky, 177–8, 185; Vasiliev, 383.
6 Bury, ERE, 292–3.
7 Theoph. Cont., 169–71.
8 Theoph. Cont., 196; Vasiliev, 277–8.
9 Theoph. Cont., 179–83; Ostrogorsky, 189–90.
10 Theoph. Cont., 185, 192.
11 Theoph. Cont., 233.
12 Theoph. Cont., 836–8; Liudprand, 8.

CHAPTER THIRTEEN

IGNATIUS, PHOTIUS AND POPE NICHOLAS I

No apology is needed for devoting a special section to the Photian-Ignatian quarrel during the years 858–67, since this is one of the few events in Byzantine history of which, owing to Rome's participation, nearly everyone has heard. Photius was not only a very great scholar and educator. He was also an unscrupulous and despotic prelate, who had very decided opinions on where his patriarchate should stand in relation both to the throne of Constantinople and to the see of Rome. It was unfortunate that, during his first patriarchate, his brother of Rome, Pope Nicholas I, was a character scarcely less assertive than Photius himself; while the civil arm on each side, represented by Michael III and Lewis II, was not in a position, or in a humour, to suppress the dispute.

The quarrel between the factions of the Byzantine Patriarchs Ignatius and Photius was in essence a simple continuation of the quarrel between the Studite zealots and the Patriarchs Tarasius (who was the great-uncle of Photius), Nicephorus and Methodius. It was, as we saw, the quarrel between extremism and moderation, between the church as a supreme spiritual arbiter and the church as a department of state; between distrust and hatred of secular learning, and love of it. No compromise was possible. No solution could, nor ever did, reconcile the opposites.

That nothing should be wanting in drama to this, the most celebrated engagement in the long war of Byzantine ecclesiastical faction, the protagonists were each of them men of high consideration, and each what seemed like an embodiment of the feelings of their parties. Ignatius was an obstinate and bigoted fanatic, who seized eagerly on any opportunity to withstand the secular government. Photius was a scholar, a gentleman, and a statesman, who (at any rate during his first patriarchate) conceived it to be the church's duty not to direct, but to act in harmony with the temporal policies of the empire. The tragedy was that they were both very good men. They in no way resembled Nicholas Mysticus and Arethas of Caesarea fifty years later, who were utterly false and unprincipled, and guided simply by fear and ambition. A sort of harmony was declared at last, when the protagonists were long in their graves; and the Synodikon of Orthodoxy solemnly anathematised those who shall speak or write anything against those saintly fathers Ignatius and Photius. But the thoughtful reader may well wonder how it could be possible to agree with one of them without at the same time disagreeing with the other.

Ignatius was of imperial blood. His father was the Emperor Michael I who, after two years of rule, had abdicated in favour of Leo V. The son, Nicetas, became a monk by the name of Ignatius, and early identified himself with the interests of his order. During the iconoclast reigns of Michael II and Theophilus, he had stood up bravely for the pictures, and had sheltered in his monastery on the Prince Islands those of his persuasion who had fled from the City. He was an austere man, uncompromising in his judgements, harsh and unyielding. A good man, I say, he certainly was; but not an attractive one.

Photius was an aristocrat by birth, and his family, if not an imperial one, was at least a marriage connection, for his father was brother-in-law of the Empress Theodora. His family's orthodoxy was beyond doubt, and he, his father and an uncle had all suffered for their fidelity to icon-worship. His learning and erudition in both fields of education, theological and secular, were well-nigh legendary: he was said to have sold his soul to the devil to acquire them. He was destined for a lay career, in education, the civil bureaucracy and diplomacy. By 858 he had risen to be head of the imperial chancery, but had during many years before this been a dominant figure in Byzantine politics and society. He started with every advantage, of birth, brains, good looks and money; and he made the most of them all. He was a close friend of the emperor's uncle Bardas, and when that statesman came to power in 856,

Photius was his most trusted adviser. But it would also be hard to think of anyone who could in all respects be more antipathetic to the Patriarch Ignatius.

The Patriarch Methodius, as we saw, died in 847; and the Empress Theodora determined to appoint Ignatius to succeed him. The decision is puzzling. There was not the smallest reason to think that the words 'moderate' and 'conciliatory' existed in the vocabulary of Ignatius, or any of his adherents. Moreover, quite apart from the consequences of such an appointment in itself, the whole business was bungled from the very start. The procedure for electing a patriarch was nomination by a synod, confirmed or rejected by the crown. While it was understood that the crown appointed, the synodical nomination was required; and Theodora, for some reason or another, perhaps from sheer incompetence, dispensed with it. It thus came about that when Ignatius had to be removed, his enemies could urge with some show of reason that his elevation had been irregular.

The prejudices of the new patriarch against the moderate party of his predecessor were manifest on the very day of his consecration, 4 July 847. The archbishop of Syracuse was Gregory Asvestas. He was a leader of the moderates, a cultivated scholar, and a friend of the youthful Photius. He appeared in the cathedral to assist at the inthronisation. Ignatius with characteristic rancour told him that, owing to some irregularities in his conduct, his presence on that occasion was improper. The whole assemblage was aghast. Gregory threw down his taper and flung out of the cathedral, muttering that they were not in the care of a pastor but in the jaws of a wolf.

No one could doubt that open war was declared. The accusation of irregularity of conduct made against Gregory was so patent an excuse that no one can now say with certainty what the alleged irregularity was. It is certain that the conduct of Ignatius caused wide disapprobation. But he persisted in it with a venom which made it persecution. Gregory was called on to answer charges. In 853 a packed synod declared him deposed and excommunicated. Gregory appealed to Pope Leo IV and afterwards to Pope Benedict III: but neither felt it in his interest to fall foul of the pro-Roman Ignatius, and both returned temporising answers. If Gregory had been an Ignatian deposed by Photius, we may conclude that Their Holinesses would have taken up a more positive attitude.

The process against Gregory was a blow against the whole cause of moderation, sensible government and secular learning: and so it was felt to be by Photius himself. He set his face against Ignatius, and began to tease him by propounding dilemmas of an absurd and unorthodox character which the ignorant patriarch was unable to solve. On one occasion Photius enunciated the doctrine that each man has two souls, one fallible, the other infallible. This theological jest caused some consternation among the simple who, regarding Photius as a prodigy of learning, really supposed there must be something in it. A remonstrance was made to him, and he desisted from this intellectual game of baiting the patriarch. But the incident may serve to illustrate the climate of opinion in ninth-century Byzantium.[1]

Ignatius, for all his stiff-necked and high-minded independence, was safe enough so long as the Empress Theodora remained in effective control. He was, after all, her appointment, and her government had an interest in supporting him, however much they may have deplored his tactless and autocratic administration of the church. Then, in 855, came the revolution. Theoctistus was murdered, and Theodora was put in retirement. Bardas governed in the name of Michael III, and a very different pattern of government was quickly seen. This government stood for everything that Ignatius disliked most, and it was soon plain that a rupture was inevitable.

Occasions of friction between state and church, we do not doubt, were found during the year 857. But, as far as our records go, Ignatius was the first to take the offensive. Bardas, the brilliant regent, fell in love with his son's wife. Whatever may be said – and much may with justice be said – of the talents of the two brothers of Theodora, Bardas and Petronas, the evidence is overwhelming that they were both of them, in sexual matters, licentious and lax to a proverb. Their general repute, or rather disrepute, in this department is illustrated by the very unedifying exposure of Bardas' remains after his murder in 866. Efforts have been made to dismiss the tale of his liaison with his daughter-in-law as slanderous: but it really will not do. His wife, Theodosia, herself complained of it to St Eustratius, and there is ample reason to believe that her complaints were but too just. The Patriarch

Ignatius saw that his moment was come. He excommunicated the detested regent, and on 6 January 858 refused him the sacrament. Bardas was now the most powerful man in the empire, and he received this rebuff with violent resentment. Prudence suggested that a less ambiguous reason should be found for the dismissal of Ignatius: but this was soon forthcoming. The dowager empress was suspected of practising by poison against her brother. The Emperor Michael determined, or was made to determine, to shut her up for good in a nunnery, and the patriarch was ordered to tonsure her. As might have been expected, he refused. On this, a charge of high treason was trumped up against him, and a synod declared him deposed. He was removed to an island in the Marmara, and is said to have been subjected to horrible maltreatment. His successor had long been resolved upon by the government of Bardas. Photius was to be the man. On 20 December 858, he was still a layman. By Christmas Day he had been hurried up the ladder of ordination and preferment, and on that day he was enthroned as ecumenical patriarch of Constantinople. He received his investiture at the hands of his friend, Gregory of Syracuse.[2]

It is idle to condemn the elevation of Photius to the patriarchate as a political job. Of course it was a political job. But so was the elevation of any other patriarch besides. What interested the government was the question of how a patriarch was going to administer his department: holiness and piety were, of necessity, secondary considerations. Ignatius was deposed, not because he was a villain, but because his policy threatened to bring government to a standstill. His removal was obligatory. He should never have been put there in the first place. The mode of Photius' elevation too, though it seemed to be wanting in decorum, was exactly parallel to that of his uncle Tarasius by the pious Irene. The extremists and the papacy naturally objected to it; but in their eyes no layman should ever be made into a prince of the church, no matter what methods were adopted at his consecration.

For the moment everything seemed to promise well. The large majority of the bishops agreed to the appointment. But this was not to last. It was customary for a new patriarch to announce his elevation by letter to his brothers of Rome, Antioch, Alexandria and Jerusalem. Photius wrote to Pope Nicholas the usual confession of faith and orthodoxy, saying nothing about the circumstances in which he had succeeded to his throne. But Nicholas was firmly convinced that the see of Rome should, in virtue of its seniority, be consulted over all such appointments. He had an idea that there was something to be enquired into in this matter, and also, perhaps, some capital to be made out of it. He therefore wrote to the effect that he could not approve the appointment until his commissioners had made a full examination of the facts of the case. And he ended by the very ingenuous proposal that it was now time that the diocese of Illyricum and the papal patrimonies in Southern Italy, removed from Rome by Leo III, should be restored to her. The inference was plain. If Constantinople would concede this secular and political demand, the pope would recognise Photius, whatever his commissioners might report. If not, not. It has been denied by honest Christians that the east-west schism was anything but a matter of deep spiritual cleavage over the nature and properties of the Holy Trinity. But it seems unquestionable that properties of a more material kind played an important, if not a dominant, role in the controversy from its inception.3

A council to regulate the affair was summoned for the month of April 861. Thither came the papal commissioners Rodoald of Porto and Zachary of Anagni. The whole proceeding was absolutely irregular. The deposition of Ignatius had been confirmed by a synod. In demanding that a council should re-try the issue the pope was interfering in what did not in the least concern him. It is astonishing that the Byzantine government should have allowed such a thing for a moment. We can only suppose that they were pretty sure what the result of such an enquiry must be, and that they thought the papal sanction for Photius' appointment worth some effort, and some irregularity, to secure in view of the great prestige of Rome in the eyes of the opposition party at Byzantium. Photius did his utmost to see that the papal commissioners were put and maintained on his side. They were splendidly entertained. They accepted lavish presents which are hardly to be distinguished from bribes. When we remember how the commissioners went beyond their own instructions in agreeing with the Byzantine government's view of the matter, we must not fail to take account of these 'diplomatic amenities'. The commissioners were kept very carefully from all contact with Ignatius or his partisans.

The council came on. Two sessions were held before, and two

after, Easter 861. Ignatius first attempted to attend in the full robes of a patriarch. This was disallowed, and he was forced to present himself in the simple habit of a monk. The grounds on which he had formerly been deposed were rehearsed for the benefit of Rodoald and Zachary. A formal ceremony of deposition followed. And Rodoald and Zachary appended their signatures to the acts of the council.4

Nothing could have displeased Pope Nicholas more. His commissioners had been entirely overreached, and had gone all lengths in support of Photius without extorting a single concession from Byzantium. Photius wrote him a polite letter protesting against the pope's strictures on his own elevation from the laity, but saying that the council had taken due note of these strictures, and that the procedure should not be repeated. He sympathised with the pope over Calabria and Illyricum, but feared the emperor could not see his way to any concession in that matter. This was not nearly good enough. The whole issue of whether Ignatius had been properly deposed and Photius properly elevated depended more and more on whether Rome was or was not to get back her spiritual authority over Illyricum. To the lay mind the two problems do not seem to be inherently connected; but they were very closely connected in the minds of the Curia, who were ready to give their support to any patriarch who would back their designs on Illyricum. It is easy to see why. Old Illyricum included new Bulgaria; and Bulgaria was shortly to become Christian. We have seen how in 863 the Khan Boris was in touch with Frankish clergy over this very question. The advantage to Rome, both spiritual and political, in having Bulgaria for a catholic, instead of an eastern orthodox, province, was enormous. Byzantium could never have allowed such an arrangement, but this was not clear to the pope, who was ready to make nearly every concession to gain his point. It is amusing to find a later admission by Pope John VIII: 'For it was on this condition that Ignatius was upheld by our predecessors, that, if he interfered with our apostolic rights in Bulgaria, he would remain under the sentence of his previous condemnation'.

While Pope Nicholas wavered and his commissioners doubted of their fate, the Ignatian firebrand Theognostus arrived in Rome. He represented in the strongest light the grievances of his party, their refusal to acknowledge Photius as their patriarch, the deference paid by Ignatius to the papal see, and finally the cruel sufferings of Ignatius himself, a story which lost nothing in the telling. Even then the pope hesitated, waiting for a word of comfort from the Emperor Michael or Photius. But nothing came. By the summer of 863 his mind was made up. A synod was summoned in Rome and the die was cast. Photius was declared once more a layman, and Gregory Asvestas, who had ordained him, was excommunicated. Ignatius was declared to be reinstated in his patriarchal throne, together with all those bishops who had resigned or been expelled rather than communicate with the usurper. Photius' own ordinations were of course declared null. The commissioner Zachary was convicted of improper action, and dismissed from his see.5

These arrogant and insulting measures aroused intense irritation in Constantinople, as they were bound to do. The annoyance of the Emperor Michael at being presented with a patriarch by an authority which did not consider itself subject to him can well be understood. But just at this time the empire itself was experiencing triumphs in east and north which were unparalleled in living memory. The papal decrees could safely be ignored, and the government pursued a judicious policy of silence. Instead, they acted. In 863 the Byzantine apostles appeared in Moravia; and by the end of 864 the Khan Boris of Bulgaria had thrown in his lot unequivocally with the orthodox religion of Byzantium. Not until then did the Emperor Michael break silence. In 865 his long-expected letter made its appearance in Rome; but his position was now so strong that there was no thought of concession. The tone of this missive, which many have supposed to be the composition of Photius, was sharp if not positively insulting. The emperor reminded the pope that at the Synod of 861 the papal commissioners had been treated with unheard of consideration. They had been allowed to attend, if not to preside, a synod over a matter of internal discipline which was no concern of theirs or his, and had in any case been closed several months before. They had been invited for a discussion on iconoclasm, not on the rights and wrongs of Ignatius. The emperor said he knew quite well the persons who were at the bottom of the whole affair. They were the slanderous and rebellious monks like Theognostus, who had sneaked off with their libels to Rome. He demanded their extradition: and if this were refused, he himself would come and fetch them.

Pope Nicholas answered by defining the claims of the Roman church in a manner worthy of Hildebrand. He said that without papal authority no council could be convoked at all, and no patriarch appointed or deposed. He reminded the emperor that until very recently both emperors and patriarchs of Constantinople had been iconoclast heretics. He asseverated that the authority of Rome, sanctified by the deaths in that City of St Peter and St Paul, extended *super omnem terram, id est, super omnem ecclesiam*. He, Pope Nicholas, therefore had the right and duty to judge the present case of the Patriarch Ignatius. As for the monks who had brought him the truth about the affair, he would not send them away. One concession he would make. If Photius and Ignatius would appear before him in Rome, he would look at the matter again, and confirm or modify the decisions of the Lateran Synod of 863. More he could not say or do.

The issues were now clear. The most important of these was the spiritual counterpart of the temporal issue which had arisen over the creation of an independent western empire fifty years before. As the Byzantines claimed universal hegemony over all territories beneath the emperor of Constantinople, and were met by the counter-claim of Charles, so now the papal claim to universal spiritual authority over Christendom was met by the counter-claim of Photius that, in removing the administrative centre of Christendom to Constantinople, Constantine the Great had removed also the spiritual centre, and vested *ecumenical* (that is, universal) spiritual authority in the church of Byzantium. Two emperors, two popes. The schism was absolute. These claims to supremacy lie at the bottom of the whole controversy: and even where the contestants seem to be laying immense stress on such questions as the marriage of secular clergy, the use of unleavened bread in the Sacrament, or even the Double Procession of the Holy Spirit, the historian must always keep in the front of his mind that these questions were symptoms of a far greater cleavage, which was nothing less that the claim of Byzantium over the bodies, and the claim of Rome over the souls of mankind. The claim of the Byzantine church to parity with, if not to supremacy over, the Roman was of course not universally received even at Byzantium. Extremist churchmen adhered to the old opinion of the primacy of the see of St Peter. But, logically speaking, the concept of Byzantine political universalism was dependent on a parallel claim to spiritual universalism. In and after the eighth century, the one implied the other.

The fulminations of Pope Nicholas could have been safely ignored by the Byzantine government if the great triumphs, both temporal and spiritual, of the years 856–65 had been confirmed and continued. But at the crucial moment when Pope Nicholas was claiming an authority which seemed to be confined to the region of speculation, an event occurred which in a moment made of that authority a very urgent, and very unpleasant, reality. The Bulgar Khan Boris–Michael, whose conversion to eastern Christianity was at once the cardinal point and the most signal triumph of Byzantine politico-religious strategy, seemed likely, only a year after his conversion, to play false. In allowing himself to be spiritually linked with Byzantium, he had obeyed the dictates of necessity, but had at the same time not fully realised just what that step implied. The temporal and spiritual arms at Byzantium worked in inseparable harmony. A convert to her faith gained her a political vassal. This must be insisted on, as it was a concept not understood in the west. The result was that, on his conversion, Boris–Michael discovered that he had acquired not only a spiritual, but also a temporal master. This was very little to his liking. He had been deeply impressed by the ceremonial of his own baptism by the patriarch of Constantinople. He applied therefore to the Byzantines for the creation of a Bulgarian patriarchate, so that these gorgeous ceremonies could be rehearsed in his own capital. He was also having difficulties with his people over their conversion to orthodoxy: might not the rigours of the orthodox canons (he asked) be here and there relaxed to assist in this great work? Here Photius blundered. The requests of the khan were brushed aside as if they had been the unreasoning demands of a tedious child. The reaction of Boris was prompt. Even before 864 he had been in touch with Frankish clergy. Now, in 866, he discovered that if Byzantium would not take him seriously, it was easy enough to apply to someone who would. In August a Bulgarian mission appeared in Rome. They asked the pope to appoint them a patriarch; and they submitted to him an enormous *questionnaire* of points touching the regulation of ecclesiastical discipline on which they had failed to get any satisfaction from Photius.

Pope Nicholas was quick to see the importance of such an approach. Roman Catholic control over Illyricum, which had seemed in 864 to be a dream that had vanished for ever, suddenly became once more a very real possibility. The pope congratulated himself as on a divine miracle. He composed a long and conciliatory answer to the Bulgarian *questionnaire*: and he sent an important delegation to Bulgaria which should refound its church on the principles and under the control of Rome.

The 'Nicolai responsa ad consulta Bulgarorum' is a document of more than ordinary care and sagacity, which shows an understanding of barbarian mentality quite beyond what was grasped by Byzantium. Where the Roman Church could, without heresy, satisfy the prejudices of the khan and his boyars, it did so. Where it could not, it gave reasons for its refusal. It saw no harm in Bulgars, men or women, continuing to wear trousers, or eating cheese and drinking milk in Lent, or in washing themselves on Wednesdays or Fridays. As for a patriarch, they could have an archbishop, and that amounted to the same thing. Polygamy, it is true – that is, having more than one wife at a time – the pope denounced; but so, after all, did Photius. All in all, the 'Responsa' made an excellent impression on the savage convertites: and Boris swore that henceforth he would be the loyal servant of the successor of St Peter.[6]

In the eight months between April and December 866, the splendid work of Bardas and Photius seemed to be toppling into irretrievable ruin. Bardas himself was murdered by an upstart adventurer. One more effort to recapture Crete had failed with the death of its promoter. And finally Bulgaria seemed to be slipping inevitably into the Roman camp, with all the unhappy consequences which that would entail. Almost as serious was the fact that in his 'Responsa' to Boris, the pope had included a number of articles which Byzantium must regard as insulting and heretical, and these insults and heresies the papal missionaries were now spreading far and wide in Bulgaria. Byzantium, said the pope, so far from being the senior patriarchate, was the fifth and most junior in rank. Clergy, in direct contradiction of Byzantine practice, were forbidden to marry. And, above all, it is now in Bulgaria, in 866, that the pope gives sanction to that doctrine or heresy which even today does more than any other question to exacerbate east-west controversy: the Doctrine of the Double Procession.

This celebrated aberration – if such it be – from the orthodox definition of 381, allows the Holy Spirit to 'proceed' (*procedere*), not from the Father only, but also from the Son: Spiritus qui ex Patre *Filioque* procedit. I shall not attempt to define the metaphysical bearing of this doctrine which, as Bury rightly says,[7] is as intelligible to an ordinary man as the postulate of a fourth dimension. The addition of *Filioque* seems to have been made in sixth-century Spain, and thence to have spread eastwards. By the ninth century it was approved by Rome, though it did not become dogma until the fifteenth. Great was the indignation of the east at this tampering with the Creed and at this corruption of the neophyte Bulgarians. And it seems to have been the article in Romish interference which chiefly prompted the retaliatory measures of the imperial government.

These measures were two. Photius resolved on calling a General Council in the summer of 867. In a voluminous letter to the eastern patriarchs he detailed the minor heresies introduced into Bulgaria by the Roman missionaries; but then:

Not merely were they deluded into these illegalities, but, if there be any summit of error, to this they have climbed up. For in addition to the said improprieties, even the holy and divine creed, which bases its impregnable authority on the decrees of all the Synodical and Ecumenical Councils, they have dared (alas for the snares of the Evil One!) to corrupt by bastard notions, and falsely inserted words, and by excess of criminal folly: for they have mischievously proclaimed that the Holy Spirit proceedeth, not from the Father alone, but also from the Son! Who has ever heard such a claim bursting from the mouth of even the most abandoned up till now? What crooked serpent has belched his poison into their hearts . . . ?

and so on. We need not follow the christological arguments of the patriarch. But he closes by adjuring his brethren to send their delegates to a council at Constantinople with all convenient speed, so that these blasphemies may be anathematised and the innocent Bulgars be snatched as brands from the burning.

Diplomacy was the second organ of imperial counter-attack, and here, too, we may see Photius as the prime mover. Pope Nicholas, in sending his missionaries into Bulgaria, had been nearly as eager to expel the missionaries of the Frankish as of the Byzantine church. He was indeed at feud with the hierarchy of Germany, into which his despotic violence had incautiously hurried him. King Lothar II had wished to repudiate his wife Theutberga and marry his beloved mistress Waldrada. The Frankish bishops of Cologne and Trier were disposed to allow this; but Pope Nicholas would have none of it. Lothar's elder brother, the Emperor Lewis II, king of Italy, a weak and unstable monarch, sided with his brother against the pope. Photius was not slow to make capital of the mounting animosity against Nicholas among western clergy and laity alike. His emissaries were in touch with the Emperor Lewis, and an agreement was speedily reached. The coming council would depose the pope, as the pope had deposed Photius three years before. Lewis would carry out the will of the Constantinopolitan council and remove Nicholas bodily from his seat. In return, the Byzantine government would do unto Lewis and his wife Engelberta even as they had done unto his great-great-grandfather Charles in 812. They would admit his imperial title, and they would salute Lewis as *Francorum imperator*.

The magnitude of this concession on the part of Byzantium should not be underestimated. It is true that there was the single acknowledged precedent for such recognition, but this had been granted in a wholly different set of circumstances. Even over the recognition of Charles the Byzantines were ashamed and uneasy. His almost equally powerful son Lewis the Pious they would not overtly recognise: to them he had resumed his rightful position of *rex Francorum*. Now, a petty king of Italy, insecure, harassed, scarcely acknowledged as emperor by his own relatives in the west, was to be saluted, not simply in Italy, but also at Byzantium, as a titular equal to the master of the world and the elect of Christ. When we assess the various factors which in the year 867 contributed to the violent unpopularity of Photius in the City, and to his unopposed dismissal in September of that year, we must not leave out of account this outrageous stroke of political opportunism. The Emperor Michael III, who, feeble and dissolute as he was, might have been expected to make difficulties over such an infringement of his own status and prerogative, in fact made none at all. Religious and political postulates which lay at the very root of his empire's existence had no meaning for that cynical and frivolous spirit who, freed from his uncle Bardas' prudent guidance, was sinking with fearful rapidity into the state of an habitual sot. To one who had promoted a groom to the throne, and was threatening to promote a creature yet more debased to the same imperial dignity, it mattered very little that the title of *basileus* should be shared with a fourth, the king of Italy.

The council met at the end of August 867. It condemned all heresies far and near, including the Roman heresies then proliferating in Bulgaria. It proclaimed Pope Nicholas deposed and anathematised. And it saluted Lewis and Engelbertha as emperor and empress of the Franks. It was Photius' last triumph for a decade. In a final panegyrical sermon, the only document which survives from the ill-fated council, he extolled the Emperor Michael the Sot as the new Christ on earth, who, with a stroke of his pen, had laid all heresy low and restored peace and unity and orthodoxy to the terrestrial universe.

Events now followed with dramatic rapidity. The Acts of the Council were dispatched to Rome. But ere they could reach the imperial frontier, the co-emperor Basil, now desperately alarmed by the insane frolics of his senior colleague, had Michael brutally murdered by a gang of bravoes. Next day, 24 September 867, Photius, whose own conduct had been closely associated with the Amorian house, was dismissed and exiled. The Acts of the Council were recalled and destroyed. Basil mounted the throne as sole emperor and, as a first step in the new epoch which was to commence, recalled Ignatius to the patriarchal chair. Basil hastily despatched an embassy to the pope to inform him that the Lateran decree of 863 had at length been implemented, and that the true patriarch was back in his palace. It came too late. On 13 November the great pope died, and the pacific Hadrian II soon succeeded him.

Such in brief was the origin of the great Ignatian-Photian scandal and of the so-called Photian schism. Scholars of west and east have long wrangled about the rights and wrongs of it and will doubtless continue to do so. Let us, however, take heed of the facts, and above all remember that we are dealing with statesmen and churchmen of the early middle ages, not of our own twentieth century, who acted from motives, and in ways, which only a strong effort of historical imagination can recreate for us today.[8]

NOTES

1 Theoph. Cont., 673; Bury, ERE, 187.
2 Theoph. Cont., 193–4.
3 Bury, ERE, 194–5.
4 Bréhier, 118–21; Ostrogorsky, 188.
5 Bury, ERE, 199.
6 Bury, ERE, 389–92.
7 Bury, ERE, 206.
8 Ostrogorsky, 178, note 3, 188–9; Bréhier, 117–21; Bury, ERE, 180–209.

CHAPTER FOURTEEN

BASIL THE MACEDONIAN

Basil the Macedonian, who seized the supreme power – he was of course already emperor, but now on 24 September 867 became chief emperor, or *autokrator* – inaugurated the greatest and most glorious dynasty ever to sit on the Byzantine throne. The so-called 'Macedonian' epoch, which lasted until the death of Basil's great-great-great-grand-daughter Theodora in 1056, that is to say, for a period of 189 years, coincided with the empire's greatest military and cultural expansion. At the beginning of this epoch, the Byzantine empire effectively controlled Asia Minor, Thrace, part of Macedonia, Hellas and Peloponnesus, and, rather ineffectively, the southern part of Italy. At its close, Byzantine power reached from the Araxes river to the toe of Italy and from the Crimea to Tripolis in Syria. Cyprus was retaken, and Crete. Above all, the north-western boundary ran once more along the Danube and the Drava to the Dalmatian coast, for the whole of Bulgaria was reduced to the imperial provinces of Sirmium, Paristrion and Central Bulgaria. The armies of Byzantium were seemingly irresistible, her treasures seemingly endless, her political and spiritual influence paramount in areas far beyond her boundaries. Such was the power and prestige of the ruling house that, when at last it declined to extinction, the eleventh-century historian and statesman Psellus could sum up its achievement in these memorable words: 'I doubt if any other family has ever been so much favoured by God as theirs has been: which is odd, when you come to think of the unlawful manner of its establishment, and how it was planted in slaughter and blood. None the

183

less, the plant took root, and sent out such mighty shoots, each bearing royal fruit, that none other can be compared with it for beauty and splendour'.[1]

It is, as the historian remarks, odd when you come to think of it: when you think of the glories of the Amorian house, when you think of the political genius of the Caesar Bardas and the military genius of his brother Petronas, and the statesmanship and cultivation of the great Patriarch Photius, all nullified by the desperate crimes of an Armenian groom. The best proof that Basil the Macedonian really was a man of no ordinary gifts and abilities, is found in the fact that his empire, so far from experiencing a decisive setback at his accession, actually continued on its path of progress and consolidation and was on balance appreciably stronger at his death in 886 than at his coming to rule in 867.

It is not to be supposed that his elevation met with no resistance. The Amorian dynasty, though fearfully and, as it proved, fatally shaken by the murder of the Caesar Bardas, was powerfully entrenched both in church and state. But that there was no strong or sustained uprising against the usurper, either in the capital or outside it, is striking testimony to the ability and tact of Basil and also to the disgust engendered by the deplorable follies of Michael III during the year 866-7.

First came the dismission of Photius, an act which cannot have been contemplated by the new sovereign without certain knowledge that this would be a popular measure. Those who try to represent it as an arbitrary and spiteful act against the Amorians, for which there was no general demand or approval, altogether forget that, had this been so, Basil could never have attempted it. He knew that Photius had disgraced himself in the eyes of the public by his condonation of the murder of Bardas, by his refusal to condemn the outrages of Michael, and by his cynical manoeuvring with King Lewis of Italy. In one of his blasphemous freaks, the late Emperor Michael had set up a buffoon called Gryllus (which means hog) to act as patriarch in some disgusting parodies of church ceremonial. 'Gryllus is my patriarch', observed his Majesty, 'Photius is my uncle Bardas's, and Ignatius is the people's'. We must suppose the Emperor Michael to have been at least as good a judge of these matters as any modern historian could be. Ignatius was thus recalled, and the Photian appointments and ordinations invalidated. But this by no means meant, as was hoped in extremist circles, a diminution in the secular authority. Basil had made the change as an act of policy; but he knew well enough who was to be master, and had no intention of reverting to the position of a Michael I or of a Theodora. In striking contrast to the cynical and irresponsible Michael III, Basil was strongly imbued with a sense of the overwhelming dignity and importance of his position. Pope Hadrian, who had inherited the policies, if not the energy, of his predecessor, and who interpreted Basil's dismissal of Photius and his consequent reconciliation with the Roman see as the weakness of an insecure upstart, soon discovered his mistake.

Basil was the first emperor since Constans II – not to say, since Justinian I – who had a settled programme for the recovery of the West, which, for him as for his predecessors, meant Dalmatia, Venice and, most important of all, Italy south of the Papal State. For success in at any rate the third of these spheres a composition with the pope and the 'Emperor' Lewis II was indispensable, and he instantly opened negotiations with both. He began by inviting Pope Hadrian to send his legates to a council at Constantinople for the healing of the schism so recklessly opened by Photius. But Pope Hadrian misunderstood the emperor's motives; and concluded that, as the price of papal support for his still precarious throne, he was prepared to concede all the supremacy demanded for the pope in the Donation of Constantine, and to repent the rebellion of his predecessor in sackcloth and ashes. The papal delegates arrived at Constantinople in 869, with the idea that they were to preside the council; and they began by demanding that all the bishops who attended it should subscribe a *libellus satisfactionis* which acknowledged the primacy of Rome. These demands created a painful impression. The emperor made it clear that the presidency was his own. And very few orthodox bishops could bring themselves to sign this libel and to attend the earlier sessions. At length the ostensible cause of the council was reached, the condemnation and expulsion of Photius. The papal legates were anxious that Photius should not be heard, but again Basil would not agree. The ex-patriarch was summoned and examined. He saw it all: and knew perfectly well that, though he would now be condemned, time was on his side if he kept his head. When he was asked for his defence, he declined to plead; and with characteristic arrogance answered only with the words of Our Saviour when examined before Pilate. A still worse disappointment awaited the papal delegates. Early in 870, when the council was still in session, the envoys of that master-tactician Boris-Michael of Bulgaria appeared before it, and asked the assembly, representative as it was both of east and west, to determine to which jurisdiction his new Christian state did in fact belong. The answer was a foregone conclusion. The papal delegates, finding themselves in a substantial minority and in the very heart of the rival citadel, made feeble protests but naturally to no purpose whatever. Basil decreed that the decision should rest with the ostensibly neutral patriarchates of the east: and these found without hesitation for Byzantium. The pope's demands were drastically edited in the Greek version of the Acts, and his reference to the 'Emperor' Lewis II was excised. His delegates left for Rome with heavy hearts. But even so their trials were not over. In the Adriatic they were set upon by Narentane pirates and stripped of all but their lives. Both the pope and the Emperor Lewis believed, or professed to believe, that this crowning insult was no accident, and that the Emperor Basil was at the bottom of the affair.[2]

To do Basil justice, he had been sincere enough in wishing for a more pacific outcome of the Council, if for no other reason than that it formed but one part of his double offensive in Italy. The other part was military, and involved the Emperor Lewis.[3] The negotiations with Lewis between 868 and 870 are obscure to us in detail, but the progress of events appears to have been as follows. During the past forty years Byzantine power in Sicily, Italy and Dalmatia had been seriously impaired by the invasions of the African Saracens. Syracuse held out. But, in Italy, the Saracen capture of Bari and Taranto in 840–1 gave the invaders a firm hold on the country during the next thirty years, a hold which could not be broken except by land and sea forces acting in concert. The area itself was partitioned between the Lombard duchies of Capua-Benevento and Salerno which Lewis claimed as vassals, and the nominally Byzantine but in fact independent cities of Naples, Amalfi and Gaeta. The Byzantine ports of Otranto, Bari and Gallipoli were in Saracen hands. Basil determined to re-establish Byzantine power over the whole area, but nothing could be done without the help of the Franks who represented the only military power on the mainland of Italy which was capable of confronting the Saracens.

The obvious policy therefore was an alliance with the Franks on the lines of that which had been attempted by Theophilus in 838. In 868, Basil dispatched an embassy to Lewis, who was then already, but fruitlessly, besieging Bari, and offered the indispensable naval support of the empire in the undertaking. He also promised to recognise the latter's imperial status, as Michael III had done in the previous year, provided that Lewis would give the hand of his daughter in marriage to Basil's eldest and dearest son, the young prince Constantine. The plan was well conceived. Lewis had no male heir; and once more the project of uniting the imperial houses and domains of east and west by a dynastic marriage seemed to be within the bounds of possibility.

This embassy was favourably received by Lewis. Basil, who had at command a splendid naval force which had been built up by the energy of the Logothete Theoctistus and the Caesar Bardas, embarked on it a considerable armament and dispatched it during the summer of 869 to Bari. The Byzantine admiral Nicetas arrived in Italy after the campaigning season was over; and he found the Frankish forces, which were in any case numerically below his expectations, dispersed in winter quarters and, as he noted with contempt, given over to wine and song. So much infuriated was he at this, that, in his message to Lewis to announce his arrival and to claim Lewis' daughter, he addressed the emperor as *king* of the Franks. A heated altercation ensued, and resulted in the departure of at least the main part of the Byzantine armament, without the Frankish princess and without the reduction of Bari. Lewis sent an embassy hard on the admiral's heels, which arrived in Constantinople early in 870, in time to coincide with the final sessions of the anti-Photian Council. This embassy complained bitterly of the admiral's insolence, and took occasion to vindicate in some detail Lewis' claim, not only to the imperial style, but also to the style of *imperator Romanorum*, with which he had been invested in 850 by papal coronation.[4]

This was a moment of very great significance in Byzantine relations with the west. The quarrel which Charles the Great had done his utmost to avoid, and which had been no more than latent during the reigns of his son and grandson, now at length burst out with fury between his great-grandson and the founder of the Macedonian dynasty. The moderate title of emperor *of the Franks*, allowed formally and with much reluctance to Charles in virtue of his European overlordship, was now discarded, and Lewis, master of less than a single kingdom, put forward the pretension to universal sovereignty in virtue of that very papal authority which Charles had disliked and repulsed. Basil's chancery drew up a *verbosa et grandis epistula*, now unfortunately lost. In it, the admiral's conduct was fully approved. Lewis was stigmatised as a usurper, along with his father and grandfather. A wealth of arguments, scriptural, dogmatic, historical and even philological, was expended to prove that the concept of empire was one and indivisible, and that this empire was the legitimate heritage of him whom Christ had set on the throne of Constantinople. It subjoined some bitter invectives against the slackness of Lewis' troops, and the baselessness of his territorial claims both in South Italy and Dalmatia. This reply was addressed to Lewis at nearly the same time as the pope's legates returned from the anti-Photian Council.

Meanwhile, with or without Byzantine naval assistance (the accounts are naturally conflicting), Bari was at length stormed in February 871. Lewis put its government in the hands of a Lombard gastald, and retired to Benevento, whose Lombard duke, Adelchis, received him with considerable coldness and misgiving. Here, sometime between March and August of 871, was composed, by Anastasius Bibliothecarius in Lewis' name, that celebrated letter to Basil which survives *in toto* in the pages of the *Chronicle of Salerno*. It is our chief source for the matter in dispute between the two empires at this time, and everyone who would understand the quarrel must study it carefully.5

The letter sets out in full the papal prerogative, according to the Donation of Constantine, of crowning and anointing the emperor of the Romans, and the claim of Lewis to be that emperor. It is in fact addressed from 'Lewis, by the Grace of God, Emperor Augustus *of the Romans*' to the emperor of New Rome: that is to say, to the emperor of that obscure *provincia* whither Constantine the Great had withdrawn. With the most provoking and wilful misunderstanding of Basil's position, Anastasius declares that, after diligent searching of the Scriptures and of profane history, he can find no support for Basil's claim that none but the Constantinopolitan emperor can be *basileus*. On the contrary: were not Melchisidek and David so denominated? Were there not *basileis* in Assyria, and Egypt, and Moab, not to speak of those among the Persians, Epirotes, Hindus, Parthians, Ethiopians and Vandals? As to the claim that all patriarchs recognise a single *basileus* only, this is repugnant to fact and common sense: for Lewis is acknowledged to be such by the eastern patriarchs (Anastasius refers to the unlucky Council of August 867), by the pope, and also by those senior sovereigns, his own uncles. The term *rigas*, with which Basil seeks to diminish him – what is that? Is it not a Greek barbarism for the Latin *rex*? And what is the Greek for *rex*, if it be not *basileus*?

All this is very diverting, no doubt; but it is mere skirmishing, and does not touch the heart of the matter. This is reached in a single paragraph where the whole theory of double empire is expounded in terms which illustrate very clearly the unbridgeable cleavage between Frankish and Constantinopolitan theory.

But, however this may be [Anastasius proceeds], if the patriarchs, during the holy sacrament and sacrifice, do make mention of a single empire only, they are right to do so. For the empire is in fact one – of the Father, the Son and the Holy Ghost: Their Church on earth is a part of it. But God has not granted it to be governed either by me or by you alone, but to us both, on condition that we should be so bound in the bonds of love that no division can be between us, and that we should be united in one single authority.

We are justified [he continues] in feeling some astonishment that your Serenity should believe that we are taking to ourselves a new and recent title. This title we owe to the author of our line, our great-grandfather of glorious memory. He did not usurp it, as you maintain, but received it by the will of God, and by judgment of the Church, on the day when he was consecrated and anointed by the sovereign pontiff, as you shall find it written in your own books. This was, at that time, no doubt a novelty. But when the first Roman princes assumed the imperial power, that too was a novelty, which in the lapse of time has acquired antiquity. All that is new is not necessarily on that account to be reprehended. For the Apostle saith to his beloved son, not 'shun the words that are new', but rather 'shun the new words that are profane'.

And finally, in words which defend the papal position and the papal right to elect the emperor *of the Romans*, the letter proceeds:

Your Fraternity should also cease to wonder that we adopt the style of emperor *of the Romans*, and not that of emperor *of the Franks*. For it imports that you should consider that, if we were not emperor of the

Romans, we should not be that of the Franks either. *It is in fact from Rome that we derive our style and our origin*; it is there that we have received the charge to protect and to enlarge that Mother of all the Churches, which conferred upon our line first the royal, then the imperial authority. Now, if you impute it for a crime to the Roman pontiff that he has conferred on us that distinction, you must also incriminate Samuel, who, rejecting Saul, whom he had with his own hands anointed, scrupled not afterwards to anoint David as king. It is the Greeks who, in their blindness and heretical spirit, have lost the faith, abandoned the city, and the seat of empire, the Roman nation and the very tongue of Rome, and migrated to distant parts.

These words breathe the very essence of the Donation of Constantine.

To this edifying epistle, which the Byzantines regarded as blasphemous nonsense, the Emperor Basil naturally did not trouble himself to reply. He had more effectual methods of bringing Lewis to reason; and the arrogant conduct of Lewis towards the Lombard duke Adelchis at Benevento played straight into his hands. With Byzantine connivance and help a Lombard conspiracy was set on foot; and in August 872, Lewis, recently returned from another brilliant victory over the Saracens at Capua, was surprised, held prisoner during thirty days at Benevento, and released only on a promise, sworn on the Holy Gospels, that he would never again come with arms into the territories of the duchy. This was the death-blow to the ambitions of Lewis in South Italy, and a splendid victory for Byzantine diplomacy. Lewis retired to Ravenna, and died four years later without leaving an heir.

Meanwhile, the western policy of Basil was pursued with energy, though not everywhere with success. The *theme* of Dalmatia was founded about 870. Missionary work was undertaken, *pari passu* with that among the Slavs of Hellas, among the Slavs of the Narenta, and a *modus vivendi* established between the empire, the Slavs and the old Roman cities of the Dalmatian coast. Venice, which had always preferred Byzantine to Frankish suzerainty, knitted her ties with the former, while prudently paying a peppercorn tribute to the *regnum italicum*. The Byzantine reconquest and recolonisation of Southern Italy steadily continued, though interrupted by some fearful defeats at the hands of the Saracens. Otranto was secured in 873, and Bari occupied in 876. The celebrated general Nicephorus Phocas, grandfather of the emperor Nicephorus II, during the years 884–6 did more than any other to consolidate Byzantine power in this area, and showed military and administrative talents which are singled out for special commendation by Basil's son and successor Leo VI. The occupation of the South Italian mainland was wisely chosen in preference to the now hopeless task of recovering Sicily, which, with the fall of Syracuse in 878, fell almost wholly into the power of the African Saracens. The foot of Italy was, about the year 892, organised into the regular *themes* of Calabria and Lagoubardia (Lombardy). This re-establishment of imperial power in Italy, on the initiative of Basil I, was a real achievement. It endured for two centuries, and was palpable witness to the never forgotten claim of the Byzantine crown to supremacy in the west as in the east.

Basil's operations in the west had, as we have seen, brought his forces into sharp contact with the Saracens of Africa and of Sicily. But in truth, throughout his reign, he was at war with Saracens by land in his eastern borders, especially with the bellicose emir of Tarsus, and by sea with the fleets of Syria, Egypt and Crete. The land fighting in Asia was carried on with varying fortune, but always with energy. The most lasting success came with the final destruction of the heretical Paulician power, which, since the persecutions of Leo V and Theodora, had grown very menacing indeed among the refugees beyond the Saracen border. They had shared to the full in the disaster at Poson in 863; but, by 870, they were again raiding the empire with the Saracens of Melitene from their fortified city of Tephrike on the border of the Armeniac province. Basil in two campaigns overthrew these gallant heretics, killed their chief, Chrysocheir, and razed Tephrike to the ground. The survivors were prudently enlisted in the Byzantine regular army, and sent to Italy, under the command of Nicephorus Phocas.

The destruction of Tephrike opened the way for a general offensive beyond the frontier, which is one of the first indications that the tide, halted in 863, was about to turn, and which prefigured the spectacular campaigns of John Courcouas, Nicephorus II and Zimiskes in the next century. The siege operations against Melitene and Adata and Germanicia were failures, it is true. But the Byzantine armies, led by Christopher and the brilliant Slav marshal Andrew Craterus, were everywhere victorious in the open field, and did enormous damage to the enemy potential, even if they did not succeed in substantially expanding the frontier. Only a severe defeat near Tarsus in 883 brought the Byzantine offensive eastwards to a temporary halt.[6]

Basil's naval campaigns are especially notable. He was excellently served by his admirals, all of whom had seen service under Theodora or Michael. Hadrian, Nasar, and above all Nicetas Ooryphas brought the reputation of the Byzantine navy to the highest pitch reached by it at any time in Byzantine history. It may well have been Basil who initiated the policy wisely pursued by his son and grandson, of developing the fleet as a specially favoured force bound by special ties to the person of the legitimate emperor: and of this we shall have more to say. But we find in the boyhood of Constantine VII veteran salts who had rowed in the galleys of his grandfather Basil, and whose loyalty and attachment to the reigning house could with difficulty be paralleled in the land forces, even among the imperial guards.

The fruits of this naval expansion were soon apparent in home waters. The Saracens of Crete had roamed almost at will over the Aegean and Ionian seas during about fifty years. The areas of their infestation are apparent from the account which Basil's grandson gives us of their depredations. They raided the Ionian Islands, they raided Peloponnesus, they raided Euboea and even Proconnesus in the Hellespont. Now they were to meet a naval power no less energetic and far more efficient than their own. In a series of brilliant campaigns Nasar and Ooryphas inflicted crushing defeats on the marauders; and there is some evidence, though of late date, that Basil actually occupied Crete.[7]

Nor must the great benefits of Basil's legislative programme go unrecorded, even in a brief summary such as this. The revision of the legal code carried out by the iconoclasts a hundred and fifty years before was by now itself inadequate, and the code of Justinian had degenerated into an inextricable confusion of precedents and anachronisms. Basil decided on a 'Purification' of the old laws, in which the common law was to be reduced to a workable system, and, where necessary, revised: especially where the gap between the civil and religious codes was too wide to allow of compromise. This immense work was begun under Basil, and completed under his son. But Basil himself published a preliminary Handbook of practical administration, which had great authority in the empire and outside it, since it was soon translated into Slavonic. Of Basil's second legal work, the 'Summary', we shall speak in connexion with the second patriarchate of Photius.

For it is time to tell of the perplexed and controversial events which marked Basil's internal government during the last nine years of his reign (877–86), and to endeavour to present a rational explanation of them. And here at the outset, a caution must be uttered. These events are narrated by our sources, with a marked degree of unanimity, in a fashion so bizarre that to a modern critic they appear almost legendary. Hence many modern historians reject them altogether, because such events would in our own day be unthinkable. But I do not believe we can afford to brush aside such testimony, any more than we can brush aside the testimony which condemns the public and private life of Michael III, as altogether partial, malicious and fantastical. I stick to my principle: Byzantine historians certainly omitted, but, generally speaking, did not invent or fabricate. They record, if not truth, at least what men of those times said and believed to be true. And it is our duty, not to reject such testimony as fabulous, but rather to criticise it as a reflection or facet of truth, if not the exact truth itself.

Photius went into exile on 25 September 867. He was, at first, harshly treated, though not by any means as harshly as Ignatius had been treated in 859–60. He was a clever man, who bided his time. He knew very well that his clerical followers were as numerous and enthusiastic as the Ignatians, and that the Ignatians simply had not got the brains or the numbers to govern the church on their own. Some compromise was sooner or later inevitable, if not another complete revolution in favour of the Photian party. It was merely a matter of patience. Meanwhile, though condemned by the Council of 869–70, he never made the blunder of setting himself in opposition to the crown, as Ignatius had done in 857: and he observed with satisfaction the arrogance of the papal delegates and the rebuffs which their arrogance called down on them.

His patience and wisdom were amply rewarded: and indeed it would have required faults and follies of a very unusual description to keep such a man, so experienced, so learned, so urbane, permanently in the background. It was not long before his expectations were fulfilled. His clergy were found to be indispensable,

especially since the return of Bulgaria to orthodoxy put a pre-
mium on clergymen of learning, ability and statesmanship. A few
years afterwards, much if not most of the missionary endeavour in
that country was in the hands of Photians, and it is easy to see
why. Ignatius wisely connived at this: for it is a truth which knows
no exceptions that to be out of office and irresponsible is an altogether different thing from being responsible and in office.
Ignatius therefore asked the pope to reconsider the validity of
Photian orders. The pope, exasperated by the loss of Bulgaria and
the resolute conduct of Basil, testily refused. Thereupon the Byzantine church went its own way without further consultation with
Rome: and something like a reconciliation between the Photian
and Ignatian secular clergy was established. After this, there could
be no reason for detaining Photius himself in exile. He was recalled – the date is uncertain, but it was probably about the year
873-4 – to Constantinople, put once more in charge of the
Magnaura University, appointed tutor to the young Emperor Leo,
then eight years of age, and given a verbal assurance that, if
Ignatius predeceased him, he should be patriarch once more.

Now, how is this restoration described in our sources? Photius,
it is said, employed an agent called Theodore of Santabaris. This
man was a thorough-paced villain and a practiser of the black art.
Photius devised and wrote out in old-fashioned capital letters a
fictitious genealogy of the Emperor Basil, which made him out a
descendant of the old Arsacid dynasty of Parthia. This rigmarole
he made an agent place in the imperial library, and produce as if
by chance. When the emperor desired an interpretation, Theodore
said that only Photius was learned enough to interpret. Photius
was therefore summoned to the palace and never returned to
exile.[8] I see no reason to doubt the substantial truth of this anecdote. If it were wholly untrue, who could have made it up? And
who but Photius knew enough about Parthians and uncial
characters to make such a tale convincing? No one would deny
that Photius was recalled as a matter of policy: but why should he
not also have tried such a trick to keep his name and learning before Basil's eye? It seems wrong to reject such a stratagem on the
part of a ninth-century prelate because we should not believe it
of the late Archbishop Temple.

Photius grew upon the emperor's affections daily. And when, in
October 877, the aged Ignatius died, Photius quietly stepped into

his shoes. Everyone acted with perfect good sense. In January 880 a council in Constantinople, attended by the legates of Pope John VIII, completely rehabilitated Photius, without any *quid pro quo* other than a recognition of Rome's primacy among the churches; and an assurance from Photius that he would be only too happy to hand over Bulgaria to the pope if the matter lay with him; but, unhappily, it did not. It was a matter for the Emperor Basil, and who could say how he might decide ?9

Who, indeed ? For he was by this time a grief-stricken recluse. And in explaining how this came about, we enter the deepest and most sinister labyrinth of conjecture which hides the last tragic years of the Emperor Basil.

Basil had a son called Constantine, born of his first wife Maria. In 865 the irresponsible Michael III had compelled his favourite to divorce his wife and to marry the aristocrat Eudocia, whom he had once thought of marrying himself. By this union Basil had three sons, Leo born in 866, Stephen in 867 and Alexander in 870. The eldest son Constantine was probably the only human creature that Basil ever loved, and he loved him with a doting fondness. He made him co-emperor in 869, and built on this lad all his hopes for the continuance of the dynasty. The boy seemed to fulfil all his desires. He accompanied his father on his Saracen campaigns and triumphed with him, clad in golden armour, and mounted on a white charger. It was he whom Basil had planned to marry to the daughter of Lewis II, and perhaps saw the boy one day as the new Augustus, stretching his power and providence over east and west, over pope and patriarch. In 879 Constantine, for whom so much greatness was planned and prognosticated, was about twenty years of age. On 3 September of that year a ceremony took place in the palace with gloomy pomp and solemnity. The Patriarch Photius stood at the gate and intoned a celebrated formula: 'Come forth, O King! Thou art summoned to appear before the King of Kings'. The unbelievable had happened. On a sudden, in the twinkling of an eye, the Almighty had put forth his finger, and the young sovereign was gone.10

It needs little imagination to understand that the effects of this disaster went very far beyond the grief experienced at the loss of a darling child and the defeat of a darling ambition. First and foremost, it meant that God had after all not forgotten the night of 23 September twelve years before, and the Emperor Michael lying in his own blood on the floor of the palace bed-chamber at St Mamas. He had thus shown His displeasure, and this displeasure was but a foretaste of the eternal torments of hell. Had Zimri peace who slew his master? The strain was not to be borne. The Emperor Basil went out of his mind, and continued during the next seven years to be subject to fits of derangement. There was a poetic justice in this, for Michael too had been nearly a madman at the end.

And now a rumour more hideous still began to spread. Photius was the man of the hour, and Photius held the half-demented emperor in the hollow of his hand. His control was made more absolute by a cunning manoeuvre. He promised to canonise the dead prince as a saint and, incredible as it appears, he kept his promise. This is a historical fact. His agent Theodore, for whom at his own restoration Photius had carved out the rich archbishopric of Euchaita, went further. He undertook the grisly task of necromancy. The emperor hid himself in a glade. All at once a familiar figure in bright arms was seen to ride towards him. Basil staggered forward to clasp the phantom, which melted away in his embrace.[11]

These, it will be agreed, are very deep waters. But we are not yet ashore. Photius and his creature Theodore (so the story goes on) then went to work to discredit the next heir, Leo, in the eyes of the deluded father. In August 883 a plot was devised which seemed to lay the prince open to a charge of high treason. He was seized, imprisoned, and was within an ace of being blinded; but this was not the intention of Photius, who was too wise and, let us admit, too good a man to allow such an atrocity. Yet the opinion was rife that Photius had practised against the imperial house with the object of putting one of his own relatives on the throne. Impossible, we are tempted to say. But was it after all quite so impossible as that?

For consider: the greatest blow to Photius' career and prospects had been the murder of Caesar Bardas. The next greatest was the murder of Michael III. Both were the work of Basil. Is it not at least possible that the proud patriarch had never been reconciled to the new order, and had always had a hankering after a return of the Amorians? One of his own relatives? Well, but Photius was a marriage connexion of the Amorian house itself. Photius was intellectually far above his contemporaries, but there is no evidence that he was morally so, nor should we require him to be. I do not say that this rumour was true. But I do say that it must be considered in all its bearings before it is rejected. It is fact that Theodore of Santabaris was Photius' agent, and was richly rewarded. It is fact that when Theodore, after Basil's death, was put to the question, he implicated Photius. It is fact that the Emperor Leo VI, after patient enquiry, believed that both were guilty of practice and treason. These, I say, are deep waters: and the reader must get himself into port as best he may.

The plot, if such it were, failed. The long and unjust imprisonment of young Leo caused rioting, and Basil, after three years, very grudgingly liberated his son. A few days afterwards, on 29 August 886, he himself died as the result of a hunting accident. The circumstances as published at the time were altogether incredible, because physically impossible. And it seems likely that Vogt is right in assuming that the fierce, mad old tyrant was murdered by his son's friends. At least this was the report which some months later leaked out to the Saracens. If it were so, the wheel had come full circle. Michael, dangerously mad, was murdered by his adopted son Basil. Basil, dangerously mad, was murdered by his son Leo. And who shall say that the middle ages were wrong in reposing their trust in the Divine Justice and Retribution ?

NOTES

[1] Psellus, I, 117.
[2] Ostrogorsky, 195–6.
[3] Theoph, Cont., 293.
[4] Bréhier, 130.
[5] Ostrogorsky, 197 and note 2, Vasiliev, 326.
[6] Theoph. Cont., 269–70, 280–1; Ostrogorsky, 197–8.
[7] Theoph. Cont., 298–312.
[8] Theoph. Cont., 689–90.
[9] Vasiliev, 331–2; Bréhier, 125–6.
[10] Theoph. Cont., 345.
[11] Theoph. Cont., 844–7.

CHAPTER FIFTEEN

LEO THE WISE

The Emperor Leo VI, known by reason of his scholarly tastes and pursuits as the 'Wise' or the 'Philosopher', governed the empire for twenty-six years (886–912). His reputation has suffered from the fact that our chief source for his reign, the so-called *Chronicle of the Logothete*, is violently prejudiced against his house, and, as is usual in such cases, shows this prejudice by the omission of anything that would redound to his credit. But, fortunately for him, there is a cloud of other witness to the essential goodness of his character and to the soundness of his policies. Anyone who reads the Chronicler's account would conclude that between the death of Basil and the rise of Romanus I nothing whatsoever was done against the eastern Saracens. This is absolutely untrue. Leo's eastern policy continued what had been started in that area, and his work was the essential basis for future advance. This is but one instance of misrepresentation, or rather of suppression.

Leo was born on 1 September 866, the eldest child of Basil I by his second wife Eudocia. As he was born while Michael III was still living, and as Eudocia had once been a favourite of Michael, malicious court gossip gave it out that Leo was not Basil's son, but Michael's. Recent scholarship has rightly come to the conclusion that this innuendo is altogether unfounded. It is true that some of the reasons given nowadays for discrediting it are not such as would stand up to a very searching cross-examination. But there seems to be one which is irrefutable: Leo was not Michael's child because Michael had no children, and in all probability could not have any, either by Eudocia or by anybody else. How far his homosexual tendency and his incurable alcoholism contributed to this state of affairs we need not now enquire, although contemporaries did; but the fact seems to be indisputable.

Leo was bred a scholar. His tastes were bookish. He was also deeply religious, and he delighted in composing and delivering sermons (of which several survive), and in writing hymns and religious homilies. There is a tradition that he was taught by the great Photius; but if this is true, it can only have been for a very short time (c. 875–7), and it certainly did not engender any feelings of gratitude or affection in the pupil, who cordially detested the tutor for reasons which we have already hinted at.[1]

Leo's character is known to us from many documents. First and foremost, he was a lovable man, capable of inspiring and retaining the affection of men of widely different views, even of men who disliked his policies. This was a very rare and a very important quality in an emperor. So far as we recollect, he was hated only by his more immediate relatives, his father Basil, and his brother Alexander: and this only for dynastic reasons. The eulogies on his charm and kindliness may in some cases be exaggerated: but nobody applied these compliments to Basil, still less to Alexander. In his youth he was choleric to excess. His outbursts of rage were dreadful to witness. But he knew his weakness and manfully, and at last successfully, strove to control it. He was also in youth given to sexual licence, but not outrageously so; and the circumstance that he married four times is no proof of licentiousness, but was dictated solely by the necessity of leaving a male heir to succeed him. His portrait survives in a celebrated monument, the great mosaic in the narthex of St Sophia, where he may be seen bending low in adoration at the throne of Grace.

Leo was just thirteen years old when his half-brother Constantine died suddenly in 879. His disappointed father Basil, who had never cared for him, now developed a violent dislike of the bookish youth, and treated him with brutality and contempt. In 882, at the age of sixteen, Leo was married to a cousin of the empress Eudocia, a plain, pious woman called Theophano, whom he never loved. He consoled himself with a mistress, and for this piece of insubordination he was kicked and pummelled by his father till the blood ran down. Shortly afterwards, in August 883, he was accused of treason and locked up for three whole years. Basil's death, as we saw, followed in August 886, soon after Leo's liberation: though whether Leo had any hand in this cannot now be certainly determined.

At once the whole administration changed. The friends of Leo, who with him had been the victims of the false charge of treason and rebellion, came to power, and began a savage persecution of their political enemies. Field-Marshal Andrew, Leo's spiritual brother, was made magister; but the chief power in the realm was confided to the father of the emperor's mistress, Stylianus Zaützes, who seems to have been partly Armenian and partly negro. He was an able man who kept his office till his death in 899, and we should not be too prone to believe the complaints of his enemies against his tyranny. Almost the first act of the new government was to depose Photius. Photius was once more ejected from the patriarchate, and induced to sign an act of abdication. And on Christmas Day, 886, the emperor's own brother, the nineteen-year old Stephen, was enthroned as ecumenical patriarch.

This appointment, which had been planned by Basil, is highly significant. It was the final step in the subordination of church to state. The Ignatian-Photian controversy, dragging on year after year, had convinced that clear-headed emperor that the sovereign could be master in his own house only if the patriarchate were vested in someone who could in no circumstances demur to imperial policies: that is, in a near blood-relative. This plan was highly successful during the five years that Stephen lived to enjoy the office: and, as we shall see, it was revived by Romanus I, who appointed his son Theophylact to the same seat.[2]

This in itself was a good reason for dismissing Photius. But there were certainly others. That Leo hated the old patriarch personally is undoubted. That Photius had acted despotically during the last years of Basil's reign and that, in his Preface to the law-book of the *Epanagoge* (or Summary), he had defined the position of the patriarch *vis-à-vis* the emperor in a manner quite irregular, and even bordering on treason, is likewise well known. But these reasons, good in themselves, were not the chief. It was asserted and believed that Photius in 883 had been involved in a substantive treason: and the government meant to get to the bottom of this. The enquiry lasted for several months, and then, in 887, Photius and his creature, Theodore of Santabaris, were confronted before an imperial tribunal in the Palace of Pege, beyond the city wall. By a lucky chance the process has survived, at least in part:

and reveals clearly what the prosecution had in mind. Theodore was interrogated by the Magister Andrew and by Photius' cousin, the Magister Stephen: 'Whom did you propose to make emperor when you advised the late emperor to blind his own son? Was it to be one of your relations, or one of the Patriarch Photius'?' Theodore said: 'I don't know what you are talking about.' Stephen said: 'Then why did you promise the emperor that you would convict the patriarch of this?' Theodore fell at Photius' feet: 'My lord', he cried, 'in God's name depose me, then let them punish me as a malefactor. I never told the emperor any such thing!' Photius said: 'By the salvation of my soul, Master Theodore, thou art archbishop both now and in the world to come.' Andrew was furious: 'Do you mean to deny', he shouted, 'that you told the emperor through me that you would prove this on the patriarch?' But Theodore continued obstinate. He was exiled and blinded. Photius retired to a monastery. The very year of his death is unknown. To such an obscure and pitiful end had come so much statesmanship, so much learning and so much glory. We need say no more of guilt or innocence.3

It is customary to represent the foreign and military policy of Leo the Wise as uniformly unsuccessful and even disastrous, and true it is that his reign was marked by some terrible reverses, against both Bulgarians and Saracens. But the results of these were, with the exception of the final loss of Sicily in 902, temporary; whereas the results of the Byzantine counter-measures, in organisation and in diplomacy, were both permanent and salutary. We may begin by sketching in outline the former and then take a look at the latter.

To begin with, Bulgaria. Since the final adhesion of that kingdom to the Byzantine sphere of influence in 870, it had remained quiescent. Boris-Michael continued the work of converting his folk to orthodox Christianity, though even in 890 paganism was still to be reckoned with. In the 870s he sent his second son Symeon (864–927) to Constantinople to receive a Christian and secular education, and he may possibly have been taught by Photius himself, along with the emperor Leo. This education was only partly successful. The youth returned to his country with some acquired cultivation and some taste for books, but his savage nature had not been tamed; and his acquaintance with the great City and its empire had filled his head with wild dreams of splendour and supremacy. In 889 the old Boris-Michael abdicated in favour of his eldest son, Vladimir; but Vladimir tried to raise the standard of paganism, and, after four years of ineffective struggle, gave way in turn to his orthodox brother Symeon, then twenty-nine years old. This terrible ruler and conqueror, who governed for thirty-four years, fought two savage wars against Byzantium, the latter of which, the eleven years war of 914–925, was probably the most destructive ever known in Thrace, Macedonia and the Greek peninsula. It has however to be remembered that on each occasion Symeon had a legitimate excuse, as well as an overweening ambition, in resorting to arms. It was certainly so on this first occasion.

The arts of peace followed by the Khan Boris had established a flourishing trade between Bulgaria and Constantinople, chiefly in the stock Slav exports of hides, furs, wax and slaves. The minister Stylian Zaützes, in an evil hour, granted the monopoly of this trade to two of his creatures; and they transferred the *entrepôt* from Constantinople to Thessalonica, besides substantially raising the customs dues for their own advantage. It is easy to see the effect of this. The Bulgarian carrying trade from the Euxine down the Bosphorus was put out of action at a blow; and the overland route to Thessalonica was much inferior to that which ran through Thrace to the capital. Symeon protested, but his protest was ignored. He was not the man to take this lightly, and in 894 he invaded the empire. The Byzantine forces were in a state of readiness, although a large force was engaged on the north-east frontier at Theodosioupolis. The command in Bulgaria was given to Nicephorus Phocas, the conqueror of southern Italy, and the fleet, under an admiral called Eustathius was sent to the Danube. Nicephorus defeated the Bulgars and advanced into their territory. Eustathius concluded an alliance with the Magyars, a Finno-Ugrian tribe not long settled in Bessarabia. In 895 he ferried these folk across the Danube and let them loose on the Bulgarian countryside. Their devastations were a foretaste of what Italy and Germany were soon to suffer, until these savages were crushed sixty years later by Otto the Great. Symeon in his agony sued for peace, and this was granted. He knew how to use his time. He over-trumped the Byzantines. He bribed an even more numerous and savage tribe of Turkic origin, the terrible Pechenegs, who came next in the conveyor-belt across the Steppe, to fall on the rear of the Magyars. The Magyars left in Bessarabia were exterminated. The remnant wandered over the Carpathians and at last, fourteen years later, they extinguished the Slav kingdom of Great Moravia, and established themselves in Hungary, where they are to this day. The Pechenegs thus moved down to the Danube, whence they stretched eastward and northward across the Russian steppe as far as Chazaria and became, in the next century, the chief preoccupation of Byzantine foreign policy.

Free of the Magyars, Symeon broke the truce and turned on the Byzantine forces. Nicephorus Phocas had been very unwisely relieved of his command, and the new commander-in-chief, Catacalon, was not equal to the task. In 896, on the field of the Bulgars' Bridge, the Bulgarians annihilated the Roman army, and began a lightning invasion of western Hellas. Leo VI sued for peace in his turn; but a large sum of money and much diplomacy was needed before the invaders would return home. Peace was not concluded till 901. The custom house at Thessalonica was shut up, and trade was resumed with Constantinople.4

Meanwhile, during twenty years the Arab raids in the Aegean had been growing in numbers and strength. The combined fleets of Syria and Crete, led as often as not by Christian renegades, were now no longer content with plundering the countryside. They assaulted and sacked walled towns. The booty to be seized in these, whether in slaves or money, far exceeded what was to be got from the peasant's hovel or byre: and the prospect of riches inspired the marauders with desperate and nearly superhuman courage. The flourishing port of Demetrias on the Gulf of Pagasae was sacked in 901, a disaster doubly severe since at just this time the fleet, sent under Admiral Eustathius to relieve Taormina in Sicily, returned with the news that this last outpost of Byzantine authority in the island had fallen to the Africans.

But a far worse blow was to come. In the summer of 904 a strong Saracen fleet sailed into the Sea of Marmara itself, and menaced the capital. This was something not experienced for nearly two centuries. Admiral Eustathius sailed out, but broke off without giving battle. Ugly rumours were abroad. The government was compelled to act quickly, and they appointed Hemerius, uncle of the emperor's mistress Zoe, to the command of the imperial navy. Hemerius was more of a civil servant than a sailor, but his loyalty and energy were past question. He presented a bold front to the Saracens, who made off down the Dardanelles and set course for Thessalonica, the second city of the empire. The government understood the threat, but had no time to meet it. The walls of Thessalonica were in disrepair. The two commanders were at odds, and issued different instructions. To crown all, the abler of the two fell off his horse and broke his neck. On 29 July 904 the walls were breached. The raiders poured in; and what the Slavs and Avars had failed to do three centuries before was now achieved by a horde of Syrian and Ethiopian pirates. The sack of Thessalonica continued for a week. At length the galleys, loaded to the waterline with human and material plunder, set sail for the south. They ran for Crete, where they sorted their spoils, then for Cyprus, and at last put in triumph into Laodicea and Tarsus.[5]

This dreadful reverse galvanised the government into action. They had a powerful force at command in Anatolia, which, under the leadership of the head of the great clan of Ducas, Andronicus, military governor of the Anatolic province, had carried out a very destructive raid into Syria in this year. In 905, a plan was devised whereby a reorganised fleet, still under the command of Hemerius, should embark this general with his army, and fall on Tarsus, a city scarcely less important to the Saracens than Thessalonica to the Byzantines. The story is confused, and only the results are beyond question. The imperial chamberlain, it is said, who hated Andronicus, had him warned secretly that the emperor suspected him of treachery, and that once he was aboard Hemerius' flagship, his eyes would be put out. One is inclined to doubt the authenticity of this story, since the chamberlain in question was of proven loyalty to the emperor; and it is more likely that Andronicus himself intended to play false from the first. At all events, when, in late September 905, Hemerius sailed into Attalia and called on the marshal to join him, Andronicus refused to budge and at length, in open revolt, shut himself up in a town near Iconium. The new admiral made up by his courage for what he lacked in seamanship. Under-manned as he was, he set sail eastwards from Attalia, and on 6 October 905 he came in sight of the fleet of Tarsus. He attacked them, and gained a complete victory. It was the first naval success in the whole nineteen years of Leo's reign, and it showed that a new spirit was at work in the admiralty.

Andronicus Ducas, the rebel, lay six months (October 905 – March 906) in his fortress by Iconium. Then, seeing that a strong imperial army was advancing to reduce him, he applied to the

Saracen government for permission to cross the frontier. This was readily granted and a Saracen force was sent out to meet and escort him. In April he arrived at Tarsus, where he was welcomed by the emir; and in October he proceeded, with his son Constantine and all his household, to Bagdad. The story has left its mark both in Byzantine and in Saracen records.

The Emperor Leo, who seems to have been cut to the quick by the treachery of a trusted commander and friend, could not believe that assurances of pardon and reinstatement, if these could be conveyed to the renegade, would fail to bring him back to his allegiance. An embassy was on the point of starting out for Bagdad, with the prime object of negotiating peace with the Saracens, and an exchange of prisoners: the captives of Thessalonica were to be exchanged for Saracens taken in 904 by Andronicus himself. A secret missive for Andronicus was entrusted to the delegation. Unluckily this missive was betrayed to the vizier. He acted promptly. All thought of using Andronicus against the empire was shelved. He was given the alternative of embracing Islam or losing his life, and he chose the former. He was, even so, closely confined, and even the year of his death is unknown. In the following year, his son Constantine Ducas, a gallant but wrong-headed soldier, did contrive to escape. He made his way to Constantinople, and the Emperor Leo received him with enthusiasm. But he added a warning against any repetition of the treasonable practices of his father Andronicus. Leo appointed him military governor of the province of Charsianon, in south-east Asia Minor; and there he remained until, unheeding the emperor's warning, he embarked on a desperate treason which cost him his life.[6]

I should not have thought it necessary to relate this story in such detail, were it not that it was symptomatic, and one of the earliest overt symptoms, of a profound disease in the body politic, which, though now embryonic, in course of time destroyed the empire as reformed by the house of Heraclius: I mean, the rise of a class of land-owning military magnates, who rapidly became an aristocracy of inter-marrying clans. Such a class was of course anomalous, and in opposition to the whole principle of the state's rural organisation. Yet it is not easy to see how its rise could have been prevented, except by draconian legislation such as only one emperor had the ability and power to enforce. The object of this class was the acquisition of land, and land was always at the disposal of one who could pay for it. Owing to heavy taxation, to natural disasters and to periodical raids by enemy marauders, there were always small men who were distressed and who were willing to sell their holdings for what they could get. Their smaller neighbours had by law an option on properties so disposed of, but could not or would not always take them up. These holdings then reverted to the crown, which was willing enough to sell to the first buyer. Once entrenched in a village commune, the big landowner found it an easy matter to extend his hold over small plots, until the whole was his estate, and the erstwhile 'free' peasant proprietors were his *parics* or serfs. It must not be supposed that this arrangement was always to the disadvantage of the serf. He got solid benefits from bartering away his 'freedom' and his land: he got that protection from oppression which only the rich and strong could give him. Besides, was he, even as a 'free' peasant, any less of a slave to the state treasury? The use of the word 'free' in Byzantine legislation is itself revealing: it means, not a free man, but a casual labourer without taxable property. The only 'freedom' lies in destitution.

We saw reason to believe that the rise of this landed class of proprietors was very materially promoted by the devastation brought about during the revolt of Thomas in 821. Certainly in the ninth century their power and prestige, as proprietors and nobles, were much enhanced. They were the main economic problem of tenth- and eleventh-century governments, which inevitably suffered by their encroachments, both in loss of revenue and in loss of manpower. But they constituted a more serious danger still, in that they were a centrifugal force, chronically opposed to the central government, and powerful enough to threaten the very existence of the state. They automatically became military governors and generals, since they, by tradition, had a monopoly of military experience and command. They were generally idolised by their own tenantry, in whose eyes they often became almost legendary figures of heroism and chivalric romance. It is (as has often been pointed out) a misnomer to call this class 'feudal' in the western sense. Yet in course of time the relationship which grew up between landlord and serf on the wide estates of Anatolia was not dissimilar in principle to that which existed in the more properly feudal system of the west.

We shall meet with these nobles, and with the largely unsuccessful measures of the government to contain them, over and over
again in the tenth century. Let us here note that in this year, 905,
the family of Ducas has already emerged with all the characteristics of the class: large property, military skill, courage, doubtful
loyalty, and an eye firmly fixed on the imperial crown.7

Thus enumerated, the military and naval disasters which overtook Leo vi's empire between 894 and 905 appear overwhelming.
But we get a one-sided picture if we dwell too much on them, to
the exclusion of an equally important work of organisation for
which Leo was responsible. This work was his greatest and most
lasting. He put through a whole series of territorial reforms
designed in each case to strengthen the *themes* and to make them
militarily more defensible. Defence in depth and defence by
fragmentation were the only answers to the perpetual Saracen inroads. Small, mobile units of cavalry, well armed, well trained
and well led, were the only effective method of defence, and these
implied the multiplication of independent provinces and independent commands. These were the reasons for Leo's *thematic*
reorganisation. But he went beyond this. It is a surprise to those
who hear of nothing but Leo's defeats to find him establishing
Byzantine power firmly in South Italy by the formation of the
new province of Lagoubardia (892); and pushing Byzantine
authority eastwards by the foundation of the new province of
Mesopotamia on the Upper Euphrates in 900. Beyond Mesopotamia stretched the Armenian principality of Taron, and by Leo's
death even this important area was well on the way to incorporation in the empire. East of Cappadocia lay a frontier waste which
divided the empire from the emirate of Melitene. This area, too,
was organised by Leo into the province of Lycandus, and re-
peopled by strong forces of immigrant Armenians. This fundamental programme of territorial reform undoubtedly strengthened
the heart as well as the limbs of the empire, and all credit should
be given to Leo the Wise.8

The imperial hand was also active in naval reforms. It is to Leo
that we must chiefly attribute the formation of a *corps d'élite* of
naval guards which were parallel to the regiments of military
life-guards. These naval guards formed the crews of two large
galleys appropriated to the emperor's use, and of the rowing-
barges maintained for the empress. They numbered about a

thousand men. The personnel of this force was recruited from the best men of the imperial navy itself, had its quarters in the palace harbour, was splendidly equipped and paid, and was given guard-duties in the palace, together with a share in palace ceremonial. The creation of this force of loyal marines was a brilliant stroke of policy. They were absolutely devoted to the person of the emperor and his family, and whatever corruption the nobles might engender in the military arm, the naval was always proof against disaffection and disloyalty.9

Nor did the indefatigable emperor fail to carry on the work of legal re-codification initiated by his father. The voluminous code known as the *Basilica* was published by him, and became the law of the land. In addition he published 113 edicts of his own on matters of civil and church discipline, all between 886 and 899. The interesting work known as the *Book of the Eparch* dates from his reign: and regulates the status of commercial guilds and conditions of sale and purchase in the capital. The tendency of all this legislative work, as has been noted, is towards imperial absolutism. Such traces as were still to be found of independent authorities in city or province are expunged, and the whole state, in all its interests and facets, comes under the direct eye and providence of the emperor and his enormous bureaucracy. Leo has been blamed for this, but he was merely putting into more efficient practice what had always been true in theory. It is certain that tighter control made for more efficient government, and equally certain that the centrifugal forces exerted by the country magnates were inimical to good government. It is no part of our task to discuss whether absolutism such as this is compatible with the higher interests and needs of humanity: we need only note that absolutism was the state theory, and that it worked in practice as long as it was allowed, and strong enough, to do so.10

Of Leo's administration of the church we shall have to speak when we come to deal with his disastrous matrimonial adventures, which revived the strife of the Photian-Ignatian church parties with a clamour scarcely heard for forty years. But what lies outside this controversy may be soon told. Leo had come to power with the support of the extremist wing, and things augured well for them when their arch-enemy Photius was deposed. But Leo was not such a fool as to try to govern with an extremist patriarch such as Ignatius had been. On the contrary, his notion –

a very sensible one from his point of view – was to make the patriarch as subservient to imperial policy as he could. He accordingly gave the office to his own brother Stephen, who held it for six years. Stephen died in 893 and the question was, since no other brother was available, who should succeed him? There could really be little doubt that if Leo wished to govern smoothly, he must appoint a Photian, little as he had liked the leader of that party. He appointed a respectable but not too zealous clergyman called Antony Cauleas, who ruled until 901. It was during the patriarchate of Antony that Leo made a gallant attempt at what so many emperors had tried and failed to do – to bring peace to the church, which was still torn between the Photian and Ignatian factions. A synod, attended by Roman delegates, was convened in 899, and the controversy was declared to be at an end. We can only contemplate this pathetic declaration with a wry smile. The exploits of Leo's last two patriarchs, Nicholas and Euthymius, are concerned almost wholly with the emperor's fourth marriage.

The final years of the emperor's reign (908–12) seemed at first likely to bring consolation for so many disasters and reward for so much toil and devotion. The succession had long been a matter of doubt. The brothers Leo and Alexander, who in name governed jointly, were always at odds and Alexander never took any hand in the government, though always a focus of potential disaffection. Between 900 and 904 the relations between the imperial brothers had been those of total estrangement, and an attempt to murder Leo in the Church of St Mocius on 11 May 903, had been plausibly laid to the charge of Alexander, though this was never absolutely proved. Alexander has indeed a strong claim to being regarded as the worst man and the worst emperor ever to sit on the Byzantine throne: the only one, so far as we recollect, of whom nobody, not even his friends, had a good word to say. To make matters worse both brothers were childless until, in September 905, a male infant was born to the fourth wife, or mistress, of Leo VI. As we shall see, his future prospects were dubious, but at least he was there. And in October of the same year, as if to confirm a return of the divine favour, the Saracen navy was defeated by Admiral Hemerius. The next five years were devoted to an intensive naval reform, which I have already referred to. Hemerius, now created *logothete*, or foreign minister, kept his post as lord admiral, and improved as a commander and as a diplomat. A great expedition was fitted out in 910, to exact vengeance for Demetrias and Thessalonica. It sailed to Crete, where a diplomatic approach was made to the emir with the object of keeping him neutral in the coming operation. This seems to have been successful; though, if the emir had known what was in the minds of the Board of Admiralty, he could hardly have been so complaisant. The fleet then turned eastwards. Hemerius steered for the Syrian coast, landed at Laodicea, sacked it, and drove into the interior, burning and plundering. The whole undertaking was a complete success, and the force returned without loss.

Having thus – as they thought – put the eastern navy out of action, the Byzantines in 911 mounted one more operation against Crete. Surely this time it must be successful. They landed on Crete in October, but they had no better success than before. For six whole months the siege dragged on, and winter gave way to spring. At length Hemerius, no doubt on receipt of news that Leo VI was in his last illness, gave up in despair, embarked his men and set sail for Constantinople. Off the north coast of Chios he met an overwhelming force of Saracen ships commanded by Leo of Tripoli, the captor of Thessalonica. The Byzantine fleet was nearly annihilated, and Hemerius himself barely escaped to Mitylene. The news of this calamity was a death blow to the emperor. Since March he had been suffering from a disease which was perhaps typhoid fever. On the night of 11 May 912, the great emperor died, leaving behind his detested brother Alexander as chief emperor, and his son Constantine, aged seven, as Alexander's colleague.

As we have seen, Leo's greatness does not lie on the surface. His triumphs lay in the less spectacular field of organisation: of territories, of churches, of legal codes, of commerce and of army and navy. Those who murmured at his military misfortunes soon had cause to regret him when the rule of Alexander and the following 'regency of the eunuchs' brought the whole might of Bulgaria about their ears. And it is with a sigh of genuine feeling that the author of the *Life of St Theoctista* refers to the lately dead emperor, 'in whose grave lies buried all the good fortune of the Roman people'.[11]

NOTES

[1] Ostrogorsky, 201–2.
[2] Ostrogorsky, 201, note 1.
[3] Theoph. Cont., 354–6.
[4] Theoph. Cont., 357–60.
[5] Theoph. Cont., 366–8.
[6] Theoph. Cont., 371–4; Bréhier, 144.
[7] Ostrogorsky, 227–30; Vasiliev, 345–9.
[8] *DAI*, 236–40.
[9] *DAI*, 246–52.
[10] Ostrogorsky, 202–4.
[11] Theoph. Cont., 376–7.

CHAPTER SIXTEEN

THE 'FOURTH MARRIAGE'[1]

We have included above two separate studies of important religious movements, or crises, those of iconoclasm, and of the Photian-
Ignatian *imbroglio*. These, as they convulsed religious and secular
society during whole decades, need no excuse for such separate
enquiries. But the fourth marriage, the 'Tetragamy', of the
Emperor Leo VI appears at first sight scarcely to deserve a detailed
and particular investigation. However, a closer look at the matter
will probably correct this opinion. In the first place, the continuance of the Macedonian house depended on the issue of the
quarrel, and with this continuance, much of Byzantine culture
and prosperity in the next two centuries. In the second place, the
quarrel was a variation of the stock theme of ecclesiastical moderates *versus* ecclesiastical extremists, which was proclaimed as
early as 787. But the variation is here as important as the basic
theme, in this way above all: that it very clearly illustrates, along
with the growth of imperial power, culture and wealth, the
parallel debasement of the public morality. The 'Tetragamy'
scandal was in many ways a repetition of the 'Moechian' scandal
which had arisen a century before over the second marriage of
Constantine VI. In each case, the ostensible issue was that of sexual
morality. But a glance at the protagonists in each is enough to
point a very striking and disturbing contrast. The Patriarch
Tarasius and Theodore of Studius were both men of principle,
who acted consistently, and in strong conviction of the righteousness of their cause. The Patriarch Nicholas Mysticus and Arethas
of Caesarea were selfish and unprincipled politicians, who cared

very little whether their emperor married four or ten times so long as their own personal interests and animosities were served. Cynical they were not; each believed himself right on every tack of his tortuous course. But this scarcely mended the matter. We can have no more respect for a man who says one thing today and the opposite tomorrow simply because he persuades himself that he is in the right on both occasions. Finally, the affair is of interest for the light which it throws on the court's own notion of the imperial prerogative at this time; and of the emperor's indefeasible right and duty, where the highest interests of the realm were threatened, to override church, public opinion and both civil and canon law – in short, to apply the theory of the emperor's own person as *agraphos* or *empsychos nomos*, 'unwritten' or 'incarnate law'.

The father of Leo VI, Basil the Macedonian, despite his humble origins and the atrocious crimes which preceded and accompanied his accession, had proved himself during twelve of his nineteen years of absolute sovereignty a talented, energetic and conscientious monarch. One lesson above all he had learnt from the circumstances of his own rise to power: the prime importance of a settled dynasty and of a constant policy arising from the idea of legitimate succession to the throne. Since the extinction of the 'Isaurian' house half a century before, the throne has been occupied by a series of rulers with divergent and often contradictory policies; and the consequent fluctuations, both in state and church, had served only to hamper and stultify the imperial objectives. Michael I was a pious image-worshipper; Leo V a determined, if rather cynical, iconoclast; Michael II had halted between two opinions; his son Theophilus was a romantic and intellectual iconoclast; his wife Theodora, who succeeded him as regent, a no less convinced worshipper of images. The conclusions to be drawn from this were plain enough. Basil rightly saw that an empire whose whole theoretical structure might be summed up in the one word *unity* must be governed continuously by a single party devoted, if not actually related by blood, to a thriving imperial family, which should in turn be supported by the favour and love of the all-important populace of the capital. His policy was therefore, as his grandson tells us, to increase the imperial family itself, so that it should never again depend for its survival on a single life; and to win for it the support of the citizenry by means of a regimen of cheap food, lavish charities, iron economic controls and scrupulously honest administration of justice. The ultimate success of this policy is striking testimony to its good sense. Basil's own son Leo VI, and his grandson Constantine VII Porphyrogenitus, were both immensely popular with the common people, whose openly manifested affection for the legitimate house was in strong contrast to their sullen toleration of, or violent reaction against, periodical usurpers, such as were Romanus Lecapenus, Nicephorus II, or Michael V. Nothing could better illustrate the enormous prestige of the imperial blood than that at the close of the tenth century the rebel aristocrat Bardas Sclerus, whose ancestors had been governors and marshals fifty years before the ruling house had emerged from the peasantry, was proud to claim descent, albeit in the female line, from Basil the Macedonian. Yet, at one moment, it seemed that this splendid growth would be choked in its infancy, and that is the moment we are now to consider.

Leo, who ascended the throne as Leo VI, had for obvious reasons little sympathy with his father's methods of government. But at least he was fully seized of the importance of legitimacy, and of the paramount duty of securing the succession. Nothing could now be done to heal the breach between himself and his wife Theophano, who lingered on for eleven years in saintly if rather querulous seclusion, while her husband returned to his old mistress Zoe. The latter bore him at least one child out of wedlock, but she was a daughter. At length, in 897, Theophano died, and Leo married his mistress as his second wife, after as short an interval as decorum permitted, that is in 898. But he still was dogged by misfortune. After only twenty months of marriage, Zoe died without further issue.

The question now arose, whether a third marriage was in the circumstances permissible. As we shall see in a moment, the canonical edicts on plural marriages (that is, marriages in sequence) had until recently differed widely from the civil; and Leo himself had been instrumental in composing this difference very much in favour of the former. None the less, the overriding importance, not only for the dynasty, but also for the court and much of the church ceremonial, of having an Augusta was strongly urged on the complaisant Patriarch Antony Cauleas, who, without very much ado, issued a 'dispensation' which freed the emperor from the canonical penalties entailed by third unions. In the summer of 900, Leo married as his third wife Eudocia Baiane, a beautiful girl chosen as empress by the last exercise of the 'bride-show', or Concourse of Beauty. The poor girl did her best. On 21 April 901, she presented her husband with a male infant. But she died in labour, and the infant hardly survived his christening. Thus, after less than forty years, the very crisis which Basil the Macedonian, in his wisdom, had striven to avoid, was upon his house. Of his four sons, two were dead, one (Alexander) was a dissolute and probably impotent wastrel, and the fourth, the reigning autocrat was, after three marriages, without a male heir. It was a dynastic crisis of the first order. So long as there was but one childless emperor the whole régime could be snuffed out by a blow on the head; and the emperor, owing to the complex imperial ceremonial, had to be exposing himself daily to the possibility of assassination. His brother Alexander, himself childless, was known to detest him. What was to be done?

That a man of Leo's tenacity of will should have resigned himself to fate's decree was not to be expected. But, warned by so many previous disappointments, he wisely decided to proceed this time with caution. A fourth marriage, which would inevitably cause widespread scandal and might at the end prove barren, would be very much more worse than useless. He resolved on a liaison: and chose for his mistress a handsome and aristocratic lady named Zoe Carbounopsina, whose family was distantly related to the celebrated chronicler Theophanes. This liaison probably started as early as the end of 901; and although it was officially discountenanced by the church, it was condoned even by its most extreme precisians, who preferred it to a public and flagrant defiance of the canons. Ill-luck continued to dog the emperor, for the first offspring of this illegal union was again female. But at last, in September 905, Zoe Carbounopsina was delivered of a male infant, who, though sickly, seemed likely to live; and did in fact live to the respectable age of fifty-four. He became one of the half-dozen Byzantine emperors of whom everyone has heard, the celebrated historian-emperor Constantine Porphyrogenitus.

The male offspring was indeed there. But the emperor's difficulties were by no means over. The mother was a mere concubine. The child was a bastard. But Leo had not gone so far only in order to stop short now. The son must be legitimized: and his mother married and crowned Augusta. It was these demands which precipitated, or revived, the ecclesiastical quarrel which had long been latent. When it was learnt, in April 906, that the emperor had, in the strict secrecy of his private chapel, actually gone through a form of marriage with Zoe, and had then with his own hand crowned her Augusta, the storm burst. The rival factions of church and state were at one another's throats in an instant. And the momentous dispute began which was composed only after fourteen years, by the Act of Union in July 920, and has never been forgotten in the annals of the Orthodox Church.

For an understanding of the merits of the rival positions, it is necessary to glance first of all at the state of canon and civil law on the question of successive marriages; next, at the factions into which church and laity were then divided; and finally at the actual persons who led the struggle on the two sides, for and against the court.

The only authoritative Scripture which was held to bear on the matter was the somewhat dubious testimony of St Paul, at I Corinthians, chapter 7, verses 2, 8 and 9; where marriage as a state is granted a qualified approval, and remarriage allowed to women; but no definition is made as to the number of wives or husbands permissible successively to any one partner. The words of Our Lord to the Samaritan woman (St John, 4, 18), 'Thou hast had five husbands, and he whom thou now hast is not thy husband', might indeed be construed as denying the validity of a sixth marriage; but they might, with equally good, or bad, logic, be construed as implying the validity of a fifth. And to the candid reader both constructions alike appear sophistical. The result was that, in the early church, especially in the West, the Fathers took their cue from the Roman civil law, and were not severe on unions contracted one after the other by the same party. We must always remember that in antiquity, and even more in the middle ages, mortality from disease and childbirth was so fearfully prevalent that the conduct of widows, and especially of widowers, presented a very real problem; witness this very case of an emperor, whose palace was secluded and had at its disposal the best medical skill then available, yet who, in the short space of a decade, could lose three wives when he himself was no more than thirty-five years of age. The third-century patriarch of Alexandria, Dionysius the Great, was especially lenient to those in this predicament. He was followed by the western Fathers, Jerome, and Ambrose, and Austin, who saw no reason to be more severe. But the ecclesiastical rule which ran in the eastern church since the fourth century was the much more puritanical edict of St Basil of Caesarea, who, in three vigorous if somewhat self-contradictory canons, expressed himself strongly against successive marriages. In canon 4, he allows a second marriage to stand, subject to a penance; to a third marriage he will not allow the name of marriage at all, but only that of 'moderated fornication', and imposes a church penalty of four years before the sacrament can again be received. His 50th canon is slightly less harsh: for he agrees that the 'trigamist' shall not be subject to a 'public condemnation', since 'moderated' is better than 'abandoned' fornication. It is not until his 80th canon that he comes explicitly to the unfortunates who have gone even beyond this mark. His edict runs: 'Upon polygamy [that is, marriages after three] the Fathers are silent, since it is a practice bestial and wholly alien to humankind. We regard this sin as worse than fornication. Therefore it is well that such sinners be subject to a canonical penalty of four years before they can again be received': that is to say, as the canonists justly gloss it, four years in addition to the four previously enjoined for trigamy, making eight years in all.

This was, I repeat, canon law, which was at variance in this, as in many other matters, with the civil; and the chasm between the stricture of the canonical and the laxity of the civil codes existed during four centuries at Byzantium. But the jurists of Basil I's reign saw fit to bridge it by reforming the latter very much more in the spirit of the former. The code of civil law which was published under the names of Basil, Constantine and Leo himself – that is, between 870 and 879 – expressed the matter in quite unambiguous language:

A law was laid down by the ancients and confirmed by the most pious Justinian, whereby those who wished might extend cohabitation as far as a fourth marriage; he had in mind, no doubt, to how many persons it naturally happens that their partners in marriage die early, when they themselves are still youthful, and nothing can resist their natural desires; so that it happens to such that they are debarred from chaste wedlock, and turn to criminal intimacies. We, who are subject to the same natural weakness, might well adhere to the ancient laws in this regard; but we see that the sacred [sc. canon] law forbids it. For this reason Our Serenity, wishing to curb the abandoned passions of those in love, forbids anyone to proceed to a fourth cohabitation, and orders that those who have proceeded to a third shall be subject to the canonical penalties of the Church; so that the same writ shall run in the case of a third cohabitation as in that of a second. Let it now be absolutely clear to all, that if any shall dare to proceed to a fourth marriage, which is no marriage, not merely shall such a pretended marriage be of no validity and the offspring of it be illegitimate, but it shall be a subject to the punishment of those who are soiled with the filthinesses of fornication, it being understood that the persons who have indulged in it shall be separated from one another.

To fly in the face of these edicts was unthinkable, even for an emperor. Infringement of the canon would automatically subject him to the penalty of long estrangement from the rites of the church, his continued absence from which must bring much of the ecclesiastical and state ceremonial to a halt. As regarded the civil law, the emperor, as the fountain of all legislation, was no doubt in theory *agraphos nomos*, a law unto himself; and Leo himself held that in matters of state the civil code could be overridden: 'For', he said, 'it is permissible for those who are charged by God with administering the things of this world, to put themselves above the law which is binding upon their subjects.' The words, uttered probably in 899, were prophetic of his attitude to the crisis of 906. Such was his resolution that he was actually prepared, it is said, to redraft the civil law once again in favour of polygamy; but even this would not have reconciled those churchmen who took their stand uncompromisingly on the canons.

The single solution open to the emperor was – once more – 'dispensation', that is to say, a decision on the part of the church that the marriage was a special case, exempt from the rulings, and hence from the penalties, of the sacred codes. This solution had been adopted in the case of his third marriage six years before; and to this solution he now once more addressed himself, with all the tenacity of his own character, and all the cunning supplied by his confidential chamberlain, the patrician Samonas.

The question was, how could such dispensation be secured? Even a third marriage was elsewhere unexampled in the imperial house (if one ignored that of the heretical Constantine v) and had only been dispensed in Leo's own case with much misgiving, and out of deference to the newly won, or newly proclaimed, peace of

899 between the contending ecclesiastical factions. Second marriages themselves were rarities. A fourth was beyond conception. Yet even this might have been allowed without too much disorder, had not some unfortunate circumstances of a personal character intervened.

The Patriarch Antony Cauleas had died in 901. Leo's policy of appointing Photian patriarchs had stood him in such good stead that he saw no reason to depart from it now: and on 1 March of that year, Nicholas, the imperial private secretary, ascended the patriarchal throne. Nicholas was one who had inherited the political principles of his party, together with much of their devotion to secular learning. He could certainly be trusted to carry out the emperor's wishes where his wishes were practicable; but these, owing to the emperor's own insistence on the preservation of church unity at almost any price, were in danger of being self-contradictory. Nicholas, like Photius, had not been bred a churchman, and was very far from being a fanatic. He was by birth an Italian, handsome, luxurious and by nature easy-going, but, when misused, rash and revengeful.

The choice of this person appeared to be a triumph for the Photian party; but at his very election he received categorical instructions from his master which were by no means to the liking of his supporters. He was indeed a Photian; but he was to govern first and foremost as guardian of the peace which his predecessor had claimed to have restored to the church. From the outset he doubted his ability to perform this task of conciliation; and he appears to have been genuinely reluctant to attempt it. But Leo used all his influence to overcome his scruples; and he embarked on his precarious voyage. Had he known just how precarious it was to be, it is safe to say that no earthly consideration would have induced him to put to sea.

He was instantly embroiled in a disastrous quarrel with his academic colleague, the celebrated scholar Arethas. The modern world owes so much to the patronage accorded by Arethas to classical letters that it seems ungenerous to insist on his very serious defects both of head and heart. Yet the series of events during the next six years cannot be understood unless it is realised that Arethas was a narrow-minded, bad-hearted man, morbidly ambitious and absolutely unscrupulous, a treacherous friend and a rancorous enemy. The whole of his public conduct presents a lamentable series of shameful betrayals and scandalous levities. He was by tradition and nurture a Photian of the Photians; and the first fifty years of his long life were devoted to classical scholarship in the school of his great master. But the brilliant revival of secular learning inaugurated – or, at all events, promoted – by Photius was, both on personal and religious grounds, anathema to the Ignatian opposition. One symptom of this animosity manifested itself at Easter 900. Arethas, who had recently taken orders as a deacon, was on a sudden accused of atheism, and hailed before an ecclesiastical tribunal presided over by the Ignatian Euthymius. There is some reason to believe that a political motive may have been behind the process; but, however this may be, the charge as framed was certainly unfounded, and Arethas was in fact acquitted. But his vainglorious and revengeful nature resented the insult in the highest manner. When, a year later, his friend and colleague Nicholas became patriarch, Arethas at once urged on him, in the name of their old friendship, the infliction of severe punishment on the Ignatian partisans who had sworn false witness against him. But Nicholas was in an awkward position. The terms of his appointment demanded a pacific policy: and he was not disposed to fall foul of the opposition on such an issue in the very first days of his patriarchate. His reply to Arethas was negative. Arethas, incensed beyond measure at what he chose to regard as his friend's treachery, became from that time his most bitter antagonist; and looked only for the moment when he should be revenged upon him. It is only right to stress the importance of personal animosity in the coming dispute.

Meanwhile, the emperor's third wife died in April 901, and by 902 his liaison with Zoe Carbounopsina had begun. If it should prove successful in its sole object of providing him with male posterity, he was in his own mind resolved, let the obstacles be what they might, that the positions of both son and mother should be legitimised. He therefore set about strengthening the ecclesiastical party which was the more likely to support him through thick and thin. In 903 the important archbishopric of Caesarea became vacant, on the death of the rabid Ignatian Stylianus. In an evil hour the emperor, relying on the hitherto unimpeachably Photian character of Arethas, nominated him to this see. It was a fatal miscalculation. Arethas saw his chance. Forsaking all ties of loyalty, friendship and tradition, he turned right about and united himself to the Ignatian wing of the church, whose leader was Euthymius. They received with open arms the adhesion of one whose long training in secular learning and Aristotelian logic would enable them to compete on equal terms with the Photian casuists. And during the critical years 906–7 he became the chief polemic in the camp of those who opposed the imperial policies.

The inevitable crisis at last arose. In September 905, the imperial concubine was delivered of the long expected male infant; and court and church were at once faced with the problems of what should be the status of the one and the future of the other.

The Ignatian wing, as might have been expected, at first absolutely refused to consider either legitimisation or fourth marriage, on the apparently unassailable grounds that these demands were in direct conflict with both canon and civil law. Their leader Euthymius, owing to his long friendship and close spiritual association with the emperor, took in public no very prominent part in this opposition. But his chief lieutenants, Arethas and Epiphanius of Laodicea, sustained the cause with clamorous ardour. The court party, headed by Leo himself, his cunning protovestiary Samonas, and his no less devoted Patriarch Nicholas, was compelled to resort to diplomatic manoeuvres. The first stratagem was the temporary removal of the chief, or at least the most vocal, of their opponents. The churches of the province of Hellas had, during the years 902–4, been fearfully desecrated by marauding Saracens. By the end of the year 905 they had been restored and were ready for reconsecration. It would appear that this was made an excuse for sending Arethas to Hellas to perform the office. He was ordered to proceed thither; and during some critical months at the end of 905 and the beginning of 906 he was absent from the scene. Meanwhile, strong pressure was applied to the Ignatian bishops to prevail on them to reconsider their position. It was emphasised that a dispensation was within the discretion of the church in a matter not involving a doctrinal heresy – the argument which had been used by the Tarasians to support Constantine VI's second marriage in 795; and that it would in the circumstances be criminal folly to provoke another schism so soon after the reconciliation of 899. These representations were so far successful that they persuaded the opposition, in the absence of their firebrand Arethas, to agree to the more important proposition, that of permitting the baptism, with full imperial honours, of the male infant. But this concession was made only on the express condition that the emperor, for his part, should agree to abandon his mistress, and banish her from the court and palace. There is, moreover, reason to believe that the Patriarch Nicholas himself achieved this qualified success only by giving a personal undertaking that he would have nothing to do with a fourth marriage except in the event of a unanimous decision of both parties to condone it. At least, it is certain that he was afterwards accused of having given such an undertaking; and that he never wholly went back on it during the next twelve months which preceded his deposition.

The emperor was seemingly all compliance. Zoe was dismissed from the palace forthwith. The baptism took place in great splendour on 6 January 906, in St Sophia, when the baby was four months old. But, to the dismay and fury of the opposition, only three days later the mistress was recalled to the palace, escorted by a detachment of life-guards. Four months later, at the end of April, the final outrage was committed. A presbyter was induced to go through a form of marriage over the imperial couple in the seclusion of a private chapel; and at its conclusion the emperor himself with his own hand placed the imperial diadem on the head of his son's mother.

Now, there can be no doubt at all that, in this unparalleled exercise of imperial authority, Leo had the private consent of his patriarch, who must have thought he could see his way to forcing through a dispensation for the marriage at a very early date. The 'marriage' that was, by every edict of church and state, no marriage at all, automatically subjected the perpetrators to total exclusion during several years from all religious sacraments and ceremonies. And that the emperor should for one moment have contemplated the possibility of subjecting himself to the canonical penance, which, however protracted, would even so not have legitimised his union, is quite incredible.

But if Nicholas had given any such assurance – and one document certainly suggests that he had – he disastrously underrated the fury of the opposition at being so overreached, and the malevolence of their spokesman Arethas. The latter, on his return from Hellas, donned the mantle of Theodore of Studius and threw himself into the struggle. The court propagandists, both lay and ecclesiastical, worked tirelessly on the opposition between May and December 906. Every argument of policy, every refinement of casuistry, and at last every menace of imperial displeasure, was exercised against the abhorring bishops. But in Arethas, trained as he was, and as his colleagues were not, in the Photian school of philosophical disputation, the party of Nicholas had found its match. They disinterred old practices of the church, dating from a period long before the formulation of the Basilian canons, which seemed to countenance any number of successive marriages; they scrutinised with all the apparatus of Aristotelian logic the very canons themselves, detected real or fancied inconsistencies in them, and proclaimed triumphantly that at least one of the canons in question could and should be construed as supporting their side of the dispute. It was to no purpose. Arethas was too many for them all. Heresy was heresy. In tortuous phrases, but with manifest justice, he defended canon law against archaic and uncanonical practice; and exposed such juggling with St Basil's edicts as impudent sophistry. Base and contemptible as were his motives, he had the right on his side, and he could not be shaken.

At length, after repeated promises of success, which were as repeatedly broken, the unhappy Patriarch Nicholas towards the close of the year prepared himself for the inevitable decision. His state was indeed pitiable. The opposition and the court were equally adamant, and he was between the upper and the nether mill-stone. If he overruled the former, he broke his pledged word, and betrayed his charge to guard the peace. If he flouted the latter, his imperial master both could and would resort to extremes. By Christmas Day 906 he was forced to admit that he could do no more.

The imperial advisers had seen this coming for months past, and were ready with sterner measures. Arguments had already given place to threats of deposition against the recalcitrant. In December it had been decided to remove Arethas for good. The old charge of atheism, of which he had been acquitted in 900, was revived against him; and there was no doubt whatever that this time the emperor would see to it that he was convicted and expelled from his archbishopric. But at the same time, an expedient as brilliant as it was unscrupulous suggested itself to the imperial conclave. The Patriarch Nicholas must no doubt be written off, as he could not override his Ignatian opponents. But – was it not possible that through Euthymius those very Ignatians themselves might be brought into the imperial camp by means of the bribe of ecclesiastical power?

The expedient met with undeserved success. Euthymius was consulted; and it was found that he himself, the saintly and austere moralist, was prepared to become patriarch and himself to issue a 'dispensation' for the marriage, if a reasonable pretext could be found. The pretext was already forthcoming. By a master-stroke the emperor appealed to Pope Sergius in Rome, and appealed not in vain. It was soon known that papal envoys were on their way to Constantinople with a favourable response; nor could the pope have answered in any other way. First, the Catholic Fathers had never been severe on plural marriages; second, the pope could certainly not resist the opportunity of once more intervening in the spiritual matters of the Eastern church; and third, he was desperate for Byzantine military aid against the Saracens in South Italy. This was all the excuse that Euthymius required. His party had always had profound respect for the authority of the pope, who had wholeheartedly supported them in their struggle with Photius just forty years before. The compact was soon reached; and by the turn of the year all was in train for the great revolution.

On 6 January 907, the emperor demanded for the last time that Nicholas should redeem his promise to release him from the ban. Nicholas, still confronted by the – to all appearances – unyielding opposition of Arethas, perforce refused. He was not asked again. One month later, on the eve of the arrival of the papal messengers, the patriarch, dining at the imperial table, was assailed by the emperor in a bitter invective, and then and there forcibly removed from the capital. His formal resignation was at once demanded through the chamberlain Samonas, and with very little difficulty accorded. He was near to a nervous breakdown, and besides, what else could he have done? The legates arrived, bearing the papal sanction. At the end of February Euthymius was installed as patriarch. Under the shelter of papal authority, he made no bones about dispensing the fourth marriage; and in the spring of 907 the long struggle which had started eighteen months before with the birth of Constantine Porphyrogenitus – for such he was now allowed to be – ended, at least temporarily, in the complete triumph of the imperial designs. It remains only to record that a week or two later Arethas, the mortal, the declared enemy of the marriage on every ground of Holy Scripture, public morals and sacred law and civil law, returned quietly to the capital, put off the mantle of St Theodore, made his peace with the emperor, and resumed his residence at the court and the duties of his diocese. Henceforward the fourth marriage of the Emperor Leo VI was to have no more ardent and convinced supporter than he.

We may here leave this disgraceful incident, and postpone its aftermath until we reach the regency of Zoe. But we may end by drawing attention to two points which it illustrates. The first of these points concerns the theoretical and practical limits of the emperor's prerogative. Many modern scholars have busied themselves with this question; and their answers to it have sometimes been conflicting. And they cannot be other than conflicting, unless it is realised that even in the most authoritarian states– such as Byzantium, or Modern Russia – parties are bound to arise with differing opinions, if not as to governing principles, at least as to how those principles should be interpreted. Party strife is no doubt a sordid affair. But no historical interpretation can be wholly valid that does not take account of it, even in a state where the word 'party' itself seems to be a contradiction in terms. That there was such a thing as a stable political theory of the emperor's position as the elected vice-gerent of Christ, whose power over all things temporal was generally recognised, and whose power over all things spiritual was from time to time forcibly vindicated, is unquestionable. But it must always be remembered that there were men, and parties, who never fully subscribed to these doctrines: who remembered that there had been a time when the emperor himself had been a pagan, or a heretic, and had cruelly persecuted Christ's church in his dominions. For these men the politic fusion of temporal and spiritual powers into one splendid, all-embracing autocracy by Constantine the Great did not seem perfect. The convulsions of the eighth century, during which imperial authority had imposed by force a manifest heresy on the church, had revived these sentiments, which remained strong for generations and were in fact never wholly allayed. A series of pious and stiff-necked patriarchs – Ignatius, Polyeuctus, Cerularius – continued to regard the spiritual arm as altogether independent of the temporal in matters of doctrine and morals. Although therefore in theory the emperor's power might appear to be firmly based on the most unambiguous and enduring of autocratic principles, we do well to remember that in this unstable, kaleidoscopic world of sense the same principles mean different things to different men at different times; and that, in studying any particular incident or epoch, it is not enough to argue from general and *a priori* theorems.

My other point is related to the former: it concerns the actors in the drama themselves. The rediscovery of the classics in the ninth century led to a reform in tenth-century historiography which conduced to a more objective and analytical study of individual characters and passions; and this allows us to see the men of that epoch as they were, rather than as their actions compelled them to appear in the prejudiced eyes of doctrinaires. This is what makes our study of this incident doubly illuminating. We see in Leo and Nicholas, not men who were either right and hence automatically angelic, or else wrong and automatically diabolical; but rather human beings, who were subject in their policies to human weaknesses as well as to dominating principles, and who, while convinced that they were right, were often hurried into doing what was wrong. Even for Arethas, whose human weaknesses, to say the truth, predominated to the almost total exclusion of any discernible principle except that of his own advancement, the same proposition may not unjustly be argued. Even at his worst, even when during ten months he argued with all his might against the emperor, and then when he abandoned his position and argued with all his might in Leo's favour, there is no reason to suppose that he was not perfectly self-deceived and self-justified. And when we come to number up his faults, many and grievous though they were, we shall I think at least not count hypocrisy among them.

NOTES

[1] See generally Theoph. Cont., 370–1; Ostrogorsky, 215; Vasiliev, 332–4; Bréhier, 142–6. But my account is based on fresh material, the letters of Arethas himself.

CHAPTER SEVENTEEN

ALEXANDER AND THE REGENCY, 912–20

The Emperor Leo VI died on Monday, 11 May 912. He had lain sick for four months, and by April he was unfit to govern. His younger brother, the degenerate Alexander, took the reins of government into his hands, and could scarcely wait for the breath to leave his brother's body. His first act, in April, was to recall the Patriarch Nicholas from his exile, and to replace in his hands the administration of the ecumenical see. On his death-bed Leo was visited by his brother. 'Ah', said Leo (and it is his last recorded utterance), 'here comes the man of thirteen months!',[1] meaning by this that his brother was of as evil omen as the intercalary year in which an extra month was inserted to square the solar with the lunar cycle. But men were quick to remember that Alexander did in fact reign but thirteen months, and to see in the emperor's very natural phrase the swan-song of prophecy uttered by Leo the Wise.

The days of the government of Alexander were uniformly evil. He was without statesmanship and without religion. If he believed in anything at all, it was in a brutal superstition deriving from classical paganism. If he had a principle, it was to reverse everything done by his brother Leo: and as Leo's policies were generally well-conceived, their reversal could not be other than unfortunate. It was early seen to what such folly would lead. Symeon of Bulgaria sent his compliments to the new sovereign, and a request for a renewal of the peace of 901. But this peace had been concluded by Leo, and Alexander therefore would have none of it. The Bulgarian delegation was repulsed with insult, and Symeon prepared for war.

The earliest months of the reign were disgraced by the unbridled vengeance taken on the Euthymian bishops and clergy by the Patriarch Nicholas, now restored to supreme power in the church. He felt, justifiably, that he had been betrayed by the Euthymians in 907, when, in defiance of their promise to stand by him over the 'tetragamist' controversy, they had first tricked him into resigning, and then, when power was in their hands, had quietly turned over and done themselves what they had refused to allow him to do: that is, to sanction the late emperor's marriage with Zoe. They had now to brave the wrath of Nicholas, who came among them like a raging bull. All that we know of the Patriarch Nicholas – and we know a very great deal – leads us to suppose that, when provoked, he was rash, hot-headed and unstable, constantly hurried by passion into proceedings which he afterwards had too much reason to deplore. A steadier man than he would have seen that his restoration should be accompanied by mercy and moderation, if he ever wished to rule over a united church. But worse counsels prevailed, and were, as might have been expected, vigorously seconded by the irresponsible Emperor Alexander.

First came the destitution of Euthymius, an act which, if done in a proper manner, would have been justifiable; but the manner was grossly improper, and drew all sympathy to the side of the victim. A *silentium*, or meeting of the privy council, was called, and Alexander took his seat with Nicholas on the bench. Euthymius was summoned and accused of adulterously entering on possession of the Spouse of Christ. The old man – he was probably near seventy years of age – said with much courage and spirit that on the contrary it was the hireling Nicholas who, by resigning, had abandoned his flock. A horrible scene ensued. Euthymius was stripped of his robe. His beard was plucked up by the roots. Two of his teeth were knocked out by blows in the mouth. He was beaten to the floor, punched, kicked and trampled. He barely escaped with his life: and he was carried thence into exile.[2]

Nicholas would have been wise to stop here. But his passions hurried him into even greater excesses. He moved his imperial master to erase the pope's name from the 'diptychs', and Constantinople ceased during eleven years to be in communion with

Rome. The Euthymian bishops and clergy were condemned *en bloc*, and ordered to leave their seats. Their ordinations were declared invalid. And their successors were appointed. But here the vengeful patriarch soon saw that he had put himself in an impossible position. It was all very well to dismiss two-thirds of the episcopal bench; but supposing they refused to go? This in fact happened in the most celebrated instance of all, the destitution of Arethas from the throne of Caesarea. No one, on a review of the past conduct of that prelate, infamous as it was, can doubt that if anyone deserved deposition, it was he. But, whatever he might lack in candour or moral principle, he certainly lacked nothing in courage. To Nicholas' manifesto he answered haughtily that Nicholas had mistaken his man. He, Arethas, was no mild and saintly Euthymius, to suffer and bow with meekness before tyranny. He flatly refused to acknowledge his deposition. If the emperor issued a mandate for his removal and sent soldiers to enforce it, he would of course comply: otherwise, not. His example was widely followed. Nicholaite bishops in the provinces, who began to evict the Euthymian clergy, provoked riots and bloodshed. The whole church was in fearful confusion from one end of the empire to another. And Nicholas, who had raised the storm, had now to spend the next seven years in trying to allay it. We can follow the poor man's desperate attempts to restore order in his diocese through his voluminous correspondence. At the end, four Euthymian archbishops, and four only, were absolutely dismissed. The rest, including Arethas, were allowed to keep their sees, or promised an equivalent in reversion. Meantime every Nicholaite bishop and abbot was ordered or supplicated to show a moderation very signally lacking in the earlier conduct of Nicholas himself. On more than one occasion the military governor of a province had to be instructed to keep the peace. So much easier was it to control a rebellion or repulse an invasion than to get two churchmen to see eye to eye.

Meanwhile the miserable Alexander sank from bad to worse. His excesses enfeebled his body. He indulged in a whole series of cruelties and follies. Once, he became convinced that a bronze boar in the Hippodrome was his fetch, and supplied it with a new set of teeth and generative organs, by way of mending his own deficiencies in those departments. He led pagan processions in which sacred vestments were misused. The only good thing about him was that he could not possibly last long. On 4 June 913, he got drunk and went to play a ball game. A cerebral haemorrhage followed. He was picked up dying, and ended his life two days afterwards, leaving the Patriarch Nicholas, with a council chiefly composed of Slavs, to govern as regents for his seven-year-old nephew, Constantine Porphyrogenitus. Such was the end of the thirteen-months man. He was forty-two years old.3

Nicholas, who now became, in addition to being patriarch, the *de facto* governor of the state, was at once confronted with a whole series of crises, which would have taxed the statesmanship of wiser men than he. At the time of Alexander's death, his brother's widow, the empress-mother Zoe, whom for obvious reasons Alexander had kept in the background, occupied the palace and began with her entourage to issue her own orders without reference to the patriarch-regent. It took strenuous action on the part of the council to evict her. In the next place, the child Constantine was undoubtedly the rightful sovereign, but only on the supposition that the 'dispensation' issued by Euthymius, which legitimised the fourth marriage of Leo, had been a valid instrument, which Nicholas naturally could not admit. He was violently prejudiced against Zoe, whom he regarded as no better than a whore, and this prejudiced his loyalty to her son. We have to bear all this in mind in assessing his future conduct.

No sooner was Nicholas master of the palace, which was also the centre of administration, than a revolt broke out in favour of the aristocratic general Constantine Ducas, who was now commander-in-chief. Considering the dubious relations into which Nicholas was said to have entered with Ducas' father, Andronicus, in 905, we may legitimately ask – as was asked at the time – whether the shifty patriarch had not suggested the whole scheme to Constantine, the rebel's son, as a means of establishing a strong aristocratic dynasty in place of the dissolute Alexander and the sickly infant Constantine VII. The small force which Constantine Ducas brought with him to the capital certainly suggests that he believed treason rather than force would unlock the palace gates at his arrival. But meanwhile Alexander was dead and Nicholas regent; and Nicholas, whatever he may have resolved on before, was now determined to preserve the substance of power in his own hands. He closed the gates of the palace and told the Magister Eladas to hold them with a force of marines. Constantine Ducas forced his way in, but his few followers were shot down or fled: his own horse slipped on the pavement, and he was brought to the ground. He was at once decapitated. The first determined bid for the crown on the part of the provincial nobility thus ended in failure. But shrewd observers and legitimists might have augured ill from the devotion with which the pretender's memory was fostered in the eastern provinces, where he became the hero of song and story, the especial paladin of the Virgin Mother of God, the Oliver or Roland of the eastern empire.[4]

The patriarch had won yet another round in the game, and once more his weak nerves hurried him into revenges which passed all bounds. The executions became so numerous and grisly that the council itself had to remonstrate, and to ask the minister of Christ by what authority he continued to order such bloody reprisals in the name of an innocent child. But the revolt of Ducas was speedily forgotten in an event which far surpassed it in importance and danger.

Constantine Ducas had been crushed in late June 913. In August of the same year, the uncountable hosts of Symeon of Bulgaria, exasperated at his rebuff by the late Emperor Alexander, appeared before the land wall of Constantinople. At first Symeon, like so many of his predecessors, thought that the defences could be breached; and, like so many of his predecessors, he quickly learnt his mistake. Indeed those walls, during centuries, suffered as little damage from sieges as a dog suffers from fleas. Symeon, whose army invested the wall from the Golden Horn to the Golden Gate, was brought to a stand. He retired to Hebdomon, and let it be known that he was ready to treat for peace. But his demands were steep. He wished for nothing less than the imperial crown, conferred by a patriarchal coronation, the title of *basileus tôn Rhomaiôn* and the hand of the legitimate Emperor Constantine Porphyrogenitus for one of his daughters. If this were granted, he would suspend hostilities. What was to be done?

It is safe to say that not one Byzantine in a hundred would have dreamt of acceding to such demands. Symeon, though an alumnus of the Byzantine university and an orthodox Christian, was in their eyes scarcely more than a wretched barbarian: and the notion that the New Jerusalem could be confided to a dynasty of Turco-Slavs, even if it were commingled with the blood of Basil the Macedonian, was too absurd for contemplation. But the patriarch-regent took a different view of the case. The legitimate house he regarded with contempt and aversion. What was more to the point, Symeon was present in overwhelming force, and, if rebuffed, capable of committing almost limitless outrages on the western provinces, if not of incorporating them wholly into the Bulgarian state. Incredible as it may seem, Nicholas at last complied in substance with Symeon's demands. He himself proceeded to the Bulgarian camp and with his own hands placed a diadem on Symeon's head (though it was a makeshift crown, improvised from his own patriarchal veil). Two of Symeon's sons were allowed inside Constantinople, and dined with their future brother-in-law, the child Constantine. After all, there was the precedent of an imperial title granted, under duress, to Charles the Great. It was bad, of course; but what could you do? Symeon, now, as he believed, an emperor and the potential father-in-law of an emperor born in the purple, professed himself satisfied. And in September, he withdrew, though without concluding any peace-treaty, to Bulgaria.5

It is scarcely necessary to say that these negotiations, and this very extraordinary investiture, had been carried out in profound secrecy. It is also unnecessary to say that they soon became, in every detail, the property of every inhabitant of the capital. This was the crowning antic of the by now hopelessly discredited regent, and even his colleagues in the council saw that Nicholas' days of power were numbered. The revolution against him broke out five months later, in February 914. At the invitation of the Magister John Eladas, the Empress Mother Zoe was recalled to the palace and she and her 'council of eunuchs' (as the Bulgar Symeon contemptuously called them) took control for the next five years.

The empress was so much incensed at the conduct of Nicholas that she actually thought of deposing him from his throne, as her husband had done in 907. But the aged Euthymius, to whom the post was offered, disclaimed any ambition to occupy it again, and Nicholas was left in possession. However, when he seemed disposed still to interfere in secular matters, the empress angrily told him to mind his business: and so he went back to his diocesan duties, and entered the cathedral in which – says one of his enemies – he had not set foot during the whole eight months of his regency.

The new government, eunuchs though they might be, started

off better than the old. Ashot, prince of Armenia, was put back on his throne by a strong Byzantine army in 914. In Italy the military governor of Lagoubardia, appointed by Nicholas, won a glorious victory over the Saracens near Capua, and restored Byzantine prestige in that country to a height unknown since the withdrawal of Nicephorus Phocas in 886. But the advent of Zoe entailed one fatal drawback, the renewed hostility of Symeon of Bulgaria. The expulsion of Nicholas of course meant that his agreement with Symeon became a scrap of paper. All Symeon's plans of alliance and fusion with the imperial house, of imperial rule in Constantinople, of founding one single great Bulgaro-Byzantine state, vanished in a second. His imperial style as emperor of the Bulgars, since it had been conferred on him by Byzantium, could not be withdrawn, and he was grudgingly recognised as an imperial 'brother'. But it was a barren triumph. It is from this moment that his implacable hostility to Byzantium must date. He began that terrible war of eleven years which all the resources of the empire could not control, and which itself destroyed many of those resources for ever. If Symeon was not to rule the empire, he would destroy it: and such was the principle on which this war was fought.

Symeon's war against the empire is one further illustration of a fact that we have often noted before: the paramount importance of the Anatolian peninsula, both as granary and recruiting-ground, to the empire. Into this area Symeon never penetrated, or penetrated but once for a few days only. When we regard the fearful havoc which he wrought in Thrace, Macedonia, Hellas and Peloponnesus, we must always remember that these areas, though economically important, were not indispensable to the survival of the empire: and it is an at first sight amazing fact that already in 923, when the war with Bulgaria was still raging, the great general John Courcouas, with a fully equipped army, was able to take the offensive against the Saracens of the east. All the same, it would be a mistake to underestimate the losses sustained. The Bulgarian hordes overran Hellas, and the letters of Nicholas himself give a fearfully vivid picture of the destruction of churches, monasteries, nunneries, cathedrals and indeed all ecclesiastical property. As for the fate of the laity, an anonymous fragment dating from these times gives some account of what happened to those who were not taken for slaves: and it is not pretty. From the year 922 to the year 925 the whole of Peloponnesus was in Bulgarian occupation, and the byzantinisation of that province seemed likely to be finally halted, since the still large Slav element in its population made common cause with the Slavonic invaders. Every kind of concession was offered to Symeon, but was contemptuously rejected. One concession only he would accept – the throne of Byzantium, which had seemed so nearly in his grasp in 913. And this of course could not be granted.

The government of the eunuchs made one single considerable effort to bring Symeon to a halt. Remembering the events of 895, they sent the governor of Cherson, John Bogas, to the savage and powerful Pechenegs, to see if they could be induced to fall on Symeon's rear. In 915 their envoys came to Constantinople, and agreement was reached: an agreement confirmed, as the inhabitants observed with horror, by the pagan sacrifices of birds and sheep and dogs. Peace was made with Bagdad, and Asia denuded of troops. A vast sum was collected by confiscation of ecclesiastical revenues. Nothing which ingenuity could suggest was omitted. Even a measure of surprise was achieved, and the Byzantine army was on Bulgarian soil in strength, before Symeon was aware of it. By August 917 all was ready. The command-in-chief was given to Leo Phocas. Leo, as even his admirers said, was more of a soldier than a general, but he got the command through his marriage to the sister of the chief eunuch, Constantine the chamberlain. The command of the fleet was entrusted to Romanus Lacapenus, who now appears before us for the first time. This very great man, as we must call him from his subsequent exploits, began life obscurely. He was the son of an Armenian peasant of Lacape, in eastern Anatolia, who had done some service to the Emperor Basil in his campaign of 871; and the young Romanus was given a career in the imperial navy. He rose rapidly, and in 912, at the age of about forty, was naval governor of the Samian province in the Aegean. At what time and by whose promotion he was made High Admiral, we do not know: perhaps Alexander's. At all events, he was now sent to the Danube mouth, to ferry the Pechenegs and John Bogas across into Bulgaria.

The strategy was good; but in the field of tactics, everything was mismanaged. The admiral reached his objective, and there fell out with Bogas. Neither would obey the other, though the position of Romanus as admiral ought to have overridden that of a military governor of Cherson, at least in a naval operation such as this. The Pechenegs, seeing that the Byzantine commanders could not agree, went home. One half of the invading force had therefore disappeared without striking a blow. The Byzantine army, fortified by sight of the True Cross, and by a handsome donative, advanced bravely along the coast of Bulgaria. They rounded the gulf of Burgas, and halted near Anchialus, on the river Achelo. Here they encountered the ships of Romanus, and received the unwelcome tiding of the Pecheneg defection. Someone else also was waiting to receive them, and that was Symeon, who was lodged in the hills overlooking the coastal plain. On 20 August he seized his moment and delivered a general assault. The catastrophe could not have been more complete. The whole Roman army broke and ran, and was massacred at leisure. Leo the Deacon, nearly a century later, states that in his day piles of skulls and bones still littered the banks of the Achelo. Thus, as in 896, at the Bulgars' Bridge, the military skill and courage of the Bulgarians were decisively evinced. It is not possible to excuse this defeat on the plea that the leadership had been confided to a civilian. Leo Phocas was bred a soldier, like all his family, and he had under him equally experienced soldiers from the great houses of Ducas and Argyrus. He had a strong force of Armenians, under the best Armenian commander of that day. Even these advantages could not avail against panic and indiscipline.[6]

The effect of this debacle was, naturally, enormous. Leo Phocas, who had contrived to escape, made his way to the City, and hastily got together the remnants of a reserve, which he sent out to meet the victorious Bulgars who were pouring into Thrace. At Catasyrtae they were the victims of a night manoeuvre, and cut to pieces. Henceforward, for two or three years, the Walls alone preserved the empire.

And now began one more struggle for the crown. The personal influence of Zoe, never a popular figure, was at an end. The Patriarch Nicholas had some show of right in bidding for the recovery of his regency, but he could scarcely govern without assistance from the armed forces. The other two contestants were the discredited general Leo Phocas, and the admiral Romanus, whose conduct on the Danube and afterwards had not been such as to inspire confidence. The situation during the year 918 was painful and confused in the extreme. Thrace and much of Hellas was occupied by Symeon. Zoe and Nicholas were jockeying for position at the centre of government. Romanus, with his imperial navy, occupied the City harbours and the Golden Horn. Leo Phocas, with an Anatolian army, lay beyond the Bosphorus, in sight of the capital. The most important feature of this four-handed competition was that Leo Phocas, who represented the military aristocracy of Asia, confronted Romanus, who represented the much more plebeian, but much more dependable, navy.

Zoe at first resolved to throw in her lot with Phocas. She very probably intended to marry him (his first wife was dead), and thus ensure to her son a powerful protector among the landed class. This was perhaps not quite impossible, but it was certainly premature. The city populace which, in the present unsettled conditions, had to be reckoned with, was, by prejudice and tradition, violently opposed to the rural barons, and only accepted them later in the century as an unpleasant necessity. By tradition it was devoted to the legitimate house and to the home fleet; and a representative of each was at hand, if only they could be persuaded that their interests were at one. The initiative was seized by the boy emperor's tutor, who got his pupil to write a letter to Romanus imploring his protection against the usurpation of Phocas. Romanus was not slow to respond. He contrived to kidnap the first minister of Zoe; and, when the empress complained, her envoys were met with a shower of stones. On 25 March 919, Romanus sailed a squadron into the palace harbour of Bucoleon, and thence he ascended into the palace. The decisive step was the adhesion of the Patriarch Nicholas to the new protector. Leo Phocas at once raised the standard of revolt in Bithynia, but his army would not second the defeated general of the Achelo. They melted away, and Leo Phocas was seized and blinded.

Romanus acted with decision. He had a pretty daughter called Helen. She was at once betrothed to the youthful emperor, and on 4 May 919, some months before Constantine had celebrated his fourteenth birthday, the young couple were married by the patriarch. The empress mother was finally remanded to a nunnery where she ended her life as Sister Anna. Romanus proclaimed himself *basileopator*, or the emperor's protector. But it was not likely, it was not even possible, that he could remain content with such a rank as this. On 24 September 920, he was appointed Caesar, that is, heir apparent to the throne. And on 17 December 920, he received the imperial crown, ruling as junior emperor to his own son-in-law. Once again, as in 610, 717 and 813, the empire, apparently on the verge of collapse, had found a strong and able man to lead it out of its distresses. As with Leo v and Basil i, the steps by which the new emperor ascended his throne were fouled with treason, trickery and bad faith. But, once established, he, like them, showed a wisdom and energy which could hardly have been expected from a simple sailor.7

It was soon apparent that at last a capable hand had seized the helm. A palace conspiracy against Romanus was instantly detected and crushed. The last survivors of the wretched regime of Zoe were rounded up and exiled. It is significant that the Colonel of the Watch who made the arrests was John Courcouas, the brilliant general who was to be the terror of the Saracens: which shows that, even before his crowning, Romanus had chosen able and devoted friends. Moreover, before his coronation came an event which we must also credit to the good sense and statesmanship of Romanus. In July 920, two months before he became Caesar, was promulgated that celebrated instrument known as the *Tomus Unionis*, which united Nicholaites and Euthymians over the thorny question of Leo vi's fourth marriage.

The return to power of the Patriarch Nicholas in 912, and his indecent savagery in taking vengeance on his enemies, had brought a hornet's nest about his ears. His correspondence between the years 914, when he had leisure to look after the church once more, and 920, when the *Tomus* was agreed, is a long catalogue of disorders, evictions, repudiations and refusals to communicate, all over his diocese. It is sometimes hard to determine, from his very elliptical and allusive manner of expressing himself, whether a particular disorder to which he refers is caused by bloodthirsty Bulgarians or equally bloodthirsty 'tetragamists'. This could not be allowed to continue. Moderation and tolerance are virtues which have never been conspicuous in the Christian church; but here they seemed to be absolutely necessary, if that church was to survive.

Romanus saw this at once. With Symeon of Bulgaria at the gates, or ranging far and wide, this was no time to be haggling about marriages or disputing imperial legitimacy. Ably seconded by Nicholas, he summoned a council in 920, which at the price of substantial concessions at length agreed on an acceptable – or at all events an accepted – formula. The council declares its intention of abolishing once for all the scandals which have disturbed the peace of the church:

> We therefore determine by our common judgment and decision, that after this present year, which is the year of the world's foundation six thousand four hundred and twenty-eight, the eighth of the indiction [920], none shall contract a fourth marriage, which is to be absolutely rejected. Should anyone do so, he shall be shut out of any and every ecclesiastical meeting, and shall not be able to enter a church so long as this union persists.

But they would not leave the matter here. Third marriages were – they said – becoming prevalent and these too must be limited. If a man was past forty and had issue by previous wives, he was not to marry a third time. If he were past thirty and a widower with children, he could marry a third time subject to four years penance. Only childless men under forty were permitted a third union without reproach. Even first and second marriages were not lightly to be undertaken, but with all purity and reverence. Clergymen who celebrated uncanonical marriage were of course to be deposed.[8]

This edict was to be read annually on the first Sunday in Lent. It is safe to say that nothing but the most violent threats and generous promises could have induced the Euthymian fathers to subscribe this document. Necessity, as we know, makes strange bedfellows. But it would have been one of the sights of church history to see Nicholas shaking hands with Arethas after the ceremony: Nicholas who had condoned the fourth marriage and then condemned it: Arethas, who had condemned it and then condoned it. It was hard to say, in such a welter of contradiction, who was right and who was wrong. But Romanus, if he could make Nicholas and Arethas kiss and be friends, could not do the same for Nicholas and the pope. Nicholas had to write three times before the pope would send delegates to Constantinople, to unsay what Pope Sergius had said in 907. Nicholas maintained that in 923 they at last did so, and all of them together anathematised fourth marriages. But, as to this, the Roman records preserve a discreet silence.

There were two potentates beside the pope who did not receive the *Tomus Unionis* with the transports of joy and gratitude which Nicholas had hoped for. One was Symeon of Bulgaria. 'We bring you tidings of great joy', wrote the patriarch, 'Our church is at one'; and added that, however unable Symeon might to be see eye to eye with Byzantium in the political sphere, he would no doubt, as a true son of the church, rejoice in the church's healing. Symeon, in a paroxysm of rage at the success of Romanus in taking a position which he regarded as his own, evinced no joy whatsoever at the exhilarating intelligence. He went on vowing slaughter and death. The other party who was equally dissatisfied was the true Emperor Constantine Porphyrogenitus. He had been forced into a marriage with the usurper's daughter (though this, oddly enough, turned out a happy one, as marriages go). He had now to stomach the implication of his clergy, that his father had been a lecher, his mother a concubine, and he himself a bastard; and this not once, but year after year on each Sunday of Ortho-doxy. It is true that by refusing to make their decree retrospective the synod had saved his mother's honour and his own legitimacy. There was a point beyond which even Nicholas could not go, and Romanus was naturally concerned to save his son-in-law's face as far as he could. But the sting dug deep and rankled. And if we are tempted to stigmatise as vindictive Constantine's later invectives against his father-in-law, we must in fairness remember this cruel insinuation passed upon him in the most impressionable years of life, quite apart from his own exclusion from effective govern-ment during the next twenty-five years. Yet, in several ways, Constantine may be accounted lucky to have lived in the tenth rather than in the ninth century. He was neither murdered nor mutilated, only married: it is impossible to believe that Leo v or his own grandfather Basil would have left alive so dangerous a focus of disaffection, or at least would have left him his eyes.[9]

During all this time, between 917 and 920, Symeon pursued his attacks on the western half of the empire. The Byzantines made two efforts to deflect him by the old diplomatic trick of rousing hostility in his rear, this time on the part of the Serbs to the south-west of him. This diversion – for it was no more – proved to be important, for it drew off Symeon in the very year (918) when the dynastic struggle was most acute. Symeon pressed his demand for the demotion of Romanus, for the cession of the Bal-kans, for his own admission into Constantinople. But Romanus was firm. Symeon began striking seals on which he described him-self as Emperor of the Bulgarians *and of the Romans*. The Patriarch

Nicholas protested in horror at this blasphemy, and tried to argue the barbarian out of his folly. He met with nothing but ridicule and menace. However, it was soon seen that a more resolute spirit was at work when Romanus himself began to correspond with his adversary. Symeon, said Romanus, might call himself the caliph of Bagdad if he cared to – no one could stop him: but this title, like the other he was usurping, corresponded to nothing in reality. In fact, with the advent of Romanus, Symeon's game was up. It took him four years to realise this and to bow to the inevitable: but meanwhile, though he won some more victories and continued to occupy Roman territory, he got not an inch nearer to his goal. And even before the truce was made, Romanus had started his series of eastern campaigns.

The end came in 924. And with the withdrawal of Symeon began that great century of nearly uninterrupted Byzantine conquest which ended only with the death of Basil II in 1025.

NOTES

1 Theoph. Cont., 377.
2 Theoph. Cont., 378.
3 Theoph. Cont., 380.
4 Theoph. Cont., 381–5.
5 Ostrogorsky, 218.
6 Theoph. Cont., 388–90; Bréhier, 157–8.
7 Theoph. Cont., 390–8.
8 Ostrogorsky, 226; Bréhier, 165.
9 Bréhier, 159.

CHAPTER EIGHTEEN

ROMANUS I

Romanus I Lacapenus, the usurping emperor who, providentially, seized power from the feeble hands of his adolescent son-in-law Constantine, wielded it wisely during twenty-four years. That is a long time, as reigns went at Byzantium, or indeed anywhere else. Few emperors since Heraclius reigned so long or achieved so much. Like all great emperors from Justinian to Basil II, he was excellently served by able administrators and generals. John Courcouas, whose family was traditionally opposed to the legitimate house of the Macedonians, served him faithfully as commander-in-chief during twenty-two out of the twenty-four years of his rule, and covered the Byzantine arms with glory. The most important of the civil advisers was the grand chamberlain Theophanes, who held the offices of master of the wardrobe and chamberlain for nineteen years. To his sage counsels the throne was vastly indebted; and on at least one occasion he showed no mean talent as an admiral. Even the 'Macedonian' apologists can find nothing but good to say of him. Happy is the sovereign who can distinguish such talents so early, and can use them so long. It must also be stated that Romanus Lacapenus, though always at odds with the wide family connexion of the legitimate house, never incurred that hatred from the city populace which was reserved for the aristocratic interlopers Nicephorus II and John I Zimiskes. His origins had been as humble as those of Basil the Macedonian himself. His tact in uniting the legitimate emperor to his own family, and in keeping Constantine Porphyrogenitus prominent at least in the hierarchy, if not in the executive, succeeded in averting popular antipathy, which could not assail him without also assailing his son-in-law; and his splendid successes by sea and land filled the populace with pride and joy after the feebleness and failures of the Empress Zoe and the Patriarch Nicholas.

The first task of Romanus was to deal with Symeon of Bulgaria. He could of course, however bad things were, have nothing to do with Symeon's primary demand for the reversion of the empire. He did what he could, and with some success, to keep alive the Serbian menace to Bulgaria; and although Serbia suffered dreadfully from Bulgarian vengeance, its intervention was of capital importance to the empire. Meanwhile, the diplomacy of Romanus was active once more among the Pechenegs, the Magyars, and even further east, among the Turkic Alans of the Caucasus. Something like a crusade was organised to put down the invincible khan, or 'emperor', as he styled himself. At this conjuncture, Symeon determined on a last desperate attempt to attain his life-long ambition. The year was 924. He got the support of the Fatimid caliph of Egypt, who promised to supply a fleet. And he descended on the City with every man he could impress into his army. Romanus was one too many for him. He intercepted the Bulgarian envoys to Egypt, and himself offered terms to the Fatimids, which were accepted. Symeon, seething with rage, set up his entrenchments, but, as always, without any success at all. He gave in, and asked to negotiate.

The aged Patriarch Nicholas, now in his seventy-third and last year, undertook to go out to his 'spiritual son' from whom he had borne so much insult and scorn in ten years of correspondence, and was to bear still more. But the humiliation of the old patriarch was insufficient for the arrogance of Symeon. He told Nicholas he would see the Emperor – or rather the usurper – Romanus. This was conceded. Byzantium had everything to gain and nothing to lose by talking; and if Romanus were needed for this, he could do it as well as another. A rendezvous was fixed on a jetty in the Golden Horn. Symeon with characteristic impudence, but with shrewdness, too, made a careful inspection of the security arrangements: he could remember the plot to assassinate the Khan Krum at that very spot a century before. He came to the trysting-place on his warhorse.

At the same time, with gorgeous pomp, the imperial galley

was propelled up the Horn and moored to the jetty. It was Thursday, 9 September. The Emperor Romanus made a commanding figure, which seems to have created some impression on his imperial brother. Romanus made him a speech which was very obviously composed by Nicholas, and which the emperor had by heart. He said he had heard that Symeon was a Christian; but the slaughter of Christian blood in which he had so long indulged made this next door to incredible.

You are [he continued] mortal. You will die and thereafter you will be judged. What will you say at the Fearful Tribunal? What defence can you make before the Searcher of Hearts, who knows the havoc you have made among His flock? Do you wish for money? I will make you rich beyond your dreams. You have only to hold out your hand. But above all, desire peace and embrace concord, and cease the shedding of Christian blood by Christian hands!

The barbarian was abashed at the emperor's confident tone and dignified rebuke. He made some shuffling reply and retreated from the scene; yet not before he had delivered a final, brutal sneer at the Patriarch Nicholas. As he remounted his charger, Nicholas made some comment on the beast. 'Yes', said Symeon, 'he was the one I rode at the Achelo, when he took the cut aimed at me no doubt as a result of your Holiness' intercession!' Nicholas was incensed. 'I don't know what you may mean by that', he said, 'I made no such prayer. I never wanted the battle at all.' 'Then why did you not stop it?' said Symeon; 'You were patriarch. You could have excommunicated the whole lot of them.' He rode away. At that same moment two eagles were seen to leave one another high in air: one flying over the City, the other winging its way northwards into Thrace. The double-eagle was once more divided.[1]

In truth Symeon's enormous efforts and towering ambitions were defeated, and he knew it. No treaty of peace was concluded, but there was no point in prolonging the war. Bulgaria was bankrupt and her populace was migrating by thousands into Byzantine territory. Symeon tried to renew hostilities in 925, but the formidable coalition raised against him by Byzantine diplomacy was poised to make an end of him if he resisted further. In 926 he sent an army into Croatia to suppress part of the threat: and this army was totally defeated. It was the end. On 27 May 927 the terrible tsar died. He was sixty-three years old.

243

Many lessons are to be drawn from the career of Symeon of Bulgaria and his wars with Byzantium. His victories were due, not to bad organisation at Byzantium, but to incompetent leadership. This lesson was learnt, once for all: and its learning is apparent in the amazing successes of Courcouas, Nicephorus II, John I and Basil II. What Byzantine armies lacked was not organisation and equipment, but discipline and *morale*. They could not claim that steady valour and devotion to a cause which would enable them to fight a soldier's battle. Only the visible presence of a loved and trusted leader, approved – who could doubt it? – by God, could give them victory; and this dependence on a single commander was as dangerous as it was necessary. Such were the lessons of the Bulgars' Bridge and Achelo. In the second place, mere losses and destruction outside Anatolia, even though they paralysed Thrace itself, were absolutely powerless to achieve any permanent result. If Symeon could have allied himself with a caliphate such as it had been in the days of Harun; and if these allies could have established themselves firmly in Amorion and Iconium, it is probable that the disaster of 1071 would have been antedated by a hundred and fifty years, though of course with very different results. In the third place the brute strength of the Walls and even more the inherited tradition of moral and political superiority which was vested in the empire, preserved the spirit of her populace in the most desperate crises. They could not be brought to believe that, however deep their sins, and however severe the punishment for them, God would finally abandon his chosen people so long as they were truly penitent.

Symeon was succeeded by his pacific son Peter, who reigned for forty-two years. On 8 October 927 Peter received the hand of Romanus' grand-daughter Maria, and in the same year peace was finally concluded. During a generation Bulgaria lived in absolute quiet as the confederate and almost the protectorate of Byzantium. The ravages of the eleven years war were quickly made good, and there is reason to believe that many of the gaps in the population of Thrace and Macedonia were filled by Slavs from Bulgaria who preferred Roman to Bulgarian rule. It was the first of the great triumphs of the reign of Romanus, and it says much for his administration that it was not also the greatest.

The earliest years of Romanus' rule were perturbed not only by the incursions of Symeon. He was, naturally enough, faced by a whole series of conspiracies set on foot in the Macedonian or legitimist interest, both at home and abroad. There were two palace conspiracies in the capital itself. There was an open revolt on the north-east frontier, in the province of Chaldia. There was a conspiracy against Romanus' military governor of Peloponnesus, which opened that territory to three years of Bulgarian occupation. And there was a disastrous rebellion in Apulia, where the military governor was defeated and killed by the Lombards. But the courage and resolution of Romanus at length prevailed, and between the years 924 and 944 he was as secure on his throne as any emperor had ever been. The legitimate heir retired, obscure and nearly forgotten, to his library, to study antiquities and history and to paint pictures with what patience he might command.[2]

The most signal triumph of the reign was won in the war against the eastern Saracens.[3] This was continued during twenty years with almost uninterrupted success, and at the end of this period the eastern frontier presented a very different picture from that of 924. The epoch of conquest began auspiciously with an annihilating victory over the Arab fleet and its commander Leo of Tripoli by the Byzantine Admiral Rhadinos at Lemnos in 923, which had the effect of relieving the islands and coasts of the Aegean from their continual martyrdom. But the steady and brilliant advance eastwards by land was the work of the great commander Courcouas, as the Greeks called the Armenian Gourgen. The Byzantine victories were undoubtedly assisted by the weakness of the Bagdad caliphate, which, during the long reign of al-Moktadir, was repeatedly hampered by internal disorders and rebellions; and only towards the end of this period was an effective resistance made against the Byzantines by the semi-autonomous emir of Mosul, the Hamdanid Saif ad-Daula.

It is important to realise that the victories of Gourgen marked a turning-point in Byzantino-Saracen 'relations'. Since the rise of the Omayyad caliphs nearly three centuries before, the empire had been almost constantly on the defensive. The defence had indeed been well organised, and a fairly stable frontier from near Trebizond to Tarsus had been maintained. But this frontier was constantly – almost annually – violated by Saracen raiders and it took all the resource and power of the frontier commanders to control and expel them. The powerful emirates across the border,

Theodosioupolis, Melitene, Samosata, Tarsus, were the centres where these raids were organised, and no peace could be hoped for while they were in enemy hands.

With John Gourgen the tide began at last to flow rapidly and decisively in the contrary direction. It is true that we must never forget the preparatory work of Basil I in rooting out the Paulicians; of Leo VI in founding the province of Mesopotamia between two arms of the Upper Euphrates; and of the Empress Zoe, in re-establishing Byzantine political influence in Armenia. But it was the genius of Gourgen that turned Byzantium into a confidently aggressive power beyond the Euphrates, humbled the power of the emirs, and carried the Byzantine arms into the heart of Armenia, beyond Lake Van, and southwards to Edessa and Aleppo.

The details of his campaigns, as they appear in Byzantine and Arab sources, look at first sight confused and capricious. But a more comprehensive view reveals the coherent strategy behind them. The object was twofold: first, to destroy the *nuclei* of Moslem power beyond the immediate frontier, and second, to establish Byzantine power firmly in Armenia. The first of these objects needs no explanation. The importance of the second needs very little. Armenia was the source of the finest and steadiest fighting and garrison troops of tenth-century Byzantium. Moreover, north of Armenia lay the Georgian principalities of the Caucasus, which controlled the oil-wells from which the Byzantines derived the prime ingredient of their most effective weapon, the Greek fire. It was therefore towards these two areas, one east and one north-east, that the main Byzantine efforts were directed. Only when the centres of power from Lake Van northward to the Caucasus were firmly held, could the Byzantines sweep southwards and endeavour to isolate the one remaining frontier-menace, the emirate of Tarsus.

The points of chief significance in this progress eastwards were first, the reduction in 932 of the cities of Perkri, Chelat and Manzikert, all to the north of Lake Van, and commanding the roads into central Armenia and Vaspurakan. Constantine Porphyrogenitus, twenty years later, emphasised the importance of these places, and the need for them to be kept firmly in Byzantine hands.[4] Next, in 934, came the final capture and garrisoning of Melitene, almost the first place of fundamental importance for imperial security which the empire had reclaimed from the Saracens since the

246

seventh century. The operations further north were hampered by the jealousy of the Georgian princes beyond the Araxes, and the counter-attacks of Saif ad-Daula. But even here diplomacy, backed by force, was ultimately successful. Vital reorganisation followed conquest, and here it is to be noted that, unlike the Saracens, the Byzantines were quick to apply their splendid provincial system to occupied territories and to incorporate these into the empire. The provinces of Mesopotamia and Lycandus, existing already in embryo, were extended east to the Euphrates; and the strong fortress of Romanopolis, the city of Romanus, was founded to secure the road through Taron to Manzikert. At last, in 942–4, a campaign southwards exposed the weakness of the Saracens and the new resolution of their enemy. The countryside as far south as Aleppo was ravaged and denuded. Amida and even Nisibis, near the Tigris, were taken. And in 944 the Byzantines laid siege to the prosperous town of Edessa. This place possessed a talisman of world-wide fame: the *mandilion*, or 'towel', on which the Saviour had imprinted the likeness of His own face, and which He had sent to King Abgarus. Gourgen saw the enormous importance of getting hold of this talisman, and offered generous terms for its surrender. The Saracens, to save their own people from slaughter, yielded. And the Holy Towel was handed over. It was conveyed with speed and reverence to Constantinople, and was added to a host of relics, equally authentic and authoritative, in the sacristy of the Chapel Palatine.5

In all these operations we observe a system and method which denotes uncommon political as well as military skill. And one of the most important features of Gourgen's conquests was the wholesale importation of Moslem captives into the homeland of Anatolia. The empire was always short of men: and the great Slavonic reservoir, which has been profusely drawn upon by the Heraclian and Isaurian governments, was not as full as it had been, despite the slave markets set up by Russians and Bulgarians. Now, the new eastern provinces were peopled by Moslems. They were converted to Christianity, took allegiance to the emperor, and were incorporated into the *thematic* system of smallholders.

But amid so much glory, it is sad to reflect that this very system itself, on which imperial manpower, agriculture and revenue in the main depended, was increasingly falling on evil days. We have seen how, even in the ninth century, the 'powerful' or *dynatoi* – that is, the rich landowners – were, piece by piece and plot by plot, encroaching upon and eating up the estates of their poorer neighbours. This process has steadily gone on; and much of the territorial and military influence of the great clans of Ducas, or Phocas, or Argyrus grew out of such methods. The Emperor Romanus was the first who tried to remedy this state of affairs by legislation. His first edict was issued as early as 922, when we must suppose that the distress caused by the Bulgarian war had reduced large numbers of the smaller proprietors in the west to penury. The edict is a categorical prohibition against any further acquisition of property by the greater landowners from the lesser. The emperor's comment is revealing. 'This system of small estates is of great value to the economy as regards both collection of revenue and discharge of military duties: which advantages, should that system fail, will totally disappear with it.' It is interesting to note, from the words of the bill, what a variety of devices was already being exploited by the wealthy to gain their ends: 'And for the future, we do forbid the powerful to receive any real property from the poor, whether by means of adoption, or outright gift, or reversion, or bequest, or simple usage, or by any protection or co-partnership: nor shall they be permitted to acquire it by exchange in localities other than their own'. These various shifts were employed to get round the right of pre-emption, which rested first in the relatives of the vendor, and next in his neighbours. If the acquisitor legally adopted the vendor, he automatically became his relative and could buy his property. Or, alternatively, no sale need take place: and the acquisitor could take over the land by 'simple usage' or 'partnership'.

It is scarcely necessary to say that this edict was ineffectual. The only way in which such economic trends can be halted is by force, and the governments of Romanus and Constantine Porphyrogenitus were not in a position to apply force to the rural aristocracy. Basil II, in and after 996, was in a position to do so, and did so during thirty years. But he was a solitary exception. The failure of Romanus' edict of 922 is seen in the fact that the same prohibitions had to be repeated, in nearly the same terms, in 934 and in 947. In the year 928 occurred an appalling winter of frost, and this was followed by a terrible famine in 929–30. Whole areas were literally starving. The consequence might be foreseen. The small estates were bought up, if not for a song, at least for a piece of bread. This was the consequence which called for the renewed edict of 934. But the government might have taken warning by an event of 932. Owing largely to the distress brought on by the famine, an agrarian revolt broke out in the Opsikion (Bithynian) *theme*, and had some success. The significant feature of this revolt was the pretension of its leader: for he gained the support of the ruined agriculturalists by pretending to be Constantine Ducas, the aristocratic hero who, twenty years before, had lost his life in an attempt on the palace. It is all too apparent that, when the government edicts stigmatised the great landlords as cruel and rapacious wolves, they were expressing not the views of the rural populace, but their own.

Now, it is plain that the most malignant feature of this disease is its effect on the armed forces and their recruitment. The 'soldiers' estates' were bound to be of a certain capital value which was calculated by the government assessors as sufficient to equip a heavy-armed cavalry man. And, in good times, it was sufficient; and the head of the family, or his son, was bound to present himself for service, provided with horse and arms out of his own means. But times were not always good: indeed during the Bulgarian and Saracen wars, and in days of drought, pestilence and famine, they were decidedly bad. And the point at which the soldier's economy was most vulnerable lay in the health or sickness of his horse: for no one is more useless than your dismounted cavalryman. Every trooper was in debt to a money-lender. The fact of the matter is that farriery is a highly skilled occupation, and horse breeding and maintenance cannot safely be left to the charge of individual peasants, however well drilled in military units. Horses, like men, get ill, grow old and die; and replacement is a costly business, especially for those who are chronically distressed in the best of times. If the Byzantine governments had had any practical sense, they would have done their utmost, cost what it might, to preserve the *morale* and loyalty of the provincial soldier by making him the *élite* of the countryside: this the great military aristocrats thoroughly understood, and were in consequence idolised by those whom they commanded. But the central government would make no exceptions in their fiscal oppression of the communes; and the peasant-soldier was as cruelly plundered as his more exclusively agricultural brethren.

A close and filial relationship between soldier and emperor the

Byzantines always postulated in theory, but seldom took any pains to foster in practice. Instead, they allowed the soldier's loyalty to graft itself on to the very class which was most threatening to the unity, the agriculture and the revenue of the state. The soldiers who fought in Crete under the great aristocrat Nicephorus Phocas regarded him very much as the Old Guard regarded Napoleon. And when he exhorted them to fight bravely for their Christ and emperor, they answered 'For you we will fight, for you we will die'. It is not strange that two years later Nicephorus was on the throne.

As yet, the cancer was still in its infancy, and during the rule of the Macedonian house it was kept in bounds. But a study of tenth-century legislation, and of the origins of the usurping emperors Nicephorus II and John I, and of the pretenders Bardas Phocas and Bardas Sclerus, will show us how seriously the whole framework of society was threatened; and how it came about that when, after the Fourth Crusade, the empire was parcelled out among western barons, who introduced their own developed feudal system into it, there was scarcely any adjustment that was needed in adapting the old system to the new.[6]

The main achievement of Romanus I, as we have shown, was in reversing the tide of Saracen encroachment and conquest. But his arms were uniformly successful elsewhere. The Russians, that is, the Norman rulers of the Slavonic tribes in Russia, had concluded a treaty of commerce with Leo the Wise in 911, and for thirty years had been content with an annual subsidy and a lucrative trade with Constantinople. But in 941 Prince Igor of Kiev determined to repeat, with better hope of success, the attempt of 860. He got together a large number of his Viking ships – the Greeks said ten thousand, but the probable number did not exceed a thousand, each manned by between thirty and forty men: and he sailed out of the Dnieper and into the Black Sea. The moment was well chosen. The home fleet was operating against the Saracens in the Aegean, or dispersed even further west: the army was beyond the eastern frontier, hammering at the gates of Erzerum. The heart of the empire seemed defenceless. The gallant chamberlain Theophanes put fifteen old hulks into commission, stocked them with Greek fire, and sailed up the Bosphorus to see what he could do. Once more this formidable weapon showed its value. The first discharge set several of the enemy on fire, and they sheered off to the Bithynian coast. Here they disembarked and began a raid accompanied by hideous cruelties. But help was at hand. Bardas Phocas, the military governor of the Armeniac province, hastened with his levies to the coast, and brought the marauders to bay; while Gourgen, with the main imperial forces, came quickly westwards, and inflicted on them a crushing defeat. They fled to their ships and tried to escape northwards. But Theophanes was on the watch, this time with a powerful squadron. His ships closed with the enemy and once more opened fire with their siphons. The effect was catastrophic. Large numbers of the Russians were burnt, and those who leapt into the sea did not escape, since the oil burnt yet more fiercely in contact with water. Almost the whole expedition was wiped out. And Theophanes was received back into Constantinople in very well merited triumph. This reverse led to the renewal of the Russo-Byzantine treaty in 945, and peace was maintained during the next twenty years.7

Romanus, preoccupied as he was, first with Bulgars, then with Saracens and Russians, did not lose sight of the west, although he could not intervene there forcibly. During the seventy years which passed between the death of Charles the Fat and the coronation of Otto the Great, the state of Italy was wretched in the extreme. It was torn by the quarrels of Lewis III and Berengar, of Rodolph and Hugh of Arles. After the death of Berengar, the very name of empire in the west was abandoned. The Saracens, in alliance with this or that petty duchy, were virtual masters of western Italy up to the gates of Rome: while, from their lair at Fraxinetum, on the Gulf of Lyons, they devastated the *regnum italicum* far and wide. The state of Rome itself cannot be recalled without a blush for the reign of harlots and favourites, of Theophylact and Theodora, of Marozia and Alberic, of Pope Sergius and Pope John X and Pope John XI. Now, if ever, seemed to be the moment for decisive intervention on the part of Byzantium, which would have every chance of speedy and permanent success. It could not be. Byzantium was fighting for her life against Symeon of Bulgaria; and thereafter every man was needed for the more pressing task of crippling the power of the eastern Saracens. The Lombard princes rose in revolt, and the Emperor Romanus, himself an usurper, could only resort to diplomacy. By a prudent stroke, taken, we cannot doubt, after the most careful consideration, he threw in his lot with Hugh of Arles, who seemed to be the most stable factor in the Italian kaleidoscope, and who, though never crowned emperor, carried in his veins the now much diluted *ichor* of Charles the Great. The alliance was maintained by Romanus with steadfast loyalty and generosity. Once more, for the last time, an effort was made to unite the imperial stock of East Rome with the family of Charlemagne. In 944 the bastard daughter of King Hugh was given in marriage to Romanus II, son of Constantine Porphyrogenitus and grandson of Romanus I. And once more the attempt failed. After five years of unconsummated union, the child-empress died.

Constantine VII devotes a whole chapter of his treatise *De administrando imperio* to proving that his daughter-in-law was descended from the Great Charles. Her mother was a mere courtesan. Her paternal grandmother, Bertha, was illegitimate. Her father died in failure and disgrace, the tool of the Marquis Berengar of Ivrea. Yet through all these murky shades the Byzantine Foreign Office could still discern the *magni nominis umbra*, the mighty ancestor who had ruled with the name of emperor over all Francia.[8]

The fall of Romanus I Lacapenus at the end of 944 was by no means expected. The legitimate heir, his son-in-law Constantine VII Porphyrogenitus, though cordially hating the usurper, had not the energy to seek ways of ousting him. He was now nearly forty years of age, and his time had been divided between his books and his bottle. In 944 Romanus had never looked more secure. He was victor in the east and north. His dynastic plans were in a fair way to fulfilment. It is often said that he wished to supplant the Macedonian house as the Macedonian had supplanted the Amorian. This appears to be untrue. He had after all married his daughter Helen to the legitimate heir, and the marriage had been fruitful. The boy who was to be Romanus II was born in 937. What might have happened if Romanus' eldest son Christopher, father of the Tsarina Maria of Bulgaria, had lived, cannot now be guessed. But Christopher died in 932, and the old Romanus had no intention of promoting his two younger sons, Stephen and Constantine, above his son-in-law. Romanus had two more sons: Theophylact, who was patriarch, and Basil, who was illegitimate, and who grew up to be the ablest man in the empire under five emperors.

The appointment of Theophylact, which was inspired by Leo VI's appointment of his brother Stephen to the patriarchate in 886, was a master-stroke which ensured the quiet collaboration of church and state for a quarter of a century. Indeed, Theophylact was no more than the head of a department, and a very lax and idle head even at that. For ecclesiastical affairs he cared not one straw, but shuffled through his official duties with what speed he could, and went off to hunt the boar or to superintend his stables. He kept two thousand horses, and would no doubt have been of more practical use as a farrier-major than as a bishop. He fed his pets not on corn and hay but on mashes of dates, figs, and pistachio nuts, steeped in sweet wines. But if he was no use, it is equally true that he was no harm; and Constantine Porphyrogenitus who, to mark his loathing of Lacapenid policies, appointed, to succeed his brother-in-law, the fanatical monk Polyeuctus, was snapped up in the jaws of King Stork and very quickly saw reason to regret King Log.[9]

In 944, then, with church and state at peace, with opposition lulled if not quite extinct, there seemed to be no reason why Romanus should not pass into a quiet old age and die, universally regretted, in his imperial bed. This was not to be. The infatuated young princes, Stephen and Constantine Lacapenus, incensed by their father's refusal to promote them over the head of their brother-in-law, and utterly deluded as to the extent of their own popularity in the City, where in fact they were regarded with just contempt and aversion, devised the frantic plan of seizing and deposing their old father and ruling in his place. On 17 December 944, this insane act was put into operation. Romanus was carried out of the palace and interned in a monastery in the island of Prote. The rumour that in these proceedings the legitimate heir to the Macedonian house had been slain provoked a reaction in the city that at once opened the eyes of the conspirators to their own wickedness and folly. The citizens rose as one man. The palace was besieged. The crowds roared for a sight of Constantine Porphyrogenitus; and it seemed likely, if he were not produced, that the whole place would be pulled down about their ears by the popular fury. Constantine, who was immersed as usual in his books, was disinterred from the library, and presented, dishevelled and dirty, at a palace window: whereupon the good citizens consented to go home. But the lesson was not lost, either on the conspirators or on the legitimists. The two Lacapenid princes laid a plot to murder their brother-in-law, but could not evade the vigilance of his wife, their sister Helen. It was clear that these lunatics could not be left at large. A second palace revolution took place on 27 January 945. Stephen and his brother were seized in their turn, and sent to keep their father company in the monastery of Prote. And at last, after twenty-four years of seclusion and abasement, Constantine Porphyrogenitus, son of Leo the Wise, the true heir of Basil the Macedonian, took over his rightful inheritance as Constantine VII.

The captive princes were no sooner put ashore on the island than their father Romanus, in the black robe of a monk, hastened down with fiendish glee to welcome them. At sight of their dejection, his face assumed a sarcastic smile, and, turning up his eyes to heaven, he detained them with the following beautiful allocution:

Now God bless the day which has moved Your Imperial Highnesses to visit my humble retreat! It was, I make no doubt, that same piety which expelled me from my palace which would not permit your longer sojourn there. But oh! well done to send me on before you! For our brethren here, devoted as they are to the divine philosophy, would otherwise scarcely have known how to receive your Majesties, unless I had gone on ahead to show them the way.

This and a good deal more was said by Romanus to his graceless sons, who, the historian tells us, looked uncommonly foolish.[10] They were removed to islands more remote. And there they were murdered or died.

Romanus himself, with his confessor Sergius, nephew to the Patriarch Photius, lived on three years in true piety, and died in 948. Seldom has an usurper had less to regret or more to be proud of. His usurpation was stained by no murder of the Lord's anointed: and was crowned with a full measure of glory. Fate in turn was kind to him. His deposition was no worse than an opportunity to reflect upon and repent his sins before he died: and, says his biographer, these were washed as white as snow, and Romanus Lacapenus went to heaven. Let us hope so. If we reckon up the list of great emperors from Michael III to Basil II, Romanus Lacapenus will assuredly come very near the top of the column. He was sterling stuff, through and through: capable, level-headed, brave and sagacious. It was indeed strange that his merits were signally ignored until, at the suggestion of John Bury, they were rediscovered in one of the earliest and most brilliant works of Sir Steven Runciman.

NOTES

[1] Theoph. Cont., 405–9; Bréhier, 161–3.
[2] Theoph. Cont., 398–401; *DAI*, 234.
[3] Ostrogorsky, 230–2; Bréhier, 170–2.
[4] *DAI*, 204.
[5] Theoph. Cont., 432.
[6] Ostrogorsky, 225–36; Vasiliev, 567; Bréhier, 164.
[7] Theoph. Cont., 423–6.
[8] Bréhier, 174–5; *DAI*, 108–12.
[9] Cedrenus, 332–3.
[10] Liudprand, 144–5.

CHAPTER NINETEEN

CONSTANTINE VII PORPHYROGENITUS

Constantine was surnamed Porphyrogenitus – that is to say, *born in the purple* – because he was born the son of a reigning sovereign, Leo VI: an 'Aetheling', as our Anglo-Saxon ancestors would have called him. This proud title, which was the badge of legitimacy and a reproach to an usurper, seems first to have been borne by the Emperor Michael III, the first emperor since Constantine VI who could lay claim to its significance. Leo VI, born just after his father Basil I had become Michael's colleague, was eligible for the description, and was in fact sometimes so described. But his son Constantine was – after legitimisation – the veritable *porphyrogenitus*, since he was the purple-born sovereign all through the long usurpation of his father-in-law Romanus I.

Constantine was an invalid, or at least sickly, all through his life, and it was an ironical circumstance that his life of quiet seclusion from the age of fifteen to the age of forty was chiefly responsible for its preservation to the age of fifty-four.[1] His years of seclusion were devoted to study and writing. He was the true son of his father, and a scholar in the tradition of Photius. He loved books. He collected a splendid library from all parts of his empire, and probably from outside it also. He was a finished classical scholar, one of the very few Byzantine scholars who had a true sense of the style and meaning of the prose writers of antiquity. Few medieval writers, in east or west, have written more gracefully; and here he was in marked contrast to his grandfather, who could not write at all, to his father, who wrote like a frigid pedant, and to his prodigious grandson, Basil II, who wrote in the idiom of a plough-boy.

256

He was also unique among emperors in being an artist. Many or most of his fellow emperors professed to patronise religious art. But Constantine actually painted with his own hands; and, says Liudprand, the palace gossip had it that his allowance from the budget of his father-in-law was so stingy that he sold the pictures he painted in order to keep himself in meat and drink.[2] This is probably untrue. After all, Romanus was the father of Constantine's wife and it is not very likely – if for that reason alone – that he would have allowed him to live on or below the breadline. But we may very reasonably wonder whether the story does not contain a germ of truth. Constantine was, in a very honourable way, an extravagant man. Being, as he rightly believed, the *de jure* sovereign of the world, he saw no reason why he should not be extravagant. He longed to spend *centenaria* – thousands of gold pieces – on gorgeous manuscripts, mosaics, pictures and reliquaries. It is more than likely that his father-in-law, faced with financial problems of which Constantine had no conception, refused rather tartly to foot the bill for these extravagances, and that the recluse scholar and his entourage were left to raise the wind where they could.

But the artistic activity of Constantine VII is of greater significance than this. In his day came that reversion to the humanistic, three-dimensional art of the Hellenistic period which is one of the principal features of the so-called 'Macedonian Renaissance'. I think it is clear that Constantine Porphyrogenitus was a, if not the, prime mover in this reversion to the spirit of late antiquity. If so, it was all of a piece with the spirit of historical writing seen in the Continuators of Theophanes, who were themselves inspired by this emperor to write of the reigns of the emperors from Leo V to Basil I. Their writings are a chief source for the ninth century, and we note in their treatment a reawakened interest in individual human character in the round, which is strictly parallel to the three-dimensional treatment of the human figure in art.

Constantine, says one of his biographers, gave assistance and encouragement, not only to literature and learning, but also to the humbler trades of craftsmen and artisans.[3] He means, to engravers, goldsmiths, jewellers and enamellers. In the cathedral treasury of Limburg is preserved one of the most beautiful and gorgeous works surviving from the middle ages: the gold reliquary of the True Cross. The gold box is covered inside and out with jewels and enamel, with chasing and filigree, with figures and inscriptions. No one who has not studied it can form any conception of the skill, artistry and magnificence of Byzantine workmanship in the middle tenth century. Around the edge run two inscriptions: 'The Emperors Constantine and Romanus [that is, Romanus II], in setting of translucent gems and pearls, have given this sacred Wood a home of wonders'; and the other, 'In deepest honouring of Christ Basil the President caused this repository to be decorated'. The young Romanus became emperor in 948, and his father died in 959. The object is thus securely dated to these eleven years, and probably to the late 950s: for Basil the President was that illegitimate son of the old Romanus who was advanced by his brother-in-law to be President of the Council some years after his father's death. The Limburg reliquary brings us very near to the Porphyrogenitus.

But his encouragement of art is not the only or even the chief reason for our enormous indebtedness to Constantine. His encouragement of, and contributions to, literature and scholarship far surpass it. It is with encyclopedism in the widest sense that we connect the name of Constantine Porphyrogenitus. Believing, as all men then believed, that wisdom resided in the past, which was the only safe guide, both in theory and in practice, to the present, he set on foot and actively fostered a huge programme of codification and extract, dealing with nearly all the departments of life and administration. Manuals of strategy, manuals of agriculture, manuals of horse-breeding, manuals of diplomacy, manuals of history, topography, ethnography, hagiography, antiquities, laws and palace ceremonial – all these he promoted with the single object of helping the future by giving ready access to the past. He had regretfully to admit the principle of excerpting: but, as he said rather plaintively, since historical writing had now grown to an intractable bulk and since industry and scholarship, like everything else, were in decline, it was vain to expect people nowadays to read original works in full: so he would skim off the cream, and hope that practical men would be prevailed on to digest it for their profit. This thirst for knowledge and this unflagging industry are the most characteristic qualities of the laborious emperor: and what on earth one of his detractors can mean by saying that he was an idler who never got anything done, and preferred the easy way out of everything, it would be hard to discover.

Dr Samuel Johnson once described the novelist Henry Fielding in Malvolio's phrase as a 'barren rascal'. 'I asked him', says Boswell, 'what he could mean by so strange an assertion?' One would have liked to have put the same question to John Scylitzes.

It was as parts of this programme of encyclopedism that the emperor wrote three works with his own hand, or at least compiled them with his own scissors and paste. The so-called *De cerimoniis aulae byzantinae* is a monumental handbook of imperial ceremonial, concerned with the ritual to be gone through at every feast, reception or investiture. It is chiefly to this work that our exact knowledge of the Byzantine theory of empire is due, for this theory is illustrated on every page by what is ordered to be said or done. The emperor as Christ, surrounded by his twelve great peers on Easter Day; the emperor presiding at the hippodrome as universal Victor; the emperor to whom the foreign nations bring their gifts as the Wise Men once brought their gold and frankincense and myrrh; the emperor as the elect of God, the embodiment of divine and universal Providence – the whole picture is before us. The Great Palace, with its gorgeous apartments, its wonderful monuments, its luxurious furniture, its nobles and high officials in their many-coloured robes of brocade or shot silk, stiff with gold and silver thread, rises before us in these pages as no other work can recreate it.[4]

But there was a department of state even more important, even more needful of guidance, than palace ceremonial: and that was the practice of government itself. In the year 952 the young Emperor Romanus II reached his fourteenth birthday. His father wished to introduce him to the technique of governing, and to the most pressing problems at home and abroad which would, in all probability, confront him. He therefore resurrected an older antiquarian work of his own which dealt with the origins of the foreign 'nations' who, in the tenth century, lived all round the borders of the empire; and on to this text he grafted some sage advice, a priceless estimate of the world situation as seen from Constantinople early in 952, and an extremely shrewd essay in diplomacy, which he was well qualified to give. The whole made up a unique book to which modern scholars have given the title *De administrando imperio*, but which its author called simply 'Constantine to his son Romanus'.

The later, political and diplomatic, parts of the book are highly illuminating. It comes as no surprise that at this period the eyes of the Foreign Ministry were turned almost exclusively to the north and the north-east, that is, to the Russian steppes and to Armenia and Georgia. The completeness of the Byzantine success in converting the Bulgaria of Symeon into a Byzantine protectorate is seen in the fact that Bulgaria, so far from being a pressing problem any more, is not even given a separate treatment in the book, but is merely mentioned in its historical and topographical relations with Russians, Pechenegs and Southern Slavs. The other old enemy, the caliphate, is not indeed ignored, but its treatment is almost wholly historical, and very little is said of Saracen matters after the time of Harun al-Rashid. Some vindication of Byzantine claims to sovereignty over Venice, Italy, Croatia and Serbia is made on the grounds of Basil I's campaigns among the Slavs and of his supposed recapture of Bari in 871. But these are not urgent problems. Sicily is written off. Spain is scarcely mentioned at all. The one urgent and paramount problem is the manipulation of the Turkic Pechenegs, who stretched across from the mouth of the Dnieper westwards to the mouth of the Danube. They were the key to the whole political complex which included Chazaria, Russia, Bulgaria and Hungary. Their enormous multitudes and horrible savagery had won them an unenviable reputation even among the no less savage Magyars, who could in no circumstances be got to look them in the face. If, says the emperor, you keep in with the Pechenegs, you need fear nothing from Russians, Bulgars, or Magyars. The Pechenegs are greedy and arrogant. They know their importance and they pitch their demands high. But it is always worth while to pay: for if you do not, the peace of the northern frontier is at the mercy of their invincible hordes.

To be short, the Pechenegs have taken the place of the Bulgars as the number one menace, and no Byzantine government must trifle with it. Every year Byzantine envoys, laden with money and cloth and silks and pepper, must contact the Pechenegs chieftains west of the Crimea and at the mouth of the Danube. The peace is to be annually resworn, promises of alliance renewed, and hostages exchanged. Only then can the empire breathe quietly. This intelligence is of first-rate importance, and was chiefly responsible for the whole book's being marked *Top Secret*. It would seem never to have left the palace, and to have circulated even there among a very limited class of diplomatists.[5]

Armenia and Georgia, after the conquests of Gourgen, are a scarcely less vital area. The principality of Taron, technically outside the frontier, is regarded as a province nonetheless. And the cities north of Lake Van, put under tribute by Gourgen in 932, must be reoccupied and firmly held. The jealous and unbelievably complicated clans of Georgians are described in detail; and the various methods which have been tried, both successful and unsuccessful, to conciliate, evict, or generally set them by the cars, are explained with a wealth of historical anecdote. Lastly the emperor turns to the organisation of frontier provinces actually within the empire, both east and south. Especial emphasis is laid on the origins of the *themes* of Mesopotamia and Lycandus, founded respectively in 900 and 916, for these are the obvious and most recent models for the planned expansion eastwards. The methods described are an astonishingly clever alternation of diplomacy and force.

A separate section is devoted to the imperial navy, and we have already noted the importance of this arm as a trusted supporter of the legitimate house. It was the sailors who had cut down Constantine Ducas; and they would infallibly have done the same to Romanus Lacapenus if he had not himself been a sailor and their own trusted admiral. Keep the navy loyal, the emperor obviously believes, and nothing very bad can happen, even at the worst.

As regards diplomacy, Constantine is in his element. His guiding principle is the principle of that art itself – to get as much and give as little as possible. There are to be no concessions to foreigners who come asking for marriage alliances, or imperial robes, or of course Greek fire. In all these departments concessions would certainly be damaging. Make any and every excuse for refusal, but always *refuse*. And it is here that the emperor gets in a venomous thrust at his father-in-law. For, respecting foreign marriages in the imperial house, suppose your foreigners say, 'Yes, but if so, how comes it that Lord Romanus gave his grand-daughter in marriage to the Bulgarian Tsar Peter?' What are we to say about that? *This* is what you are to say about it: Lord Romanus was an illiterate boor, a common fellow, who was too ignorant to know what was right, and too arrogant to listen to reason. 'Of course, you may say, the Lord Romanus was a usurper and his son was a cypher, so what did it matter? But in fact it mattered a great deal. The scandal he caused was immense; and was largely responsible for his own deposition, and for the just detestation in which his memory is universally held even at the present day'.[6]

I ought to say, in all justice, that though Constantine's resentment against Romanus was understandable, if not excusable, he is here altogether unfair to his father-in-law. The marriage of Maria Lacapena to Peter of Bulgaria was, on the contrary, a stroke of profound policy, which amply repaid the very slight derogation of imperial dignity, and secured peace in the Balkans for about twenty-five years. Moreover Peter's father Symeon had been granted imperial status in 913: wrongly, no doubt, but the grant had been made. And, barbarous as the Bulgars appeared to be, they were anyhow orthodox Christians, so that no charge of heresy could lie against them. If we compare the marriages of Constantine's own sister Anna to Lewis III of Italy, or of his own son Romanus to the bastard daughter of King Hugh, we shall not be in any doubt which of these three unions was the most politic, and the most respectable.

Apart from such lapses as these, which are dictated by personal rancour, the *De administrando imperio* is the work of a very clever man. The book is also, needless to say, much more than a diplomatic handbook. It contains a wealth of historical information on the origins of modern Europe about which we should, without it, have no ideas at all, or only very hazy ones. Where they can be checked, Constantine's accounts of the nations are nearly always right, and modern scholars are at last coming round to the realisation of their essential accuracy.

In his practical policies Constantine has been almost universally condemned. He 'seemed' to govern, says Gibbon. He was at the mercy of his intriguing wife Helen. He was prejudiced and implacable. He drank too much. And so on. If he did indeed drink too much (and 'too much' is a relative term), his industry is proof that this failing did not interfere with his duties. He was no Michael III.[7] Among the many arts which he cultivated was the art of diplomacy; and his activities in this field were assiduous and highly beneficial. The year 949 was the year of western embassies. Envoys from Otto of Germany, Berengar of Italy, and Abd ar-Rahman of Cordova all came to Constantinople. And these embassies will lead us to a brief consideration of Byzantine policy in the west at this time.

The western policy of the legitimate, Macedonian, house had

tended towards Germany rather than Italy ever since the days when Basil I had opened communication with Lewis the German in opposition to his nephew the 'Emperor' Lewis II (872–3.) This policy was shrewd: since the German princes were further removed from, and more alien to, the papal authority than were the petty kings and marquises of Italy. On the deposition of Romanus I, his son-in-law Constantine at once reversed his policy. King Hugh and his son Lothar were abandoned with little regret to the untender mercies of Berengar, the marquis of Ivrea; and in 945 negotiations were begun between the Byzantine government and Otto the Saxon.

These negotiations were continued, with growing cordiality, during the next five years. Once again, fragmentary as are the records, we seem to discern an effort on the part of Byzantium to weave the familiar pattern of an east-west alliance, cemented by a royal marriage, against the Saracens of the Mediterranean. The same attempt, by precisely the same methods, had been made by Theophilus in 838 and by Basil in 868. In 949 came the ambassadors already enumerated, from Germany, Italy and Spain: and it is reasonable to suppose that they all came about the same business. Otto's envoy Liutefred came perhaps to discuss a marriage between the young widower Romanus II (whose child-wife died in this year) and Otto's niece, Hedwig or Hadawig of Bavaria. We know that Greek teachers and courtiers were at once sent to Germany to instruct the young princess, and that these tutors were still at Otto's court in 952. The ambassador of Berengar, who came with Liutefred, was none other than Liudprand, later bishop of Cremona, who has left us a lively account of the court of Constantine Porphyrogenitus, but, significantly, very little account of the business he was sent to transact. Yet it is not difficult to guess what this business was. Constantine Porphyrogenitus, now the ally of Otto the Saxon, was manifestly interested to persuade Berengar, then the most powerful man in Italy, to submit himself to Otto, which, as is well known, he did in 952. The third group of envoys were those of the Omayyad caliph of Cordova. The common aim is clear enough, and clearer still when we remember that, in this very year, Byzantium mounted one more massive invasion of Crete. It was the old story of east-west collaboration. Otto was to be bound by a Byzantine marriage, and to intervene in South Italy, his rear being secured by the settlement with Berengar. And the Spanish caliph was to join in action against his enemies the African Saracens, in Sicily.

Constantine's plans for this alliance against the Saracens failed; but that is not to say that they were misconceived. The plans of Theophilus and Basil I, of which Constantine's was simply a re-suscitation, also failed, for reasons beyond their control. Where Constantine can probably be censured is in his related plan for the capture of Crete. In 949, as in 842, the expedition sailed to Crete, and as in 842, it totally failed. There was no shame in such failure: half a dozen previous attempts had failed, and twelve years later the greatest general then living succeeded indeed in the enterprise, but succeeded by only the narrowest of margins. The fact is that Crete was a Moslem island with a distinct culture of its own: and not a Christian island yearning for 'liberation'. This the Byzantines knew very well. They wanted to occupy Crete not to liberate a non-existent Christian population, but simply in order to save their own coasts and islands from continual rapine. And when they referred to Crete, it was the island itself that was 'God-damned', and not just the Moslem occupants of it. However, the command of the expedition was entrusted by the emperor to one Constantine Gongyles, a eunuch, a diplomat, and a one time minister of the Empress Zoe. Just what amount of responsibility for the failure can be attributed to Gongyles is not clear. The chronicler says that he neither fortified his camp nor sent out scouts, which seems almost unbelievable. At all events the Cretans attacked him, routed and took prisoner his whole force, and compelled him to take ignominious refuge on his flag-ship.[8]

It was, we have said, in this year that the celebrated Liudprand of Cremona first came to Constantinople. He has left us a charming account of his mission, which brings us nearly as close to the emperor as does contemplation of the Limburg reliquary. He left Venice on 25 August and arrived in Constantinople on 17 September. He was received by the emperor in the throne-room of the Magnaura palace:

Before the emperor's seat [says Liudprand] stood a tree, made of gilded bronze, its branches filled with birds which uttered various cries according to their species. The throne itself was of enormous size and guarded by lions, made either of bronze or wood and plated with gold, which beat the ground with their tails and roared with open jaws and

moving tongues. After I had made a triple obeisance before the emperor, with my face to the floor, I looked up and found he had meanwhile changed his clothes and was sitting on a level with the roof. How
it was worked, I could not imagine: perhaps by the sort of device we
use for lifting the timbers of a wine-press. The emperor did not on this
occasion speak to me personally: even had he wished to do so, the distance between us would have made conversation impracticable. At a
nod from the interpreter, I left his presence and retired to my hotel.[9]

On Christmas Day 949 Constantine asked Liudprand to dine in
the Saloon of the Nineteen Couches. A juggler came in, balancing
a 25-foot pole on his forehead. Two boys swarmed up the pole
and did gymnastics on the top, before sliding down to earth. The
pole remained motionless on the man's forehead. The emperor,
seeing Liudprand's stupefaction, sent to ask him which he thought
the cleverer, the man or the boys? Liudprand could only say,
rather feebly, that he didn't know. Constantine laughed good-
naturedly: 'Well, well', he said, 'I don't believe I know either':
and went on eating fruit. There was a time when this sort of
anecdote was considered beneath the dignity of history. But I
fancy that few of us would be of such an opinion today. It is plain
that Liudprand thought his host a thoroughly good fellow, which,
by all accounts except one, he certainly seems to have been.

The western alliance was not the only occasion for Constantine's diplomacy. There are long accounts extant of his reception
of Saracen delegates in 946, who came to negotiate an exchange of
prisoners, those of Gourgen against those of Saif ad-Daula of
Mosul. In 949 the Magyars sent a very high delegation, which
submitted to baptism and concluded a treaty of non-aggression.
May we not see in this mission yet one more facet of the grand
alliance between east and west – the desire to protect Otto's rear
from Hungarian attack, while he came southwards to expel the
Saracens from Italy? In 957 came the emir of Diyarbekir; and on
Wednesday, September 9, of the same year came Princess Olga
of Russia, the widow of Igor and the mother of Prince Svyatoslav.
It cannot be doubted that all this diplomacy did an enormous
amount of good, not least in what would now be termed 'cultural
relations'. There are good grounds for believing that Constantine's
accurate and detailed information about the origins of the Magyars came from the Hungarian ambassadors of 949. In the same
year he sent to the caliph of Cordova splendid manuscripts of

Dioscorides and Orosius, adding, rather pedantically, 'The Dioscorides will be of good use to your Excellency, if you can find a medical man with a knowledge of ancient Greek to explain it to you. As for Orosius, he is no problem, as you will doubtless easily find someone who knows Latin'. The imperial missive was written in golden letters on a purple parchment and sealed with a golden bull, bearing on one face the effigy of Jesus Christ (on Whom be peace, adds the Moslem annalist). It was enclosed in a case of chased silver, with a golden lid on which was enamelled the emperor's portrait, and this casket in turn was enclosed within a tapestry-covered coffer.

I dwell with complacency on the arts of peace and diplomacy pursued by the Emperor Constantine Porphyrogenitus, since they form a pleasant interlude in the monotonous catalogue of defeats and victories. But it would of course be a mistake to suppose that his reign was free of fighting; and we have already noted his plan to rid the inland sea of the Saracen marauders. The war on the eastern front was never at rest. It was pursued with various success, but without any significant disaster and one very notable triumph, the capture of Adata. The important thing to note about these campaigns is that the imperial armies were almost all commanded by aristocrats. Bardas Phocas commanded in chief. His son Nicephorus was military governor of the Anatolic province. His younger son Leo was military governor of Cappadocia. Pothus Argyrus commanded a troop of lifeguards and was appointed *generalissimo* against the Hungarians in 946. The one exception to the rule was Basil, the illegitimate but most able son of old Romanus I, who made up in natural parts what he lacked in experience, and was thus able to lead an army with success even against the formidable Saif ad-Daula.[10]

Constantine governed during fifteen years, that is, from the fall of his father-in-law in 944 to his own death in November 959, at the age of fifty-four years and two months. Three years before his own death died his disreputable brother-in-law, the Patriarch Theophylact, as the result (characteristically) of a riding accident. To mark his disapproval of the lax régime of Theophylact, the misguided emperor, in an evil hour, chose a monk, the fanatical Polyeuctus, as his successor. Polyeuctus – as might have been expected – soon showed that he was in the tradition of Ignatius and Theodore Studita. Even at his institution, there were angry. mur-

murs from moderate churchmen. Almost at once Polyeuctus began his tiresome career of protest and complaint. He put the palace in an uproar by publicly accusing Basil the chamberlain of greed and extortion, when Constantine himself was on his way to church on Easter Saturday. Constantine received this attack on his brother-in-law and favourite minister with the highest resentment. Polyeuctus next insisted on digging up the nearly forgotten relics of Leo vi's fourth marriage, and demanding that the Patriarch Euthymius, who had, with Rome's consent, issued dispensation, should be re-inserted in the holy diptychs. This was to undo all the work of the Act of Union and the claim was very rightly rejected. Constantine's last three years were embittered by these quarrels. He had long been ailing; and his infirmity grew apace. He crossed to Bithynia to consult the bishop of Cyzicus on the possibility of dismissing Polyeuctus; and then went on to pay a farewell visit to the monks of Mount Olympus. They warned him of the approaching end, and he returned to the City to die. His relatives surrounded his bed in tears and there is no reason at all to believe that their grief was insincere.

Constantine had six children by his wife Helen: the boy Romanus, born in 938, and five girls. He was an affectionate father, and his relations with his daughters remind one of the saying of old King George iii, 'I have no Goneril and Regan, only three Cordelias'. In appearance he was tall and broad shouldered, upright and manly, with a ruddy complexion, a long face, an aquiline nose, blue eyes and a long black beard. We have several portraits of him, of which the best, datable to early in 945, is an ivory in the Museum of Fine Arts in Moscow. To his intense regard for the dignity and importance of his imperial office he united the enthusiasm of a scholar and an artist. In practical affairs he was by no means the fool he has been made out to be: he had a clear view of the needs of his empire, and he very properly relied, where he could, on diplomacy rather than war to satisfy them. He was not a great conqueror, but he was a good and conscientious ruler. As a writer, our debt to him is beyond measure. Let us for a moment try to imagine what our ignorance of the Middle Byzantine polity would be if all that he wrote, and all that he caused to be written, were lost to us.

NOTES

[1] *DAI*, 5.
[2] Liudprand, 91–2.
[3] Cedrenus, 326.
[4] Ostrogorsky, 233.
[5] *DAI*, 48–56.
[6] *DAI*, 72–4.
[7] Cedrenus, 325; Bréhier, 183–4.
[8] Cedrenus, 336; Leo Diac., 7.
[9] Liudprand, 154–5.
[10] Ostrogorsky, 235; Theoph. Cont., 461–3.

CHAPTER TWENTY

ROMANUS II AND NICEPHORUS II

The new emperor, Romanus II, was, on his father's death, just twenty-one years of age. There was never the smallest doubt about his legitimacy, and no one could taunt him with a father's lust and heresy. He mounted the throne with the happiest auspices, perhaps, of any Byzantine sovereign. His empire was great and growing, in the arts of war no less than in the far nobler arts of peace. Its prestige was at last fully restored, owing to the energies of his great-grandfather, his grandfathers and his father. He combined his father's commanding presence with his mother's beauty. He went out of his way to cultivate and patronise the noble families who were the backbone of his empire's military strength; and in this, if in this alone, he showed a wisdom singularly at variance with the thoughtless irresponsibility with which the enemies of his house were eager to credit him. He was, indeed, fond of hunting and polo: but if these manly sports are to be set down as blemishes, some august personages, even in our day, are likely to incur a low estimate from their posterity. He reigned only three years. But during these years the empire was governed with a sagacity, accompanied by triumphs abroad, which says a great deal for the character of the juvenile sovereign.

He had, indeed, in the days of his father, committed an imprudence which, in a youthful prince, we shall consider pardonable. On the death of his child-bride, the Italian Bertha-Eudocia, in 949, the Byzantine Foreign Office had, as we saw, arranged for him a marriage with Hedwig of Bavaria, the niece of Otto the Great. It would have been well if this union could have been brought to consummation: I mean, well for the state, though certainly not for the emperor's domestic happiness, for Hedwig, later Duchess of Suabia, grew up to be a Tartar. But Romanus fell in love with an innkeeper's or huckster's daughter, and in 956 he married her, despite anything his father or the Foreign Office could urge to the contrary. His bride Theophano was unfortunately a woman of ambition, cast in the mould of Justinian's Empress Theodora and the Empress Zoe, her husband's own grandmother. It is perhaps the moment to trace the further splendour of this God-guarded family. Romanus and Theophano had a daughter Anna, who was married in 988 to Vladimir, Prince of Russia. Her grand-daughter Anna, born to her son Yaroslav I, married in 1051 Henry I of France, the grandson of Hugh Capet. In this way during nearly eight centuries the blood of Basil the Macedonian ran in the veins of the kings of France.

Theophano has been credited with a whole series of the blackest crimes known to man. It is said that she poisoned her father-in-law and, at least by implication, her first husband: and that she betrayed her second husband to the daggers of his assassins. As regards the first two charges, there is not a tittle of evidence. Constantine Porphyrogenitus died probably of typhoid fever, like his father. And as for Romanus II, we do not know why he should have died at twenty-four; but we can at least say that no one suffered more by his death than his wife, who, incidentally, had given birth to her daughter Anna only forty-eight hours before he did die. The reckless irresponsibility with which charges of poisoning are bandied about in medieval and modern chronicles should make us extremely chary of accepting rumours of this nature for facts, or even for probabilities.

The reign began well. The principal offices of government were – as was usual at a demise of the crown – shuffled, but not so thoroughly as had been customary. The command-in-chief of the armed forces was confirmed on the great general and aristocrat, Nicephorus Phocas. The confidential office of Grand Chamberlain was indeed removed from Basil, the son of old Romanus. But his talents for diplomacy and indeed general statesmanship were kept at command. He was given the title of President of the Senate. In his place as chamberlain was set Joseph Bringas, who had until that time been high admiral of the fleet.

And now, after so many decades of tribulation in the Aegean, it was time to deal once for all with the island of Crete. A late Arabic source suggests that after the disastrous failure of Constantine Gongyles to recover the place in 949, Constantine Porphyrogenitus had tried to win by diplomacy a part of what force had failed to achieve. According to this source, he proposed to the emir that Cretan piracy in the Aegean should be halted, the desolate islands be repopulated, and in return a very handsome subsidy, yielding twice the sum to be gained by marauding, should be paid to the emir. No evidence of this transaction survives in Byzantine documents, though the story is very far from improbable. But such a settlement could not be other than temporary. The new emperor felt strong enough to try once more where so many had failed. There was a sharp division in the council. A majority seems to have deplored the undertaking and made much of the losses in blood and treasure hitherto sustained in similar enterprises; and their point of view was understandable if Constantine VII had in fact bought peace in the Aegean. But the emperor and the ex-admiral Joseph bore down all opposition, and the expedition was determined on. Nothing needful for success was wanting. The numbers given for the flotilla are startling. The squadron of liquid-fire ships is put at two thousand; the great troop-carriers at a thousand; and the supply ships at 308. The army was composed of the best fighting elements: Armenian cavalry, Russian axe-men, and picked regiments of Slavonic guards. Their number is not given, but it was probably not less than fifty thousand. The command-in-chief was entrusted to Nicephorus Phocas.

On 13 July 960 this vast armada hove in sight of Candia. Its arrival seems to have been a complete surprise. Many of the chief Saracens of the city were in *villeggiatura*. Nicephorus landed unopposed on the sandy coast at Halmyros. From far and wide the residents of the countryside abandoned their dwellings and rushed for cover behind the walls of Candia. Nicephorus was not to be hurried. He began by constructing a fortified camp, almost a walled town, at Phoenicia, the 'Place of the Date-Palms'. He issued strict orders against straggling, pillage and drunkenness. Only by iron discipline could success be achieved. The wisdom of these orders was soon painfully apparent. The harvest was ripe and Nicephorus despatched a strong force, under one of his lieutenants, Pastilas, to collect provender and forage. Pastilas, deceived by the lack of opposition, allowed his men to forget their orders and become disorganised. The Cretans, lurking in the hills, rushed down on them and cut them off to the last man. Pastilas himself was slain.

This was a serious setback; but, apart from it, all at first went well. The siege was laid in due form. Two sorties of the besieged were repulsed and at last the whole of the land side was blockaded. However, the sea was still open, since in the absence of any haven Nicephorus could not keep his ships at sea, and had to draw them up on land. Swift galleys were dispatched from Candia to Egypt and Spain, to announce the investment and to implore Saracen aid to the threatened city. This was not forthcoming: and, after enquiry, Cairo and Cordova abandoned Candia to its fate. The besiegers behaved with atrocious cruelty to their captives, with the idea of breaking the spirit of those within the walls. But in this they probably achieved the reverse of what they intended. For all was by no means over. Winter came on, and with winter came famine. The harvest had failed in Thrace, and the price of bread rose alarmingly, even in Constantinople. The army before Candia began to go short and to show signs of mutiny. This was exactly the danger-point, the point at which so many expeditions had failed in the past. It took all Nicephorus' personal influence to allay the discontent. The home government, harassed as they were, made extraordinary efforts to collect grain and ship it to the island. Fortunately it arrived in time, and the danger passed. In February two attempts to carry the walls were beaten back. But on 7 March 961, after eight months of blockade, the fortification was breached, and the victorious Byzantine army burst into the stronghold.

And now a condign vengeance was to be wreaked for 135 years of misery and ruin and slavery. No quarter was given. The rich and flourishing city, stuffed with the spoils of a century's pillage of so many Aegean towns, churches and monasteries, was abandoned in its turn to a general sack. The island was pacified in the most effective manner. The Arab chonicler Nuwairi puts the number of the slain at two hundred thousand and the number of the en- slaved at the same: this may be an exaggeration, but even if we cut his figure by fifty per cent, the devastation is still enormous. It has been maintained that the island still housed a large Christian population, but, after 135 years, this is highly improbable. And we have evidence of the difficulties experienced by the Byzantine missionaries who were soon sent to the place.[1]

It is difficult to overrate the effect which this splendid victory had on both the spirits and the economy of the empire, and on those of the Moslem world. The Byzantines were in transports of joy which even the personal unpopularity of the victor in their city could not repress: while in Egypt and Palestine the event was followed by the very rare expedient of persecution of the Christian subjects of the caliph. It was plain that Byzantium was on the eve of an era of reconquest: and the panegyrical poem of Theodosius the Deacon on the Cretan campaign ends with a significant warning to the frontier emirate of Tarsus to look to its defences.

Indeed the whole empire seemed to be inspired with the confidence of victory which it had probably never known till now. The spirit of the Christian empire of Rome had been by definition pacific. The proper Byzantines had hated war; and one of the most urgent duties of their emperors was the preservation of peace, after the pattern of that Prince of Peace Whom they claimed to represent. They wanted not power or empire, for these were theirs already. They wanted not riches and plunder, since in theory all the world and its riches were theirs already. Military glory, involving as it did the slaughter of innocent blood, was seldom an incentive, since it was frowned on by the church in whose interest they governed and whose counsels they claimed to direct. Only the harsh facts of absolute necessity had compelled them, century after century, with mounting losses and impoverishment, to defend themselves and their empire. It was God's will and they submitted. But the empire was naturally at a serious disadvantage in struggling with the Saracens, who regarded the 'Jihad', or truceless war against the infidel, as a part of their creed, or with the Normans, Franks and Bulgars, who regarded war as a man's profession which was joyfully embraced by all who could lay claim to courage or bid for a fortune.

In the ninth to eleventh centuries Byzantium abandoned her age-old view of warfare and was animated for two centuries by the fierce spirit of Crusaders. From defence they went over to attack. It is necessary to say that the great Armenian barons of Eastern Anatolia were in the forefront of this great spiritual revolution. The admirable courage, the fearful savagery, and the remorseless discipline of the Byzantine conquerors, were products of a baronial aristocracy, whose properties and whose lives depended on the inculcation of these very qualities in the armed forces of the state. As always in these circumstances, a tradition of chivalry and towering courage rooted itself deeply in the breasts of the fighting men, who saw their captain or general riding at their head, and striking down with his own hand the strongest champions of the enemy. The discipline, as well as the courage, of the great aristocratic leaders, was phenomenal. Nicephorus Phocas imposed an exactitude and implicit obedience to orders which reminds us of the Cromwellians. Spirit and discipline were all that were needed to make the Byzantine armies invincible.[2]

The conqueror of Crete, Nicephorus, had vacated the command of the eastern armies, but this was happily supplied by his brother Leo Phocas (it may be wondered if any family in history has had such a record of military genius, generation after generation). The Abbasid caliphate was in process of dissolution, and the wretched caliph, al-Muti, who nominally governed during about thirty years, was in fact a prisoner in his capital. But the virtually independent Hamdanid dynasty of Mosul, which, in the person of Saif ad-Daula, we have seen competing with even honours against the great John Gourgen in the time of Romanus I, was still menacing under the same old and experienced chief, who long since had moved westwards into Syria and established himself in Aleppo, a city which became celebrated for its arts no less than for its riches. The emir of Aleppo now carried on the annual raids into Romania which had been Saracen policy almost since the establishment of the Syrian caliphate. But Nemesis had nearly caught up with him.

In 960, while Nicephorus was preparing to lay siege to Candia, the Emir Saif's raiders poured through the defiles of the Taurus and burst into central Asia Minor, beyond the Halys river, and sacked the city of Charsianon. This time they were not to return in triumph. Leo Phocas hurried to intercept them. All along both sides of a narrow defile, which the Byzantines called the 'Pipe', he hid his troops in close ambush. The Saracen cavalry, escorting the prisoners and baggage-trains, quite filled the pass when Leo gave the signal for attack. Avalanches of boulders rolled down on the enemy, and then the troops fell upon their flanks. Saif, inarticulate with rage, hewed wildly about him till his gigantic stallion was hamstrung. Then, on a servant's horse, he broke away and made for the mouth of the defile. He was hotly pursued but, scattering gold coins by fistfuls in his wake, he made good his escape; and with three hundred cavalry only made his way back to Aleppo. All the rest were killed or taken. His force was said to have numbered thirty thousand.

This was a foretaste of what was to come when the terrible 'White Death' of the Saracens, as they called Nicephorus himself, began his war of conquest in the east. In 961, on his return from Crete, he was instantly restored to his eastern command and told to continue his brother's work. During seven years, as marshal and later as emperor, he pursued it mercilessly until, at last, no Saracen force could be collected who would face his terrible cavalry. It is to be noted that whereas John Gourgen had operated mainly beyond the northern and central areas of the eastern frontier, Nicephorus attacked the southern sector, clearing Cilicia of Saracen forces, and then going on to reduce Tarsus and Aleppo and Antioch. The reason for this is clear. In Gourgen's time the most dangerous of the immediate Saracen threats was the emirate of Melitene. In Nicephorus' decade, it was that of Aleppo. The striking feature of Nicephorus' strategy is that his armies were thus headed directly for the Holy Land and Jerusalem; and in fact his successor John I came in sight of Jerusalem. Only death prevented his occupation of it. This is all of a piece with the new crusading spirit which animated the troops of the eastern aristocrats; and it was only reversed by the accession to power of the legitimate emperor Basil II, who naturally reverted to the old concept of Universal Rome, and turned his eyes once more towards the west.

Nicephorus took the offensive in February 962. His army was launched like a thunderbolt into the Cilician plain. There was virtually no resistance. In a campaign of twenty-two days the Byzantines made themselves masters of fifty-five walled towns in the region of Tarsus. After a break for the celebration of Easter, the indefatigable commander renewed the assault. He drove on past Tarsus, and in three days reduced the strong city of Anazarbus. Syria now lay open. He forced the Syrian Gates near Alexandretta, and appeared suddenly before the walls of Aleppo. The city fell. Booty undreamt of was left in his hands. The Emir Saif fled from his own capital. On 23 December 962, the Byzantines were masters of all but the citadel, and the citadel all but fell.

275

Nicephorus withdrew unopposed to Caesarea. But before he could renew his assault, events of great moment had occurred in Constantinople.3

On 15 March 963, the young Emperor Romanus II died. We have seen that his ambitious Empress Theophano was said to have poisoned him and also that there is no evidence at all to support such a slander. Indeed, she was placed by her husband's death in an exceedingly awkward position. Romanus left two sons behind him, the rightful Emperors Basil and Constantine. But the elder was only six years old, and the younger no more than three. The government was in the hands of the able but unscrupulous minister Joseph Bringas: and Bringas, a true son of Constantinople, detested the house of Phocas like the plague. While Romanus II was alive, Nicephorus and Leo Phocas could be occupied on the eastern border and beyond it. Now, all was uncertain.

The empress distrusted Bringas, and feared for her two sons. She therefore determined to put herself under the protection of the strongest power in the state, that of Nicephorus himself. The city populace, who mistrusted warlords, strongly disapproved of this alliance; and all kinds of stories were set on foot to show that she had schemed with the conqueror before her husband's death. She was innocent then, and comparatively innocent now. If she broke with the house of Phocas and threw in her lot with Bringas, how long would it be before the chief of that house appeared before Constantinople at the head of his invincible army, flushed with the conquests of Crete and Aleppo? And what would happen to her children then? What would happen to anybody, for the matter of that? If, however, she made an alliance with Nicephorus, even a marriage, was it not at least possible that Nicephorus would protect his stepsons as Romanus I had protected his son-in-law Constantine VII?

At all events, the conquering war-lord was summoned. He was admitted to the city. He celebrated a splendid triumph. And he began a secret negotiation with the empress. That he also began a liaison with her, that he fell in love with her, or that she seduced him, are suppositions in the highest degree improbable. Nicephorus was a man past fifty years old, who, moreover, was a proven ascetic. He wore a hair-shirt next his skin and often proclaimed his desire of retiring to a monastery. That Theophano can have loved him is next door to impossible. His physical appearance was repelling, even if we allow for the malice of Liudprand, who has left us a detailed account of it. He gave his word to Theophano that he would protect the rights of the child emperors in return for the imperial crown, and he kept his promise. It was a sensible business deal, and nothing more.

But the negotiations reached the ear of Joseph Bringas. He roused a riot and Nicephorus, whose army still lay in the east, was compelled to take refuge in the cathedral. But here he found an unexpected ally in the Patriarch Polyeuctus, to whom the genuinely pious and ascetic character of Nicephorus warmly commended itself. The combined influence in the council of throne and church was too much for the minister. Nicephorus was taken out, under mutual promises of good faith. He was reappointed to his command, and to the minister's fury was sent out of the city and back to Caesarea, where, at the head of his troops, he was once more beyond the reach of harm. Bringas could think of no resource but to dispatch him by conspiracy. He suborned two of Nicephorus' commanders, John Zimiskes and Gourgen, to go after the general and do away with him. But Bringas was out of the frying-pan into the fire. The two supposed conspirators at once revealed the whole plot to Nicephorus, whom they urged to take the initiative, proclaim himself emperor and march on Constantinople with all his forces. Nicephorus, after some decent show of reluctance, submitted. On 3 July 963, he donned the scarlet boots, and was saluted as emperor by his army.[4]

This usurpation caused a profound shock in Constantinople, and Bringas was quick to make the most of it. Rioting broke out and much damage was done to Phocas' property in the city. Old Bardas Phocas and his son Leo sought asylum in St Sophia. But once again the opposition could affect nothing against empress, court and patriarch. Nicephorus was coming up by forced marches. On 16 August 963, the gates were opened. Nicephorus on a white charger rode in triumphantly, this time with a considerable force of his household troops. He was crowned on the same day by the patriarch.[5]

Now the second part of the bargain had to be fulfilled, the marriage with the dowager empress. There were certain difficulties in the way. Nicephorus was himself averse to marriage on religious grounds. He was, we have seen, an ascetic, who ate no meat and wore the shirt of a penitent. But his monkish friends overcame this scruple, and he consented to the union. But soon a more ugly rumour began to be noised abroad. Nicephorus had stood god-father to the young Emperor Basil in 958, and hence he and the empress were spiritual brother and sister. Marriage was therefore impossible. Needless to say, the Patriarch Polyeuctus seized the occasion to protest: 'For', says Leo the Deacon, 'he was full of divine zeal and thought no shame to withstand the emperors themselves'.[6] However, he was made to see reason. Nicephorus swore it was his father Bardas, and not he, who had been sponsor on the occasion, though it is not easy to see how this mended the matter. But in truth, reasons of state made the union imperative. The alternative might well have been civil war. In the autumn of 963 the marriage was celebrated. Nicephorus was now chief emperor, stepfather of the legitimate sovereigns, and for practical purposes Mayor of the Palace.

Nicephorus II was a conqueror, and the six short years of his reign are years of conquest and expansion. We need not rehearse the details of his campaigns, but a summary account of his exploits will give some idea of the completeness of his success. In 964 he entered Syria once more. His expedition was scarcely opposed, but no permanent or spectacular results attended it. The year 965 was the year of decisive progress. In the summer, a splendid army under the three greatest generals of the day – the emperor, his brother Leo and John Zimiskes – laid siege to Tarsus. For nearly two hundred years, since its re-founding by the Caliph Harun, this city and fortress had been the base of every Saracen incursion into Cilicia. Its emir was nearly an independent despot, though subject in theory to Bagdad and later to Aleppo. A glance at the map will show the importance of the place, lying as it does near the sea, close to Cyprus, and far inside Anatolia, that is, west of the longitude of the Cappadocian Caesarea. Its time had now come. Neither Bagdad nor Aleppo could relieve it. After a brief investment the city of St Paul surrendered on terms.

In the same year, as a corollary to the reconquest of Tarsus, the Byzantine fleet occupied the island of Cyprus. This island had been since 688 a neutral condominium of Byzantines and Saracens, who collected taxes from it and used its ports as temporary naval bases, but laid no claim to sovereignty over it. The treaty had on the whole been loyally kept during nearly three hundred years by both sides. But now, with the Saracen power retreating

out of Anatolia and into Syria, the arrangement was an anachronism. Cyprus was turned quietly into a Byzantine *theme*.
What the inhabitants thought about it is not recorded; but they
probably deprecated it, for obvious reasons.

It was now no longer a question of whether the Saracens could
mount a counter-attack; but simply of how quickly and how far
the Byzantine armies would advance to east and south. The
gallant Emir Saif of Aleppo lost heart. Menaced by revolt and
treachery at home and discouraged by continual rout whenever
his forces met the Byzantines, he gave up the struggle and died in
967. After this, it was merely a question of time before Antioch
fell. In fact, some resistance was encountered here by Nicephorus,
and it was not until the year of his own death, 969, that the great
city on the Orontes capitulated to his marshal Vourtzes. Aleppo
became a Byzantine vassal and protectorate. And the way was
open to Phoenicia and Palestine. In this way the great Emperor
Nicephorus undid the work of the great Caliph Moawiya.7

In other directions Nicephorus was not so politic or so successful. We may reserve some account of his relations with the Emperor Otto the Great, for this is a subject of such importance that
it cannot be summarised in a paragraph. But Otto's aggression
was to some extent precipitated by a disastrous attempt on the
part of the Byzantines to expel the Saracens from Sicily. It is plain
that anyone who aspires to the empire of the inland sea must hold
the three great islands of Cyprus, Crete and Sicily. Nicephorus
captured Crete in 961, and Cyprus in 965. In 964 he sent a large
naval force under his nephew Manuel Phocas to invade the third
island. Manuel, unlike most of his family, was destitute of military
ability. He rehearsed all the blunders which his uncle had so
studiously avoided in Crete. The result was a foregone conclusion.
His force was cut to pieces and he himself was slain. The experi-
ment was not repeated.

Nevertheless, the unexampled successes of Nicephorus in the
east seem to have bred in him what the French call 'folie de la
grandeur'. He became imbued with the notion that all the power
of Augustus and Justinian was not merely his in theory, but
actually within his grasp. The days of compromise and concession,
he thought, were over: and in this conviction he acted towards
both Bulgaria and Italy. By the prudent settlement of Romanus I,
Bulgaria had been converted from a savage and ruinous enemy

into a warm and benevolent friend, in return for a marriage alliance and for some very trifling favours which included an annual grant of money. Late in the year 965 the Bulgarian envoys arrived in Constantinople to claim the subsidy. They could scarcely have come more inopportunely. Nicephorus, elated by his triumph over Tarsus and his annexation of Cyprus, was in no mood to welcome them. 'Confound it!', he exclaimed to his father, 'have we Romans, hitherto triumphant everywhere, sunk so low that we must pay tribute to this hideous race of beggars, to these Scythians of Bulgaria ?' Then, turning to the envoys, 'There, be off with you!' he cried, 'and learn in future a proper respect for the Roman name, you that are triple slaves, the sons of dogs': and the disconsolate ambassadors departed with this answer for Preslav.

A little reflection would have taught the emperor and his council the prudence of leaving the existing settlement as it was. Bulgaria was not only a buffer state between the empire and the Magyars and Russians: it was also, and seemed likely to remain, a friendly buffer. To tamper with the arrangement was to expose the empire gratuitously to fresh dangers, and to commit it to a war on two fronts, which had so often brought it so near to extinction. But Nicephorus felt that only blood could wipe out the insult. A *casus belli* was soon found. An infamous pact was made with the Russian prince Svyatoslav, who undertook to chastise the Bulgarians as the hireling of Byzantium. In 968 his invasion began. Too late the Byzantine government realised the consequences of their folly. Svyatoslav was not out for booty, but for annexation and empire. Bulgarian resistance was impossible. The Russians stormed Preslav and took the new Tsar Boris II into captivity. By 969 Byzantium had on her doorstep, no longer the pacific Bulgarians, but the warlike and ferocious Northmen of Kiev.[8]

The arrogance of Nicephorus, moreover, rendered his government at home as unfortunate as his western and northern policy abroad. In order to understand the sentiments of nearly universal hatred which he aroused in his capital, we have to remember, first that he was rightly regarded as an interloper, if not as an usurper against the legitimate heirs of Basil the Macedonian; and second, that he was a typical representative of the Anatolian military aristocracy. The interests of this class were diametrically opposed to those of the central government. The nobles cared first for landed property and second for the soldiers under their command, and the citizenry had no interest in either of these: indeed, they looked on the rule of Nicephorus, backed as it was by an invincible host of eastern heretics and barbarians, as an enemy occupation. The army was always before their eyes, to remind them of their servitude – training, drilling, manoeuvring, or, what was worse, drunkenly roistering and despoiling. The emperor was deaf to all complaints that his darling troops were to blame. 'Pooh!' he said, 'in a large force of this kind, you are bound to have one or two who will get out of hand!' In his eyes a soldier could do no wrong. He pressed the Patriarch Polyeuctus to canonise any soldier who fell fighting against the infidel as a Christian martyr. But Polyeuctus, who, to do him justice, was never afraid to stand up against what he believed to be wrong, would have nothing of such blasphemy.

Nicephorus yielded on this point, but made it very clear that he would be master in his own house. The edicts passed by him bore heavily on church holdings. Though himself half an ascetic, and a genuine friend to the humbler followers of Christ, he had a rooted and justified dislike of ecclesiastical wealth and property. Lands were continually accruing to monastic foundations, which were unable to exploit them, so that some of the best agricultural areas of Anatolia were waste: or, on the other hand, revenues due to the poor were misappropriated to the benefit of the trustees. Nicephorus, in short, faced the very problem which, two centuries before, had been solved in so drastic a fashion by Constantine V. A celebrated law of Nicephorus absolutely forbade the alienation of land to the church: those who wished to give money might do so in restoring ruinous or abandoned monasteries, but there were quite enough of these already without adding to the number. This was a bold and sensible attempt to correct a real social evil; and it is possible that, had he stopped there, the church might have been brought to accept it. But a second edict made it clearer that he desired absolute power over church administration: for in this it was laid down that all appointments to bishoprics must be subject to the emperor's approval. While the emperor's right to nominate bishops in individual cases was never in dispute, no such wholesale supervision as this had ever yet been demanded by the crown; and in fact the edict remained only five years in force.

Nicephorus thus, in two years, had succeeded in alienating two important departments of state, the civil bureaucracy and the church. To make matters worse, the whole empire was bled white to pay for his wars in east and west. The spoils of his victories he gave to his soldiers. The civilians should be made to pay for the coats on their backs and the swords at their sides. Basil II never committed this blunder, and was able by adroit financial management even to remit taxes, despite his continuous wars. No doubt his sagacity took warning from the errors of his stepfather; but Nicephorus, as a wealthy aristocrat himself, could not afford to be a radical.

In fact, Nicephorus naturally legislated in favour of his own class. The right of pre-emption – that is, the prior right of a neighbour to bid for vacant properties in his commune – was withdrawn and lands could now be purchased by anyone who chose to put down the money. This played directly into the hands of the acquisitive property-owner. Secondly, Nicephorus effected a radical change in the valuation of the 'soldiers' estates' themselves. These had hitherto been required to be of the value of 4 lbs gold (or 288 gold pieces) in order to supply the equipment of a heavy-armed cavalry man. Nicephorus at a blow raised the minimum value to 12 lbs (or 864 gold pieces), and thus turned the cavalry-man-peasant into an esquire. This was a long step in the direction of feudalism, properly so denominated. It meant the decentralisation of command and the reorganisation of the provincial troops into a hierarchy based on landed property. It was one further barrier erected between the emperor, who personified the central government, and his loyal peasant-militiamen: and one further prop for the authority of the great military aristocrat. The 12-lb estates presuppose a substantial encroachment of the rich on the estates of the poor: and the squire of such an estate now led into the field his own band of tenants, instead of being one of a body of equal soldiers from a commune of neighbours.[9]

I make these comments because they are indicative of the way things would certainly go if, or when, the baronial families – as we may begin to call them – established their control firmly. At last they did so: but only in the late eleventh century and after struggles with church and bureaucracy which had been ruinous to the empire.

NOTES

[1] Theoph. Cont., 473–81; Leo Diac., 261 ff.; Ostrogorsky, 237.
[2] Ostrogorsky, 240.
[3] Bréhier, 190–1.
[4] Cedrenus, 345-8
[5] Cedrenus, 351; Leo Diac., 48.
[6] Leo Diac., 50.
[7] Ostrogorsky, 240–1; Vasiliev, 308–9.
[8] Ostrogorsky, 242.
[9] Ostrogorsky, 238–40; Bréhier, 195–7.

CHAPTER TWENTY-ONE

NICEPHORUS II AND THE WEST: JOHN I

We have given some account of the home policy of the aristocratic usurper Nicephorus Phocas, and of the reasons why this
policy set him at odds with all parties and classes in his realm –
bureaucrats, church and commons – except the army. But
Nicephorus had not yet exhausted every resource for making himself unpopular. It is important that his western policy should also
be scrutinised, since western sources state unequivocally, and with
some show of reason, that this was a prime cause of his downfall.

Here we must go back a little. We saw how, on the deposition
of Romanus I, his son-in-law Constantine Porphyrogenitus, the
legitimate emperor, had in 945 reversed the western policy of the
Byzantine empire: and, instead of bolstering the last sad relics of
the Carolingian line in Italy, had allied himself with the strong
and vigorous German dynasty. The death of the first wife of the
young Emperor Romanus II in 949 had opened the way to a
dynastic alliance between Romanus and Otto's niece: and while
there still seemed a possibility that this union might be brought
about, Otto had carefully abstained from running foul of Byzantine influence in Italy. But, as we know, this plan failed. Romanus
had married the Byzantine Theophano: and in 959 his father, the
faithful ally of Otto, died; so that there was now no longer any
diplomatic obstacle to bar German intervention in Italy.

That country was at the mercy of the Marquis Berengar, and of
his son Adalbert. Berengar was nominally the vassal of Otto, who
in 952 had assumed the title of king of Italy. But he behaved as an

independent tyrant and even made his hand heavy on Rome. Pope John XII, the last and most disreputable pontiff of the disreputable line of Marozia, appealed in 961 to Otto, whose prestige was already very great owing to his crushing defeat of the Hungarians on the Lechfeld in 955. This time Otto came for good. In February 962 he was crowned emperor of the Romans in Rome by the pope; and the whole problem of two emperors of Rome, which had scarcely counted in Byzantine politics since the death of Lewis II in 873, was in a moment resuscitated.

Otto's assumption of the imperial crown, and his consequent degradation of the Master of the World at Constantinople to the status of a provincial *imperator Graecorum*, took place when Romanus II was still on the throne, and he was not likely to pay much attention. But his successor, the arrogant Nicephorus II, was an altogether different proposition. A clash was bound to occur over the Byzantine provinces of South Italy. In these provinces Byzantine rule had always been at odds with the Lombard principalities of Capua and Benevento, which had more than once risen in revolt. The defeat of Nicephorus' fleet by the Sicilian Saracens in 964 precipitated the inevitable conflict. Pandolf Ironhead, the prince of Capua, threw off his nominal allegiance to Byzantium. He invited Otto's invasion. And in 967 Otto was ready to fulfil the dream of Lewis II and make himself master of the whole peninsula.

Yet even now, the persistent vision of dynastic union was still floating before the eyes of East and West. Otto was prepared to treat: let the Byzantines send the purple-born princess, daughter of Romanus II and Theophano, to be the bride of Otto's young son Otto II (crowned co-emperor in 967), and thereby acknowledge his own imperial status: and then western aid, with a guarantee of Byzantine territorial integrity, might be forthcoming. 'Such a marriage', Otto said, 'is worth Apulia and Calabria'. And so it was, for the provinces in question might well be ceded as part of the bride's dowry. Refusal of the terms meant war.[1]

Late in 967 a German embassy was dispatched, headed by the Venetian Dominic, which was met by the Emperor Nicephorus in person in Macedonia. Otto's envoy seems to have exceeded his instructions. The Byzantines overreached him, haggled over the terms, and finally elicited from him a promise that Otto would respect Byzantine South Italy without themselves making any very clear concession. Otto, naturally enough, found this unsatisfactory. He believed, in all probability rightly, that a sudden and successful stroke in Apulia would force the hand of the Byzantine government; and, without delay, but with some show of bad faith, he pushed into the Byzantine domains and laid siege to Bari. Here, however, he showed a lack of historical knowledge and also of logistics. Lewis II had besieged Bari during four years and found it impossible to reduce as long as it was open to supplies by sea. It was the same story now. Though Otto was master of the open country, the Byzantine garrison of Bari laughed at his siege: and the resurgent might of Byzantium had infused an altogether different spirit into her armed forces, whether they were in attack or on their defence. By early summer Otto was reluctantly convinced that negotiations must be reopened, this time under very unfavourable auspices.

A second embassy to Constantinople was therefore determined on which should renew the offer of an imperial marriage alliance and a settlement of the west: an embassy which obtained a celebrity perhaps more universal than that of any other diplomatic mission in history. For Otto's envoy was Liudprand, bishop of Cremona; and his report of it is, in a literary point of view, one of the most masterly, if one of the most malicious documents ever penned by a diplomat: the so-called *Relatio de legatione constantinopolitana*, written in the year 969.

If the letter of Lewis II to Basil I, almost exactly a century before, is to be considered of the first importance in any study of Byzantine relations with the west during the period under review, the *Legatio* must be regarded as scarcely inferior to it; and it is instructive at the outset to note the humorous, even flippant, tone which characterises both documents, a levity which is without parallel in any document of comparable importance emanating from the east. But, with all its malice and all its prejudice, the *Legatio* contains so accurate a statement of the fundamental issues at stake between the parties, and withal so lively a picture of Byzantium and her court at the period of her great glory, that its historical importance, quite apart from its literary merit, is incontestable.[2]

It is to be remembered that Liudprand, who reached Constantinople on Thursday, 4 June 968, arrived in most inauspicious circumstances. The agreement which had been reached only a few months before between Nicephorus and Dominic had been violated at once by Otto; and although Otto had claimed that his envoy had acted *ultra vires*, that is, without his own sanction, in promising to respect the Byzantine territories in South Italy, his action in invading them appeared very naturally as the grossest bad faith in the eyes of Nicephorus. Moreover, Liudprand's own self-love was bitterly wounded. He, who had been received with honour and generosity by the Emperor Constantine VII, he who knew Greek (of which he was intensely proud), he who was now the emissary, no longer of an Italian marquis, but of the powerful emperors of the west, had expected that he should be received with a deference and consideration suitable to his position, and far above those shown to any other envoy. Instead, he was received, not indeed with inhumanity, far less with cruelty, but with an in-difference and disdain which accorded only too clearly with the estimate in which the Byzantine court held his master's dignity. Not many of us can lose our tempers and at the same time remain lucid and witty: it was unfortunate for the reputation of Byzantium that Liudprand was one of the few who could. But we must remember than when he describes his isolation and discomfort in the diplomatic hostelry, he was receiving only the treatment accorded to all envoys at Byzantium, which had the phobia against spying common to all east European nations; when he describes the food at the imperial table as 'pretty filthy and dis-gusting', and the wine as undrinkable, it was the food and wine which he had eaten and drunk twenty years before without com-plaint; when he decries the squalor of the imperial and court vesture, this was the very vesture which he was trying, by in-judicious and arcane purchases, to introduce into the German court; and when he answered the arguments of the Byzantine government about their grievances, if indeed he did answer them with the freedom recorded by him (which we may take leave to doubt), he did so with a deliberate misunderstanding of their point of view which, in one who professed to be an expert in Byzantine policy and manners, was inexcusable.

The foreign minister, Leo Phocas, the emperor's brother, re-ceived him on 6 June, and went straight to the point. His govern-ment could not, he said, recognise Otto and his son as emperors, but merely as kings. Liudprand pretended in reply, as Lewis II had pretended a century before, that the two words (*basileus* and *rex*) meant the same. The foreign minister thereupon reprehended his insolence and refused to receive Otto's missive. The emperor himself interviewed Liudprand on the following day, and launched a bitter invective against Otto's whole Italian policy. A long recrimination followed, at the close of which Liudprand repeated his offer: if the Byzantine princess were sent, he was empowered to offer such and such terms, which included a total evacuation of Apulia by the Saxon forces. On the 9th, he renewed this offer in writing; and on the 13th Basil the chamberlain, the most powerful man in the empire after the Emperor Nicephorus, communicated his answer: a princess of the purple – though this was an unheard-of concession – should be sent, if Otto would cede Ravenna, Rome, all eastern Italy, Istria and the north coast of Dalmatia. These terms, which implied an evacuation of Italy by the Germans, were of course derisory, and were not intended for serious consideration. In any case Liudprand would not have been competent to agree to them, as he bore written instructions stating just how far he was empowered to go.

Nicephorus saw that the situation was past mending by diplomatic means. He confined the unhappy envoy in his lodgings, and during the next six weeks collected a large naval force which was dispatched on 13 July to operate with Adalbert of Ivrea against Otto in South Italy. During these weeks Nicephorus himself was preparing for an eastern campaign, and had little time for his guest, except to see him now and again at dinner and to torment him with reproaches that his master should call himself emperor, and with demands for the evacuation of South Italy and for the surrender of the rebel Pandolf Ironhead of Capua. At length the emperor left for the east, and Liudprand had at last some reason to think that he might be set at liberty. But, on 20 August, came a message from the west which put an end to his hopes of freedom and even, for a time, of life. Pope John XIII, Otto's nominee, at Otto's instigation, advanced an appeal to Nicephorus which was intended to further the negotiations initiated by Liudprand, but in which he was tactless enough to refer to Otto as the 'august emperor of the Romans' and to Nicephorus as 'emperor of the Greeks'. The rage of the Byzantine chancery knew no bounds. It was fortunate that Nicephorus himself was absent from Constantinople; but, even so, Liudprand never knew how the bearers of such an impious document escaped with their lives. Much of the resentment overflowed upon himself, even though his own credentials had made no such distinction. There were ominous references to sewing up in sacks and submersion in the Bosphorus. At last, on 17 September, he was again summoned to the foreign ministry, and, amid a tumult of objurgation and insult, asked to explain this extraordinary piece of insolence on the part of the pope. Liudprand, for all his boasted courage and resolution, was reduced to an abject apology: and though he himself, as an experienced and intelligent western diplomat, saw very clearly that his masters would have to adopt the papal idea of an ecumenical *imperium Romanorum*, he on this occasion thought discretion the better part of valour, and promised, in the pope's name, that future letters should be inscribed 'John, pope of Rome, to Nicephorus, Basil and Constantine, the great and august emperors *of the Romans*'.

After this he was allowed to go; but not before being examined rigorously by the imperial customs, who removed from his baggage all the purple cloth which he had bought to adorn his imperial masters and his own church. In vain he pleaded that Constantine Porphyrogenitus had placed no such embargo upon his exports in 949. It was made very clear to him that times had changed, and that the Otto of 968 was not the desirable ally that he had seemed to be twenty years before. At last on 2 October, after a hundred and twenty days of mortification, discomfort, doubt, sickness and failure, he shook off the dust of the city 'full of lies, tricks, perjury and greed, the city rapacious, avaricious and vainglorious'.

The war of course broke out in Italy. A Byzantine force surprised the Lombards and even succeeded in capturing Pandolf Ironhead, who was sent to captivity in Constantinople. But retribution was swift. Otto's forces inflicted a heavy defeat on the Byzantines, who, committed now to a full-scale war on the east and in Bulgaria, could not reinforce their Italian arms. The whole of Byzantine Italy appeared about to fall irrevocably into the hands of the western emperor. But, at this precise moment, the Emperor Nicephorus II was murdered.

There is much in this *coup de théâtre* that has not been explained. According to the chroniclers, the tireless and redoubtable Empress Theophano was at the bottom of the whole conspiracy against her second husband.3 As she was also believed to have murdered her father-in-law and her first husband, it was inevitable that she should have been implicated, and implicated in the basest and most detestable fashion. But, whatever may have been her part in the matter – and it seems clear she knew of what was afoot – we must be very careful about attributing to her any but a subordinate rôle in the proceedings. The prime mover in the affair was the handsome and popular general John Zimiskes, who made himself emperor next day. Of course it was said that Theophano was his lover, and that she set him on to supplant an elderly and ascetic husband by the most effectual means. But it is clear that Nicephorus had other grounds for distrusting Zimiskes, whom he had deprived of his command and exiled to his estate. It is altogether probable that we have here to deal with a much wider and more ramified conspiracy than can be confined to a mere sordid intrigue in the women's quarters of the palace.

Nicephorus, whatever his eulogists might say in his favour, was universally unpopular in his own capital. The citizens detested his manners and policy and even more they detested the licence and cruelty of his garrison. Only a week or two before his murder, a bloody clash had taken place in the city between the emperor's Armenian bodyguard and the citizens, who were aided by the traditionally loyalist corps of marines. Nicephorus well understood his danger, and fortified his palace; but rumours and prophecies were afloat which boded ill for him so long as he remained in the seat of government. His prestige as the conqueror of Crete, Tarsus and Antioch undoubtedly stood high. But his arrogance had gratuitously involved the empire in wars simultaneously with Svyatoslav of Russia in Bulgaria and Otto the Great in Italy. Moreover, he was in bad odour with the church, which was furious at his intervention in ecclesiastical administration. To crown all, hunger and distress afflicted his citizens. A series of bad harvests sent up the price of bread: and where the Macedonian sovereigns had been prudent enough to keep down the cost by artificial means in times of famine, Nicephorus was suspected of making capital out of the scarcity, as one more device for wringing out money to pay for his wars.

When all this is considered, we may plausibly assume that the conspiracy of Zimiskes had a very wide measure of support in Constantinople: and the fact that the murder of Nicephorus was received in profound quiet throughout the city merely confirms the assumption. It is likely that Zimiskes had the support of the clergy and even of the patriarch: at all events he made no bones about fulfilling every demand afterwards made on him by Polyeuctus. It is certain that he had the full support of the power-ful chamberlain Basil, who equally certainly disapproved of Nice-phorus' policies in the west. All in all, we may conclude that no one, except the small party devoted to the interests of the clan of Phocas, regretted his release from an arrogant and despotic tyrant, whose genius and valour were undoubted, but whose ill-judged and nearly insane policies threatened disaster both at home and abroad.

The account of the murder surpasses most fiction. On the night of Friday, 10 December 969, the emperor retired early to rest. The empress left him to see after her guests – two Bulgarian princesses whose hands were destined to the young Emperors Basil and Con-stantine – but asked her husband not to bar the door against her return. Nicephorus prayed and read the Scriptures for an hour or more, and then lay down, not in his imperial bed, but on the floor, beneath the icons of Christ and His Mother. Outside, a north-easterly gale was blowing, and it was snowing hard. At eleven o'clock a skiff, with the conspirators aboard, put into the palace harbour of Bucoleon. A basket was let down by a windlass from the palace roof, and one by one the murderers were hauled aloft, Zimiskes himself last of all. They crept down inside the building, and made their way silently to the imperial bedchamber. With drawn swords they stole to the bedside; and then there was a moment of panic – for the bed was empty. But only for a moment: closer search revealed the emperor sound asleep on a panther-skin rug on the floor. He was kicked awake: and merci-lessly dispatched. His severed head was displayed at a window, while Basil the chamberlain, with a strong force of soldiers, went through the streets at dawn to proclaim the new sovereign, 'Johannes in Christ faithful emperor and autocrat of the Romans'. Never was a crime better conceived, prepared and executed. No one stirred a finger. And the empire woke to find itself firmly in the grasp of its new master.[4]

The new emperor was at first sight a mere duplication of the old. Neither had any legitimate claim to rule. Both were Mayors of the Palace, the protectors of the legitimate boys, Basil (now eleven years old) and Constantine (now eight). John Zimiskes (which means a native of Tshemeshgadzak, near Melitene) was a typical Anatolian military aristocrat. He was grand-nephew of Romanus I's general John Gourgen, and his mother was a Phocas. All his career (and he was now forty-five) had been spent in the field. Despite his small frame, he was immensely strong: it was said of him that he could jump over three horses standing side by side, and could, at full gallop, knock a leather ball out of a glass vase without cracking the vessel. His brilliant qualities as a general had been fully proven in the eastern campaigns of Nicephorus, and were to be demonstrated even more strikingly during the next six years of his reign.

Yet he differed in some ways strikingly from his predecessor. He had seized power as the result of a compact between himself and two estates of the realm which were not aristocratic, the bureaucracy and the church. To the one he owed it to base his foreign policy on sensible principles: and to the other to rescind the anti-ecclesiastical legislation of Nicephorus. His subservience to the church was most striking. At the behest of the Patriarch Polyeuctus he tore up the decrees of Nicephorus and put away the shameless woman Theophano, as the price of his own coronation. He is even said to have subscribed publicly to the dogma of Photius, that emperor and patriarch formed independent powers in the state, the one to order men's bodies, the other their souls. These notable concessions have been used by some modern historians to illustrate the growing power and independence of the church. With all submission, I suggest that they illustrate no such thing. Zimiskes gave in to Polyeuctus as part of a bargain, without which he could not have been crowned. His position was an extraordinarily weak one: he was an usurper of the imperial power, and, what was worse, had used murder as the means of his usurpation, the stain of which could be effaced only by a patriarchal coronation. He was compelled to yield to the church on her own terms. Those who argue that the church, by some strengthening of her position, was now on equal terms with the crown, should stop to ask how the church was treated by Basil II during the next thirty years, when no concessions had to be made. Even Justinian the Great could not have regarded her temporal interests with more contemptuous indifference.5

The first tasks of the Emperor John I, as we may now call him, were the consolidation of his own position, the settlement of affairs in the west and the Russian war in Bulgaria. The thoroughly

discredited Empress Theophano was hustled with scant ceremony into a nunnery, where we may take our leave of her. If
reports say true, she was a very bad woman indeed. But report is
not always just. She was much loved by her father-in-law and
her first husband. She was the mother of the most extraordinary
man who ever sat on the Byzantine throne. And she was also the
mother of the future western empress, called like herself, Theophano. John then made a marriage with a lady of unexceptionable
legitimacy and virtue, Theodora, daughter of Constantine Porphyrogenitus, and in this way became the uncle, as well as the
guardian, of the two infant emperors.

The western policy of Nicephorus was almost at once put into
reverse. The arm of Otto was poised to strike at the Italian provinces of Byzantium, and John was only just in time to save them.
The captive Pandolf Ironhead was instantly set at liberty, and sent
on an embassy to Otto. The hand of the *porphyrogenita* Theophano, which Nicephorus had so contemptuously refused to
Otto II, was once more offered. This time it was accepted. A
treaty was arranged in virtue of which the Byzantine territories in
Italy were guaranteed against all aggression from the north. The
Princess Theophano was sent with a splendid escort and even
more splendid gifts, to the Eternal City and there, on 14 April 972,
she was married to the Emperor Otto II, then seventeen years of
age.

The marriage was remarkable in more ways than one. In the
first place it was a success, among so many failures, in bringing
about a union between the imperial lines of east and west. It is not
easy to over-estimate its importance for that reason alone. True
Leo VI had married his daughter Anna to the Emperor Lewis III,
but Lewis was never more than a *fainéant*, and the offspring of the
marriage, the Prince Carl Constantine ended his life as a humble
duke of Vienne. This marriage was different. Otto the Great, the
imperial father-in-law, was no *fainéant* sovereign. He was the
undoubted emperor over Germany and Italy, and his posterity
was likely to inherit an empire hardly less magnificent than that of
Charles the Great. The precise degree of empire that Byzantium
was prepared to concede to him is not known; but Byzantium
certainly acknowledged that he was an emperor of the west. It is
true that the bride's brothers, Basil (II) and Constantine (VIII) were
juveniles, from whom a numerous posterity might be expected.

Nevertheless the offspring of Otto the younger and Theophano could become the lawful heir to the entire dominion of Caesar Augustus: and, but for mischance, it would probably have become so.

In the next place, Theophano was a Greek: she had been brought up in the Great Palace of Constantinople, and her first language was Greek. Through her, Byzantine influence on the western conception of empire was bound to be considerable: and, as it turned out, it was enormous. Her son Otto III was, to all intents and purposes, a Byzantine (or Roman) emperor. Her court was Byzantine, and her education and abilities were such as to permeate that court.

Lastly, we have to note that she was, and still is, the centre of an historical quarrel which has been pursued during the past eighty years with such minuteness and industry that I cannot wholly pass it by. The western Empress Theophano purported to be, and in all probability was, the daughter of Romanus II and his wife Theophano; the grand-daughter of Constantine Porphyrogenitus, and thus great-great-grand-daughter of Basil the Macedonian. However, an unlucky remark of the nearly contemporary German chronicler Ditmar tends to throw doubt on this identification. He states, that when she arrived in Rome, she was found to be not the *virgo desiderata* (i.e. the girl they wanted) but another, a niece of the emperor John Zimiskes, and thus not a *porphyrogenita* of the legitimate dynasty. Otto the Great, adds Ditmar, was urged by his council not to put up with this substitute and to send the lady packing. But he decided to put a good face on it, and so the marriage was celebrated. Now, to refute this calumny it is scarcely necessary to do more than to state it. Is it for a second probable that John should have played such a trick, or that Otto would have stomached it? The questions answer themselves. But, as several of the greatest living Byzantinists, after minute research, accept Ditmar's version of the affair, it is not possible quite to leave it at that.

The chief argument urged against the lady's credentials is that in Otto's diploma announcing his marriage she is referred to, not as daughter of Romanus II, but as niece of John I. Quite so. John Zimiskes, as we saw, interdicted willingly or unwillingly from marriage with the dowager-empress Theophano, had married her sister-in-law, Princess Theodora, and thus he became in fact the uncle of the lady in question, and she his niece. Ditmar, having the common western conviction about the treachery of all Greeks, sprang to the conclusion that John Zimiskes had resorted to deception. But, say the lady's detractors, why call her *niece of John*, instead of *daughter of Romanus*? The reasons are obvious enough. John, interloper though he might be, was the senior Byzantine emperor. His fame as a conqueror was world-wide. Saracens and Normans fled before him. He was the avowed friend and ally of Otto the Great, and had, on his own initiative, settled the disastrous east-west dispute opened by the arrogance of Nicephorus Phocas. How was the young empress of the west more honoured – by describing her as John's niece or by describing her as daughter of a youthful and undistinguished emperor, and sister of two boys not yet in their teens? Again the question answers itself. If John's claim to imperial power was doubtful in point of legitimacy, was Otto's any less dubious? I must incline decisively to the opinion of von Ranke, that Theophano was what she purported to be.[6]

Having prepared the way to peace in the west, John could at once turn his attention to facing the danger of the Russian Svyatoslav in Bulgaria. It was high time. The Russian prince at the head of sixty thousand of the bravest and hardiest troops in the world, had, by the folly of Nicephorus, been called in to chastise a friendly and orthodox kingdom, whose only danger to the empire lay in its temporary weakness. But Svyatoslav had no idea of acting as a paid vassal of Byzantium. His designs were those of Symeon and later of Samuel and Dushan: to carve out a great Byzantino-Slav empire with its capital on the Bosphorus. It is amusing to note this early instance of a plan which perplexed and terrified European chanceries from the days of Tsar Peter the Great to those of Tsar Nicholas II. Some historians whisper that the plan is still not regarded as wholly abandoned in the counsels of the Kremlin today: and that the ultimate hope of Russians, after as before the Revolution of 1917, is to found the empire of the Third Rome in the seat of the Second.

It was soon clear that Nicephorus had sown the wind only to reap the whirlwind. Too late he realised his blunder; and in the last days before his murder he had hurriedly projected a Byzantine-Bulgar alliance against the invader whom he himself had invited.[7] In his supreme contempt for the legitimate house, and for Byzantine public opinion in general, he summoned two Bulgar princesses, probably sisters of the young Tsar Boris II, to be married out of hand to the two young Macedonian Emperors Basil and Constantine; and to this high-handed and insulting project much of Basil's inveterate hostility to the Anatolian aristocracy, and to Bulgaria itself, must in fairness be set down. But Nicephorus was murdered, and the foolhardy plan fortunately came to nothing.

Svyatoslav, aided by the confusion caused by the murder of Nicephorus and the transfer of power to John, did not let the grass grow under his feet. In 970 he crossed the Balkan, stormed Philippopolis and burst into Thrace. In a few weeks he would be below the walls of Constantinople; and who could say what might happen then ?

But Svyatoslav was unfortunate in the moment of his attempt. The military reforms of Nicephorus himself had placed his successor in an altogether invincible position. The spirit of the armed forces, now commanded in person by an emperor not inferior in military skill to his predecessor, was to prove decisive. In truth, the whole method and morale of warfare had undergone a profound change since the days when Symeon had routed the might of the empire at Achelo, fifty years before. It can scarcely be doubted that if in 970 the Byzantine army had been commanded by generals such as those of the Empress Zoe in 917, it would have experienced an even more inglorious disaster and annihilation. But it was not. The period of personal command by the sovereign, the period of knightly deeds, of heroic encounter, of single combat, reminiscent of the days of Homeric warfare under the walls of Troy, had succeeded to those of armies splendidly equipped by industry and bureaucracy, but commanded by generals of doubtful loyalty or by eunuchs of inadequate military skill. And here we must note two of the most significant factors in this reform of the military: the exploits of general officers, and the dilution of the cavalry arm into small separate commands of the esquires whom the legislation of Nicephorus had called into existence. What more than anything characterises the new pattern of warfare is that the generals are fighting men; and not only so, but the best and strongest of their armies. When in 1693 King William III met Marshal Luxembourg at Landen, Macaulay said it was a battle between a hunchback dwarf and an asthmatic skeleton. Epic warfare is not like this. When Hector meets Menelaus, there is no place for Thersites. The rival generals not infrequently challenge one another to a single combat. Any general who led his men from behind could not hope to maintain their allegiance for five minutes. But, obviously, there are dangers in this mode of warfare: for what happens if the general gets killed? This is where the esquire, or regimental officer, steps in. General panic is avoided since every company is an army in little, with its own commanding officer, whom every trooper knows as well as, or better than, he knows the general. This superb organisation explains the victories of John over the Russians at Preslav and Silistria. They were hard-fought and often doubtful fields, such as Byzantine armies, hitherto accustomed to win or lose in the shortest possible time, had not been known to contest before. In every case the cavalry was decisive. Splendidly trained and officered, their *morale* was unshakable. They needed only a skilled and dashing cavalry general, and in John they found him. The champions who formed the general staff of the emperor were of course all aristocrats from Asia Minor. The two ablest marshals of John were Bardas Sclerus and Bardas Phocas, both Armenian nobles, and both considering that they were at least as much entitled to the imperial crown as Nicephorus or John. This of course was where the danger lay. It was excellent to have an invincible army led by a brilliant general. But the central government could never be quite easy as to which way the army might move.

The shape of things to come was early seen when the Russians in the spring of 970 invaded Thrace and arrived at Arcadiopolis near Adrianople. They were thirty thousand men, most of them Northmen who would die rather than yield, and whose outlandish howling encouraged themselves and dismayed their foes. To meet them Bardas Sclerus had but twelve thousand, but they were a *corps d'élite*. His first charge threw the enemy into disarray. Two champions stood forth to rally the ranks, but Bardas and his brother cut down both with their own hands. Such resolution and skill were invincible. A combined charge of fresh troops on either wing settled the matter. And the few Russians who escaped disappeared northwards beyond the Bulgarian border. Of the Romans only twenty-five fell.[8]

The rest of the war was a repetition on a larger scale of the battle of Arcadiopolis. It lasted from April to July 971. John commanded in person, and was conspicuous by his golden cuirass wherever the fighting was hottest. In May he stormed Preslav, put the Russian garrison to the sword and rescued the Tsar Boris from their hands. In June he reached the Danube and laid siege to Silistria, where Svyatoslav himself, with the core of his Varangians, lay encamped. At the same time, with superb precision, the imperial navy sailed up the river, dropped anchor and began to torment Silistria with discharges of the horrible and dreaded liquid fire. Svyatoslav came out and engaged the emperor in three pitched battles. It is unnecessary to say that these were fiercely contested. But it was all to no purpose. Each time, at the crucial moment, the drumming of innumerable hooves announced the insupportable shock of the Byzantine cavalry. The Russians were finally enclosed in the fortress, and closely invested. It was a choice between peace and starvation, and Svyatoslav chose the former. He would go back to Kiev. Never again would he invade or make war on the emperor's dominions. He spoke more truly than he knew. On his return to Russia he was set upon near the mouth of the Dnieper by the Pechenegs and put to the sword. We may surely regard this brilliant Balkan campaign of April–July 971 as the summit of Byzantine military achievement. The Tsar Boris II was formally dethroned and Bulgaria, or at least eastern and maritime Bulgaria, was made into an imperial province.9

By comparison with the Russian war, John's eastern campaigns were mere reconnaissances in force. The internal and external difficulties of the once proud caliphate of Bagdad were constantly increasing: and the wretched al-Muti was virtually a prisoner in his own palace. The influence of Bagdad in Armenia, paramount half a century before, was now a cypher: while from Egypt the independent caliphate of the Fatimid house had occupied Palestine, and was casting eyes on Damascus and the Byzantine protectorate of Aleppo. There was virtually no force east or south of Antioch which could face or long delay a Byzantine push eastwards: and had not John died in 976, there is every reason to think that in a decade East Rome would have recovered nearly all she had lost to the Caliphs Omar and Moawiya.

John began by a recruiting tour of Armenia. Here he concluded a treaty of friendship with the Prince of Princes, Ashot III, similar to that which Leo VI had concluded with Ashot's grandfather Sembat the Martyr. He followed this by a destructive raid far into Mesopotamia and northern Syria. This was but preparation for his greatest and, as it proved, his last campaign, which he has described in his letter to King Ashot. In 975 he turned southwards against the encroaching Fatimids. In April he set out from Antioch, received the homage of Emesa and stormed Baalbek. Damascus threw open its gates and yielded an immense tribute. Thence he drove on to the Lake of Tiberias 'where (says His Majesty) our Lord Jesus Christ performed His miracle with two fishes and five loaves of barley'. Tiberias and Nazareth surrendered at the first summons. Encamped on Mount Tabor, the site of the Transfiguration, John received the envoys of Jerusalem itself, who implored his mercy and promised tribute. All Palestine was his without his striking a blow. He turned westwards to the coast, expelled the Fatimid garrison from Caesarea, and received the surrender of Acre, Tyre, Sidon, Beyruth and Tripoli. All this huge area was put under Byzantine protection. Seldom has more been done at less cost in so short a time. One of the emperor's comments deserves special notice: 'It had been our desire to free the Holy Sepulchre of Christ from Mahometan outrages'. This is the very spirit of the Crusaders, and John had performed their task for them a century before they undertook it. But there was a difference. The Byzantine never felt for the Holy Places that romantic attachment which century after century captivated the west of Europe. The reason is that in his eyes his own City was the New Jerusalem on earth, and far more important than the old. This explains why, although the Sepulchre possessed some intrinsic interest for John personally, it had none whatever for his successor Basil II. And though Basil could have occupied Jerusalem at any time he chose to send an army there, he never gave any sign of wishing to do so.[10]

John was already sick when he returned to Constantinople at the end of 975. He was dying of typhoid fever, though – need it be said? – he was confidently stated to have been poisoned: not, curiously enough, by the Empress Theophano, but by the chamberlain Basil, who took over the administration. John died on 10 January 976, after ruling just six years. He was fifty-one. It is impossible not to wonder what would have happened if he had lived, as he might easily have done, until the year AD 1000. As it was, his death at last cleared the way for the legitimate Emperor Basil II.

NOTES

[1] Ostrogorsky, 241–2; Vasiliev, 327–8.
[2] Liudprand, 175–212.
[3] Cedrenus, 375; Leo Diac., 84 ff.
[4] Cedrenus, 375–6; Leo Diac., 87–8.
[5] Bréhier, 197–9; Ostrogorsky, 243–4.
[6] Ostrogorsky, 246, note 1.
[7] Cedrenus, 372.
[8] Leo Diac., 108–11; Cedrenus, 384–8.
[9] Ostrogorsky, 244–6; Bréhier, 206–9.
[10] Ostrogorsky, 246–7; Bréhier, 205–6.

CHAPTER TWENTY-TWO

BASIL II

The reign of Basil II, and indeed his own character, are two of the profoundest puzzles in all Byzantine history. The very facts, when stated, seem to be nearly incredible. To start with, the heredity: Basil's father Romanus II, his grandfather Constantine VII and his great-grandfather Leo the Wise, had none of them shown the smallest interest or skill in military command: Basil II was the greatest military genius and the greatest military organiser of his time, one of the greatest of all time. His father had been a youthful voluptuary; Basil was ascetic and hardy, to a nearly unbelievable degree. His father and grandfather had been tall men with long thin faces and long thin beards: Basil was short, round and ruddy-faced, with little beard but abundantly bushy whiskers. His grandfather and great-grandfather had been scholars, devoted to books, art, music and learning: Basil despised all such pursuits, and was very imperfectly instructed even in Greek grammar, such as it then was. His forebears had been eager to impress on their subjects the majesty of their position by lavish expenditure on gorgeous appointments and exquisite objects of art: Basil was avaricious to a fault, and went about his capital in dingy, dirty garments which would have disgraced a well-to-do tradesman. His forebears had all been greatly influenced, sometimes inordinately so, by the opposite sex: Basil never married, and kept all women at a distance. The eleventh-century historian and politician Michael Psellus, who in his youth could just remember this emperor as an old man, and who was familiar with many who had known him intimately, has left us an unforgettably brilliant portrait of Basil's

301

personal appearance and character.[1] If any were to read this passage without prior knowledge that it was the portrait of a Byzantine sovereign, I wonder what his guess would be as to the identity of the person depicted? I know what mine would be: that this was an astonishingly accurate portrait of a Norman ruler of the high Middle Ages: of a William the Conqueror, let us say. I have spoken of Basil's mother, the Empress Theophano, and I have tried to show, or at all events to believe, that she was not as bad a character as she has often been said to have been. But that she was sexually promiscuous cannot, I fear, be doubted. This circumstance, taken in conjunction with the proclivities of her terrific son, gives rise to certain painful reflexions. And when we recollect and enumerate Basil's affinities with Norman, rather than with Byzantine, despots; and when we remember that, since 911, there had been a sizeable contingent of Varangian Northmen among the palace guards, we shall, I hope, be doing no very substantial injustice to the empress-mother if we suggest the possibility (for it is no more) that Basil II had a recent infusion of Norman blood in his veins.

Yet, after all, heredity is a peculiar thing, as they tell us. Characteristics may lie dormant for many generations, and burst out afresh after hundreds of years. Now, the wife of Basil the Macedonian, whom he married in 865, was daughter of a certain Inger, that is, Igor, who was almost certainly Scandinavian in origin. And it does not seem wholly incredible that Basil was a throwback to the family of his great-great-grandmother, which had abandoned the icy regions of Norway for the civilised and luxurious climate of the Bosphorus. This – let me emphasise – is the purest conjecture: so let us get back to the solid basis of historical fact.

When John Zimiskes died in January 976, Basil was eighteen years old. But he was still quite without experience, either of war or of government. The whole of the administration fell into the more than capable hands of the eunuch chamberlain Basil, who had lent his wise counsels successively to Constantine Porphyrogenitus, Romanus II, Nicephorus Phocas and John Zimiskes. He is said to have deliberately encouraged the young emperors, his great-nephews, in careers of licence and frivolity, in order to retain power in his own hands. In the case of Constantine, no encouragement was needed. But if the minister supposed that he could relegate the young Basil to the permanent status of a *fainéant*, he soon had too much reason to think again.

The external position of the empire had never been stronger. Her armies were everywhere victorious. But, as I have shown, this very strength brought with it a profound internal weakness. The chief aristocratic contenders for the mantle of Zimiskes were two: Bardas Sclerus and Bardas Phocas, the latter a nephew of the Emperor Nicephorus II. Sclerus came of an old Armenian family of aristocrats, who appear in history as generals and governors already by the very beginning of the ninth century, fifty years before the peasant lad Basil the Macedonian had come to seek his fortune in Constantinople. Sclerus' sister had been the first wife of John Zimiskes. He was himself a brilliant general. He had defeated the Russians at Arcadiopolis in 970, and distinguished himself greatly in the Danubian campaign of 971. When John died, Sclerus was commander-in-chief of all the armies of the east, those armies which had received the homage and submission of Aleppo and Damascus and Jerusalem.

The probable outcome was obvious to eyes far less keen than those of Basil the Eunuch. He tried to forestall the danger by prompt action. Sclerus was dismissed from his command, and given instead the military governorship of the frontier province of Mesopotamia, where it was hoped his resources for mischief-making would be curtailed.[2] This manoeuvre failed. On the news of his demotion, Sclerus at once donned the purple boots, proclaimed himself emperor, raised an army of provincials and Saracens, seized the revenues of the east, and marched on Caesarea. In two pitched battles, late in 976 and early in 977, he was completely victorious against the imperial armies, and in the second encounter the imperial commander, Peter Phocas, was slain. The provincial navy of Attalia, with its Admiral Curticius, went over to the rebel. Sclerus hastened across Asia Minor to the shores of the Propontic, reduced Nicaea, and, early in 978, began the investiture of Constantinople by sea and land.

Hitherto all attempts to check him had failed. But now, like so many of the City's besiegers, he was to find that his task was only just beginning. The government, despite repeated misfortunes, remained firm. The splendid imperial navy, traditionally loyal to the ruling house, sailed out in overwhelming strength and annihilated the rebel fleet. And Basil the Eunuch, by a master-stroke, induced Bardas Phocas to take the command of the land forces against Sclerus.

It was indeed a master-stroke, but must to many have appeared no more than a counsel of despair, like calling on Satan to fight against Sin and Death. Phocas was already in prison for revolt against Zimiskes. In point of hereditary ambition and disloyalty, there was little to choose between Phocas and Sclerus. They might well have joined forces against the capital; and indeed, less than ten years later, they actually did so. But what else could be done? The whole skill and experience of the military arm was an aristocratic monopoly; and only a member of this caste stood any chance of success against another. The risk had to be taken, and this time, in the end, it justified the taking. Phocas knew where his strength lay, and he escaped through the rebel lines into the heart of Anatolia, where he soon collected a strong force. Sclerus was compelled to break off the siege and follow him. The first engagement between the champions was favourable to the rebel. But Phocas was not without fresh resources. He fled to Iberia, where his friend David, the Georgian prince, soon supplied him with splendid new troops. In March 978 the two contestants met once more, near Amorion. True to their traditions of chivalry, the two generals challenged one another to single combat in sight of their armies. The account reads like a page from the *Iliad*. Sclerus got in the first blow, but missed his aim, and only cut off the ear of his opponent's charger. Phocas aimed better. He dealt the rebel such a cut that he fell, bleeding and unconscious, to the ground. His army broke and fled and was mopped up at leisure. Sclerus was spirited away by his followers, brought round, and conveyed over the frontier to Bagdad, where, much to the embarrassment of the Saracen government, he took refuge during the next seven years. And, after three whole years of bloodshed, ruin and devastation, the first civil war of Basil's reign was at an end.3

There is no doubt at all that this revolt was decisive in the making of the young Emperor Basil's character. If he was ever to restore his dynasty, the task must be his and his alone. He was just twenty-one years of age; and according to our accounts it was at this time that he experienced what later ages would have called a 'conversion'. It was then that ease and pleasure, delicate foods and charming society, were relegated suddenly and finally to the past. He put away childish things. His body and mind began to assume those deeper lineaments of sternness and inflexibility which characterise his later years. The harsh lessons he had to digest were two: he must break the territorial power of the barons, and he must break their strategic monopoly: and the two were in fact two aspects of a single problem. If the aristocratic stranglehold on Asia was to be broken, force must be used, and only someone outside the closed circle of aristocratic generals could be trusted to use it.

The problems may well have seemed insoluble by a youth of twenty-one. It was a century since a legitimate emperor had led his army in the field, and the tradition had to be relearnt. It was seventy years since a legitimate emperor had been in absolute control of all departments of state. This control too must be resumed. The sources leave us quite in the dark as to the courses of study mastered by Basil in the years 980–5, but we may certainly conclude that military strategy was the chief, and that this was combined with a minute investigation of recent developments in internal administration. By 985 he was obviously nearing a *coup d'état*. The minister Basil the Eunuch saw that his days of power were numbered, or he would never have committed the desperate treason laid to his charge. He began to tamper with the loyalty – never very secure – of Bardas Phocas, whose services in the late revolt had been rewarded with the command of the east. The vigilance of the young sovereign was not to be eluded. On a sudden it was learnt that the all-powerful minister had been arrested, sentenced and exiled. His ostensible crime was malversation. He had, or was said to have, repeatedly taken bribes in return for winking at the alienation of crown lands: and had by these means amassed an enormous fortune. Now, all his property was declared confiscated to the crown. And even the revenues of the monastery of St Basil, which he had erected at vast expense and handsomely endowed, were impounded. This gave rise to a celebrated witticism on the part of the emperor. 'As for those monks', he said, 'I have turned their refectory into a reflectory – for they may now sit there and reflect upon where their bread is to come from'. The minister could not survive the disgrace at the hands of a great-nephew whose throne he had preserved. His mind gave way under the shock. He, who had been celebrated for the firmness of his understanding, now declined into doting imbecility, and died shortly afterwards. Basil II had taken his first step to supremacy.4

But he was still very far from being out of the wood. It was one thing to be master of the Great Palace. It was quite another to be master of the army. This, however, the as yet inexperienced young emperor sought and claimed to be. The forty years war with resurgent Bulgaria, which Zimiskes had apparently crushed and occupied, broke out shortly after Zimiskes' death. The causes and circumstances of this protracted struggle we shall have to examine briefly in a moment. Suffice it to say that by 986 the great Bulgarian hero Samuel Cometopoulos had invaded Hellas and Peloponnesus and was inflicting damage on those countries such as they had not known since the year 924. Basil, with too much self-confidence, set out at the head of an army, into the heart of Bulgaria. The result was a terrible reverse, which, if anyone but Basil had sustained it at the very outset of his military career, would have been fatal to himself and his house. As it was, the consequences were appalling.

The first of these was a return to the empire of the old rebel Sclerus. He represented to the caliph that now he must succeed: and he undertook, upon success, to surrender some important fortresses to the Saracens. The caliph, with some misgiving, agreed that the attempt should be made. He released Sclerus from his prison at Bagdad, gave him men and supplies, and sent him across the frontier to Melitene, where once more he proclaimed himself emperor. It was the spring of 987. This was bad enough, but far worse was to follow. The whole military aristocracy of Anatolia, jealous for their hereditary control of the army, was up in arms against an emperor who had dared to invade Bulgaria without so much as consulting the uncles, brothers, cousins and nephews of Phocas and Zimiskes. They regarded Basil's defeat, with good reason, as the inevitable consequence of his folly; and they regarded it, this time incorrectly, as a sign that the crown must now again be the property of one of their own order. Bardas Phocas, the nephew of the Emperor Nicephorus, and the commander of Asia, was the obvious choice. He mustered his order. In August 987 it rallied to him in the princely mansion of Eustathius Maleinus, one of the most powerful landlords in the provinces of Charsianon and Cappadocia. Every commander of note or experience was there. And on 15 August, Bardas Phocas himself assumed the imperial dignity, and was saluted by such a distinguished general staff as had seldom been congregated in one place.5

There were now four emperors: two in Constantinople, one in Charsianon, and one in Melitene. Phocas saw at once that to march directly on Constantinople leaving Sclerus in his rear would be mere madness. He therefore opened negotiations with his fellow-rebel. He would proceed to the capital and secure the crown: and after this, a partition of Anatolia would follow, according to which the western half would go to the new emperor and the eastern to Sclerus. Sclerus, against all advice, fell in with the plan, and dropped his guard. Phocas, with a resource equal to his treachery, surprised him and sent him to confinement in a fortress. Then, his hands free for the main undertaking, he made straight for the capital, and reached Scutari at the end of the same year 987.

And now what chance had Basil II? His army was defeated: and what was left of the troops of the western provinces was far away, striving to hold the victorious Bulgars in check. He had his guards and nearly nothing else. He could not think of facing in the field the seasoned warriors of Asia, commanded by the most various and dazzling array of military talents. But, whatever faults Basil had committed, his courage and resolution never failed him for an instant. There was one force, and one alone, which, if he could command it, would bring him through to safety: the Northmen of Kiev. Imperial warships were swiftly dispatched to Cherson, and negotiations were opened by Basil's ambassadors with Vladimir, the prince of Kiev.

Vladimir was one of the three sons of Svyatoslav, who had been expelled from Bulgaria by Zimiskes, and killed by the Pechenegs in 971. He was a barbarian of the most cruel and licentious species. Though his grandmother had accepted Christian baptism, he was a pagan, who propitiated his deities with bestial and human sacrifices. His sexual proclivites were terrific. He had at least three wives, and no fewer than eight hundred concubines. Yet he was not without a certain shrewdness and sense of his position. His father Svyatoslav had been also the father of Russian imperialism: and Vladimir was able to see that for any power aspiring to greatness, paganism was anachronistic. The legends of his casting about for a civilised religion to adopt, are certainly legends: but they correctly illustrate his policies. After considering in turn the relative advantages and demerits (most of them very gross) of Judaism, Islam and Western Christianity, he had sent his ambassadors in 987 to Constantinople, to try his luck with the Orthodox. On 8 September a splendid service was celebrated for them in the Cathedral, and they were in ecstasies of rapture. They thought they were in Heaven, and that during the service the angels of God (who were in fact mosaics seen behind fluttering candles) had come down and floated about their heads. The Byzantine clergy gravely assured them that such was undoubtedly the case. They returned to Vladimir full of praise for the imperial religion, and their prince was about to cast in his lot with Orthodoxy when the imperial embassy arrived to bring news of the empire's deadly peril, and to implore the aid of his invincible arms.

Vladimir was clever enough to see that the game was in his hands. He made the most of his luck. He would send a company, or *druzhina*, of six thousand Varangians with all speed, and he would become an Orthodox Christian. But in return he must have for his bride the Princess Anna, own sister of the emperors, born in the Purple Chamber and daughter of one who had there been born. The insolence of the demand was breath-taking, as he well knew; but he also well knew that it could not be refused. The capital was closely besieged. Other help than his was non-existent. The Iberians of the Caucasus were solidly behind the rebel. Haggling would have been worse than useless. With that good sense which the Byzantine government always showed when there was no help for it, the terms were accepted with a minimum of delay: and the ardent young emperor sat down to wait for their fulfilment with such patience as he could command. He had to wait about twelve months, every day of which must have been torture. The whole of the Bithynian coast was in the hands of Phocas. The only card in Basil's hand was control of the sea. Inside the capital, the populace, who remembered Nicephorus II, and were not at all eager to repeat their experience with his nephew, remained steadfastly loyal. But the church seized the occasion of Basil's embarrassment to make demands which he was forced to concede, but never forgot. In the idle year 988 the patriarch enforced a complete repeal of Nicephorus' ecclesiastical legislation over the matter of monastic properties, one of the most sensible of that sovereign's edicts, as Basil, better than most, knew it to be. It was unwise to submit such a man as Basil to *force majeure*. Basil, says his biographer, seldom or never forgot an injury: and when his day of absolute power dawned, it was with ineffable contempt that he dismissed all patriarchal protests against his ruinous taxation of ecclesiastical properties.

At length, at the turn of the year 988–9, the stalemate was broken. Along the open sea-way from the mouth of the Dnieper to the Bosphorus came the Viking ships that brought salvation. Six thousand Northmen warriors, whose backs no enemy but Zimiskes had ever seen, landed safely in the Golden Horn. With a sigh of relief the young emperor began to plan his counterattack. It was excellently conceived. The main camp of Phocas was at Scutari – or Chrysopolis, as it was then called, – in full sight of the Walls across the strait. On a night late in February 989 the priceless Varangians were ferried across into Asia, and concealed within striking distance of the enemy concentration. At dawn, while the enemy were still snoring in fancied security, six thousand howling barbarians, of enormous stature and ferocity, were let loose upon them. It was not a battle, but a massacre. The emperor in person directed the operation. Scarcely any of the rebels escaped. The three commanders were delivered alive into Basil's hands. They were impaled and crucified.

Bardas Phocas himself, who lay with a strong force at some distance, was spurred into activity. He moved his troops westward to Abydos, the imperial customs-house, and laid siege to it with the idea of transporting his army into Thrace. But the sea was Basil's, and the besieged city was at once relieved by the imperial navy. The imperial army, with the Varangian Northmen at its head, came up fast. In the middle of April they had raised the siege, and the two main forces were at last confronted in the plain. Bardas Phocas, already incensed by the defeat and massacre of his adherents at Chrysopolis, watched from a height the progress of the two emperors, Basil and Constantine, as they rode along their lines. At length, he could no longer contain himself. He called for his horse. The charger stumbled and fell, but he mounted another, and, with a gesture to a body of Iberian troops to follow him, he spurred across the plain directly to the point where the two young emperors stood. This was a crucial moment. If Basil had now shown the white feather, all would have been lost. But he did no such thing. He drew his sword and quietly awaited the onslaught of the heir of the house of Phocas. The rival armies looked on in breathless astonishment at this singular *dénouement*. As the rebel approached his antagonist, it was seen that something was amiss. He swayed in his seat. At a short distance he slackened speed, guided his horse to a low eminence, slid from the saddle, and died almost immediately. He had suffered a cerebral stroke. The Varangians made short work of the discomfited host, and the chief threat to the crown was removed.[6]

Even so it was but the chief threat of many others, both at home and abroad. At home the senior rebel Sclerus, interned in a fortress on the eastern frontier, at once regained his liberty after his rival's sudden demise. Months went by before Basil succeeded in bringing him to terms. It is more than likely that, had Sclerus been the Sclerus of 970, and even of 987, the terms would have been refused. But he had recently been stricken with the cruellest of diseases, blindness, which threatened to become total. He saw that nothing more could be done. His son had deserted him, and the terms were generous. None of his followers was to be demoted or punished: and this was as wise a condition for Basil as it was for Sclerus, for his general staff contained some of the best officers of the empire. He was indeed not to call himself emperor, but he might count himself next in rank to the reigning emperors. And, after submission, he could keep his eastern command. Basil crossed to one of the imperial estates in Bithynia, and there, beneath a gorgeous tent and seated on a golden throne, he awaited his old antagonist. At sight of him Basil could scarcely command his countenance. The old general, nearly blind, was led in by two ushers. 'Is that the fellow', said Basil, 'who has scared me out of my wits? And now he has to be brought in and shown his way'.

Psellus, who has left us an account of the conversation which ensued, tells us that, over dinner, Basil condescended to ask the advice of Sclerus as to his future policy. In reply Sclerus said: appoint no military leaders out of the wealthy class; oppress this class by penal and unjust fines and taxation, so that all their energies will be absorbed in their own personal affairs; and, lastly, allow no woman to have any influence whatever in the government of the state. We may be tempted to suppose that this witness is *ex postfacto*, for it was in fact on these principles that Basil conducted his government – so far as he could – during the next thirty-five years; and in any case he must already have known their wisdom better than Sclerus could teach it to him. But I record the incident because it shows that the aristocratic menace to the state was as obvious to contemporaries as it is to us; the only question was, whether any lasting remedy could be applied. The answer to this, of course, was no: Basil was powerless to put back the clock. But he could and did stop it for a generation, and this in itself was an extraordinary achievement.7

So ended twenty-five years of aristocratic usurpation and rebellion during which two usurpers had mounted the throne and two rebels convulsed the whole empire in their efforts to do so. It was a period of the utmost social, economic and military significance: it was also significant for its effect on the temper of Basil II. This temper was now ulcerated by repeated misusage and misfortune. If he had a ruling passion, it was his deadly hatred of the Byzantine aristocracy and the Bulgarian tsar. If his severity and even savagery were phenomenal, it is only fair to remember the terrible wrongs under which all his youth had lain.

Basil was now master of Asia. But he was still under threat from the north. There seems to have been some hesitation – no doubt as a result of popular clamour – in fulfilling the terms of the treaty with Vladimir, that is, in sending the *porphyrogenita* Anna to be his bride. But Vladimir soon showed that he was not to be trifled with. At the first hint of reluctance on the part of Byzantium, he seized the Byzantine fortress of Cherson in the Crimea, which was the lynch-pin of imperial relations with Patzinacia, Russia and Chazaria. And he intimated that if there was any more shilly-shally, he would do unto Constantinople even as he had done unto Cherson. Basil saw the game was up. The arrival of ten thousand hostile Varangians on the Bosphorus, whom Basil's own Varangian guards would instantly join, would be the final straw, as Vladimir very well knew. The poor princess, twenty-five and still unmarried, was informed of her doom. 'You send me into slavery', she said, 'I would rather die here'. Romantic historians make much of her sorrows; but was she after all so much to be pitied? She was a humble instrument in the Christianisation of Russia, and of her line sprang the Bourbon kings of France. But her first experiences of the land of Midnight were undoubtedly discouraging. She fell desperately ill, and it needed a miracle to save her.

Free of the rebel and Russian perils, Basil could set about the main task of his life, the final reduction of Bulgaria. Here again, his policy is at first sight something of an enigma. The Bulgarian war, now resumed, lasted near thirty years. Its object was to bring under effective imperial control all that vast territory which lies between Macedonia and the Danube, the Euxine and Adriatic, and to make Bulgaria, free and independent since the days of the Heraclians, as much an imperial domain as Thrace or Bithynia: to restore, in other words, the Balkan frontier of the empire as it had been in the days of Justinian and Maurice. That the plan was feasible is shown by its accomplishment. That it was wise in the long-run must remain doubtful. For three centuries the salvation of the Anatolian state had lain in the strong independent buffers of Bulgaria and Armenia. The dangers of weakening either buffer had been only too apparent less than twenty years before, when the Russians of Svyatoslav had poured into the vacuum left by the enfeebled realm of the Tsar Peter and the Tsar Boris. But we have always to remember that the whole theory of empire was based on the conception that God's Will had decreed that one day, when the sins of the people were washed away (that is to say, when the empire was strong enough), Byzantium should resume the government over the domains of Augustus and Trajan, and indeed more yet than those. This theory was as strong in the tenth as in the fourth century; and in the fifteenth as in the tenth. Hence, throughout Byzantine history, whenever conquest or encroachment were possible, all considerations of strategic advantage or balance of power, so well cogitated in times of weakness and retreat, vanished like mist before the flaming sun of the Almighty's decree. To be able to vanquish and romanise Bulgaria, and to abstain, out of worldly considerations, from doing so, would be to ignore the *fiat* of God, and would certainly entail far worse disasters than any to be apprehended from straining the state's resources. If it was His Will that Byzantium should (to put it vulgarly) bite off more than she could chew, He would strengthen the jaws and fortify the digestion.

Yet, when all is said, there seemed to be in Basil's enduring hatred and resentment towards Bulgaria something that in these days would be called pathological. His conquests in the east, splendid though they were, show none of that morbid pertinacity with which he trampled on and extirpated the Bulgars. Is it possible that he had a more personal motive than the Will of God?

Is it conceivable that this motive was bound up with the most powerful of human instincts, and the most sensitive area of human pride? In 969, for purely political reasons, his hated step-father had betrothed him, then a boy of eleven, to some Bulgarian princess. The insult may have rankled, more fiercely than we know, in that stern and unforgiving breast.

At all events, the provocation at least was all from the Bulgarian side. The origins of the war are very doubtful, and an enormous amount of argument and hypothesis has been put forward about them. Zimiskes, by his expulsion of Svyatoslav and his deposition of the Tsar Boris II, had seemed to have done Basil's work for him. Yet, in the very year of Zimiskes' death (976), Bulgaria was ready with leaders and an organised host to rebel against the empire. Whether or not it were, as many have maintained, that there then existed a West Bulgaria as a more or less separate entity, at least it is certain that Zimiskes' settlement scarcely touched the large area which stretched westwards of a line from Silistria to Adrianople. In the area of Macedonia was a certain Count Nicholas, who, from his title, presumably held some nominally Byzantine administrative office. He had four sons, upon one of whom fell the mantle of Symeon the Great. The origins of the family are obscure: one of the eastern sources says that it was Armenian, and this is possible, in view of the large numbers of Armenians settled in the west during the past hundred years. But as the sons were called Moses, Aaron, David and Samuel, we might with equal reason suppose them to have been Jews. However, the probability is that they were Bulgars, who had long resented the degradation of their country to a Byzantine protectorate in 927; and that the Jewish names given to the children – the Cometopuli, as they were called – of Count Nicholas were a reminder that they were marked out to deliver their people from the house of bondage and to restore its former greatness.[8]

The only son with whom we have to deal was Samuel Cometopulos. He was a foeman worthy of Basil's steel. He was quick to capitalise the seething resentment felt by his proud race at their subjection by John Zimiskes. No sooner was Zimiskes dead than he rose in revolt: and, taking advantage of the simultaneous revolt of Sclerus in Asia, he led his followers southwards and began to plunder the now prosperous provinces of Thessaly and Hellas.

For about ten years the fate of the Greek peninsula is as dark to us as it was in the eighth century, or during the years 917–25, when it was occupied by Symeon. We can probably conclude that while Samuel failed to capture Thebes, or Athens, or Corinth, he effectively occupied the rest. Basil, fighting for throne and life against rebels within and without his capital, could do no more than Romanus I to liberate it. Certain it is that by the end of this decade things had become very bad indeed. Larissa, the Thessalian capital, after a gallant defence during a series of sieges, at last threw open its gates in 985. In the spring of 986, Samuel stormed Berea: and Berea, as St Paul discovered, is only a few hours' distance west of Thessalonica. Just at this moment, the first of Sclerus' revolts collapsed, and Basil was free to take such action in Bulgaria as he saw fit.

His disastrous campaign has already been alluded to, but passed over in order to complete the story of the aristocratic revolts. Like many great soldiers – Julius Caesar and Frederick for example – he had to learn wisdom by unhappy experience. The strategy was excellent, and was later repeated with complete success. It was the discipline that broke down. Basil's two lieutenants, Melissenus and Contostephanus, were at loggerheads. The artillery was manned by bunglers, who could not even defend their pieces, let alone fire them. The commissariat was in the hands of swindlers. The expedition set out in June 986. The object was to march on and lay siege to Serdica, or Triaditza. This, we repeat, was sound strategy, for Serdica was the nodal point of Bulgarian communications to the north-west and south-west; and it lay on a practicable route from Constantinople – the very route that the Sofia-Istanbul railway follows today. The army traversed the valley of the Maritza and passed through the celebrated defile of Trajan's Gate, which divides the northern slopes of the Rhodope from the sóuthern slopes of the western Balkan. They reached Serdica and began the siege; but with such poor success that ammunition and food were exhausted before any impression could be made. At last, on 15 August, it was seen that a retreat must be made. But it was too late. Samuel had returned by forced marches from Berea and had occupied the high ground on either side of the defile of Trajan's Gate. On Tuesday 17 August, while still in the defile, the Byzantines were attacked and routed with great slaughter. Basil and his two generals got away into Thrace. Most of the rest were lost. The first round had gone to Samuel; and seldom has a great warrior's career begun more unpromisingly.[9]

Thereafter, as we have seen, the second Anatolian revolt pre-occupied the emperor during three more years. But when he returned to Bulgaria in 990, he was a very different commander from the one who had been so ignominiously expelled from it. This is a convenient point to pause. From 963 to 976 Basil had been a ward of two mayors of the palace: from 976 to 985 he had been his grand chamberlain's puppet: from 986 to 989 he had been defeated by Samuel the Bulgar and Bardas Phocas, and blackmailed by Vladimir of Russia. A lesser man would have succumbed. Basil's firmness only grew more firm. And the era of his triumph and absolute mastery, bought as they were at the price of humiliation and disaster, it will be our more pleasing task to trace in the next chapter.

NOTES

[1] Psellus, I, 21–3.
[2] Cedrenus, 416–8.
[3] Bréhier, 213–4.
[4] Psellus, I, 12–4; Ostrogorsky, 249.
[5] Cedrenus, 438.
[6] Cedrenus, 443–4; Psellus, I, 9–11.
[7] Psellus, I, 14–9.
[8] Ostrogorsky, 250 and note 2.
[9] Cedrenus, 436–8; Leo Diac., 171.

BASIL II
(CONTINUED)

We left the great Emperor Basil II at what seemed to be the nadir of his fortunes, yet, owing to his courage and determination, inspired no less by bad than by good qualities, poised to begin the ascent which should lead him to the summit of human grandeur, never ascended by any Roman emperor since Trajan, or ever to be ascended again. We left him encompassed by a sea of misfortunes and menaces. And it is impossible to withhold our admiration for the presence of mind, the coolness, the statesmanship, and the sheer dogged obstinacy with which he made his way to shore.[2]

Nothing could better illustrate the unquenchable spirit and vigour of the young emperor than his conduct in the autumn of 989. As soon as Bardas Phocas was dead, and while Sclerus was still in arms, he dispatched a powerful force under John of Chaldia to punish the Georgian princes who had aided the chief rebel. David, the prince of Tao in South Georgia, who in 978, while he was aiding the then loyal Bardas, had been granted temporary possession of the Roman territories north of Lake Van, had continued to support Bardas when the latter had himself revolted in 987. He was now to make atonement. Basil's terms, accepted by David in 990, were characteristically farsighted. David might retain the lands ceded to him in 978, and be invested with the high imperial title of 'curopalate'; but at his death, all his lands, including his native Tao, were to fall to the Byzantine crown. By this politic settlement Byzantium was assured of her title to all, and much more than all, her former domains on her north-eastern frontier.

At the end of the same year, 990, Basil embarked on his second Bulgarian campaign, which occupied him almost without intermission until 995. In 991 he restored the position at Thessalonica by the recapture of Berea; and then began a systematic pacification of the enemy's territory. Details are wholly lacking; yet there is reason to think that he devoted special attention to establishing a firm hold on the area about Serdica, the importance of which was to be demonstrated during the years 998–1003: that is to say, he embarked with better success on the strategy that had failed through indiscipline in 986. A vivid impression of his general plan is conveyed by a brief passage of Yahya of Antioch:

> During four years [i.e. 991–5] Basil made war on the Bulgarians and invaded their country. In winter time he marched upon the most remote provinces in the Bulgarian territory, assailed their inhabitants and took them prisoner. During this time he stormed a number of fortresses, retaining some and destroying others which he thought he had not means to hold.

It was in these years that Basil himself developed from the inexperienced youth who had fled from Trajan's Gate into the wary and ruthless slayer of the Bulgars; and perfected that scheme of warfare which made him invincible whenever he took the field. This scheme was the annihilating progress through a specific area by an overwhelming force, perfectly equipped and perfectly disciplined, which could be neither openly encountered nor surprised. Such a method of warfare called not so much for brilliant generalship as for meticulous organisation: and here Basil was in his element. His exactitude and attention to detail were phenomenal. Nothing more was needed. His soldiers grumbled to his face at his minute punctilio; but he blandly assured them that by such means, and by such alone, could they hope to return safe to their families and homesteads. One more lesson of cardinal importance he had learnt: that for a legitimate emperor supreme command in the field was essential. Here Nicephorus II and John Zimiskes were the models. It was all very well for a Leo VI or a Constantine VII to sit at home, writing encyclopedias, composing prayers and declaiming sermons. The intervening thirty years had shown that only the commander-in-chief was master. And this Basil

317

determined to be. He may probably not have known that the word 'emperor' means 'commander-in-chief'. But he had discovered it by painful experience.

At the same time Basil was busily engaged in strengthening his position in Bulgaria's rear by diplomatic means. In March 992 a treaty, long in preparation, was concluded with Venice, whereby the tolls payable on Venetian cargoes trading with the empire, and the method of their exaction, were regulated on terms highly favourable to the republic. Venice, for her part, undertook police and carrying duties for Byzantium in the Adriatic. In the same year, while still encamped in Bulgaria, Basil negotiated an agreement with the Serbs, which probably had the effect of drawing to his side John Vladimir, the powerful ruler of the Serbian principality of Dioclea.

The progress of these necessarily protracted operations was interrupted during the winter of 994-5, when they were still far short of completion. A disaster on the Syrian frontier compelled the emperor to proceed thither in person. Since 992 the Hamdanid emir of Aleppo, a Byzantine protectorate, had been under pressure from the encroaching power of the Egyptian Fatimid Caliph Aziz. The emir appealed to Basil, who in 994 sent reinforcements to Antioch, with instructions to its governor to intervene. The governor, Michael Vourtzes, was old and incompetent. He advanced languidly to the Orontes. The Fatimid commander, a Turk called Manjutekin, hurried westwards from Aleppo to meet him. On 15 September he forced the ford of the Orontes, turned the Byzantine position and routed the Roman army with great slaughter. Vourtzes fled back to Antioch. The emir of Aleppo dispatched a second appeal to Basil, who was wintering in Bulgaria. The emperor was quick to see the danger, which now menaced Antioch itself. He gathered some levies, which included newly recruited Bulgarians, and, travelling by forced marches, crossed his empire from west to east, a distance of some six hundred miles, in twenty-six days. At the end of April 995 he appeared unannounced beneath the walls of Aleppo, at the head of seventeen thousand men. At the mere report of his presence Manjutekin threw up the siege of Aleppo and retreated in haste to Damascus. Basil received the homage and thanks of Aleppo; then, turning south, sacked Rafaniya and Emesa, and penetrated as far as Tripoli, burning and pillaging as he went. On his return he garrisoned Tortosa, and, after appointing Damian Dalassenus to govern Antioch, with instructions to continue the policy of annual demonstrations in force, made his way back to Constantinople. In less than six months the eastern situation was restored.

His homeward journey could be taken more leisurely; and he was able for the first time to see for himself the vast encroachments which during the past century the Anatolian aristocracy had made on the lands of the village communes and on the estates of the crown. Eustathius Maleinus, the old rebel, on whose estate Bardas Phocas had set up his standard in 986, and whose properties spread mile after mile over the provinces of Charsianon and Cappadocia, received his sovereign much in the style of a powerful independent prince. Basil saw, as his predecessors had seen, that while this immense and growing influence was wielded by military magnates jealous of, and hostile to, the crown, the legitimate emperor could never be master of his own soldiers and his own revenues. But where Basil differed from his predecessors was in his ability to apply a practical remedy. He was now the head of the strongest military force in Christendom; and his remedy was soon forthcoming. On 1 January 996 was promulgated a comprehensive law for the repression of landed estates. This celebrated edict combines a searching demand for titles to landed properties which is reminiscent of *Quo Warranto* with a ban on the alienation of estates to the church which is reminiscent of *Mortmain*. As the law then stood (the law of Romanus I), forty years of undisputed tenure were required to establish rights of ownership and disposal. But it was easy enough for a powerful proprietor, whether by bribery or brute force, to suppress any claims for restitution during the period of suspense. The provision was openly derided; and estates held by no legal title whatever were handed on from father to son as though they had been the real properties of the testators. This provision was now repealed. Estates which had been held, and could by properly authenticated documents be shown to have been held, during seventy-five years or more, were confirmed on the possessors. The rest were to be handed back, without compensation, to the original proprietors. But for crown lands seized and held through bribery of government inspectors, no time limit less than one thousand years was to be valid, and the proprietor was required, with grim humour, to cite a title dating from the reign of Caesar Augustus.

Documents emanating from the treasury and purporting to make grants of such land in the imperial name were revoked. In particular, a demand was made for the revision of all deeds of grant issued between the years 976 and 985 in the name of the chamberlain Basil the Eunuch. These were submitted to the personal scrutiny of the sovereign: and all which were not accorded his 'endorsement', written in his own hand, were declared invalid.

The effects of this radical enactment were felt even before its formal promulgation. Maleinus was summarily expropriated and imprisoned for life. The estates of the Phocas family were drastically curtailed. The grasping protovestiary Philocales was evicted and humbled to the status of a peasant. The Mousele family was reduced to beggary. These were examples *in terrorem*: 'so that', as the emperor bluntly expressed it, 'the powerful may take note of it, and not leave this sort of inheritance to their children'. The law was thereafter enforced for thirty years with unceasing rigour; and all the great properties, whether military, civil or ecclesiastical, suffered substantial diminution if not wholesale extinction. Yet even this was insufficient. Eight years later (1003–4) the terrible emperor imposed a yet more crushing burden on the estates of the 'powerful'. The groups or communes of villages were assessed at an annual sum which all the proprietors were jointly held liable for subscribing. This system had borne harshly on the 'poor', and Basil determined to relieve them. The *allelengyon* (as it was called) now became the sole responsibility of the 'powerful' land-owner: that is to say, that, when the sum of taxes on a provincial commune was found to be deficient, owing to the failure or desertion of a peasant-landowner, this deficit was no longer chargeable on his peasant fellow-proprietors, but on any great land-owner who had bought up property in the district. This final blow fell most heavily on the church properties, which had fewer resources to meet it. The 'ministers of God', who, says the chronicler, 'were reduced to the extreme of penury', urged the Patriarch Sergius to repeated protests (1004, 1019); but these were dismissed with contempt.3

Basil remained at home during the unusually long period of two years and a half (January 996 – midsummer 998). The wide application of his land law demanded his presence: for his draconian measures provoked serious disaffection. Ecclesiastical and diplomatic affairs of grave import also claimed his attention. In 996, after the ecumenical patriarchate had been four years vacant, he appointed to the see a layman, the well-known physician Sisinnius, and set him to work towards a rupture with the papacy. At almost the same time a yet bolder design occurred to him: of placing a Greek prelate on the throne of St Peter. Bishop John Philagathus, a Greek-speaking native of Calabria and a protégé of the late empress of the west, Theophano, was sent to Constantinople in the summer of 996 to negotiate the betrothal of Basil's niece Zoe to the young Emperor Otto III. The tenor of these negotiations is unknown; but the consequence is notorious. On his return to Italy early in 997, Philagathus, trusting to the anti-German reaction in Rome fostered by the patrician Crescentius, allowed himself to be chosen anti-pope in opposition to the German Gregory V, the cousin and nominee of Otto himself. The manoeuvre miscarried disastrously. After a short term of ineffectual presidency, the upstart was seized by the Ottonians, horribly mutilated and thrown into prison (998). Thereafter, negotiations between Basil and Otto, though not entirely suspended, were indecisive during three years.

Meanwhile, Basil's withdrawal from the west in 995 had led to a dangerous revival of the power of the Bulgarian Samuel. In 996 he ambushed and killed the governor of Thessalonica, Gregory Taronites, and took prisoner successively Gregory's son Ashot and his *remplaçant* John of Chaldia. Samuel then swept south into the defenceless province of Hellas, and ravaged it down to the Isthmus of Corinth. Basil, pre-occupied at home, could not intervene. But he sent to Thessalonica, which still held out, the ablest and most fortunate of his marshals, Nicephorus Uranus, who in 997 encountered the returning Bulgars on the river Spercheius, and inflicted on them a bloody defeat. Samuel himself was wounded, and barely escaped. Uranus seized the opportunity to advance into the centre of Bulgaria; and such was the completeness of his victory that during a progress of three months he met no opposition. From 997 until 1001 Samuel's arms were not seen in eastern Bulgaria or Macedonia. Indeed, he seems for a moment to have thought of submission. But events of the same year caused him to think again. 4

In 997 died the Croat princeling Stephen Drzhislav, to whom the Byzantine government had granted the title of king and entrusted the protection of their province of Dalmatia. His death inspired Samuel with the grand design of carving out a fresh and unassailable empire in the west. From this time may be dated the truly imperial policy of Samuel. He proclaimed himself tsar. He seized and garrisoned Dyrrhachium. He invaded Dioclea and took prisoner its prince, John Vladimir, whom he married to his daughter. He advanced up Dalmatia, where, though its maritime cities repulsed him, he was soon master of the hinterland, hitherto under Croat protection. He then turned north-eastwards into Bosnia; and in or about the year 1000 he set the seal on his triumph by concluding a marriage alliance between his son and heir Gabriel Radomir and a daughter of King Stephen of Hungary.

His power in the west of the peninsula was now enormous. But Basil was more than a match for him. The emperor's first counter-stroke was the transfer of the protectorate over Dalmatia from the feeble successors of Drzhislav to Venice. The doge's eldest son, John Urseolo, hastened to Constantinople (997–8), and the bargain was soon struck. John returned to Venice with the promise of a wife from the imperial house; and in 1000 the doge himself, in a splendid progress down the Adriatic, received the grateful homage of his new protectorate. Meanwhile Samuel had virtually abandoned his territories east of a line from Vidin through Serdica to Vodena, and Basil was not slow to take advantage of the respite. When Samuel returned eastwards in 1001, it was too late.

Basil's strategy in the Bulgarian war from 998 to 1003 is clear enough. It was a steady progress outwards from the centre, each advance being secured by the garrisoning of strong points along the route. Philippopolis was first made into a strong base camp, with a permanent governor. Next, the forts about Serdica must be occupied, for they commanded the routes north-westward to Vidin and the Danube, and south-westward to Skoplje and Ochrida. If the centre were firmly held, each of these routes could be pursued in turn. A chain of Byzantine garrisons on the Danube would prevent the crossing of any reinforcements from Hungary or Patzinacia, a danger always present to imperial governments of that time. An advance on Skoplje would menace any Bulgarian thrust south-eastwards, and would concentrate Bulgarian defences on the threatened capital at Ochrida. Basil took the field in the summer of 998, and had carried out the first part of his programme, the reduction of fortresses about Serdica, by the following spring. In 999 he was urgently recalled to the Syrian frontier, in circumstances precisely similar to those of 995. But this time he could safely leave western operations in the hands of his marshals. In 1000 Xiphias and Theodorocanus overran the Dobrudja, and established the Byzantine arms firmly on the lower Danube. They returned without loss.

In July 998 the energetic governor of Antioch, Dalassenus, was accidentally slain during a campaign against Apamea. His troops at once broke, and were massacred. Basil saw that it would be necessary to repeat the lesson administered four years before. He arrived in Syria in September 999, with the invincible Russian troops of his household, and during three months spread devastation far and wide, though once again he had to fall back before the impregnable defences of Tripoli. He appointed Nicephorus Uranus to succeed Dalassenus at Antioch, and in January 1000 went into winter quarters at Tarsus.

But he had other work to do in the east and this was the time to do it. In April, as he lay at Tarsus, came news, not unexpected by him, of the murder on Easter Day of the curopalate David, prince of Tao, whose rich legacy must now be occupied in force. Without delay Basil, at the head of his army, pushed north-eastwards through Melitene and Hanzit and Erez, settling local affairs by the way. At Hafjij, a fortress on the south bank of the Phasis river, the Georgian and Armenian potentates were gathered to receive him. A bloody encounter between the emperor's Russians and the Iberian levies, which may have been accidental but was certainly impressive, preceded the assize. The chief of the despots to be reckoned with was Bagrat, King of Abasgia and Prince of Karthli, whose southern frontier marched with that of Tao, now annexed to the empire. He was given the title of 'curopalate' in succession to his deceased cousin, and his borders were carefully defined and agreed upon. The assize, which included a tentative towards the annexation of Vaspurakan, was followed by a progress through the recovered territories north of Lake Van, and thence into the heart of the new province of Tao itself. Late in the year Basil returned by way of Theodosioupolis to Constantinople. In the following year, 1001, the Fatimid caliphate signed a ten years' truce with the empire.[5]

Matters being thus satisfactorily settled in the east, the emperor at once resumed his interrupted campaign in Bulgaria. In the spring and autumn of 1001 he made two short but fruitful forays into the southern area, capturing Berea and Serbia in the first, and rooting out Bulgarian garrisons from Thessaly in the second. Samuel, now effectually roused by the Byzantine menace, advanced eastwards and made an attempt to recapture Serbia, but was repulsed. Late in the year Basil returned to Constantinople, to renew and this time to complete the negotiations for the marriage of his niece with the western emperor. But here, once again, his western diplomacy miscarried. The princess, magnificently escorted, set out for Italy in January 1002, only to learn on her arrival at Bari that her betrothed, in the flower of his 'sweet years', had passed away.[6]

We have more than once referred to this interesting dynastic plan of Basil II: and it calls for more than a passing mention. We have to look on it in connexion with the whole series of similar tentatives which were made in the period under review, with the object of re-uniting east and west, and doing away with the anomalous – nay, blasphemous – condition entailed by two separate empires. Constantine VI and Charlemagne's daughter; Charlemagne himself and Irene; Basil I's son and Lewis II's daughter; Lewis III and Anna; Romanus II and Bertha; Romanus II and Hedwig of Bavaria; Otto II and Theophano: these were the most important of the matches projected or consummated, always with the same end in view. But none of them could compare in promise or importance with the match projected by Basil II. Let us consider the circumstances. Of the two legitimate emperors at Constantinople, Basil was unmarried, and his brother Constantine had three daughters, of whom one, the Princess Zoe, now offered, was eminently nubile. She was twenty-three years old. She was the undoubted heiress of the line of Basil the Macedonian; and she was *porphyrogenita*. Her bridegroom himself, aged twenty-one, was no less undoubted emperor of the west, being third in the direct line from Otto the Great. But he was more than this. His mother Theophano was also a Byzantine princess, in – as I believe – the direct line of Basil the Macedonian: and, if so, the betrothed couple were first cousins. Young Otto III had been brought up by his mother in the traditions of Byzantine rather than western imperialism. He was a Roman rather than a German emperor: crowned by the pope of Rome and ruling in the Eternal City. If he and his cousin had had male issue (as seemed highly probable), what pretender in east or west could have stood for a moment against such unquestionable and enormous authority? Meanwhile the bride's uncle, Basil, was rapidly reducing to Roman authority the territory that lay between the Euxine and the Adriatic; while Otto himself was master of Germany and, in all but name, of the whole of Italy besides. A son born to the young couple would have been in his early twenties when his great-uncle and grandfather died (1025, 1028): and would have inherited a dominion extending unbroken from Armenia to the Gulf of Lyons, from the confines of Persia to the confines of France. Many believe that the cleavage between the Greek and Roman worlds was already far too wide to be bridged by any mere dynastic fusion: and I do not say that they are wrong. What I do wish to bring out is the implications of such a match as they presented themselves to Basil II. It was a grand conception: and it seemed a stroke of Providence itself that it was not given a chance to be fulfilled. Basil had now tried to put a Greek pope in the chair of St Peter, and a Greek princess, his own heir, on the throne of the west. Both tentatives had failed. Only the third alternative, that of conquest, remained: and if he had lived till 78 instead of 68, he would have tried this too, and very probably succeeded.

The year 1002 Basil devoted to extending the work of his marshals on the Danube. He hastened to the north-west, and, probably in March or April, laid siege to Vidin. The town, defended strongly by art and nature, resisted for eight months. Samuel tried to relieve it by a destructive raid on Adrianople, far in the emperor's rear. Basil was not to be deflected; and at last the fortress surrendered. Samuel was now forced to make a serious attempt to stem the tide of Byzantine invasion. In the spring of 1003 Basil advanced to the Vardar and menaced Skoplje. The Bulgarians lay in strength on the opposite bank of the swollen river. Samuel repeated the blunder which had cost him the battle at the Spercheius six years before. He trusted too much to the natural barrier, and kept slack guard. Basil forded the river by night, and massacred his army.7 This was the turning-point in the war, and even Samuel's allies saw that it was so. Nothing could now prevent the final and total victory of the Byzantine arms, however long it might be in coming; and the navy of Venice presented an insuperable barrier to Samuel's establishing an Adriatic power. In the summer of 1004 the grand Veneto-Byzantine

alliance was confirmed by the marriage in Constantinople of John
Urseolo with Basil's second cousin, Maria Argyrou, at which the
imperial brothers acted as groomsmen. In the spring of 1005 the
bridal pair returned in triumph to Venice; and in the same year
Dyrrhachium, Samuel's all important outlet on the western sea,
was surrendered by his own father-in-law to a Byzantine fleet.

The last sparks of Bulgarian resistance were not finally trampled
out until 1019. This was partly due to the tenacious spirit of the
Bulgarian people and to the natural strength of many of their
fortresses, impervious to any siege which even Basil could mount
against them; and partly to the fact that, now Samuel was incapable of serious resistance in the field, the occupation could be
slower and more methodical, and more time be given to consolidating the revolutionary progress made both at home and
abroad in the years 996–1004. For these reasons, we have almost
no details, apart from scattered and unreliable hints, about the
annual incursions into Bulgaria during the next decade. It is certain only that many or most of them were undertaken in winter
time, when the flocks were down from the hills and the peasant at
his fireside, and that they were accompanied by systematic destruction, pillage, and mass deportation. When the curtain rises
again in 1014, the aspect of the war has changed, very much to
Samuel's disadvantage. Northern and central Bulgaria were now
firmly held; and Basil, in his gradual progress towards the heart of
Samuel's dominion at Ochrida, had during successive campaigns
entered Bulgaria from the south, by way of Serres, the pass of
Rupel and the Long Plain, the 'Campulungu', of the Strumnitsa
valley, between the mountain barriers of Ograzhden and Belashitsa. The tsar, in this year, made a final and desperate effort to
halt the ruinous advance. With fifteen thousand men he blocked
the pass near Kleidion; and sent another force across the mountain
to Doiran, in order to menace Thessalonica. Both manoeuvres
failed. The diversionary force was cut to pieces by Theophylact
Botaneiates, the governor of Thessalonica; while from the Long
Plain Basil sent a detachment over the Belashitsa, which, on 29
July, fell suddenly on Samuel's rear. The tsar himself got clear to
Prilep. His army fell, almost to a man, into Basil's hands. Then
was committed the savage crime which has left a lasting stain on
the memory of that great emperor. The number of the prisoners
was fourteen thousand. Basil put out the eyes of ninety-nine in

every hundred, leaving the hundredth wretch one eye to guide his fellows back to their prince. This fearful instance of severity has been received with scepticism by some writers in our own age; but nothing we know of Basil's character or of his conduct on similar occasions gives us any reason to doubt it. Basil was no lover of cruelty for cruelty's sake; but he was not a man to do things by halves, or to strike two blows where one would suffice. The punishment was inflicted, as always, with a politic end in view, and this end was achieved. The sight of his mutilated host as it stumbled towards him broke Samuel's heart. He fell down in a seizure, and died two days afterwards, on 6 October 1014.[8]

Thereafter the very name of Basil, the very report of his presence, were dreadful to his victims. On one occasion, a Byzantine detachment was cut off and surrounded. Basil called for volunteers and rode off to the rescue. At sight of the imperial standard the Bulgars raised a lamentable cry, 'Run, run, it is the Tsar!': and they ran.

The end of the whole gigantic undertaking was now in sight. Sporadic and unorganised opposition was encountered from Samuel's son Gabriel Radomir (died 1016), and from his murderer John Vladislav (died 1018). Basil never relaxed. He was everywhere, mopping up resistance, storming and garrisoning fortresses, disposing of the royal and noble personages who fell into his hands, riveting the chains of Byzantine control and administration on one area after another. By 1019 nearly the whole of the vast domain was an integral part of the Byzantine empire. It was parcelled out into the three provinces of Bulgaria in the centre and Sirmium and Paristrion on the upper and lower Danube. These, as imperial provinces, were now entitled to the imperial philanthropy; and they were administered, especially in the collection of revenue, with a leniency demanded by their ravaged and ruinous condition. Serbia (Dioclea, Rascia, Bosnia) and Croatia were allowed to remain self-governing dependencies; but their proximity to the Byzantine provinces of Dyrrhachium, Dalmatia and Sirmium, as well as to the Adriatic power of Venice, rendered them powerless to harm.[9]

Basil's ambitions were directed toward the west, which was the goal of that stupendous career; but during the past five years the unquiet state of affairs far to the north-east, on his Georgian borders, had disturbed the settlement of 1000, and led him in 1021 to undertake his third and last progress in the east. In 1014 died the curopalate Bagrat of Abasgia, and his son George at once broke through the agreement. With Armenian aid, he invaded and occupied Tao and Phasiane. Basil had no time to deal with him personally, though in 1016, as a preliminary step, he sent a naval force to occupy the Chazar ports in the rear, that is, to the north-west, of George's dominions. In 1021 the emperor's hands were free. He recovered Phasiane, and pushed on beyond the frontiers of Tao into inner Iberia. A drawn battle was fought near Lake Palakatzio; but after it George abandoned his gains in Tao and fled northwards into Abasgia. In the following year, though he was able to incite Basil's trusted marshal Xiphias to an abortive revolt in the emperor's rear, he was finally defeated in September near the Phasis river. Menaced both by land and sea, he left his infant son a hostage in Basil's hands, and retired, this time for good, beyond his frontier. Basil, as was his wont, improved the occasion by making a wider settlement of the east. He compelled John Sembat, king of Armenia, as he had once compelled David of Tao, to bequeath his lands about Ani to the Byzantines, a legacy which fell to them in 1045. He then turned south and occupied the territory of Vaspurakan, to the east of Lake Van, whose ruler Sennacherib, alarmed by the first ripple of the swelling Seljuk inundation, had in the winter of 1021-2 ceded his lands to the empire.[10]

When Basil returned to his capital early in 1023, the Byzantine empire had, through the energy and resolution of one man, achieved a territorial extent combined with internal economic security which it had never known before and was never to know again. From Azerbaijan to the Adriatic the emperor was absolute master. In southern Italy a dangerous Lombard revolt, which broke out in 1011 and was rendered yet more dangerous by the adhesion of the earliest Norman invaders, had been crushed in a second *clades Cannensis* (1018) by the governor Basil Boiannes.[11] Four years later the same Normans, now prudently enrolled in the imperial service, repulsed from Byzantine territory the last of the Saxon emperors, Henry II. At home the land-holding aristocracy, though seething with resentment, was held powerless in an iron grip; and the old system of 'free' peasant communes and soldiers' estates, relieved of the crushing burdens of taxation which had ruined them in the past, were enjoying a halcyon interlude of prosperity and devotion to the central government. Moreover, the solid strength of the empire had, as was natural, enormously enhanced its political influence beyond its borders, of which the most spectacular symptom was the firm establishment of the imperial religion and culture in Christian Russia. The achievement was so splendid and astonishing that it demands a brief review of the circumstances which made it possible.

Of all the emperors of Byzantium Basil II, in his own person, came nearest to the imperial ideal of boundless power and boundless providence. He seemed to have been sent by Heaven to show that, in a set of highly exceptional circumstances, it was humanly possible to put the age-old theory into practice. He was supreme, exclusive pantocrat; over the army, over the civil administration, over the church. His fiat seemed to be invested with a godlike omnipotence and inexorability. At his nod, Russians and Slavs threw back his enemies in South Italy: Armenians fought on the Danube: Bulgarians were settled in Vaspurakan. His treatment of the church is especially worthy of notice, in view of a modern tendency to misconceive the nature and extent of its authority at Byzantium.

It is sometimes said – very erroneously – that emperor and patriarch governed the bodies and souls of men in an amicable dyarchy: and scholars have pointed to the definition on these lines put out in 879 by Photius, and reaffirmed to John Zimiskes by Polyeuctus. But they fail to observe the exceptional circumstances in which these declarations were made by the spiritual, and acquiesced in by the secular, authority. In 879 the Emperor Basil I was nearly out of his mind and fit for nothing; and in 969 John Zimiskes had usurped through murder an empire in which his own position was most insecure. The Patriarch Cerularius, as we shall see, vindicated his independence in face of the feeble Emperors Constantine IX and Michael VI: but no sooner had the strong Emperor Isaac I mounted the throne than he was dismissed without out ceremony. The emperor chose his patriarch. The emperor could and often did dismiss him. The emperor defined dogma either directly or else by the simple expedient of refusing to allow the promulgation of any dogma he disliked. 'Amicable dyarchy' seems in the circumstances a misnomer: and, as we have repeatedly emphasised, in the political theory of the Byzantine imperial constitution the patriarch was no more than the head of a department of state.

Now to apply this principle to the strongest of emperors, Basil II. Basil appointed three patriarchs of Constantinople, of whom one was a layman and the other two were ciphers. They were wholly subservient to his policies, especially where these concerned his relations with the west. Before the first and second of these appointments he allowed the see to remain vacant during a total of more than seven years, for no better reason than that he was absent from the capital and could not, or would not, make time to nominate. He rusticated the patriarch of Antioch (989) and seven years later deposed him, nominating as his successor a creature of his own. He detained the patriarch of Jerusalem at Constantinople from the year 1000 until his death in 1004. His ambition, we have seen, may not have stopped short of appointing a Greek pope of Rome. His ecclesiastical settlement of conquered Bulgaria made of it an archbishopric, the appointment to which was in the emperor's own personal gift, without reference to the patriarch of Constantinople. His legislation bore as hardly on church as on lay property, and he was deaf to all remonstrance against it. There was, plainly, no room for a Polyeuctus or Cerularius in the economy of this sovereign autocrat.[12]

In his diplomacy he was not less independent and despotic. His dynastic marriage of a *porphyrogenita* to Vladimir of Russia in 989 has often been cited as a breach with tradition, committed under duress; but the marriage of Maria Argyrou to John Urseolo and the betrothal of the *porphyrogenita* Zoe to Otto III were no different in principle. Of the Byzantine tradition of learning and education, which his own ancestors had done so much to foster, he was openly contemptuous. To the end of his life he spoke and wrote, plainly and forcibly indeed, but without the smallest regard to grace or propriety. Extravagant ceremonies and pageants he disliked in themselves and because they cost money. His financial administration was not the least brilliant of his achievements: though he spent half a century in continual and costly warfare, and though he reduced the taxes on all the poorer estates in his realm, he left at his death no less than fifteen millions of gold pieces, with other treasures worth many times more than this. Some money he did spend on architecture. When the dome of St Sophia fell down, he put it up again; but this was from political rather than from aesthetic or pious motives. In these departments, as in all others, his word was absolute. The unity of the world under the elect of Christ, which the sovereigns of the ninth and tenth centuries had postulated, and for which they had striven, was finally consummated in the person of their prodigious off-spring.

Yet the very qualities required to achieve this consummation – the unswerving resolution of a dedicated ruler, the strategic grasp of a commander-in-chief united to the meticulous precision of a drill-sergeant, the practical talent and farsightedness of a states-man, the laborious fidelity of an administrator, above all, perhaps, the physical toughness and endurance of a body insensible to fatigue and privation – were so various that they could never again be united in a single frame. The flaw in the noble structure built by Basil, as in many of the structures of Byzantine archi-tecture, was that it was built for the day without regard to the morrow. The internal forces which threatened disruption were held in check by his arm alone. The military aristocrats he could humble by economic oppression; and he could and did submit their rash and hot-headed methods of warfare to the iron discipline of his imperial military machine. But even he could not do with-out them. If he had found it as easy to recruit capable general officers from the ranks as to recruit capable clerks for administra-tion, he would have dispensed with the services of the military even more readily than he did with those of the bureaucratic grandees. But this was impossible; and throughout his reign Dalasseni, Melisseni, Argyri, Comneni, even Phocae, are found in high command. Abroad, Normans and Seljuks were at his death already on the western and eastern borders of his empire. The inevitable result of his being succeeded by his brother and his nieces must have been clear to eyes far less sharp than his. Yet he 'put out no roots for the throne'. He probably never married, and certainly left no heirs of his body. He was and remained an unique phenomenon.

Bulgaria, Georgia, Armenia had not sated that thirst for con-quest. In 1025 he sent his marshal Boiannes into Sicily, to prepare his way. He was about to follow in person; but, on 15 December, in his sixty-ninth year, he died.

NOTES

[1] The contents of chapter 23 are, with a few slight alterations, reproduced from *Cambridge Medieval History*, vol. 4 (new edition), by kind permission of the Cambridge University Press.

[2] The Byzantine sources for the second part of Basil's reign are meagre. Scylitzes' version is confused, and Psellus scarcely mentions external affairs. The facts are mostly to be found in Gustav Schlumberger, *L'épopée byzantine à la fin du dixième siècle*, Part II, 'Basile II le tueur de Bulgares' (Paris, 1900).

[3] Ostrogorsky, 253–4; Bréhier, 217–8; Vasiliev, 347–9.

[4] Cedrenus, 449–50; Ostrogorsky, 256.

[5] Cedrenus, 447; Bréhier, 228–9.

[6] Bréhier, 229.

[7] Cedrenus, 454–5.

[8] Cedrenus, 457–9.

[9] Ostrogorsky, 257.

[10] Bréhier, 233–4.

[11] Bréhier, 236–7.

[12] Bréhier, 218–20; Ostrogorsky, 258.

CHAPTER TWENTY-FOUR

CONSTANTINE VIII TO CONSTANTINE IX

The historian who treats of the forty-six years between the death of Basil II (1025) and the battle of Manzikert (1071) is, inevitably, conscious of an anti-climax, and may be excused for dealing with the political events in a rather more summary fashion. During this period, which was less than that of the single rule of Basil, no fewer than ten emperors or empresses ruled, off and on; and the story is one of steady and accelerating political decline. If the engine of your motor-car cuts out on an upward incline, the vehicle will continue to move forward for some yards, will come to a halt, and will then, unless you apply the brakes, begin to run backwards downhill: and this descent will be accelerated if there is a powerful hand on the bonnet which is assisting the force of gravity. Something akin to this took place in the Byzantine empire after 1025. Here and there the momentum supplied by Basil's energy continued to operate during a year or two: thereafter the backward movement set in with fearful swiftness.

To the modern historian who examines the state of the empire during these years, in the pages of Scylitzes and Psellus, of Cecaumenus and Attaliota, the predominating fact is not an external circumstance, but an internal contradiction. The Seljucid Turks, who in 1055 seized the empire of Bagdad from the effete drivellers of the house of Abbas, certainly constituted a threat which had not been presented from that quarter for close on two hundred years. But it was a threat at which Basil would have laughed. The meteoric careers of the sons of Tancred in Italy and Sicily between

1040 and 1071 were perhaps more serious for the empire. But Italy was far off, and even if the worst came to the worst, the Byzantine possessions in that peninsula were more a matter of prestige than of vital importance; and, on an impartial view, were probably more nuisance than they were worth. The Turkic tribes of the Steppe, under further impulsion from Asia, were, to be sure, unquiet. But the Danube defences were sound and well manned. All these threats put together could not amount to one tenth part of the dangers which the empire had faced in the seventh and eighth centuries, and had gloriously surmounted.

The great danger lay within. It lay in the suicidal contest for political and territorial power and influence between the civil (or bureaucratic) and the military magnates. The bureaucracy of the Byzantine empire, inherited from the later Roman empire, is its most characteristic feature; I mean, the feature that distinguishes it from all other medieval states of the western world. The bureaucrat was the Byzantine *par excellence*: he came of a class of highly educated laity, from which many of the ablest and most eminent patriarchs had been recruited by the crown. He knew his Homer and even his Plato. He loved to compile those glittering but meaningless edifices of euphuism which are the despair of the modern historian and translator. He patronised art. His supremacy rested on culture rather than on birth, and hence his class was recruited from those with natural abilities and taste rather than from an hereditary aristocracy in our sense of the word. His pride and arrogance, his subtlety and unscrupulousness were proverbial. He hated and despised all foreigners as brutal and barbarous, if not heretical. His wealth was amassed out of administration and traffic. And this wealth he laid out in territorial aggrandizement, and so became a third competitor, along with the military barons and the church, for the lands and labour of Anatolia and the Balkans. He thus developed an intense antipathy to everything military: and, when in power, did all he could to deride, weaken and dissolve the military organisation.[1]

This savage hatred and, where possible, depression of the military might of the empire brought about its ruin in an unbelievably short space of time. There was seldom a time in the history of the Middle Byzantine Empire, after the ninth century, when her foes within were not many times more dangerous than any to be apprehended from without. Two of the internal dangers were the destruction of the social and economic system by the aristocracy, and the usurpation of a successful general. No doubt these dangers were grave. But they were nothing like as grave as those entailed by a succession of weak emperors, however legitimate, and a succession of inexperienced commanders, however loyal, who could in a very short space of time bring about a situation in which there would no longer be any territories left to covet, or throne to usurp. Basil II had known how to reconcile the contending factions of civil and military aristocracies, that is, by ignoring the one and persecuting the other. But no subsequent emperor possessed a tithe of his power or sagacity: and, moreover, the legitimate house of the Macedonians, which possessed such vast prestige in the eyes of commons and nobility alike, became extinct a few years after his own death. After 1028, when his elderly brother died, the barriers were down and the battle was joined. The crown became the plaything of whichever of the two factions could by force or influence possess it. And here it was soon seen that, contrary to what we might have expected, the cards were nearly all in the hands of the civilian bureaucrats.

To start with, these civilians were all-powerful in Constantinople herself, which had always exerted a predominating influence in the empire. She had often seemed to stand alone when all else was lost. She was the only possible centre of government; and the only possible centre of ecclesiastical administration. She was, according to the old folk-song, worth any fifteen of the strongest cities in the world: and this was no idle boast. Her walls were impregnable. Her treasures were fabulous. Her market engrossed the trade of Europe and Asia, and her workshops and looms supplied the barbarian with an ample recompense for his furs and hides, his wax and his slaves. She was peculiarly the care of Christ and His Mother. Relics the most authentic, religious pictures and jewellery the most superb, were multiplied in the 360 churches which abutted on her streets.

But, more important than all this, her citizenry, amounting at that time to probably not less than a million souls, was solidly anti-military. Their pride in their City was intense; and this pride had been cruelly outraged at the City's occupation by the Armenian levies of the usurper Nicephorus Phocas. This anti-military prejudice in the very heart of an empire which could only survive by means of continual warfare is a paradox; and I lay stress on it, for it is of the highest importance for an understanding of Byzantine history, and especially of the catastrophic decline of Byzantium in the eleventh century under a series of anti-military and civilian sovereigns. There was assuredly much in the concept of pacifism which commands respect. But in all Byzantine theories of life and government, there was a profound cleavage between faith and fact. The plain truth is that the empire could not afford such indulgence in theory. And when, through their predominant influence in Constantinople, the anti-military party forced one after another of their own representatives into power, and then set about oppressing and destroying the military organisation of the empire – by extortion, by sales of exemption, by purchase of military estates – they could not see that their policies, however much justified in theory, were ruinous and fatal.

Yet there was in truth much to excuse their blindness and folly after 1025. At Basil II's death, the world seemed to have reached that state of peace which Basil's wars had been fought to achieve. As far as the eye could reach, both west and east, the sky was serene and unclouded. Storms were gathering below the horizon, but who could foretell this? Far off in Transoxiania, east of the Aral, things might be unquiet, but the eastern frontier was splendidly fortified. In South Italy the Normans had shown their mettle, but they were no more than a handful, and as yet submissive to Byzantium. Mutterings could be heard from enslaved Bulgaria, but surely Basil had not spent fifty years for nothing in settling that problem? The conclusion seemed to be that no extraordinary efforts need be made to foster and strengthen the military arm. On the contrary, it could and should be reduced and enfeebled, more especially since the military aristocracy were always threatening a seizure of power, and any care or money bestowed on the provincial forces would merely strengthen their hands. This line of thought soon showed itself to be fallacious, and worse: but it was at the start not destitute of some show of reason.

I propose in the remaining four chapters to give some account of political and social developments from the death of Basil II to the death of Romanus IV Diogenes: to describe the circumstances of the religious schism which widened the rift between the Catholic and Orthodox churches: to give an account of the campaign of Manzikert in which Byzantium's place as a world-power was finally and irrevocably lost; and lastly to summarise the course and significance of the events and tendencies which we have passed under review.

The death of Basil – as has been truly said – was a turning-point in Byzantine history. He left no one who was remotely capable of continuing his policy, which was the policy of unity of all departments of state, including the church, under the legitimate emperor, crowned by God. Henceforward unity was a dead letter, even as a principle; and the great division which had during centuries rent the bosom of the church found its counterpart in the bosom of secular society.

Basil's brother, Constantine VIII, was now sixty-five years old. He had nominally reigned as his brother's co-emperor, but had shown no aptitude or eagerness to govern. He was in every way his brother's opposite: voluptuary where Basil had been ascetic; idle where Basil had been energetic; weak where Basil had been strong.[2] The military aristocracy rose nearly as one man, which shows the strength of their resentment against Basil's land-laws, and also the strength of Basil's arm in being able to suppress them. In a few months almost all the great families were either in open revolt, or making preparations to become so. Nicephorus Comnenus, Romanus Courcouas, Nicholas Xiphias (Basil's old marshal), and of course another Bardas Phocas and Basil Sclerus, were all on the move. If they could have agreed to unite behind one of their order, there is little doubt that they could have toppled the aged voluptuary from his throne. But they acted piecemeal, and as the bulk of Basil's splendid army still held loyal to the ruling house, they were suppressed in detail. Constantine, who had learned Basil's policy of suppressing the clans without learning his skill in suppression, acted like a frightened dotard. Fear made him inhumanly cruel, and his severity merely increased the resentment of the nobility against him. Many perfectly innocent men were punished without mercy on mere suspicion. Any successful general could now be slandered and accused of treachery by a jealous rival, in the knowledge that the slander would be received, the victim relieved of his command, and, as likely as not, mutilated into the bargain. This was fatal to any sort of military loyalty to the central government, who themselves could supply no commanders that the troops would follow.[3]

On the other hand, Constantine was quite unable to resist the pressure of both parties, civil and military, for a repeal of Basil's edicts against acquisition of land. Here all the 'powerful' were at one. The part of Basil's legislation which was most obnoxious to the landowner was of course his penal taxation in favour of the smallholder. By this provision, as we saw, any deficit in the annual tax on a village commune had to be made good by the rich proprietors who had made any purchase of land in the area. There was, to be sure, no justice or even equity in this provision: it was simply an act of expediency, designed to ruin the larger landowners and to keep their hands off the soldiers' estates. No government with a power and determination less than Basil's could enforce such an edict for long. The big proprietors paid up while he was alive, simply because they knew that the emperor was longing for an excuse to evict them, and that refusal to pay would mean a very prompt and very unpleasant visit from a company of imperial troops. Constantine VIII could not act in this autocratic fashion, because he himself was not the empire's war-director. Even in the short time of his independent rule the hateful edict had become a dead letter, and the emperor had perforce undertaken its formal repeal. This was good enough for the magnates. During thirty years their teeth had been drawn. They were now up once more and snarling over every piece of land that could be snapped up. And just at this time, for ten years or more, Anatolia and Thrace were visited by a series of droughts and plagues of locusts. Whole areas of Anatolia were denuded. The distress was such that the smallholders were ready to sell, not only their properties, but even their own children, for a crust of bread. This was all the exploiters needed to complete their triumph. The great estates expanded with a rapidity proportionate to their enforced contraction. And Asia became once more, as in the sixth century, a country of *latifundia*, owned by military or civil landlords and worked by serfs.4

With the consequent decay of the 'free' peasant's estate and, more important, of that of his soldier-peasant neighbour, the military system of the empire finally broke down. A clear-sighted statesman would instantly have seen that the empire's survival now depended on one thing: the coming to power of the military aristocrats and the subjection of the civilian. Ultimately this unpleasant truth was realised. But not before many years of blindness had reduced the state to the verge of extinction.

Constantine, fool as he was, seems to have had a glimmering of the truth. He had no son but only three daughters. The eldest of them need not concern us. She was early pitted by the smallpox and retired from the world. With the second daughter, Zoe, we have already made acquaintance: for she was betrothed by her uncle to the western Emperor Otto III. This marriage, as we saw, was frustrated by the death of the bridegroom: and thereafter no suitable match could be arranged for her. Now, in 1028, she was fifty years old: and in the next fourteen years she made up for lost time by marrying three times. She was destitute of any political sense or ability: and, if rumour said the truth, her spinsterhood had been far from respectable. But she had two solid advantages: she was the legitimate heir of the Macedonian house and, as such, she was enormously popular with the citizenry of Constantinople, who called her their Mama. The third daughter, Theodora, was an equally inept but far less attractive woman. She was unmarried, and stayed so.

Any dynastic plans which could now be formed must centre round the ageing Zoe. She was, barring a miracle, past the age of child-bearing, but marriage to her would confer legitimacy on her husband. Her father at first bethought him of the military aristocrat Dalassenus, son of the intrepid marshal who had taken over the government of Antioch from Vourtzes in 996. As the Dalasseni were one of the few military families which had a record of unswerving loyalty to the Macedonian house, the choice seemed a good one. But it aroused clamorous opposition in Constantinople, where an emperor in the tradition of Phocas and Zimiskes was the very last thing the bureaucracy wanted. They put forward their own candidate, one Romanus Argyrus, the Mayor of Constantinople, who was connected with the house of Romanus I, and was probably Zoe's third cousin: and they surrounded the emperor's death-bed and urged his claim. Constantine weakly yielded. Dalassenus was told to stay at home; and Romanus was elected as the future bridegroom and emperor. Still, there was a difficulty. Romanus, a man near sixty years old, was happily married already. He was told to put his wife away, and threatened with mutilation if he refused. His wife cut the knot, and retired of her own accord into a nunnery. On 15 November 1028, the marriage with Zoe took place; and on 18 November,

339

Argyrus succeeded to the throne of his father-in-law as Romanus III.[5]

Romanus reigned six years. His career as a civil magistrate had been respectable and he was not destitute of ability. But imperial power turned his head. He was a keen student of Roman history, and could even, it was said, read Latin. He saw himself as a reincarnation, not of Heraclius or Basil, but of Trajan and Marcus. He would restore the east and the west to the Roman dominion. Though he had never seen an engagement, he convinced himself that he was a divinely gifted strategist, and spent his time devising campaigns and ambuscades, sieges and sorties with the perseverance, but with none of the experience, of my Uncle Toby and Corporal Trim. In 1030 an occasion arose to put this expertise to the proof. The emir of Aleppo, who had taken the measure of the incompetent governor of Antioch appointed by Constantine VIII, had begun to raid the rich territories of Hollow Syria; and Romanus set out, his head stuffed with stratagems and plans, to chastise him. He entered Antioch in triumph. In vain his marshals begged and implored him to desist. In vain the emir offered peace and reparation. He was deaf to all remonstrance. He marched out with a splendid force and made for Aleppo. The emir posted a small force of cavalry on the heights which dominated a defile through which the enemy must pass. On a sudden, the Saracen horsemen showed themselves on the flanks, raised a fearful din, and began galloping about in a very determined manner. Forthwith, the whole Byzantine army broke and fled without striking a blow.

It was [says the historian][6] a sight which surpassed all expectation or belief. Here was an army which had conquered the world, an army so equipped and deployed as to be invincible by any number of barbarians, but which was now unable even to look the enemy in the face. The very life-guards of the emperor wheeled about and galloped off without drawing rein. And the unfortunate monarch, who had hoped to shake the earth, as nearly as possible fell into the enemy's hands.

The military historian will find much matter for reflexion in this reverse. Basil had been dead just five years when it took place. To such a pass had a single quinquennium of military disaffection and civilian mismanagement brought the strongest and best disciplined army in the world.

Romanus, defeated and disgraced, withdrew to Constantinople. He was hopelessly discredited. He now devoted himself to civil government and building. But his weakness and folly were pitifully apparent in these departments also. In finally repealing Basil's tax-law he was probably doing what could not be avoided: and was merely implementing the promise of his predecessor. But he completed the demoralisation of the rural economy by reviving the pernicious system of farming the taxes, a system so dirty that – as we know from more than one contemporary authority – no decent man would touch it. The farmers contracted with the treasury for a fixed sum, and the government washed its hands of all responsibility for the means whereby this sum, or double or treble this sum, was to be wrung out of the miserable taxpayers. As the big landowners were too powerful to submit to oppression, this naturally fell on the small man, who, equally naturally, was only too ready to make over his person and property to a stronger arm who would protect him.7

Romanus blundered wherever he went. He began to neglect his empress, who was the prime source of his authority. He secluded her and even cut down her allowance. She was outraged, and soon found a way to disembarrass herself of her futile and pompous consort. One of the high palace officials was a lowly born eunuch called John. He had, among other offices, become the trustee of the imperial state-orphanage, and hence was known as John the Orphanotrophus. He had a youthful and personable brother called Michael, who soon caught the empress' eye. She was already fifty-four, but not too old for love. Michael and Zoe became lovers in 1033, and on 11 April 1034 Romanus III was found dead in his bath. Zoe married her lover on the same day, and he was crowned emperor shortly afterwards as Michael IV. He reigned seven years and eight months.8

I say he reigned. But the substance of power was in the hands of his scheming and capable brother, John the Orphanotrophus. This person is well known to us from one of the most percipient works surviving to us from the Middle Ages, the *Chronography* of Michael Psellus. Psellus was a man who seemed to epitomise in his own character and achievements all the virtues and vices of the bureaucratic aristocracy. His parts were brilliant. His learning was universal and encyclopedic. He knew his Homer by heart, and his Plato. His rhetorical style, though odious and prolix to a modern who has been educated in the purity of the Attic masters, was such as to move his contemporaries to transports of admiration and applause: and to this, perhaps more than to any other acquisition, he owed the phenomenal influence which he exercised on Byzantine politics during forty fateful years. His origins were humble. He belonged by birth to what would now be called the 'bourgeoisie', or middle class. Psellus is often – perhaps universally – condemned for his faithlessness and want of honour and scruple in his political career. To me this seems very unjust. He was a man of his age and class, a selfish, ambitious and agile politician, neither better nor worse than a hundred others of his own day. Psellus is singled out for obloquy, ironically enough, not so much because of his vices, but because of his virtues. He writes so much like a clever, educated man of the present day that we insensibly apply present-day standards to his moral character; and, naturally, find it wanting. If he had never written a line, we should regard him, not as a scoundrel, but merely as a Byzantine.

This brilliant and witty character-monger, who may rank in this important department of letters with Francis Bacon, Lord Clarendon and James Boswell, wrote the reigns of the emperors from Basil II to Michael VII. Of all the imperial personages in and after the reigns of Michael IV, he wrote from personal knowledge. Those who search his pages for a factual account of the earth-shaking events which were even then taking place in and outside the empire, will search in vain. These events are touched on merely by implication, as they affected the fortunes and characters of the principals in his narrative. Psellus' *forte* is in character-drawing: he knew it and he stuck to it. And I do not believe anyone has ever done it better.9

During the administration of John the Orphanotrophus, Psellus was beginning his political career. And this is the sketch which he has left us of that all-powerful minister: –

For myself, who often dined and drank with him, it amazed me that this man, drunkard and buffoon as he was, yet contrived to preserve the balance of the Roman empire on his shoulders. Even when he was drunk, he could follow all that was passing through the minds of each of his boon-companions, and, catching them (as it were) upon the hip, would afterwards call them to account for what they had done or said in their cups; so that they came to dread him drunk even more than they dreaded him sober. He was a strange mixture: he had long worn the garb of a monk, but he never thought of observing the decencies of conduct which such a habit imposes; and yet such duties as the divine law prescribes for that profession he made some outward show of performing, and those who wasted themselves in riot and wantonness he absolutely despised. But if any chose an honourable life, or passed it in the liberal exercise of the virtues, or enriched his mind with classical learning, of all such he was the enemy, and would do all he could to vilify to each the object of his devotion. Such was his singular conduct towards the generality; but towards his brother the emperor he still preserved the same disposition, with an unchanging, undeviating firmness of demeanour.[10]

The régime of John was chiefly notable for fiscal extortion. New taxes multiplied at such a pace that few could enumerate them. As the rich refused to pay, more had to come from the poor. This principle was applied with disastrous results to Bulgaria. Basil II after pacifying that country, had with characteristic statesmanship adapted both civil and ecclesiastical administration to the local customs and usages prevailing there hitherto. 'The Emperor Basil', says the chronicler, 'had no wish to make any revolutionary changes in the system of government applied by Tsar Samuel: so he taxed each Bulgarian peasant in kind, at the rate of one bushel of corn, one bushel of maize, and one pitcher of wine per head: but now the Orphanotrophus decided that these taxes must henceforth be paid in cash'.[11] This injudicious measure was the last of a series of paltry vexations to which Bulgaria had been subject since 1025. And here I may observe that the outspoken contempt of all proper Byzantines for the Bulgarian race and the Slavonic tongue was a very foolish indulgence in those who aspired to maintain an empire; and moreover one which has left a bitter legacy down to our own day. It is an interesting question why the Byzantines early came to terms with the heretical Armenians on their eastern borders, but could never or would never do so with the orthodox Bulgars on the north. A typical comment is that of Princess Anna Comnena, the twelfth-century historian, who says that the 'very body of history is disfigured by Slavonic names'; and Psellus still calls them barbarians, two centuries after their conversion. As the largest part of the population of Anatolia were of Slavonic stock, one can only wonder at the universal dislike and contempt with which they were regarded in high places.

At all events, in 1040 Bulgaria rose in revolt. That this was possible so soon after Basil's death shows the extent of Byzantine misgovernment. Peter Delyan, bastard grandson of the Tsar Samuel, led the revolt, and he was soon joined by his legitimate cousin, Alusianus, on whom Basil had conferred a high Byzantine command. Delyan threw off the Byzantine yoke from western Bulgaria, and, like Symeon and Samuel, invaded the west of Greece. He stormed Dyrrhachium, which gave him an outlet on the Adriatic. He annexed the province of Nicopolis, which brought him as far south as the Gulf of Lepanto; and then he laid siege to Thebes, the capital of the province of Hellas. This was beginning to look unpleasantly like the events of 921 and 996. Fortunately, a timely quarrel between the two insurgent leaders reduced their effectiveness. A brave sortie from the gates of Thessalonica destroyed the army of Alusianus, and thereafter the revolt petered out, more by good luck than good management, in 1041. The Emperor Michael, who had been directing operations in person, came back in triumph to Constantinople; but came back only to die. He had long suffered from epileptic fits, which made him an unfit companion for the empress; and now he was stricken with a horrible malady which caused his limbs to swell. These afflictions were of course God's punishment on him for the murder of Romanus III. He retired with all speed to a monastery, and died there on 10 December 1041.[12]

At this pass, the cunning Orphanotrophus was not found wanting. Eager at all costs to keep himself and his family in power, he induced the helpless empress to adopt his nephew, a worthless and reprobate youth, as her son and co-ruler; and he now presented himself to the world as Michael V. However, he was soon to find that there was a point at which the Byzantine populace drew the line: and that he was that point. Michael V, son of a Paphlagonian dock-worker, seemed the ultimate degradation to those who remembered Basil II. After four months of follies and indiscretions, he was mad enough to try and confine the Empress Zoe in a nunnery. The people rose unanimously in defence of their dear Mama. Michael and his uncle were seized and blinded: and the Paphlagonian house disappears from history, unregretted and unmourned.

The imperial sisters, Zoe and Theodora, now essayed to reign jointly, but they could not agree, and at last after two months, it was decided that Zoe, now in her sixty-fifth year, should give her hand for the third time in marriage, and elevate her husband to the throne. The choice of the emperor was yet one more triumph for the bureaucratic aristocracy: for the elect was Constantine Mono-machus, who in June 1042 was proclaimed as Constantine IX.

This emperor reigned for the – at that time – exceptionally long period of twelve years. As he comes in the middle of this period of decadence and irresponsibility, so he may be said to epitomise it. And this is not simply a modern judgement. It was widely felt at the time that his reign precipitated the fearful decline. 'I feel bound to say this', says the eleventh-century historian Scylitzes, 'that from this emperor's prodigality and ostentation the decay of the Roman empire took its origin. From this time onwards even to today, things have by little and little gone the wrong way, until we have arrived at the present universal decrepitude. His unrestrained liberality degenerated into insane prodigality'.[13]

He mounted the throne in a period of apparently profound peace. The calm was to be sure more apparent than real, and the means for preserving it were scarcely apparent at all. By the time he died, the Seljuks were masters of Bagdad, and the terrible brood of Tancred de Hauteville were in a fair way to becoming masters of Byzantine Italy and Sicily. The Danube frontier had been breached by the Pecheneg and the Uz; and two dangerous revolts by the nobility had only been repressed by the most out-rageous run of good luck. The religious schism between Rome and Byzantium had been fatally widened by the Patriarch Cerularius. The treasury was empty, and the coinage debased. And all that was left to show for such profusion were a few ostentatious buildings and a School of Law. Seldom are we presented with a more degrading spectacle than the governing triad of an emperor, his vacuous face forever on the grin, toying with his wife's niece, and two miserable old women, gloating over coffers of gold or boiling up messes in a cauldron. Efforts have been made to relieve this picture of some of its darker colours. Pretty books were written – it is said – and pretty poems, and pretty churches and chapels built and decorated. But it will not do. The contemporary testimony to the general folly and vice of Constantine's government is explicit and unanimous.

He was scarcely proclaimed when revolt broke out in the west. The greatest of the military magnates who survived in the tradi-tion of Nicephorus and Basil II was George Maniaces. He had done splendid service against the eastern Saracens, and had now been sent to complete the work of Basil by clearing Sicily of the Africans. Assisted by King Harald Harderaade, he set about the task with characteristic energy and splendid success. The inevitable fate befel him. His successes aroused jealousy and jealousy begat slander. In 1043 he was accused of rebellion and dismissed from his command. He crossed into Italy and there proclaimed himself emperor. He passed into Greece and the imperial forces at Thessalonica went out to bar his path. He was brushing these aside when he was suddenly slain by a lance-thrust. And with his fall Byzantium lost the best and ablest of her field-marshals. Four years later a very similar revolt was crushed only because of the crass folly of the rebel, Leo Tornices, who this time led his forces to the very walls of Constantinople. He overwhelmed the feeble band sent out to oppose him, but then neglected to observe that the gates had been left unguarded. So his opportunity passed.[14]

Meanwhile Constantine lived with the niece of his second wife, a girl of the Sclerus family. Zoe, the titular empress, raised no objection, and the girl was seated with the imperial family on all state occasions. The rude burghers expressed their disapproval in a very palpable fashion. But the courtiers were charmed by her beauty and wit. It is of her that is told the anecdote of the adroit courtier, who on seeing her, said in her hearing 'it is no wonder', the first two words of *Iliad* 3, 156: the passage runs, 'It is no wonder that Trojans and Greeks should suffer so long for such a woman: for she is in face much like an immortal goddess'. The young lady called him, and rewarded him suitably; but the compliment was double-edged.[15]

The significance of all this profusion and waste lies in the means which Constantine took to supply it. If there was one sound military part of the empire, it was to be found, as usual, in the Armenian and Georgian highlands. The province of Georgia had an army of fifty thousand, according to an accurate computation.[16] They were first-rate troops, second only in quality to the Scandinavian mercenaries from Russia. Constantine suggested to these peasant-soldiers that they should contract out of military service on payment of a fee. Nearly all of them did so, and another prop of the empire was broken in two. Even these means were insufficient to restore the finances. Constantine took the final step of a bankrupt: he debased the gold coinage. It used to be thought that only after Manzikert did Michael VII resort to this deperate expedient; but recent researches prove that it was Constantine who did so, for no reason at all save wanton extravagance. It is the final drop in his cup of infamy. He died in January 1055. His portrait may be seen on the wall of St Sophia.

NOTES

[1] Ostrogorsky, 265; Vasiliev, 351 f.
[2] Psellus, I, 25.
[3] Cedrenus, 481–3.
[4] Ostrogorsky, 266–7.
[5] Cedrenus, 484–5.
[6] Psellus, I, 38.
[7] Ostrogorsky, 273–4 and note 3.
[8] Psellus, I, 44.
[9] Psellus, I, liv-lix.
[10] Psellus, I, 60–1.
[11] Cedrenus, 530.
[12] Psellus, I, 76; Cedrenus, 527–33.
[13] Cedrenus, 608–9.
[14] Attaliota 18–30; Ostrogorsky, 275.
[15] Cedrenus, 556; Psellus, I, 146.
[16] Cedrenus, 608.

CHAPTER TWENTY-FIVE

THE 'SCHISM' OF 1054

I want now to try very briefly to explain what went on in Constantinople in the month of June 1054 between the ecumenical Patriarch Michael Cerularius and the Roman Catholic delegation headed by Humbert, cardinal of Silva Candida. In effect, the ecclesiastical rupture, which is often said to have become final and unbridgeable in 1054, was a symptom rather than a cause of the quarrel between Eastern and Western Christendom. This cleavage is of vast importance for the history of Europe and hence for the history of mankind; and it still, in all its essentials, exists today.

To begin with: the Greek East and the Latin West. The hostility between the two is of pre-Christian origin. The Hellenistic Greek, whether he were or were not of Hellenic stock, believed with some justification that he was the heir to a culture which stood incomparably higher than any to be found in Italy. But, unhappily, by the second century before Christ, the Hellenic genius was moribund, and the Hellenic arms were feeble. The wretched *epigoni* of Leonidas and Agesilaus and Alexander were no match for the legions of the Tiber. Greece fell a prey to the conquests of Mummius and Sulla. And not only Greece. All that great territory stretching from the Black Sea to Egypt, whose culture was based on Hellenic letters, was engrossed in the Roman Empire.

It was here that the trouble started. The Romans and Greeks were respectively at stages of development which made any basic fusion impossible. The Greek was far too much civilised to yield up his language and culture to the invader. But on the other hand the Roman of the second century before Christ was on a far higher level of culture than Alaric or Attila. He could not romanise the Greek, but he could not himself be grecised. We often speak of our Graeco-Roman tradition of culture: and the culture of the early Roman Empire could scarcely be better described. Roman literature owed much of its inspiration to the Homeric poems, to the great writers of prose from Herodotus to Aristotle, and – perhaps most of all – to the Hellenistic writers of the Alexandrine school: and in this last department the Roman writers of course far surpassed their masters. The more intelligent Romans of the last two centuries of the Republic acknowledged the unique source of so much intellectual grandeur; and eagerly studied the Greek – that is the Attic – language, in order to be able to read these stupendous works in their original tongue. The Greek universities of Athens were thronged by the Roman youth.

Yet in nearly all ages the 'proper' Romans looked on these Hellenic tutors with a dislike and contempt such as Dr Johnson reserved for a Frenchman. Juvenal's *graeculus esuriens* might instruct in a language which, half a millenium before, had been the vehicle of splendid literary masterpieces. He might teach the Roman sculptor to mould his brass or marble into statuary which seemed to breathe and move. He might initiate the Roman architect into those technical mysteries which had erected the temples of Athens, or the throne of Pergamon. Yet, after all, he was but a slave, fit only to instruct his master in sciences which many, whether out of pride or ignorance, were inclined to think better untaught. In the year 86 BC the great proconsul Sulla laid siege to Athens. Out of the city came three orators, who detained him with long and prolix harangues in the Attic dialect of four hundred years previously, and dwelt on the splendour and magnificence of the Athenian cultural and military tradition. Much mention was made of Marathon, and of Salamis. Sulla heard them for some time without rebuke. But at last boredom overcame civility. 'There, that's enough, my little men, run along'; he said 'I did not come here for a lesson in history, but to put down a rebellion'. The satires of Juvenal written about two hundred years later evince the same bitter contempt for the Greek, now spread over the whole Near East and, in purely Roman eyes, characteristic of a bogus culture and a swindling charlatanism. 'Romans', said Juvenal, 'I can't stand a *Greek* city': and he went on to enum-

349

erate the – often disreputable – professions by which these Greek professors obtained their livelihood in the imperial capital.

During the first five hundred years of our era the hostility between the western and eastern halves of the Mediterranean was latent, though it never died away. The empire, whether governed from Rome or from Constantinople, was a unity, under one emperor, and with one official language, Latin. But the Greek-speaking, Hellenistic East, nurtured in the tradition of Greek letters, never ceased to regard the western empire as foreign, barbarous and intrusive. The fact that the sacred and patristic books of Christianity were largely written in Greek contributed to this pharisaical feeling. The Greek-speaking part of the empire made no attempt to learn Latin or to assimilate Latin thought and culture. Why should it? In its view, what the west had of culture all came from the east. Why should Greeks go to school to the Latins? And when in the seventh century Greek became officially, as well as in practice, the language of the eastern empire, the linguistic division was absolute.

The most important of the areas in which the incompatibility was manifest was of course the area of ecclesiastical doctrine and government. It was natural and right in the eyes of the Byzantines that the see of Constantinople should be no less supreme than the imperial throne. But here the emperors were to find that it was easier to transfer the privileges of an empire than those of a church. The Romans, who, as Rome believed, held an apostolic tradition reaching back to the reign of the Emperor Nero, were very unwilling to yield their pride of place, or even to allow that the upstart Constantinople was entitled to any ecclesiastical privileges at all. They would allow that the patriarchates of Antioch and Alexandria were apostolic foundations, and therefore acceptable centres of the dioceses of Syria and Egypt – always of course bearing in mind the supremacy of Rome herself. But who or what was Byzantium? She had been until the fourth century a mere suffragan of the archbishopric of Heracleia. In vain was the Council at Chalcedon induced to vindicate for the bishopric of Constantinople a parity with Rome in the hierarchy, 'because Constantinople is the New Rome'.[1] The Romans would never accept it, and continued to regard their city as *prima* among the *pares* of herself, Antioch, Alexandria and Jerusalem.

Byzantium naturally was not behind in maintaining her own

position. As early as the sixth century she began to claim that her patriarch was 'ecumenical', a term exasperating to the papal court, which translated the word as *universalis*, and understood it in that sense. It has been claimed that this is a mistranslation, and that all that the Greeks meant by the 'ecumenical' title was that the patriarch of Constantinople was supreme wherever the eastern emperor's writ ran. It is hard to subscribe to this view of the case. It is true that 'patriarcha terrarum habitatarum' would be verbally a more accurate rendering; but how does this mend the matter? Were the western lands uninhabited? And did the eastern emperor not lay claim to them as part of his historic, nay of his divine inheritance? Rome again and again protested against this usage, and with good reason. There were doubtless several misunderstandings in eastern and western relations which were due to linguistic ignorance on both sides; but this, I submit, was certainly not one of them.

The question of the primacy of the see of St Peter had for centuries been the chief cause of ecclesiastical friction between East and West. The bases of the Roman claim to spiritual seniority were substantially three: first, the words attributed to Our Lord in St Matthew's Gospel, chapter 16, verse 18: 'And I say also unto thee, that thou art Peter, and upon this rock I will build my church; and the gates of Hell shall not prevail against it. And I will give unto thee the keys of the kingdom of heaven, and whatsoever thou shalt bind in earth shall be bound in heaven, and whatsoever thou shalt loose on earth shall be loosed in heaven'. Second, the apostle so privileged was stated to have travelled, in or about the year AD 42, by way of Corinth to Rome, where he became bishop of the Roman Christian community for twenty-five years, and was martyred about the year AD 67. This established the connexion between the senior of the apostles and the Eternal City. Third, there was the *Constitutum Constantini*, or 'Donation of Constantine', with which we have already had to deal. According to this document, the Emperor Constantine the Great, when transferring his capital from the Old to the New Rome, had recognised the supreme spiritual authority of the Roman see, as well as according to Pope Silvester a temporal authority over the western half of his empire.

Now, it is important to note that the Byzantine opponents of these claims did not go about the task of confuting them as a scholar of modern times would do. Nowadays, a scholar would begin, not with the significance of such claims or documents, but with their credentials. For example, as regards St Matthew's text, he would speedily note that the words which accord such imprescriptible authority to St Peter are found in St Matthew's Gospel alone, though the incident out of which these words arose is recorded both by St Mark and St Luke. The omission of the words from St Mark's Gospel is especially noteworthy, since it is a chief source of Matthew's and Luke's versions, and since, by a very old tradition, St Mark derived much of his information from St Peter himself: which, if true, would render the omission inexplicable. These considerations are of course not decisive against the authenticity of the passage, at least as it may have stood in the earliest version of Matthew. But when they are put alongside the anomalous reference to 'my church', it becomes virtually impossible that Jesus Himself uttered the words.

Our scholar then turns to the claim which connects St Peter with the city of Rome and the Roman see. Here he would have to conclude that, while there is excellent evidence that St Paul came to Rome and lived there, such evidence is almost totally lacking in the case of St Peter. The testimony of tradition, as opposed to historical evidence, is undoubtedly very strong in support of the story; and no historian nowadays underrates the importance of tradition, or at any rate neglects the task of examining the origins of it. But in this case, while he cannot say that the story is absolutely impossible, there is yet much which renders it dubious and improbable, and the earliest statement of the tradition cannot be pushed back further than c. AD 170.

Then, turning to the 'Donation of Constantine', he finds at once that this is universally admitted to be a bare-faced fraud, concocted at the end of the eighth century or the very beginning of the ninth, by or at the instance of Pope Leo III, with reference to the new situation brought about by the Frankish empire of Charlemagne.

Having thus exposed the essential weakness of the substructure, our modern scholar will perhaps not waste very much time on study and interpretation of the superstructure; still less in trying to prove it a genuine antique. But the Byzantine apologists did not go to work in this way. The soundness of the foundations was universally assumed: even the Donation of Constantine was accepted as genuine. And the whole of their ingenuity was devoted to examination and interpreting of the documents as they stood.

As thus: Our Lord no doubt confided his church to St Peter: but in so doing, He meant the whole of His church, not just the Roman church, which could thus not claim an exclusive authority and predominance over all Christendom. Or again, if the Roman church had been founded by Peter, the Byzantine had been founded by Andrew, and he was senior to Peter, the 'Peter-before-Peter'! Or again, with respect to the Donation of Constantine, no doubt that emperor had given the pope the widest spiritual and temporal authority in his proper domain; but that authority was derived *ex hypothesi* from the temporal sovereign, over whom the pope could claim no jurisdiction without invalidating his own pretensions. Or again, Constantine had transferred the whole administration lock, stock and barrel to Constantinople, leaving in Rome only a bishop whose successors were now heretics and hence of no account. So their subtle minds wove their webs. But behind it all lay the hard, practical and all-important question of the Byzantine imperial principle: the principle that the emperor must be master in his own house, without interference or dictation from his bishops. And, according to the doctrine of empire, Italy was a part of this empire and Rome a town in Italy: an important town, no doubt, and the seat of an historic bishopric, but with no more right to freedom and independence of judgement, still less to overriding authority, than Thessalonica or Corinth.

This was the crux of the whole affair. So long as Rome was a part of the *Roman* empire, I mean, the empire administered from Constantinople; or so long as Rome formed a small independent state, with its own territory and with the free exercise of choice in its episcopal elections, Byzantium had little or no uneasiness about her. She could never be dangerous, and could on occasion be useful, as in the instance of the fourth marriage of Leo VI. Irritating quarrels, both doctrinal and administrative, had subsisted for centuries between the two sides: the Procession of the Holy Ghost, the title of 'ecumenical', the jurisdiction over Illyricum, and the papal patrimonies of South Italy, are examples. But these, though fierce, were intestinal disturbances in one single organism. The decisive event which made division final and inevitable was the foundation of a strong, secular western empire by Otto the Great in 962, and the subsequent efforts, often successful efforts, to convert the papacy into a department of the German state even as the Constantinopolitan patriarchate was a department of the Byzantine. When, as in 968, the pope began to write 'in the name of his imperial masters the emperors of the Romans' (Otto I and II) to the 'emperor of the Greeks', the Byzantines were quick to see the dangerous implications, and their resentment was unbounded, as Liudprand discovered to his cost.

An ominous sign of the times had shown itself in or after 1012. The official indication that the church of Byzantium was in communion with the church of Rome was the reciprocal commemoration of their patriarchs in the liturgical *diptychs*, those tablets on which the heads of Christ's church were wont to be inscribed. In 1012, on the death of Pope Sergius IV, there were two popes. The German emperor Henry II chose in favour of Benedict VIII, and in February 1014 Benedict crowned his patron emperor of the Romans, giving into his hand an orb which betokened the mastery of the world. Benedict VIII was not included in the Byzantine liturgical diptychs, nor has any pope after him been so included. The churches were, officially speaking, in schism from that date: and for reasons at least as much political as doctrinal.

Yet all was not quite lost. In 1024, the last year of Basil II's life, Byzantium was at the topmost point of her glory, strength and prosperity. It was decided to negotiate once more with the papacy. The terms were exceedingly moderate; amounting to a recognition of equality of ecclesiastical status between Rome and Byzantium, and a declaration that each was sovereign in her own ecclesiastical sphere. These proposals would have many advantages. On the one hand, their acceptance would be a recognition of the existing state of affairs; though it is true that medieval states were always extremely reluctant to make recognitions of this kind. On the other, it would solve the vexed question of the so-called 'ecumenical' title claimed by the Byzantine patriarchate, since this term would be no longer construed as universal, but merely as covering the lands of the eastern empire. The terms were very nearly accepted by Pope John XIX: very nearly, but not quite. Parity with Byzantium stuck in the gizzards of Italian and French churchmen alike. Protests poured into the Vatican: and Pope John resiled, and sent back Basil's commissioners empty-handed.[2]

It would be very incorrect and misleading to convey that politics were the field in which the battle was ostensibly fought.

The avowed causes of the dispute were of course doctrinal. In the course of centuries had arisen several divergences, mostly – to a modern eye – so trivial that, *ceteris paribus*, nothing but a little good will was needed to iron them out. There was the question of the unleavened bread used by the Romans in the sacrament, while the Greeks 'animated' it with leaven. There was the addition of water to the sacramental wine. There was the question of fasting on Saturdays. There was the question of the marriages of the secular clergy, encouraged by the Greeks, but eschewed by the Romans. There were various questions touching baptism or anabaptism. There was the Greek excommunication of priests who shaved their chins and cut their hair. There was the matter of eating strangled meat. The list is endless.

But the doctrine over which there was the most acrimonious disagreement between east and west, and which, in appearance, contributed most to making religious schism complete and inevitable, the doctrine which combined a high degree of importance with an almost equally high degree of incomprehensibility, was of course that of the 'Procession' or *ekporeusis* of the Holy Spirit. It is not for a layman to discuss this doctrine; but I have been assured by more than one Catholic clergyman that the question is of very little importance to the faith and salvation of a Christian: and even if its importance were (as was pretended) infinite, it was irrelevant to ninety-nine out of every hundred Christians, medieval or modern, who simply could not grasp what it was all about.

We have already met with this doctrine in connexion with the struggle of Photius with the papacy in 866 and 867. Very briefly, the points at issue were these. The creeds of Nicaea and of Constantinople had dogmatised that the Holy Spirit proceeds from the Father: and the Council of Ephesus had condemned all who should seek to alter or emend the final formula of perfect and absolute Truth. However, in the sixth century, in far-off Spain, the Catholics began to add the words – or rather word – *Filioque* to the symbol, thereby stating that the Spirit owed a *Double Procession*, that is, from the Father and the Son. At first, very little attention was paid to this. No doubt the addition was unauthorised by an ecumenical council, and hence uncanonical; but it seemed to Rome that it did no great harm. It merely expanded the expression of what was self-evidently true. Gradually, however, this addition to the Credo spread eastwards into Germany, and took root in the church of Charlemagne. At the Council of Frankfort (794) the Double Procession of the Holy Ghost was received for truth; and the Byzantine Patriarch Tarasius was rebuked for maintaining that the Spirit proceeded from the Father *through* the Son, instead of *and* the Son. Pope Leo III, who subsequently crowned Charles the Great as emperor, protested against this finding, upheld the Single Procession, and vindicated the orthodoxy of Tarasius on the point: a circumstance which put later Catholic apologists to some confusion and embarrassment. But subsequent incumbents of the chair of St Peter acquiesced in the novelty (if such, after 250 years, it can be called); and German and Roman missionaries in Bulgaria in the later 860's taught the doctrine without papal protest.

The metaphysical implications of this question are of course highly abstruse. They involve Essences and Hypostases, which none but a theologian can attempt to understand. But it may be useful, on the rather lower plane of theological history, to suggest how the dispute came about. The chief enemy of orthodoxy in the west, above all in Visigothic Spain, was Arianism. The heretical Arius had taught what in substance amounted to a doctrine that the Son was both posterior and inferior to the Father: and there seemed, at least on the basis of Scripture, to be some grounds for this opinion: since the Son was *ex hypothesi* begotten, and had Himself stated that His Father was greater than He. This difficulty was, as we know, got over by the doctrine of the Two Natures: but, in contending with western Arians, it was vital to affirm the equality of Father and Son, and therefore that what had 'proceeded' from the One must also have 'proceeded' from the Other. In the east the situation was the exact contrary. Here from the third to the seventh centuries the chief enemy of orthodoxy had been monophysitism. This doctrine seemed to minimise the importance of the Son's humanity, and thus to stultify the all-important theory of the Divine Incarnation. The task of eastern orthodox divines was therefore to define and distinguish, as closely as might be, the separate Persons or Hypostases of the Triune Deity. Double Procession seemed to them to jumble this nice distinction.

The outward circumstances of the rupture of 1054 were such as called for no disturbance between east and west. On the contrary, circumstances seemed to call for closer collaboration. Both Byzantine and papal states were menaced by the rising Norman power in South Italy, and there was everything to gain by joint action between Bari and Rome, whether or not one shaved one's beard or fasted on a Saturday. The crisis was brought on by the confrontation of powerful personalities, who were unwilling to yield an inch of ground to their opponents. It was the clash between Photius and Nicholas all over again.3

In 1043 the emperor Constantine IX appointed Michael Cerularius to be patriarch of Constantinople. The appointment promised well, since Cerularius was in the tradition of Tarasius and Photius rather than in that of Ignatius and Polyeuctus. He was indeed a monk, but this was purely coincidental. A few years before he had been implicated in a conspiracy against the Emperor Michael IV, and had been compelled to receive the tonsure. When the Romans called him a 'neophyte', who had become a monk 'through fear', they were right enough, as far as that went. Cerularius would have been a good patriarch under a Nicephorus II, or a Basil II, since he was a competent administrator and a clever man. But under a Constantine IX he was a disaster. Proud, despotic, overweeningly ambitious, he soon saw that his master was too weak and indolent to oppose his schemes, which were centred on nothing less than the ecumenical triumph of eastern orthodoxy.

On the other side of the fence was Pope Leo IX, appointed by the German Emperor Henry III. He seems himself to have been a just and reasonable man, but he stood at the beginning of that reformation of the papacy which is associated with the Cluniac movement, and which brought it to the pinnacle of its influence and power under Gregory VII. This Gregory, or Hildebrand as he then was, was a close friend and adviser of Pope Leo IX, as was also Cardinal Humbert of Silva Candida, who took the chief part in the dramatic events of July 1054.

Cerularius' attack on the Roman beliefs appear at first sight quite gratuitous. He may have thought, comparing the temporal power of Byzantium with that of Rome, that the time was come for one more assault on the west: or it may have been that, in his desire to bring the Armenian churches into uniformity with the Orthodox, he was drawn to a realisation that many irregularities indulged in by the Armenians were practised also by the Romans.

Suddenly, late in 1052, the patriarch ordered all Catholic churches in his diocese to conform to orthodox usages; and, on their refusal, he closed them. This high-handed action was followed by proceedings yet more unwise. Cerularius moved the head of the Bulgarian church, the Greek Leo of Ochrida, to compose a flaming denunciation of Roman practices, especially as touching the 'unleavened' bread; and this letter was addressed to John, bishop of Trani, the Orthodox Church's representative in Italy, with instructions to communicate it to the most reverend pope and to all the bishops of the Franks.

It is pretty clear that Cerularius in all this was acting without the emperor's sanction. If Basil II had been emperor, Leo of Ochrida's letter would never have been sent without imperial command, or, if it had been, Leo would shortly have found himself thinking the matter over in Cyprus or the Crimea. Even the Emperor Constantine seems to have been shocked by his patriarch's folly, just at the moment when the Byzantine and papal armies had been defeated by the Normans, and Pope Leo IX was actually in Norman hands.

Emperor and patriarch thereupon each wrote a letter to the pope in a wholly different strain. The emperor asked for closer political relations: and the patriarch asked for a renewal of their reciprocal commemoration in the liturgical diptychs. No mention was made of Roman practices or aberrations. But alas, the harm had been done. The pope and his adviser Cardinal Humbert resented Leo of Ochrida's letter in the highest manner. No notice was taken of the more recent conciliatory approach: instead, Humbert directed a furious answer to Cerularius, in which he reasserted the primacy of the Roman see, invalidated Cerularius' ordination, reproved him for interfering with matters outside his own diocese, reprehended his impertinence in venturing to criticise Roman usages, and ended by saying that His Holiness was dispatching to Constantinople some commissioners who hoped that they would find the patriarch in a state of sincere repentance.

These were not the words which turn away wrath. But worse was to follow. Chief among the papal commissioners who arrived in Constantinople in April 1054 was Cardinal Humbert himself, who acted as courier for his own dispatch, signed of course by Pope Leo. The antics of both sides during the next three months were – to say the least of them – unedifying. To start off with,

Pope Leo died on 15 April, and so, nearly from its inception, Humbert's mission was devoid of any official sanction whatsoever. Humbert was truculent and insulting. Cerularius was haughty and repulsive. Humbert delivered his letter. Cerularius made him wait in a queue of metropolitans. Cerularius published an answer to the papal letter, by the pen of the Studite monk Stethatus. Humbert published an answer to Stethatus in which he said that the monk's name meant 'belly-crawler', and that the monk himself seemed to smack of the brothel rather than the cloister. Then, as the patriarch continued aloof, Humbert took the final step. On the morning of Saturday, 16 July 1054, the Roman commissioners strode into the cathedral of St Sophia, and laid on the altar a verbose and abusive tract, in the Latin language, which detailed the heresies of Cerularius, and ended thus:

Wherefore we, abhorring the violence and insults done unto the Holy and First Apostolical See, and seeing that the Catholic faith is many ways violated, do by the injunction of the Holy and Indivisible Trinity, and of the Apostolical Throne (whose messengers we are), and of all the orthodox Fathers of the Seven Councils, hereby subscribe that anathema which our Lord the most reverend Pope hath passed upon the said Michael and all his followers, (if they be not penitent), in these terms – Michael the pseudo-patriarch, the neophyte, who donned the monastic garb merely out of human fear, and is now notorious as the author of dreadful crimes; and with him Leo, so-called Bishop of Ochrida, and Nicephorus, chancellor of the said Michael, who in sight of all trampled on the sacrifice of the Latins with his feet; and all who follow them in the heresies aforesaid and the crimes aforesaid: shall be *anathema maranatha*, together with Simoniacs, Valesians, Arians, Donatists, Nicolaïtes, Severians and Manichaeans, and with those who teach the animation of leavened bread, and with all other heretics, nay, with the devil himself and his angels; unless they do turn aside: Amen, Amen, Amen.

Such, says the Greek commentary of Cerularius, was the content of this impious and unholy script.

Even here, in this would-be dignified gesture, there was an unseemly element of farce. The officiating Byzantine sub-deacons seized the script from the altar and hurried after its depositors, who were ceremoniously shaking the dust from their shoes outside the door. They tried to get the commissioners to take back the document. In the confusion they dropped it. It was retrieved and sent to Cerularius, who at once translated it into Greek and sent it to the emperor. He summoned the commissioners for an explanation, but they had left the city at once, and they refused to come back.

Opinions differ as to the historical importance of Humbert's action.[4] Some see it only as an incident in the long and inevitable process of estrangement which culminated in 1204. Others see in it a decisive and final act which forever sundered east and west. Good arguments can be marshalled on either side, and I shall not recapitulate them. But I would repeat this point: the balance between east and west depended, not on religious practice, but on physical power. It does today, and it always must. The really decisive date in the eleventh century is not 1054 but 1071, which saw the final occupation of Byzantine Italy, and the irremediable destruction of the Byzantine army at Manzikert. These were the events which led, slowly but inevitably, to the Fourth Crusade.

NOTES

[1] Ostrogorsky, 50; Vasiliev, 106.
[2] Bréhier, 219–21.
[3] Bréhier, 262–6; Ostrogorsky, 278–9; Vasiliev, 337–9.
[4] Ostrogorsky, 279, note 1.

CHAPTER TWENTY-SIX

MANZIKERT

We must now go back to the sorry story of political history, and briefly review the reigns of Theodora, Michael VI, Isaac Comnenus, and Constantine X Ducas, which occupied the years 1055–67; and give some account of the celebrated campaign of Manzikert.

The Empress Theodora was, at the death of her brother-in-law Constantine IX, the sole survivor in the direct line from Basil the Macedonian. She was an old woman, and unmarried. It was supposed that she would appoint some prominent administrator to be her consort; but, warned by her sister's fate at the hands of three worthless husbands, she refused to do any such thing, and elected to govern on her own account. There had always been a doubt whether this was or was not a constitutional proceeding, and it will be remembered that the Empress Irene, who governed alone after putting out the eyes of her son Constantine VI, had styled herself 'emperor', and had even so failed to win recognition in the west. But the popularity of the house of Basil was such that, except in one quarter, no question as to authority was raised, and she ruled for twenty months, and then died. The one quarter where disapproval was voiced was of course the patriarchate. Cerularius, triumphant over the west, and himself immensely popular in the city owing to his personal stand against the papal commissioners, had become a figure of great importance. In a minor degree he worked in the same direction as his more celebrated contemporary, Pope Gregory VII. For with Cerularius we can at last mark a change in the relationship between church and state. The series of incompetents who occupied the Byzantine throne in the second and third quarters of the eleventh century naturally weakened the control of the central government: and, since this period coincided with the rise of Cerularius, it is not surprising that the church made some encroachments on the realm of the state. This was simply one more indication that things were getting finally and fatally out of balance. Cerularius himself, who, at the time of the conspiracy against Michael IV had been the conspirators' own choice for emperor, attempted with some success to exercise imperial functions from the patriarchate. Whether he really intended to govern as a spiritual head of state with a puppet emperor of his own nomination, is a question. At least he was intimately familiar with the text of the Donation of Constantine, and seems to have applied to himself many of the privileges therein claimed for the pope.

The only other interesting feature of Theodora's reign – and yet it is most interesting and informative – is the character of the empress' chief minister, Leo Stravospondylos, or 'Crook-back'. He was, by the united testimony of friend and foe, a man of sterling rectitude and integrity. See now, how the most characteristic of Byzantine politicians, Michael Psellus himself, whose lack of principle is a by-word, comments on these qualities:

This man was found by most people to be quite unbearable. He was neither courteous nor affable, and showed everyone the rough side of his nature. He avoided all interviews if he could; and if anyone did not go direct to the heart of the question, but put forward some introductory matter, he growled, lost his temper, and cursed him all round: so that no one would go near him unless he was absolutely forced to. Well; for my part, I can admire the firmness of such a temper, but it seems to me to be better adapted for the next world than for this one. Total insensibility to charm or passion is doubtless to be highly extolled: only I think that life in this worldly body has to be more 'politic' and more adapted to actual circumstances, and therefore a sensible soul is more at home in a fleshly body.

This is a highly important and significant judgement. The qualities of principle and inflexibility are stigmatised as more suitable to the ascetic than to the politician. Politics is an affair of swift and subtle manoeuvre, unhampered by too much integrity and oiled by the delectable lubricant of rhetoric. It was to this last accomplishment that Psellus himself owed the chief part of his political

influence under seven sovereigns who hung with varying degrees
of intoxication upon his lips. And a minister who cut through his
mellifluous exordium with a curt demand to come to the point,
was naturally very little to his taste.[1]

Theodora died in September 1056. Before she did so, the
chiefs of the civil bureaucracy had induced her to appoint one
of their own number and faction to succeed her. Of all their
choices during this fateful half-century, this may fairly lay claim
to being the worst: for Michael VI was even more of a dotard than
Constantine IX. To start with, he was already a very old man. His
whole life had been spent in the civil service, and he was what we
in England should call the Permanent Under-Secretary to the
War Office. The reason for his popularity among his deluded
colleagues was his known and rooted dislike of everything military, which he had doubtless derived in the War Department
during many years of insults and menaces from aristocratic
generals. It was a sign of the times that this idiotic old man should
have been put in the seat of Basil II. He at once set to work to cut
down all military expenditure, and to show in all possible ways
his hatred of the officer-class. During the last week before Easter
it was the custom for the emperor to distribute his largesse to the
deserving. At Easter 1057 the civil magnates appeared and were
munificently rewarded. Then came the turn of the military. How
they fared may best be seen in the spirited account of Psellus, who
was actually present:

Well, the soldiers – I mean, the generals and other senior officers –
came to Byzantium, supposing they should receive as much as or more
than the civilians. They had been appointed a day of access to the
emperor, and I was myself standing by His Majesty. They came in,
these brave fellows – proper heroes they were – and ducked their heads
and gave the usual salute, and were told to stand on one side. And then,
when we expected His Majesty to single each of them out and to say
some words of noble and dignified gratitude, he began instead with
some general reprehensions, and then told the two chiefs (Isaac
Comnenus and Cecaumenus) to stand forth. Isaac he drenched with
ten thousand insults: 'You as good as lost Antioch! You have destroyed
your army! You have never done anything worthy of a general, or
even of a common soldier! All you can do is to take people's money!
Your only principle is insatiable avarice!' Isaac seemed to be stunned by
the sudden and unexpected nature of this invective. Some of his col-

leagues endeavoured to speak a word in his defence, but the emperor cut them short. I do not say that he had no grounds for dissatisfaction with the rest, but Isaac he should have treated with all kindness and honour. However, he did the reverse.[2]

The result of such infatuated conduct could not be doubtful. The armed forces, as the result of thirty years of starvation and dissolution, were indeed not what they had been. But there still was an army, and an army devoted to its hereditary leaders. The return of Isaac to his country domain in the Anatolic province was the signal for a general revolt. The families of Sclerus, Vourtzes and Botaneiates rallied to the cause of their insulted relative. And on 10 June 1057 Isaac was proclaimed emperor by his troops.

Among the other insurgents who had been gratuitously insulted by the Emperor Michael vi, was one whom the Greek Chronicle calls 'Hervevios', that is, the Frenchman Hervey. Hervey was an old servant of the Byzantine crown, who had campaigned in Sicily with George Maniaces and Harald Harderaade in the time of Michael iv. He had been granted an estate, or fief, as we may now more properly call it, in the Armeniac province. And about him, we must suppose, on estates of less worth, settled several hundred Frenchmen who served under his command. He chose on this occasion three hundred of the best of those, and with them made common cause with the Turkish emirs of Media.[3]

This leads us to a brief consideration of one of the changes in military organisation to which the social revolution which followed the death of Basil ii had given rise or impetus. We have seen how Basil was the last emperor who tried to maintain the old organisation, introduced by the house of Heraclius, of soldiers' estates among the free peasant communes in Anatolia. His drastic legislation and irresistible power had been able to put back the clock for about forty years, and the old system was actually made to work again. Basil not only restored it, but developed it. In the true spirit of the Heraclian house, he imported Slavs and Bulgars and Asiatics by thousands and settled them in communes, generally far away from their country of origin. Whatever they had once been, they now became byzantinised. And the empire was much strengthened by this influx. The total abandonment of this system to the rapacity and land-hunger of the wealthy – whether military, lay or ecclesiastical – was the really important political fact of the years following Basil's death.

One of the earliest felt and most disagreeable consequences of the revolution was the lack of a native militia. As the peasant-soldiers sank one after another into the state of peasant-serfs, it naturally was of the first importance to supply their places in the ranks or squadrons. For this purpose, the expensive and otherwise unsatisfactory system of importing foreign mercenaries was widely resorted to. In addition to the Varangians of the guard, Italians, Germans and Frenchmen came in considerable bodies to join the imperial service. These soldiers could not, like Harald Harderaade, be paid in cash, for there was no money left to meet such a charge. Instead they were given a life or shorter interest in a landed estate, of which they enjoyed the full and free revenue, not subject to state taxation, and over which they dispensed justice from their own baronial courts. This system of land-holding was called *pronoia*, that is to say, 'care' or 'providence', and the recipient was called *pronoiarios*, which meant one who was given the care over the property. It will be seen at a glance that this tenure of property expressly in return for military service is scarcely distinct from western feudalism; and, since the beneficiaries largely came from the west, it is probable that the system of military *pronoia* derived thence, although there are isolated instances of the usage in favour of civilians before this time. So that, to sum up, what we find increasingly in Asia Minor is, no longer the free peasant and peasant-soldier commune, but on the one hand the large estate of the civil or military magnate, which, however acquired, is now hereditary in the family, and on the other the crown property handed out in *pronoia* to a foreign adventurer who will supply his men and his own services during the campaigning season. It is unnecessary to say that the Byzantines strongly resented this latter system. They complained that, instead of being freemen, the Romans now worked as serfs on the estates of foreign masters: a complaint all too just. And to the resentment felt by the native serf we must add the always doubtful loyalty of the foreign *pronoiar*, who was simply out for profit, and whose interest in Roman victories was no more than that of freedom to pillage. The case of Hervey who takes his Frank tenants across to the Turks, is characteristic. One is glad to learn that after some very uneasy relations with the enemy, the renegades were tricked into an ambush and massacred by their new allies.4

The disaffection caused by the gratuitously insulting conduct of the dotard Michael brought about – as we saw – the election as emperor by his troops of one of the greatest of the military magnates, Isaac Comnenus. This celebrated family now advances into history, though it had already a long career of military glory and nobility behind it. Isaac's nephew was Alexius I; Alexius' son, grandson and great-grandson, during a century strove to uphold the ruined state against the Saracen and the Crusader. They did what probably no other family could have done. If only Isaac Comnenus had reigned twenty years instead of two, and had then handed over the empire to Alexius, unbeaten, or probably victorious, at Manzikert, the eleventh- to twelfth-century history of Byzantium would have been vastly different. Lastly, Alexius' daughter was Anna Comnena, who wrote the *Life and Times* o her father, and, as a woman of letters, is unique in the middle ages.

Isaac easily made good his claim to imperial power. Aided by the supple Psellus who saw that, even in Constantinople, the cause of Michael VI was lost, he entered the capital; and with the energy and ruthlessness of his caste, he at once put in hand a complete military reform. Pacific policies went by the board, and Isaac appeared on his coins with the sword of redemption and regeneration in his right hand. Almost at once, a recovery set in. The eastern garrisons, properly supplied and organised, revived like grass after an August thunderstorm. Like Nicephorus II, Isaac rode roughshod over bureaucratic and ecclesiastical interests. Money was needed, and the parasites and leeches of the commonwealth should supply it. Michael Cerularius, who had domineered over Constantine IX and the even feebler Michael VI, soon found himself brushed aside. A synod was convened to depose him and he died in 1058 of rage and a broken heart. How long and how far this promising recovery would have gone on if allowed to do so, we cannot tell. What Isaac did achieve in two short years is astonishing, and shows that there was still time for revival if the misguided and selfish bureaucrats could be kept in their places. But Isaac was stricken by a mortal disease and died in 1059. The bureaucratic faction was at once resurgent. And before any concerted move on the part of the military could be made, the crown was clapped on the head of Constantine Ducas, the chief of a family once distinguished by military talents, but now, during many generations, gone over wholly to the civilian faction.5

The eight years of the rule of Constantine x completed the disaster, temporarily checked by Isaac. Constantine was not content with ignoring the military arm: he took active steps to destroy it. Military supplies were cut to the bone. The garrisons were literally starving, and consequently mutinous. All the emperor cared about was law. Educated in the Law School established by Constantine ix, he was enamoured of the pursuit of legal rhetoric and the fantastic pantomime of pleading before the legal tribunals, at which he loved to preside. The most characteristic feature of an educated Byzantine was a desire to talk at enormous length, in euphuisms and sophistries which he fondly believed were in the tradition of Demosthenes and Lysias. This was a harmless pursuit for a leisured class, so long as a man of sense was at the helm. But Constantine was not such a man. And by offering the ablest men in his empire the choice between starving in Theodosioupolis or Romanopolis, or waxing fat in a rich house at Constantinople, for the very small labour of mastering the tricks of Hellenistic oratory, he was doing his empire a signal disservice. Nor must we omit to notice a crowning blunder on the part of this infatuated ruler, his bloody persecution of monophysite Armenians. It was the same blunder as had been committed by Maurice and Heraclius four centuries earlier: the coercion of a heterodox Christian population in a key position on the very eve of a Moslem invasion. The resentment and retaliation of the Armenians were fierce. And the considerable Armenian force which under Romanus iv met the Turks at Manzikert was among the first to desert the Roman ranks.6

Things could not go on so. During the reign of Constantine x almost every frontier was threatened simultaneously. The Normans were firmly established in South Italy. The Pechenegs and the Uz (a Turkish horde) were already on the Danube. And, worst of all, the Seljuk Turks, now masters of Bagdad, were encroaching further and further into the Anatolian homeland. At length, in the very last year of Constantine's reign, 1067, they burst into the heart of Romania and sacked the Cappadocian Caesarea. The crisis could no longer be denied or ignored. A strong military ruler was the only hope of survival. At length, in the teeth of violent bureaucratic resistance, Romanus Diogenes, a capable soldier and administrator, was chosen, and crowned as Romanus IV on 1 January 1068. He was married to the dowager empress, the widow of Constantine X Ducas. But his position was not the stronger on that account. The whole Ducas family intrigued against him from the start, and their favourite Psellus was deeply implicated in their treachery. Romanus IV was a brave man, who staved off despair by shutting his eyes to danger. Yet even his sanguine spirit was appalled when he summoned his troops to the rendezvous in the province of the Anatolics. Those who obeyed his summons were not an army but a disorganised and demoralised rabble, without pay, without provisions, without equipment. The ragged regiments paraded with pruning hooks. The cavalry were dismounted. The horses were sold or dead, and no one had bothered about remounts. Their very standards were filthy and unserviceable. It was, says the chronicler, so long since an emperor had taken any interest in these matters that the military art had died away.7 Worse still, the decay of the *thematic* system had destroyed the very foundation on which recovery could be built, even if there had been time to set about it. The only resort was the recruitment of expensive and often disloyal mercenaries. Moreover, the whole general staff was rotten with disaffection. Such were the resources with which the empire was left to confront the bravest, best disciplined and most enthusiastic conquerors which had opposed her since the Saracens had emerged from the Arabian peninsula and advanced to the Yarmuk.

For, about the time when Basil II was settling the eastern and north-eastern frontier by establishing a protectorate over Vaspurakan and a right of succession to the most important domains of the Prince of Princes of Armenia, ferment was growing in the fair land of Transoxiania, east of the Caspian Sea. Here had dwelt, for many centuries, a Turkish race of innumerable horsemen and bowmen, who, in the early eleventh century, came under the leadership of a chieftain called Seljuk. As so often before, ferment was to lead to explosion and expansion. The grandson of Seljuk was the renowned Toghrul Beg, whom the Greeks called Tangrolipex, and who was destined to unite his countrymen and to discharge them with sudden and terrible force on the decaying empires of Byzantium and Bagdad.

The explosion took place in the fourth decade of the eleventh century. In the year 1038 Toghrul, leading between a hundred and two hundred thousand fierce but disciplined Mahometan horsemen, pushed southward into Eastern Persia. The disorganised dynasty of the Ghaznevides, who exercised a loose supremacy from Persia to Afghanistan, was swept eastwards into India. The Seljucid Turks seized and held the central stronghold of Merv. And they began a swift advance westward. Bagdad, where the Abbasid Caliph al-Kaim held a position of nominal sovereignty even more despicable, if that were possible, than that of his predecessor al-Muti, fell in 1055, and accepted with relief the powerful protection of Toghrul Beg. Toghrul died in 1063. But his equally able nephew Alp Arslan, the 'Victorious Lion', took his place. And the Seljuk and Byzantine forces were soon confronted in the very areas which the folly of Constantine IX had denuded of any power to resist: that is, in Armenia and Georgia.[8]

The Emperor Romanus IV for two years held his own. But the reason for this was rather the prestige of his empire than the strength of his arm. Observers noted ominous symptoms of disarray. The mercenary forces would not cohere. If a Russian contingent were engaged, no other contingents could be induced to go to its support. There was a total lack of drive and enthusiasm. More than one opportunity was presented of decisive victory which, if presented to Nicephorus or Basil, would have led to the enemy's annihilation; but which, now, was thrown away by an army which repelled an assault and then halted in listless indifference.[9] At last, in 1071, Romanus saw that an all-out effort must be made to crush the Turkish power before his own army disintegrated and was mopped up in detail. An imperial army was with much difficulty gathered, and advanced to the disastrous campaign of Manzikert.[10]

In any review of the campaign which overthrew the empire's military might, certain circumstances are to be borne in mind. The first is this: Nicephorus, John or Basil would never have lost such a battle as that of Manzikert; or, if they had, the consequences would have been trivial. Indeed, even as it was, the consequences were only momentous in the long run, since two whole years elapsed after the battle before the Seljuk occupation of Anatolia began systematically; and two months would have sufficed for Basil to repair all, and more than all, the damage sustained by a single reverse. If such a battle had been fought in 1021, instead of fifty years later, it would scarcely have obtained a mention in our history books. So rotten was the state of the empire in 1071, that there were in its own home and kernel of Anatolia neither men nor money, neither skill nor resolution, to mount a second campaign.

The second point, which arises out of the first, is that the Byzantine army, poor in quality as it was, was not beaten in the field since it never fought. Treachery spread a panic in the undisciplined ranks; and panic led to rout. All the Turks had to do was to cut down the caitiff host at their leisure. The Byzantine empire was a hollow nut with a crumbling shell eaten out by vermin. The slightest pressure sufficed to crush it into dust.

The third point to be borne in mind is that the Seljuk Sultan Alp Arslan, had no intention whatever at this time of making war on, far less of conquering, the Byzantine empire. He could not regard such an undertaking as anything but extremely difficult, if not wholly chimerical. The contemporary historians tell us expressly that the Saracens, despite the follies of Romanus III, still shook in their shoes at the names of Nicephorus and John and Basil. But more than this. Alp Arslan had succeeded to the traditions as well as to the rule of the Abbasid caliphate. During centuries the conception had been fortified that the east was divided between two powers of the first rank, the Roman and the Saracen, just as in former days it had been divided between the Roman and the Persian. During all that time these two powers had been at war, with varying fortunes. But it had been a warfare of incursion and counter-incursion, an affair of prisoners and plunder. Neither side, since 718, had dreamt of exterminating its rival. Accessions or losses of territory had certainly accompanied the eastward campaigns of Gourgen and Nicephorus and John: but it is very significant that even Nicephorus had made no drive directly on Bagdad, which, however, he might easily have done, with a fair prospect of success. The frontiers of Byzantium now lay as far east as Vaspurakan, and as far south as Lebanon; but at no time did she threaten to engulf Iraq.

As the sultan saw it, his relations with Byzantium were merely a continuation of the old condition: plundering but indecisive raiding by one side against the other. The Turkish raids which during 1067–1071 had devastated central Anatolia, and had resulted

in the sack of Caesarea, Amorion and Chonae, had been undertaken without his assistance and perhaps even without his sanction,
just as in the old days the emirs of Tarsus and Melitene had
mounted their own offensives against Anatolia without help from
the central government.

Moreover, the sultan had a much more pressing reason for
avoiding any large-scale operations against the empire: and that
was the aggressive and encroaching policy of the Fatimid caliphate of Egypt. The Egyptian power was firmly entrenched in
north Syria, and had only been brought to a halt by the strong
arms of Zimiskes and Basil. It had ceased to be a menace to
Byzantium, but was very definitely hostile to the Seljuk domination of the Abbasid inheritance. If Byzantine diplomacy in 1070
had been what it was in 1020, there is little doubt that the Roman
foreign office would have estimated at its true value the extent of
the Seljuk danger, and would have concluded a firm military
alliance with Egypt against it. But, like everything else in this
dreadful half-century, Byzantine diplomacy had gone to pot.
And when the Seljuk sultan sent to demand of the Empress
Theodora that, in the prayers offered at the Saracen mosque in
Constantinople, the name of the Abbasid caliph should be restored and that of the Fatimite expunged, this infatuated sovereign
acquiesced at once. What did it matter to her?

For all these reasons, then, the Byzantine collapse was neither
planned, nor forseen, nor hoped for, by the Sultan Alp Arslan. It
seems certain that until it happened he never considered it as a
possibility. Why then were the Byzantines hurried into this
disastrous engagement? The chief reason is that the army so
painfully collected could, if left idle and then disbanded, scarcely
be mustered again. Moreover Romanus, though his eyes were
open to the weakness of his own forces, thought, with some
justice, that the sultan's own troops were equally vulnerable, and
that a decisive victory over Alp Arslan would mean the end of the
Turkish threat. Hindsight suggests that he should have fortified
the eastern frontier at Romanopolis, or else halted to receive the
Turks at Theodosioupolis. But the choice of a battle-field was
irrelevant. Wherever the encounter had taken place, indiscipline
and treachery would have seen that there should be only one end
to it.

The emperor had – it is said – put three hundred thousand men

371

into the field. It is probable that this figure should be cut by at least fifty per cent, but even so, it was, to all appearance, a formidable force. Since the disgraceful muster of 1068, some money and time had been spent on equipment and the restoration of *morale*. In 1071 the emperor determined to restore the position in the vital area north of Lake Van, where the old imperial strongholds of Chelat and Manzikert were now held by the Turks.

The imperial dispositions on and off the field of Manzikert showed the inherent weakness of the army. The Byzantine left wing was composed of Uz, or Ghuzz, who were blood-brothers of the Seljucid Turks themselves; and the right wing, of Turkic Pechenegs, who cared for nothing but plunder, wherever it might come from, and who were not even Christians. The rearguard was commanded by Andronicus Ducas, whose main, if not his only, object, was to overset the Emperor Romanus and replace his first cousin Michael Ducas on the throne. By a fatal division of strength, the Russians and Normans, commanded by the Frenchman Roussel, were twenty miles in the rear; and with them lay the traitorous Georgian Tarchaneiotes, who commanded another body of mercenaries.

To oppose this mass of troops, Alp Arslan could muster about twenty thousand men. But of these, fourteen thousand were a compact and highly trained force of Turkish cavalry, heavily armed, superb horsemen and archers, and above all devoted to their leader. In order to defeat them it would be necessary to cut them off to the last man, and that would be no easy task. Even so, the sultan's heart failed him. It had been whispered to him by his subordinate Afshin, who had penetrated deep into the empire and come off scatheless, that the whole empire was a gigantic imposture, which had no means or spirit to defend itself. But this the sultan could not believe. Was it really possible that the emperor of the Romans, with a hundred thousand troops at his back, would yield to a force one fifth as strong as his, and open the path to the subjugation of an empire against which Chosroes and Moawiya, Suleiman and Harun al-Rashid, had striven in vain ?

On Wednesday 17 August 1071, the rival forces were at last confronted near Manzikert, which lies south of the river known as the Murad-cai, about thirty miles to the north of Lake Van. The day passed in skirmishing, between the Byzantine-hired Uz and their relatives, the Seljuks, skirmishing which was followed by the general staff with deep apprehension, since they were well aware of the danger of confronting the enemy with a force of the enemy's own speech and religion. However, no substantial defection resulted, and the *status quo* was preserved. The emperor sent off a swift dispatch to the *masse de manoeuvre*, to inform them that a decisive encounter was imminent, and that they should advance at once in support of the main body. The receipt of this dispatch showed the depth of treachery that lay in his rear. Tarchaneiotes summoned the Frank Roussel and represented to him in the strongest terms that the emperor's position at Manzikert was hopeless. He, Tarchaneiotes, would disobey his orders, whatever Roussel might do. In the end, they agreed. And both the commanders of the vital reserve turned westwards and galloped off as hard as they could to the confines of Anatolia.

They, therefore, who had been strongest in forcing the emperor to risk an encounter, were the first to desert him. Yet still, their desertion was more fatal to him in his being unaware of it than in its actual event: for he waited for their arrival too long before, on 19 August, he gave the signal for a general advance.

The sagacious Arslan retired in excellent order, covering his withdrawal with a cloud of arrows. The terrain favoured him, and he knew that any force except the most rigidly disciplined is disorganised by unopposed advance as much as by retreat. At last, in the later afternoon, Romanus found that he had gone forward into a position where it would be impossible to encamp for the night, and the Turks had still not been brought to an engagement. He decided on the hazardous but necessary manoeuvre of a retreat in face of the enemy. The standards were reversed, and the regiments about-faced. The inevitable at once occurred. A cry of *sauve qui peut* was set up from the rearguard, commanded by Andronicus Ducas. And the whole host broke and fled. This was the moment which Arslan had been waiting for: and he let loose ten thousand fresh cavalry on the Roman rear.

We may in mercy draw a veil over the sequel. The might of the empire was destroyed, and could never be rallied. The emperor fell into the sultan's hands, where he met with a courtesy and kindness not shown by his treacherous relatives in Byzantium. Within two year the Seljuks were firmly established in the vital homeland of Anatolia, hitherto free of enemy occupation, the source and supply route of men, food and money.

It is unnecessary to make any more reflexions. It is best to leave the curtain to descend in silence.

NOTES

[1] Psellus, II, 74–5.
[2] Psellus, II, 84–5; Attaliota, 53.
[3] Cedrenus, 616–21.
[4] Ostrogorsky, 273–4.
[5] Cedrenus, 641–4.
[6] Attaliota, 76; Ostrogorsky, 282–3.
[7] Cedrenus, 668; Attaliota, 103.
[8] Cedrenus, 566 ff; Attaliota, 43–5; Bréhier, 258–9; Vasiliev, 351–8.
[9] Cf. Attaliota, 112–3.
[10] Cedrenus, 692–9; Attaliota, 148–63: Ostrogorsky, 284, and note 3; Vasiliev, 356–7.

CHAPTER TWENTY-SEVEN

SUMMARY

I should like to end this survey with a brief article, part recapitulation and part reflexion. Even for the recapitulation no apology need be offered, since many things said before can now be seen to have greater significance when the whole story has been unfolded and the background painted in.

First of all, then: as to the period itself. The choice of the seventh to the late eleventh centuries has, I hope, justified itself as tolerably complete and coherent historically, if not also socially and ideologically. There has been a great deal of discussion on the divisions of Byzantine history: for example, on such questions as 'When does the Roman become the Byzantine Empire?' 'How do the two differ essentially from one another?', or 'Can Byzantine history itself, in any significant way, be labelled early, or middle, or late?' The divisions most in favour, which I do not think likely to be substantially modified in the future, are those put forward by Ostrogorsky in 1941. He maintained that the period from the foundation of Constantinople in the fourth century down to the accession of Heraclius in the early seventh should be called Late Roman, or, at most, Early Byzantine. During that period the continuity of the Roman Empire as established by the house of Julius is far more apparent than any divergences from the original. Latin remained the official language in west and east. The empire, though governed from New Rome or Constantinople, remained a Mediterranean empire; and, for a time, the Emperor Justinian I ruled in Asia, the Balkans, Italy, Africa, and even in a part of Spain. After him came the deluge. In the hundred years between

570 and 670 the whole face of things was, in a political point of view, radically changed: with the coming of the Lombards, the Slavs and the Saracens. The Byzantine state was long confined to Asia Minor and Thrace, and long involved in a life and death struggle with Saracens and Bulgars. It was, during that time, re-peopled by Slavs and Armenians, and by many other immigrants numerically less important. It was torn by religious controversies which reflected deeply seated racial, as well as ideological, divisions. Through all these vicissitudes the Christian-Imperial idea and a version of the Greek language exerted a cohesive force which at last kneaded the diverse elements into a more or less consistent whole. Leaders of genius in war and administration led it forward once more on a path which was truly imperial. To those who looked at it in the third decade of the eleventh century, it seemed that it was after all, under God, to realise its age-old profession, and to reunite the Mediterranean under the sceptre of a new Augustus or Trajan. The precise opposite, as we know, came in the event. Within fifty years the resurgent empire was struck down, never to rise again: not so much by external powers or pressure as by malignant internal diseases, which sucked the marrow from its bones and left it an empty shell.

The most fatal contradiction in all the Byzantine polity was the contradiction between tradition and practice. The old Roman imperial tradition envisaged a state, all of which, behind distant and far-flung frontiers, enjoyed profound peace. War was something which threatened and was confined to the borders. The new 'empire' of the seventh and later centuries made nonsense of this concept in the sphere of real and practical policies, where war, and not peace, was the general condition of all its people, and not simply of its now much contracted frontiers. This was at once realised by the Heraclian emperors, who reorganised the whole state on a war-footing; and it was soon realised by the great territorial magnates, whose tradition and trade were military through and through. But, as always at Byzantium, practice made very little impression on theory. In the City the old tradition of universal, imperial peace survived. The citizens and the bureaucracy detested war and everything connected with it; and would never realise or come to terms with the stark truth that survival, not to speak of progress, depended on continual military preparedness and efficiency. Thus when the triumphs of Basil II seemed for a moment to have restored the *Pax Romana* they were too ready to assume, in defiance of all experience, a return of the Kingdom of Saturn. They dropped their guard, and insulted their defenders. Retribution was prompt.

This period, then, we call the 'Middle Byzantine'. When it is subjected to a chronological analysis, certain fixed points begin to stand out above the tide. The repulse of the Saracens from the gates of Constantinople, by Constantine IV in 678 and by Leo III in 718, are events of world importance, which ensured the survival, not merely of Byzantium herself, but of Christian civilisation. The reign of the drunken and dissolute Michael III (842–67) provides no fewer than three dated events of capital importance: and indeed his reign, though not he himself, must be regarded as marking the commencement of Middle Byzantine greatness. In 843 the 120-year-old ecclesiastical quarrel over images was finally liquidated, a triumph – as we saw – for Graeco-Roman tradition over oriental asceticism, the significance of which can scarcely be over estimated. In 863 the emir of Melitene and all his forces were annihilated at Poson, which showed – almost for the first time – that the Saracens were not invincible in the field, and could by proper tactics be outmanoeuvred and destroyed. This victory presaged the eastward advances of Courcouas and Nicephorus and Zimiskes. Third, in the following year, 864, the Bulgar Khan Boris was converted to orthodox Christianity. When we remember that this reign also saw the literary and educational triumphs of the Caesar Bardas and Photius, and – for obvious reasons – a splendid revival of painting, which culminated in the awe-inspiring apse mosaic of St Sophia, we shall get some idea of the Byzantine achievement between 840 and 870, and of the strength of the forces making for recovery.

The next century (860–960) is one of gradual expansion and consolidation in which, with many more or less superficial setbacks, the empire grew in territory, in riches, and in military might. It was the heyday of the native Byzantine armies of Anatolia, in which area economic stability bred confidence, and confidence bred victory and pride. And here we have to observe two symptoms of immense significance, the one prosperous, the other malign. The new populations of the East Roman Empire, after about two hundred and fifty years, had gradually made of their multifarious elements something of a unity which begat a feeling indispensable to greatness: I mean, a feeling of what I can only call 'nationalism', though this was in theory opposed to the spirit of the empire. Shall we coin an ugly word – *uniculturalism*? On the other hand, the greatest triumphs were won only through the devotion of the soldiers to leaders who generally detested the central government of educated bureaucrats and tax-gatherers in the capital. This conflict – I say it again – is really the cardinal problem of the Middle Byzantine Empire: and was justly realised as such by successive imperial governments during all the tenth century.

A sort of equilibrium, unstable as it often was, between the crown and the magnates, endured for the first three-quarters of that century, and was chiefly instrumental in preparing for and in consummating the great imperial effort which ended only in 1025. It was Basil II who, conscious of his enormous power, and embittered by the revolt and treason of the houses of Phocas and Sclerus, finally declared a truceless war on the nobility of Anatolia.

The next most significant date is the death of this Basil II, in 1025. It is indeed in this year that Ostrogorsky would place the end of the Middle-Byzantine period itself, though this is perhaps more commonly put in 1071, which saw the Norman capture of Bari and the defeat of Romanus IV at Manzikert. But Ostrogorsky, as usual, has a point. He sees in Manzikert and the subsequent occupation of Asia Minor by the Seljuk Turks merely the inevitable results of a process of internal decay and dissolution which began as soon as Basil's strong hand was removed from the tiller. The actual date of Manzikert is of little significance: the disaster would have happened anyway, sooner or later. The really important date is the point at which the process of destruction started: and that is 1025, or rather the five years after that date, during which the radical land-laws of Basil were repealed, and the 'common responsibility' tax removed from the shoulders of the wealthy and replaced on the shoulders of the poor. Thus in five short years the whole Middle-Byzantine structure was put finally into reverse. The extinction of the Macedonian house, followed by a whole series of civilian incompetents on the throne, completed the process of economic and military disintegration. Our only wonder is that it should have been so rapid. But slavery, says the old Greek proverb, takes away half a man's life: and by the end of the eleventh century, it was very little to the once sturdy freeman, soldier and taxpayer, whether he worked as a serf for a Byzantine, a Frank or a Turkish master. With the year 1071, then, begins that Turkish drive westwards, first Seljuk then Ottoman, which was not decisively halted until, five centuries later almost to the day, the Ottoman fleet was destroyed at Lepanto.

We may perhaps be allowed to recapitulate in brief the main reasons why the survival against seemingly overwhelming odds under the house of Heraclius, the recovery under the Isaurians, and the splendid triumphs of the Macedonians, were possible at all. These reasons are of two kinds – first, theoretical; next practical; and it would be a bold historian who awarded the palm to either.

In the first place, the *faith* – I mean the faith in the divinely decreed destiny of the empire – so far from dying away in the Heraclian epoch, was very notably reinforced by a mystical tendency which had hitherto been alien to the imperial theory. If we say that Justinian I was more of a Roman than of a Christian emperor, the statement requires several qualifications. But it none the less embodies a profound truth. Justinian I was in thought far more akin to Constantine the Great, or, for that matter, to Augustus Caesar, than to Heraclius, who was so much closer to him in time. Would it be going too far to suggest that the Christian religion to Justinian was scarcely more than a prop or adjunct of Roman imperialism and unification, whereas to Heraclius and his successors it was the inspiration, the justification, the very marrow of that concept?

This is what gives to the Persian wars of Heraclius the tincture of a crusade. I suggest that without this strong conviction of God's support and decree, no political recovery would have been possible. It is significant that the unanimous opposition which manifested itself in Constantinople to the plan of Heraclius to remove the empire's capital to Carthage, as Constantine had removed it to Byzantium, was headed by the Patriarch Sergius. The theory of Christ's appointment of Byzantium to be the centre of this earthly kingdom, and of its inhabitants to be His Chosen and Peculiar People, had already struck firm root.

Throughout Byzantine history, even at its very end, this undoubting faith in God's decree was passionately held. I will cite a single example, which is frequently quoted, but not more frequently than it deserves to be. In or about the year 1394, when Byzantium was a small state, less powerful by far than half a

379

dozen city-states in Italy, and incomparably less powerful than France or England at that epoch, the Grand Prince of Moscow, Basil Dimitrievich, seems to have thought that a more realistic appraisal of the political situation was overdue. He wrote to the Patriarch Antony of Constantinople that the Russians recognised the Orthodox faith, but could no longer recognise the Constantinopolitan emperor. 'My son', wrote the patriarch in reply, 'it is not well that you should say "We have a church, but we have no emperor": for I tell you that it is not possible for a Christian to have church without emperor. Empire and church are a single unity, and to separate them is quite impossible'. Never was the age-old dogma more nakedly expressed. Christ, emperor: emperor, Christ: you cannot have one without the other. And to pretend to be a Christian without loyalty to Christ's representative at Constantinople is rank hypocrisy, heresy and blasphemy.

So much for the faith. But no mere faith however firmly planted and maintained, will preserve a state during a thousand years, against odds which seem at first sight insuperable. Avars, Slavs, Bulgars, Pechenegs, Saracens, Franks, Russians, Magyars: how could mere faith in the decrees and purposes of God prevail against these successive assaults of warlike and uncountable multitudes, careless of all but slaughter and pillage? The fact that, after centuries of such continuous shocks, Byzantium not merely survived, but survived, in the tenth and eleventh centuries, as the strongest, richest and most cultivated power in the western world, is not quite miraculous, but is at all events not indicative of decline or degeneracy. It implies, in addition to the faith, a very effective combination of brains, energy, organisation and courage. Heaven helps those who help themselves.

It is obvious that in a state constantly at war the armed forces of the crown must be of the first and greatest importance. Whatever the Christian faith might say of war, or however the bureaucracy and populace of the capital might belittle its importance, this practical truth was firmly and conscientiously vindicated by every emperor worthy of the name, from Heraclius down to the end of the Macedonian dynasty. The most effective emperors, Heraclius, Leo III, Constantine V, Leo V, Basil I, Nicephorus II, John I and Basil II, were all generals who took the field at the head of their armies. Even the civilian emperors such as Leo VI and his son Constantine VII did what they could to cherish the bond which they postulated between the crown and the soldier. If, said Constantine VII, the state is a body, the army is its head; and he went on to proclaim that his own troops were his spiritual children, who partook of him in a mystical communion, even as the Christian worshipper partook of his Lord. This is very striking testimony from one whose lifelong preoccupation was to avoid, by the most skilful and adroit diplomacy, a resort to force and bloodshed.

The new army of the Middle-Byzantine state, painfully evolved in the course of about three hundred years, reached at last a pitch of perfect efficiency under the aristocratic generals of the middle and later tenth century, against which nothing could prevail. The basic unit was the brigade of heavily armed cavalry, recruited from the Anatolian peasant soldiery, and drilled into discipline by generations of gifted military governors and their junior officers in the *themes*. It was thus that the age of the Byzantine epic and chivalry was born. Courage bred victory, and victory courage. At last, towards the end of the tenth century, the very report of the Byzantine 'cataphract', with his charger, his lance and his arrows, was terrible to the brave but undisciplined hordes of Syria. Cavalry tactics were developed to a high art; and, when practised by the hereditary skill of Zimiskes or the native genius of Basil, were almost everywhere victorious.

But this mode of warfare was vulnerable at several points. To start with, it cost more money than the rural taxes could cover: and it had to be heavily subsidised by the imperial treasury. The moment when the fatal division between the provincial military and the civil bureaucracy became acute (that is, in and after 1025), the latter could, and ultimately did, destroy the former by the simple expedient of cutting the military appropriations and raising money by sale of military exemptions. In the second place, the whole system put far too much power into the hands of the big provincial families, whose representatives were the only leaders whom the provincial levies would follow. An uniquely powerful emperor, Basil II, even though he came of a non-aristocratic family, could at length take over the machine and make it work; but even he relied on six thousand Varangian mercenaries, and had to contend with two serious and nearly fatal aristocratic rebellions. This was the reverse of the medal, and remained dark even when the obverse of victory and prestige shone brightest.

So, in the end, it was all a matter of military *morale*. 'The genius of Belisarius and Narses', wrote Gibbon, 'had been formed without a master, and expired without a disciple. Neither honour, nor patriotism, nor generous superstition, could animate the lifeless bodies of slaves and strangers, who had succeeded to the honours of the legions. Their vices were inherent, their victories accidental. and their costly maintenance exhausted the substance of the State which they were unable to defend.' Almost all of this judgement is simple nonsense, except as regards the expense. Bury, on the other hand, goes much too far in the other direction: 'Up till the end of the eleventh century, the Byzantine army was beyond comparison the best fighting-machine in Europe. When a Byzantine army was defeated, it was always the incompetence of the general, never the inefficiency or cowardice of the troops, that was to blame.' If uncertain *morale* ranks as cowardice, the statement is untrue. Bulgarogephyron, Achelo, Manzikert, what lost these and a dozen other fields except sudden panic rushing through the ranks of an intact, greatly superior, and potentially victorious army? The feelings of national *morale*, which have often sustained armies in adversity when deprived of supplies and leadership, were wanting to the heterogeneous and polyglot levies of the medieval empire, who would thus only fight bravely for a leader whom they knew and could see, not for one who was unknown to them and whom they believed to have fallen.

In this manner, by faith and by strength, the Middle-Byzantine Empire grew from the ruins of the Later Roman, waxed in splendour and majesty, and then, for reasons almost wholly social and economic, withered and collapsed. Our final question must be: what, against the wider background of human history, was the significance of it all? What did this specifically Byzantine empire achieve that remains of permanent value, that is with us today, and without which the modern world would be other and poorer than we find it to be? Or must we leave the question in abeyance, as simple Kaspar had to leave the results of the Battle of Blenheim?

> And everybody praised the Duke,
> Who this great fight did win.
> But what good came of it at last?
> Quoth little Peterkin.
> Why, that I cannot tell, said he,
> But 'twas a famous victory.

The positive merits of the empire of East Rome have been, during more than a millennium, consistently ignored or despised in Western Europe. The savage and suicidal hatred and mistrust of the east for the west is a phenomenon which declared itself almost as soon as the two halves of the Roman world felt themselves to be separate entities; and it is very nearly as strong today as it was in the time of Charlemagne. The hatred of the East European communist for the Free World is no mere doctrinal hatred. It goes far deeper than that. It is an *instinct*, inherited and ingrained in the Byzantine character during centuries of religious and political conflict. Let me recall what the Byzantine historian Nicetas thought about the West at the end of the twelfth century: 'And so, between us and the Franks, is set the widest gulf. We have not a thought in common. We are poles apart, even though we may happen to live together in the same house. They are arrogant for the most part, and proudly make pretence of an upright carriage, and affect to look down on the smoothness and modesty of our manners as base and fawning. But *we* regard their arrogance and boasting and over-bearing as a flux of the snivel which keeps their noses in the air, and we tread them down by the might of Christ who giveth us power to trample unhurt upon the viper and the scorpion.' Animated by these feelings, neither side was likely to do justice to the other. We can afford to be more impartial.

The contribution of Byzantium to world culture varies with the progress of time, from positive to negative, between the ninth century and fifteenth. The first and greatest of the positive contributions was the conversion and civilisation of the barbarians in the ninth century, a contribution of inestimable value not merely to Byzantium but also to Europe. Missionary work was linked with Byzantine imperialism as a definite and recognised political activity. The two, as the Patriarch Antony observed, could not be disjoined. Here the Byzantine empire is to be compared with the Spanish, and to be contrasted with the Roman and English. The Roman citizen, if he went through a few formal gestures of respect to the emperor, was free to believe what he chose, and, within very broad limits, to worship according to his beliefs. The English in India very wisely adopted a similar policy. They never attempted to cram Christianity down the throats of Moslems and Hindoos; and among the Christian missionaries of India it was commonly said that the

383

British Government looked on all religions with favour except the religion of Jesus Christ. The Byzantines could not be equally tolerant. To be Christian and orthodox was the *sine qua non* of a Byzantine subject, for loyalty to the emperor was indivisible from orthodox religious belief. But, inversely, the conversion of the outsider to orthodox Christianity automatically made of that outsider a Byzantine subject, since, with the supremacy of Christ, he had also to accept the supremacy of Christ's elect, the Byzantine emperor. It can thus be seen that missionary endeavour was a political instrument as effective as, and far less costly than, conquest by war. It did not always work quite according to theory: things hardly ever do. Bulgaria and Russia and Serbia were orthodox, but this did not stop them from attacking the empire from time to time. But there was always an element of shame and uneasiness in such wars, on both sides: the feeling that brother was murdering brother, and that the angels looked on with sad and wondering eyes to see the children of Christ shedding one another's blood. To estimate the value of this christianisation of mainly Slavonic peoples, we have only to consider what those people were like before the conversion took place: ignorant, brutal, without letters or art, worshipping pagan deities with bloody rites and sacrifices. To these people much of the gospel message filtered through, and with it, some at least of the Graeco-Roman culture in which that religion was embedded, and some knowledge of the splendid art-forms through which it was illustrated. When Gibbon states that his history of the empire's decline recounts 'the triumph of barbarism and religion', he altogether forgets that the barbarism was there already, and that, without the religion, it would have been far more barbarous than it was. It is a truism that the culture of Eastern Europe springs from Byzantium: indeed it is, in the matter of moulding of thought, far truer than most of us realise. The literary and educational tradition of Byzantine Hellenism was a barren culture, but still, it *was* a culture; and the splendid monuments of Byzantine art still surviving in Russia and Bulgaria, Serbia and Greece, give us some idea of the inspiration of splendid craftsmen by Christ and His saints.

It is indeed with unfeigned diffidence that I speak of Byzantine art. But to omit all mention of its cultural and religious influence outside the bounds of the empire would be to leave out the greatest achievement of Byzantine civilisation, beside which the literature – if you can call it that – and even the admirable series of historical writings, are as nothing. It is a highly significant circumstance that the various manifestations of Byzantine culture are more or less successful as they are nearer to, or further from, Christian inspiration. Byzantine art is a religious art, one of the most successful ever practised. As a vehicle for the expression of the transcendent truths of the Christian religion, it is unsurpassed. Formal and dignified, literal and detailed, combining exquisite restraint with profound emotion, it makes the religious art of the European Renaissance look vulgar by comparison, if not blasphemous and disgusting. Its influence on Western Europe was far-flung and everywhere beneficial: and whatever else the west disliked and despised about the east, its mosaics and enamels, its textiles and ivories, its pearl and onyx, its paintings and its goldwork were eagerly coveted and jealously guarded in western treasuries.

The same principle holds good when we come to the written word. The religious productions, whether dogmatic, hagiographic or liturgical, while decidedly not of the first order either in charm or acumen, are greatly superior to those which set out to exercise and preserve the grace of antique diction and rhetoric. The Byzantine rhetoric which, like its predecessor Hellenistic rhetoric, formed the basis of all polite education, was the curse of the later as of the former age. In their endeavour to seize the vocabulary and nuances of a tongue far removed in pronunciation, construction and diction from their own, the Byzantines puzzled their wits and obfuscated their minds. Poetry disappeared, and what passed for it was no more than rhetorical versification, at best ornate and insipid, at worst a detestable jargon. All originality, all freshness, all emotion were stifled. And this was inevitable when writing was practised only in what amounted to a complicated medium never spoken spontaneously by any human being, and therefore useless as a vehicle of thought.

Yet we cannot wholly regret these, in themselves, ridiculous and stultifying exercises: for they were responsible for the greatest incidental boon conferred by Byzantium on mankind, which in sum outweighs all the positive contributions rolled into one: I mean the preservation of the Ancient Greek classics. These, with the exception of Homer and Demosthenes, were scarcely studied by Byzantine scholars before the twelfth century, when the sense of Byzantium's decline as a world empire of Rome led her folk to search for other props to support their inbred conviction of their own ineffable superiority. Sometimes it was touch and go: and it is terrifying to think how nearly Sophocles, for example, came to being totally lost – except for some elegant extracts in anthologies – between the fifth and eleventh centuries. As it was, an inestimable treasury of drama and lyric poetry disappeared, and will probably never be recovered. All the same, we must be thankful for what we have; and we must be thankful to Byzantine schoolmasters, even though their interest in these texts was almost entirely grammatical and lexical.

In the third book of the *Iliad*, Helen ascends the walls of Troy with Priam, and tells her father-in-law about the Greek heroes who appear on the plains below them. After enumerating the chief of them, she says there are two she cannot see – her own brothers, Castor and Polydeuces: 'Perhaps', she says, 'they stayed at home: or perhaps they are here, but daren't show their faces because of their sister's shame'. And then Homer goes on: 'So she said: but them already the life-giving earth held in her embrace, far off in Sparta, in their own native land.' The poetic and emotional impact of these lines is terrific. They convey – as is Homer's trick – the maximum of effect with the minimum of effort. Nothing could emphasise better the folly and degradation of the whole miserable seduction, elopement and adultery, than this simple and terse statement that, for these reasons, the lady's own brothers were dead and she didn't even know it.

The best Byzantine commentator on Homer, the twelfth-century Eustathius of Thessalonica, who has here and there a glimmering that Homer's text is after all something more than a medley of unusual words and abstruse constructions, can find on this passage nothing more to say than that Helen knows she has done wrong and that Paris had probably concealed from her the death of Castor and Polydeuces, so that she should not spoil her pretty face by crying. He then enters *con amore* into a long, and erroneous, disquisition on the derivation of the word *physizoos*. Well: what does it matter? The point is that owing to the Byzantine's interest in any aspect at all of classical letters, even the driest and least important, these letters are preserved to us. And we are quite capable of making our own comments on them.

And we can turn, without regret, but yet not without a thought of gratitude, from the meagre fruits of Byzantine literature, to that amazing liberation of the human spirit, that intoxicating realisation of the richness and beauty and strangeness of the world about us which flooded the consciousness of Renaissance man, but to which the Byzantine eyes were for ever closed. This tremendous discovery raised the poetry of the western Renaissance to heights never before achieved by poetry, and in all probability never to be achieved again.

A short passage or two will better illustrate the contrast between Byzantium and the new spirit of the western world than would hours of literary and historical criticism:

Pandora:
> Give me a running streame in both my hands,
> A blew kings fisher, and a pible stone,
> And Ile catch butter flies upon the sand,
> And thou Gunophilis shall clippe their wings.

Stesias:
> Ile give thee streames whose pible shalbe pearle,
> Love birds whose feathers shalbe beaten gold,
> Musk flies with amber berries in their mouthes,
> Milke white Squirrels, singing Popiniayes,
> A boat of deare skins, and a fleeting Ile,
> A sugar cane, and line of twisted silke.

So Shakespeare's contemporary, John Lyly. Or there is John Fletcher, another contemporary:

> He shall have chariots easier than air,
> Which I will have invented; and thyself
> That art the messenger shall ride before him,
> On a horse cut out of an entire diamond,
> That shall be made to go with golden wheels,
> I know not how yet.

The Byzantines believed that the present dispensation would come to an end with the close of the seventh cycle of one thousand years, dating from 5508 BC. In a way, they were right: for the seventh cycle ended with the year AD 1492, in which Columbus sailed to America. And it is wholly appropriate that Ariel should have sung his incomparable lyrics of yellow sand, coral and pearls in the islands of the New World.

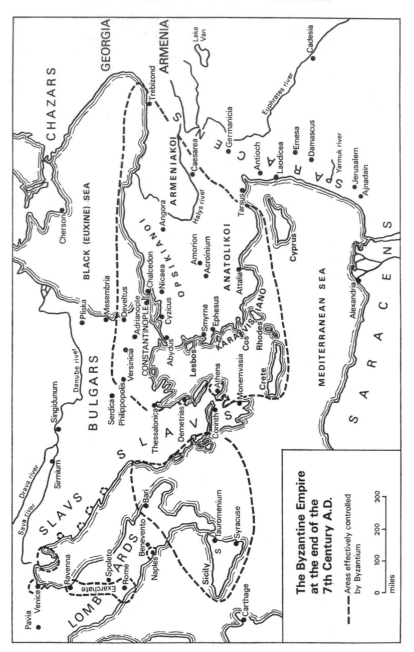

The Byzantine Empire
at the end of the
7th Century A.D.

- - - Areas effectively controlled
by Byzantium

0   100   200   300

miles

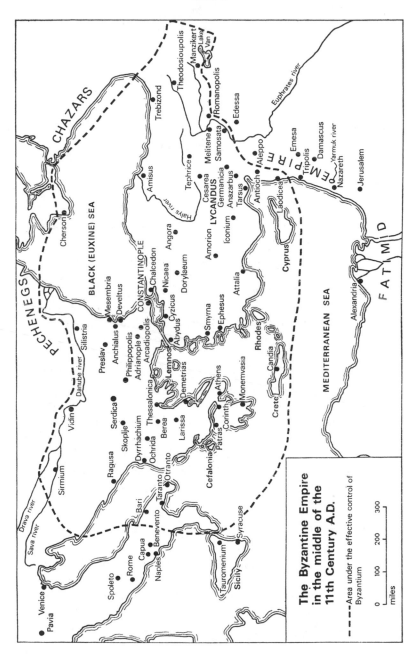

The Byzantine Empire in the middle of the 11th Century A.D.

– – – Area under the effective control of Byzantium

miles

0   100   200   300

BIBLIOGRAPHICAL NOTE

A ORIGINAL SOURCES

Theophanes, *Chronographia*, Ed. C. de Boor, vol. 1, Leipzig, 1883
(Theophanes)
Nicephorus, *Historia syntomos*, Ed. C. de Boor, Leipzig, 1880
(Nicephorus)
Theophanes Continuatus, Ed. I. Bekker, Bonn, 1838 (Theoph. Cont.)
Constantine Porphyrogenitus, *De administrando imperio*, Ed. Gy.
Moravcsik, Budapest, 1949 *DAI*
Leo Diaconus, *Historiae*, Ed. C. B. Hase, Bonn, 1828 (Leo Diac.)
John Scylitzes = George Cedrenus, *Historiarum compendium*, Ed. I.
Bekker, vol. 2, Bonn, 1839 (Cedrenus)
Michael Psellus, *Chronographia*, Ed. E. Renauld, 2 vols., Paris, 1926, 1928
(Psellus)
Michael Attaliota, *Historia*, Ed. I. Bekker, Bonn, 1853 (Mich. Att.)
Liudprand of Cremona, *Opera*, Ed. J. Becker, Hannover and Leipzig,
3rd edition, 1915 (Liudprand)

B MODERN WORKS

L. Bréhier, *Vie et mort de Byzance*, Paris, 1947 (Bréhier)
J. B. Bury, *A History of the Later Roman Empire from Arcadius to Irene*,
vol. 2, London, 1889 (Bury, *LRE*)
J. B. Bury, *A History of the Eastern Roman Empire from the Fall of Irene to
the Accession of Basil I*, London, 1912 (Bury, *ERE*)
The Cambridge Medieval History, vol. IV, Ed. J. M. Hussey, Cambridge,
1966

G. Ostrogorsky, *Geschichte des byzantinischen Staates*, 3rd edition, Munich, 1963 (Ostrogorsky)
(An English version of the above by J. M. Hussey was published by Blackwell in 1956 and by Rutgers University Press in 1957)

A. A. Vasiliev, *History of the Byzantine Empire*, 2 vols. (continuously paginated), Madison, 1961 (Vasiliev)

INDEX